A problem without a solution may interest the student but can hardly fail to annoy the casual reader. Among these unfinished tales is that of Mr. James Phillimore, who, stepping back into his own house to get his umbrella, was never seen again in this world.

Sir Arthur Conan Doyle

Other Books in the Dead Men Do Tell Tales Series by Troy Taylor

* Dead Men Do Tell Tales
* Bloody Chicago
* Bloody Illinois
* Bloody Hollywood
* Suffer the Children
* "I Want to Come Home Tonight"
* One Night at the Biograph
* Fear the Reaper (with Rene Kruse)
* One August Morning
* The Two Lost Girls
* Fallen Angel
* Murdered in Their Beds
* Murder by Gaslight
* Blood, Guns and Valentines

Without A Trace

Unsolved Disappearance & Mysterious Vanishings

Troy Taylor

This Book is Published By:
American Hauntings Ink
Jacksonville, Illinois | 217.791.7859
Visit us on the Internet at
http://www.americanhauntingsink.com

Second Edition – February 2020
ISBN: 978-1-7324079-7-8

INTRODUCTION

I've had the file cabinet for years. It's an old, beat-up thing that has moved from place to place so many times that I've lost count of everywhere it's been with me. I'm not even sure where I got it, but I know that I've had it for more than two decades now. As for its contents, well, they're a little strange. They'd even be considered by most people to be disturbing if they didn't know what I do for a living.

The cabinet contains records and remnants of the vanished – people who walked away one day, or were taken, and never returned. They just disappeared, without a trace.

I have been fascinated —– perhaps even obsessed —– by unsolved disappearances for as long as I can remember. Like many other people, I have always been intrigued by the idea of a puzzle that cannot be solved. Perhaps for this reason, I have voraciously read, collected, and written murder mysteries, stories of unsolved murders, and tales of ghosts and the supernatural. In the course of my collecting and writing, I have learned that real life is not like the stuff of fiction. In a fictional mystery, the detective always solves the case in the final pages of the book or the last reel of the film. Real life, however, is not so simple. There are far too many mysteries that simply cannot be solved —– especially when it comes to those who disappear without a trace.

History is filled with mysterious vanishings, which is why I filled my cabinet with such accounts. It's been said that in the United States alone, as many as 10 million people are reported missing each year. The majority of them return home within hours or days but there is a small percentage of them that go missing forever. It seems like this would not be an easy thing to do in this modern age, but it occurs more often than you'd like to think. The accounts of those vanishings have all the ingredients of a mystery story, except for the ending, of course.

It is these stories, that we are left to speculate, wonder, and lose sleep over.

Many of the circumstances around unsolved disappearances are often bizarre, sometimes ridiculous, but in the end, always inexplicable —– even when it seems that the event should be impossible.

How does a person, a plane, or a ship disappear without a trace? In some cases, people vanished into the uncharted wilderness, a victim of the elements and of a place for which no map existed. Or perhaps the weather played a crucial role, washing over ships at sea and snatching airplanes out of the sky. Many disappearances can be blamed on man. Brutal murders have occurred for which no clues have been found and the bodies of the dead have never been discovered.

But what if, sometimes, things are even weirder?

There are some who believe there are "holes" in the fabric of time and space into which people, animals, and objects have involuntarily and unexpectedly slipped. Many of them are unable to return to the world from which they came, creating mysteries that can never be solved. The American writer and researcher Charles Fort, who spent years in libraries collecting accounts of oddities and bizarre happenings and who compiled several books of such things, concluded that these mysterious "portals" were not only possible, but that they actually exist. As strange as this might sound, Fort was not alone in this idea. There are a number of scientists and researchers who theorize that such "doorways" just might explain the mysterious disappearances of people in cases where no normal explanation can be found.

But can we relegate all unexplained vanishings to the world of the supernatural? Of course not, for there have been thousands of disappearances that are undoubtedly linked to historical mysteries, the wrath of the elements, and the bloodthirsty nature of man. In the pages ahead, we will explore scores of intriguing mysteries, from both centuries past and modern times. You will find accounts of lost explorers, kidnap victims who were never returned, missing ships —– and an uncomfortable number of cases for which no logical explanation exists.

As I sorted through the piles of papers, books and materials in my cabinet, I found cases that involved every type of disappearance.

* During the Spanish War of Succession, from 1701 to 1714, an army of 4,000 trained and fully-equipped troops marched into the Pyrenees mountains that form the border between France and Spain and were never heard from again. Despite numerous searches, no trace of them was ever found. They had camped one night by a small stream and the next morning, they broke camp and set off into the foothills of the mountains. They marched into oblivion.

* In 1858, 650 French soldiers vanished during a march on Saigon, in what is now Vietnam. There had been rioting in the city and 500 well-trained French Legionnaires, along with 150 Spanish recruits, were dispatched to restore order. They were last seen marching across open country about 15 miles from Saigon, but they never reached the city and they never returned to their base. A search was conducted but the soldiers had simply disappeared.

* In 1915, three soldiers claimed to be witnesses to the bizarre disappearance of an entire battalion during the infamous Gallipoli campaign of World War I. The three men, from a New Zealand field company, said they watched as a battalion of the Royal Norfolk Regiment marched up a hillside in Suvla Bay, Turkey. The hill was shrouded in a low-lying cloud, into which the English soldiers marched without hesitation. They never came out. The cloud burned away in the sunshine and was gone —- apparently taking the soldiers with it. After the war ended, assuming that the battalion had been captured and held prisoner, the British government demanded that Turkey return them. The Turks insisted, however, that their army had neither captured nor contacted the English soldiers. The battalion was never heard from again.

* In June 1874, a stern-wheeler called the *Iron Mountain* vanished on the Mississippi River. The massive riverboat was more than 180-feet long and had five huge boilers to provide steam enough for her giant

paddles. The vessel, which sailed from Vicksburg, Mississippi, was loaded with cotton and molasses from New Orleans and carried 57 passengers. The steamboat was bound for Pittsburgh, via the Ohio River, when it sailed, towing a string of barges behind it. As she reached midstream, the pilot gave a couple of long blasts on the whistle to warn small boats out of the way and then she rounded a bend —– and was never seen again. The *Iron Mountain's* barges were later found adrift on the river, their towing ropes cut cleanly through. No trace of wreckage from the steamer, nor bodies of passengers and crew, were ever found. Hundreds of miles of river bottom were dragged, but without success. Other riverboats should have seen the *Iron Mountain*, but none of them had. No adequate explanation for the disappearance of the ship has ever been found.

* On October 13, 1913, early American aviator Albert Jewell disappeared off Long Island, New York. No trace of him was ever found. Jewell was on his way to Staten Island, where he planned to take part in the *New York Times* American Aerial Derby. The race had been organized to commemorate the 10th anniversary of Orville Wright's first flight on December 17, 1903. The race was a series of timed flights over a 60-mile course, starting and ending in Oakwood on Staten Island.

Jewell held a pilot's license issued by the Aero Club of America and at the time of his disappearance, he had been flying for six months (which made him a veteran aviator in those days). He was also an instructor at the Moisant Aviation School, though he had little experience of flights of the distance he was attempting.

His last flight was planned to be from the Moisant Aviation School near Hempstead, Long Island to the Oakwood airfield from which the competitors in the race were due to depart. Soon after he left the ground, witnesses said that it looked as though his lightweight airplane was blown out to sea. The captain of a fishing vessel reported seeing an aircraft resembling Jewell's off Sandy Hook a short time later. Unfortunately, Jewell was unable to swim. There were no safety devices on the plane and the only part of it that would actually float was the inner tube of a tire. It was unlikely that he was skilled enough to ditch the aircraft at sea and get clear of the wreckage.

But did he crash? No one knows. Extensive searches on land and sea were conducted for Jewell and his aircraft. The Moisant Aeroplane Company sent six motorboats to search for Jewell and several automobiles joined the land search. Several of the aviators present in the New York area took part in these search efforts. Searchers concentrated on Jamaica Bay and the sea off Rockaway Point where Jewell was last sighted. No signs of Jewell or of the wreckage of his aircraft were found. He had simply vanished.

Several rewards were offered for information about Jewell and a possible accident. Although several bodies were subsequently discovered in the ocean off New York, none of them turned out to be the unlucky aviator.

No trace of him was ever found.

* On July 2, 1948, a socially prominent man named Orja Glenwood Corns, Jr. from Winnetka, Illinois, vanished after spending the night at the Parody Club on North Clark Street in Chicago. With his wife and child out of town for the Independence Day holiday, Corns went looking for some diversion. He spent the evening mixing with strippers, prostitutes, and shady characters and then disappeared. Allegedly carrying $150, he was thought to have been murdered for his money, but a gas station owner swore that he saw Corns on July 6 driving his 1947 green Oldsmobile.

Corns and the car were never seen again.

* Captain Mansell James took off in his own airplane from Lee, Massachusetts, on May 29, 1919. He planned to land at Mitchell Field, Long Island, but like Albert Jewell, he vanished without a trace. He was last seen flying over the Berkshires but was never seen again. Five days later, after several search parties failed to turn any clues, the Army sent planes over the area in hopes of locating some wreckage. Nothing was found. Local newspapers carried stories, rewards were offered, and telephone companies called all their subscribers and passed along

information about the missing flier. Captain James and his plane flew off into the wild blue yonder and never came back.

* A Danish training vessel called the *Kobenhoven* set sail from Montevideo on the morning of December 14, 1928 and was never seen again. The ship was staffed by 50 cadets and sailors. The cadets had been taking part in a ceremony at the Danish consulate and were excited to set back out to sea. The *Kobenhoven* steamed out of the harbor, past a couple of small fishing boats, and vanished. Whatever happened to her must have occurred in only a few minutes for incoming ships, which sighted the same fishing boats a few hours later, never saw the *Kobenhoven*.

On May 15, 1970, a wealthy couple from Arlington Heights, Illinois, Mr. and Mrs. Edward P. Andrews, attended a cocktail party at the Chicago Sheraton Hotel and were seen leaving the hotel's parking garage at 9:30 p.m. People attending the party later stated that Mr. Andrews seemed to be ill, complaining that he was hungry after having only canapés to eat during the event. Mrs. Andrews appeared to be crying by the time the couple reached their black and yellow 1969 Oldsmobile. The garage attendant saw them drive away on Lower Michigan Avenue, going south toward the Michigan Avenue Bridge that spans the Chicago River.

The couple was never seen again.

Their luxurious home, their extensive bank accounts, their stocks and bonds, and their 14 credit cards, were never touched. The Andrews simply disappeared.

* In October 1964, a retired paint contractor named Charles F. Holden from Oakland, California, disappeared while on a hunting trip with his son and brother-in-law. While the other men planned to hunt, Holden merely wanted to paint and sketch in the woods. The three men stopped on the highway east of Crescent City, California, in the middle of the afternoon on October 11. While the two younger men went to scout the area for game, Holden set up his sketching board. Albert, his

son, glanced back at him as he started up the trail and saw his father bent over the paper, lost in thought.

This was the last time that he would ever see him.

When the two men returned, about 45 minutes later, Holden had vanished. He left no footprints, discarded sketch paper or cigarette butts behind —– he was simply gone. Sheriff's deputies and forestry officials conducted an extensive search of the area but found no evidence that Holden had ever been there at all.

* Some places gain a reputation for swallowing people up and causing them to vanish. Mount Rainier in Washington is one of those places. In July 1999, the 65th person in history to vanish on Rainier walked into the wild and did not return. Joe Wood, a Bronx-born journalist who worked as an editor for a New York book publisher, was in Seattle attending a minority journalists' conference. On July 8, he decided to hike up Mount Rainier National Park's Mildred Point Trail. Wood was no novice in the outdoors, having been an Eagle Scout, but he may not have been prepared for the conditions in the park that day. Rainier had received its fifth heaviest snowfall in its history and the six-mile hike was made treacherous by ice and was lined with tree wells and dangerous snow bridges. On the trail, Wood ran into Bruce Gaummond, a retired Boeing aircraft employee who came forward after Wood was reported missing. Gaummond told representatives of the National Park Service that the two of them had chatted briefly about birds, the length of the trail, and a slippery creek crossing ahead. After that, Wood was never seen again. Searchers scoured the area for five days after he was last seen but no trace of him was found. A final search was conducted in September 1999 and after that, Joe Wood was added to the list of those who walked away —– and never came back.

* On June 29, 1919, Arthur Phillip Wentz, a seven-week-old baby boy, vanished from a baby carriage in front of a department store on Third Avenue in New York. His mother, Elsie, had left him sleeping for a few minutes and returned to find the carriage empty. The police interviewed a number of people who were standing outside the store at the time and they claimed to see a young woman in a white blouse and

skirt bending over the baby just moments before his mother returned. Despite a thorough search, reward posters, and newspaper stories, little Arthur Wentz was never seen again.

* A boy named John Patterson, age 14, vanished on September 1, 1873, in Albany, New York. He was running an errand for his mother and never came back. The boy was no adventurer. He was devoted to his mother and spent most of his time reading books, and yet he vanished without a trace. His mother offered a $500 reward for information leading to his discovery, but the reward was never claimed. She spent several years visiting morgues and viewing the bodies of unidentified young men, but John was never found.

* One of history's strangest disappearances involved an elderly man named Owen Parfitt from Shepton Mallet, England, who had been paralyzed by a massive stroke. In June 1763, he was seated outside of his sister's home, enjoying the warm evening and wearing only his nightshirt with a light blanket on his lap. He was 60-years-old and virtually unable to move. When last seen, Parfitt was sitting quietly watching some farm laborers across the road finishing up their work for the day. Around 7:00 p.m., Parfitt's sister, Susannah, noticed that a summer storm was approaching and went outside with a neighbor to help Parfitt back into the house —– but he was gone. His chair was empty, and the carefully folded blanket had been left behind. Investigations into this mysterious disappearance were carried out as late as 1933, but no clue as to Parfitt's fate was ever uncovered.

* In 1975, a young couple, Jackson and Martha Wright, were driving from New Jersey to New York through the Lincoln Tunnel. According to Jackson, who was driving, he stopped just after passing through the tunnel to clean condensation off the car's windows. Martha offered to clean off the back window and both got out of the car. As soon as Jackson finished, he looked for his wife —– but she was gone. He neither heard nor saw anything unusual take place, and a subsequent investigation could find no evidence of foul play.
Martha Wright had just disappeared.

* On September 25, 1981, Thelma Pauline Melton was hiking the Deep Creek Trail in the Great Smoky Mountains National Park with two friends when she vanished. She was last seen just after 4:00 p.m., at the same time that she suddenly sped up her pace and walked ahead of her companions. They saw her walk over a hill on the trail and vanish from their view. When they didn't see her on the trail ahead, they assumed she had returned to the campground where she and her husband had parked their Airstream trailer. But when they arrived there at 4:30, there was no sign of Thelma. Her husband was inside the trailer when they group left for their hike and had not seen his wife since that time.

Park rangers were contacted about Thelma's disappearance around 6:00 p.m. A search immediately began but there was no sign of the missing woman. She had been familiar with the trail she had been hiking and there were no signs that she had veered off the path. She did not have any cash, identification, or medication with her when she disappeared —– only a pack of cigarettes.

Although Thelma's day-to-day life before her vanishing seemed ordinary, there were a few troubling things that came to light. She had followed her normal routine on the day of her disappearance, with one exception. Thelma usually volunteered every day at a center that served meals to senior citizens but had not shown up for her shift on September 25. Her supervisor at the center told police that Thelma never used the telephone at the center but had placed a call to an unknown person on the day before her disappearance. The person on the other end of the line remains unknown.

Thelma had suffered from bouts of depression in the recent past. She used Valium frequently in 1979 but it was believed that she had stopped using the drug by 1981. Her minister volunteered the information that she had been grieving the death of her mother, who had died earlier in 1981, and that there were rumors that she had been involved in an affair with another man. There was no evidence of this, however.

Thelma Melton simply vanished from the Deep Creek Trail, just steps ahead of her friends, and was never seen or heard from again.

* And this may be the strangest one of all.

On August 12, 1973, a search was called off for a seven-year-old boy named "Larry" who claimed to be lost in the New Mexico mountains. Why would the authorities stop searching for a boy that hundreds of people were convinced was lost in the wilderness? That seems like a good question ——- but the answer is stranger than you might think.

Five days earlier, on August 7, CB operators in the southwestern states of New Mexico, Arizona, and California began receiving some very strange transmissions. The voice on the other end of the radio seemed to be from a seven-year-old boy. The boy called himself Larry and he claimed to be speaking from the inside of an overturned pickup truck. His sobbing —– along with a static on the airwaves —– made it hard to understand what he was saying, but most believed that he said that his dad, who lay beside him, might be dead from a heart attack.

He and his father had been out rabbit hunting, possibly in the Red Rock Canyon region of New Mexico, when his father collapsed at the wheel. The red and white pickup truck landed upside down in a ditch. His father had not moved since the accident.

Soon, other CB operators began to hear Larry's panicky cries. They were reported in New Mexico, California, Wyoming, and even in Canada. Some heard the story a little differently. His father might not be dead. He might have just hit his head. Some heard that Larry was outside the truck, not inside of it. Despite the inconsistencies —– and the fact that no one could get Larry's last name —– the calls were reported to the authorities, who took them seriously.

Hundreds of people gathered to search for the boy they believed was somewhere in New Mexico's central mountains. A helicopter rescue team flew over the area. Military aircraft, with radio tracking devices, were sent into action. A rescue worker in one of the search helicopters spoke to a young boy through the radio but he found no trace of the truck. At one point, Larry told an Albuquerque radio operator that he could see airplane searchlights that had flown over the mountains, south of Albuquerque. And he was right, there was a plane in the air at that time. Meanwhile, the authorities checked for any reported missing child named Larry or a father and son disappearance but found nothing.

Larry didn't seem to know how to properly use the radio and he switched channels often. As days passed, his signal got weaker, likely due to a low battery. On August 12, the signal disappeared, and the search was called off.

Four directional finding stations had been established to pick up any signals that could pinpoint the boy's location. More than 150 people had joined the search on the ground. Over 30 civilian and military aircraft had been employed to track him.

They all found nothing.

The authorities quickly wrote the whole thing off to a hoax —– but was it really?

If a little boy had really been lost in the desert, he would have died after five days, which explained the end of the radio calls. Some didn't believe the radio's batteries would have lasted as long as they did or that the signal would not have reached as far as it did. Others argued this was possible, though.

The radio operators who spoke to Larry were adamant that it was a real child in need of help. One of them, an army sergeant, claimed he spoke to Larry for three hours. Others believe that perhaps the first call was real, but the others were from copycats. But if that was the case, how did a fake caller spot an aircraft that was flying over the mountains at the same time and know it had been looking for Larry?

To this day, no one can say for sure if "Lost Boy Larry" was a hoax, or a real missing boy. All that we do know is that no trace of him was ever found.

These accounts —– and dozens of others just like them —-- only scratch the surface of the record of the vanished. There are hundreds of cases locked up in my file cabinet and thousands more in archives, libraries, and police stations across the country and around the world.

The stories that follow are an updated group of cases that I found the most intriguing, compelling, and downright chilling, but please don't mistake them for a complete list of everyone who has disappeared without a trace.

These dead men do tell tales, but their voices come from a place from which they will never be found.

Troy Taylor
Winter 2019–2020

1587: Croatoan

It is one of the greatest unsolved mysteries in American history —
- what happened to the Lost Colony of Roanoke Island? How did they
vanish so completely, leaving only a single clue behind, that we are still
searching for any trace of them more than four centuries later?

It seems fitting to begin this book with one of the most enduring
mysteries of all time. There have been more people trying to solve the
mystery of the Lost Colony than perhaps have tried to solve all the
other cases in this volume combined.

And yet, as with all the others, it, too, remains unsolved.

As the English privateer ship *Hopewell* approached Roanoke
Island on August 17, 1590, Captain Abraham Cocke fired off a cannon
to announce the arrival of the vessel. Governor John White was on
board. Three years earlier, acting on behalf of Sir Walter Raleigh, White
had established what was meant to be the first permanent English
colony on the American East Coast. After establishing a settlement on
the island, White sailed for England to bring back badly needed
supplies. He had left behind 90 men, 17 women and nine children in
the wilderness in August 1587. Among them was White's daughter,
Elinor Dare, who had just given birth to a girl named Virginia, the first
European child born in the New World. He planned a short journey but
tragically, three years passed before he could return.

As the ship neared what would become the North Carolina
coastline, White looked anxiously for some sign of the settlers. He had
expected a joyous greeting but there was no one on the beach.
However, there was a thin plume of smoke wavering out of the trees. It
was assumed to be coming from the cook fires of the settlement. As the
sailors rowed White to the island, they shouted, sang, and blew
trumpets to get the attention of the colonists. But no one came to greet
them. In fact, as they ventured inland, they found the smoke in the air
was not from a tended cook fire, but rather from a brush fire that was
likely caused by a lightning storm.

The men hurried to the village and found it empty. White's daughter Elinor, his granddaughter Virginia, and all the rest of the colonists had vanished without a trace, leaving nothing behind but wrecked, abandoned homes, a mysterious message, and what has become more than four centuries of unanswered questions. The only clue that had been left behind were the letters "CROATOAN," which had been carved into a post. A short distance away was possibly a duplicate of that message that was started and never finished. It spelled out simply "CRO."

White could only assume that the missing colonists had carved the word before abandoning the settlement, but what did it mean? Specific instructions had been left that the settlers should carve a cross on the post if they were in trouble. Did this mean that they had left the colony willingly? If so, where had they gone? Could they have joined the friendly natives on nearby Croatoan Island? If they had, this ignored White's orders. He had told the colonists to head north towards Chesapeake Bay if they were in danger, but Croatoan was to the south.

Several search parties were sent out to look for the missing settlers, but bad weather forced the *Hopewell* to return to England. The colonists were abandoned to their mysterious fate, but they were not forgotten. Years later, John Smith would launch several expeditions from the Jamestown Colony to try and determine the fate of those who went missing at Roanoke. He never learned what happened to them and neither have the scores of historians, archaeologists, and curiosity-seekers who have followed in his footsteps.

America's first colony had vanished, never to be heard from again.

The sixteenth century has often been called the "Golden Age of Exploration." European governments were anxious to stake their claims in the New World and England was no exception. Queen Elizabeth granted dozens of charters to men who were willing to finance expeditions and to start colonies in America. By using private funds to launch English colonies, the money would not be taken from the official coffers and yet England would be able to lay claim to land before France or Spain could do so. The investors would then receive enormous land holdings and hopefully, wealth and great status. Rich men jumped at the chance to start their own colonies, never realizing the great risks involved.

In 1584, Queen Elizabeth granted a charter to a favorite of the royal court, the privateer Sir Walter Raleigh. He quickly organized a voyage to the New World and appointed Philip Amadas and Arthur Barlowe as captains of two of his vessels. They departed from England in April 1584 and a few weeks later, landed on one of the islands that now form the Outer Banks of North Carolina. They stayed for a few months, exploring the area and meeting with a tribe of American Indians who lived on Roanoke Island, which was located between the Outer Banks and the mainland. Amadas and Barlowe returned to England with two of the Indians and with reports of timber, wild fruit and forests, and water teeming with game and fish. The Queen was impressed with their reports and she dubbed the new country "Virginia."

The next spring, Raleigh sent seven ships, carrying 108 men, back to Roanoke Island. Their mission was to establish an outpost there and to set up a base for attacking Spanish ships. England and Spain were at war at the time and Raleigh made his fortune seizing ships as a privateer.

The leader of the expedition, Sir Richard Grenville, abandoned the fledgling colonists at Roanoke and set sail back to England for more supplies. The colonists were left behind with Governor Ralph Lane and John White, the expedition's artist and map-maker. The men initially searched for mineral resources in the area but soon became bored and impatient for Grenville to return. The men constructed a fort at the north end of the island and while they waited for supplies, they refused to hunt or fish and began taking food from the local tribes. At first, the natives were as generous as they had been with Amadas and Barlowe, but eventually, they began running out of food they could share. When they turned away the colonists, the settlers became enraged and raided their village, burning their homes and slaughtering the people, including the chief who had befriended them. The Indians did not retaliate openly, but for the next several months, quietly raided the settlers' fish traps. The friendly relationship between the Native Americans local tribes and the colonists had come to an end.

Meanwhile, Grenville's return to America with supplies was delayed and he did not leave England until the spring of 1586. In June of that year, while Grenville was still making his way across the Atlantic, Sir Francis Drake happened to anchor off the Outer Banks and some of his ships sailed to Roanoke. There, the sailors found the colonists in a sorry state. A number of the men had died from disease, their supplies were gone, and the fort was in ruins. Hungry, miserable, and desperate, they managed to convince Drake that they were in danger of imminent attack by the Indians. Drake, unaware of the incident that had occurred with the village, offered to take the colonists back to England.

Two weeks later, when Grenville arrived, he found the fort deserted. But unwilling to abandon England's claim in the New World, he left 15 men at the outpost with two years' worth of supplies and again returned home.

Even after Raleigh received word about how poorly the Grenville-Lane colony had fared, he refused to give up. He had already lined up several dozen volunteers for another colony, this one to be started near Chesapeake Bay. He promised each of them land grants of 500 acres or more. Raleigh appointed John White as the governor of the colony. White already had experience in America, having been a part of Lane's original colony. He was convinced that the new settlement would succeed.

On May 8, 1587, White and the colonists set sail from Portsmouth, England on three ships. The group included White's daughter, Elinor, her husband, Ananias Dare, and the two Native Americans who had been brought to England with Amadas and Barlowe. White's pilot was Simon Fernandez, a Portuguese navigator who had also been part of the 1584 voyage. The journey from England to America, with a stop in Puerto Rico, took about two and a half months.

Although they had planned to sail straight on to Chesapeake Bay, White decided to stop at Roanoke Island on July 22 to check on the status of the 15 men who had been left there by Grenville. This simple plan sealed the fate of the colonists and their journey took them no farther.

There had been tensions between White and Fernandez throughout the trip. They had begun when White prohibited him from raiding Spanish ships during the journey and, by July, Fernandez was anxious to return to England. When the group reached Roanoke, he refused to take them on to Chesapeake Bay. He stranded the settlers on Roanoke Island.

They did not receive a pleasant greeting when they arrived. The fort that had been built by Lane's colonists had been destroyed. Of the 15 men that Grenville had left behind, all trace of them had vanished, save for the skeleton of one man that was found in the ruins of the fort. The colonists nervously took up residence and began to try and salvage what they could from the outpost. A few days later, one member of the colony, George Howe, was killed by Indians while fishing for crabs. The settlers retaliated by attacking the village they believed belonged to the hostile Indians, but killed a member of a friendly tribe, a Croatoan, instead. Luckily, one of the men who had returned from England with them was also a Croatoan and he interceded to prevent more bloodshed.

Over the course of the next month, the settlers organized all their supplies from the ships and started rebuilding the fort. They also constructed a small village of homes to live in. On August 18, Elinor Dare gave birth to her daughter, Virginia. She was appropriately named for the colony and for the Virgin Queen, Elizabeth I. The birth of the little girl was a joyous time in the colony, but dark days were still ahead.

During the month that was spent revitalizing the remains of the first colony, hurricane season began to approach. Simon Fernandez was anxious to set sail for England. It was too late in the year to plant crops and the colonists had only a few months' worth of supplies, so it was decided that someone would have to return to England with Fernandez and bring back food and provisions. The leaders asked that John White take the responsibility and he reluctantly agreed. A short time later, he departed with Fernandez, leaving his family behind. He had arranged with the colonists that, if they moved their settlement from the fort, they should carve their destination in a visible location. If they had to leave because of an attack, they were told to add a Maltese cross to the carving.

Ocean storms prevented White from reaching England until November. Once there, he hurriedly gathered food, supplies, and weapons and within four months had a fleet of ships together to sail back to Roanoke. Before he could leave, though, it was learned that Spain was organizing an armada of ships with which to attack England. The English navy needed the ships that White planned to take to America and White was left with only the two smallest vessels in his fleet. He re-organized and then finally set sail. Unfortunately, during the journey, the captains of the two ships tried to seize a French vessel and their ships were badly damaged by the larger ship. They were forced to return to England.

White spent the next year and a half unsuccessfully trying to get ships and supplies for the Roanoke colony. Desperate, he was finally able to buy a passage to Roanoke with a fleet of privateers in 1590. On August 17, they anchored off the Outer Banks. From their position, they saw a column of smoke rising from Roanoke and White was hopeful that his family and the rest of the colonists were still alive.

What he found on shore was a mystery.

White discovered that the abandoned homes of the village had been wrecked and the area around the village had been surrounded by a barricade made from fallen tree trunks —– as if the settlers had been trying to protect themselves from something, or ward off an attack. The settlement was overgrown and silent, but there were no human remains and no signs of slaughter or death. It was as if everyone had just walked away and left the cryptic message behind. There had been no Maltese cross added to the words, which must have eased White's anxiety somewhat. It was bad enough to find that his friends and family had vanished, but it would have been worse to know they had been in mortal danger when they fled.

White led his men to nearby Town Creek, located south of the settlement, where the settlers moored their boats and where they had fortified the outpost with several small cannons. Both the boats and the cannons had also vanished. The rescue party was faced with an immense wilderness to search and no clues to follow. White was saddened, but not without hope. He believed that, with no sign of the Maltese cross, that the colonists had left Roanoke voluntarily. He could only pray that they were safe. He had no choice but to return to England. Unable to raise the money to come back and search for them again, and he died in 1606, never knowing the fate of his family who had disappeared in the New World.

The colony was simply considered "lost" and no one searched for them in earnest until after 1607, when the Jamestown colony was founded. Sir Walter Raleigh had been in no position to look for his lost colonists. He had secretly married while all of this was occurring in America and when Queen Elizabeth found out, she did not take it well. She imprisoned her former lover and his new bride in the Tower of London, and when he was released, he was exiled from the court. In 1595, Raleigh set sail for South America, the problems of the lost Roanoke colony all but forgotten. If he could claim that the colonists were probably alive somewhere, and their bodies were not found, Raleigh could maintain his patent on the colony. He did send a party to make a quick search for the settlers in 1602, but they found no trace of them, alive or dead.

In 1607, the first successful American colony, Jamestown, was founded in Virginia. The settlers there made several attempts to find the lost colonists from Roanoke but could discover no evidence of where they had gone. In 1608, John Smith was told a chilling story by Powhatan, the Algonquin chief and the father of Pocahontas. According to Powhatan, the Roanoke settlers had lived with the Chesapeake tribe for a number of years but had then been massacred by a confederacy of Indians led by Powhatan himself. He even showed Smith a few metal items that he claimed had belonged to the murdered colonists.

John Smith believed the story, but many others did not. For that reason, the true fate of the Roanoke colonists has never been determined. No physical evidence has ever been found to show what route they took when they left the fort and no one, living or dead, was ever found and proven to be part of the Roanoke settlement. Over the years, the lost colony has entered the realm of legend and lore.

What became of the settlement at Roanoke? Historians have posed a number of theories as to the settlers' fate and one is that John Smith was correct, and that Powhatan's confederacy did kill the settlers. Such a massacre would obviously explain why no trace of them has ever been found.

Another theory is that the colonists went to live with the friendly Croatoan tribe, which fits with John White's finding of the word "CROATOAN" carved into the post. This theory has been questioned, though, based on White's own writings. In 1587, he noted that the Croatoan feared that the English settlers would wipe out the ir already limited supply of corn. This suggests that they had didn't have enough food to support their own people, let alone 100 additional colonists. Some believe that perhaps the Croatoan assisted the settlers in leaving the Outer Banks and that the colonists then joined up with a tribe on the mainland. Eventually, they were assimilated into the tribe, explaining the legends of pale-skinned Indians with blue eyes that became a part of Outer Banks lore.

It has also been suggested that perhaps the Croatoan killed the colonists. This seems unlikely given that the Croatoan had always been supportive of the settlement. But could there have been tensions that Governor White didn't know about, just as there had been with the original settlement? Perhaps, but we must remember that there were no signs of violence at the fort and nothing to indicate that any of the colonists had been killed. This theory, along with the idea that a group of Spanish explorers attacked the colony, is further questioned because of the lack of a Maltese cross at the site. This was the agreed-upon sign of danger and yet it was nowhere to be found.

Historians and archaeologists have searched for clues as to the fate of the lost colony for decades. Occasionally, tantalizing clues come to the surface. At one point, two independent teams found archaeological remains suggesting that at least some of the Roanoke colonists might have survived. Their findings led them to believe that the colonists split into two groups and each of them assimilated itself into different Native American communities. One team excavated near Cape Creek on Hatteras Island, while the other uncovered artifacts about 50 miles northwest of Roanoke Island.

Cape Creek was once the site of a major Croatoan settlement and trading hub. In 1998, archaeologists stumbled upon a unique find from early British America — -- a 10-carat gold signet ring engraved with a lion or horse, believed to date to the sixteenth century. The ring's discovery prompted later excavations at the site, which unearthed a small piece of slate that was apparently used as a writing tablet and part of the hilt of an iron rapier, a type of light sword used by the British at the time of the colony. In addition, they also found an iron bar and a large copper block. Native Americans lacked such metallurgical technology at the time, so they were believed to be European in origin. It was possible, scientists believed, that the items belonged to Roanoke colonists.

A watercolor map that was drawn by none other than John White inspired the search at the other location, near Edenton, North Carolina. The map shows the East Coast of North America, from Chesapeake Bay to Cape Lookout. White began drawing it in 1585, two years before he became governor. In 2012, researchers using X-ray spectroscopy and other imaging techniques spotted a tiny four-pointed star, colored red and blue, concealed under a patch of paper that White used to make corrections to his map. The star marked a location some 50 miles inland, which White alluded to while trying to attempt to return to the colony. The theory among researchers was that this could have been a reasonable destination for the displaced settlers from Roanoke.

During excavations at the site, archaeologists found shards of what was known as Border Ware pottery, which was typical of other pottery that was dug up on Roanoke Island, as well as at Jamestown, but was no longer imported to the New World after the early seventeenth century, when most of the area was settled. They also found other items like a food storage jar known as a baluster, pieces of early gun flintlocks, a metal hook of the kind used for erecting tents, and more.

Based on these findings, the researchers surmised that some of the Roanoke colonists moved inland to avoid hostile Native Americans after White left.

Of course, these discoveries don't solve the lingering historical mystery of the Lost Colony, but they do offer some intriguing ideas about the colonists' fate. Until then, many people continue to search, waiting for the missing pieces of the puzzle to appear. Until that happens, though, we are left with many unanswered questions about one of the most enduring riddles in America's strange and often troubling history.

1813: "Dear Theodosia"

The story of Theodosia Burr began not with her birth in 1783, but with her disappearance in 1813. That story deepened into macabre legend nearly six decades later when a doctor named William Gaskins Pool was called to help a sick old woman named Polly Mann. Dr. Pool was on vacation at the time, staying near Nags Head, North Carolina, but the dedicated physician traveled to a nearby, ramshackle old home to help a patient in need. When he and his daughter, Anna, entered the dark, dust-covered home, they were drawn to a portrait that was hanging on the wall.

"It was a beautiful young woman, about twenty-five years of age," Anna later recalled. It stood out amidst the squalor of the rest of the house.

After he questioned Polly Mann about the painting, he realized that he was staring at the portrait of the long-vanished Theodosia Burr Alston. It was a portrait that might hold the key to her disappearance, he thought.

But it likely didn't. After all this time, she is still missing. Her fate remains unknown.

Today, most of us know little about Theodosia, aside from the lullaby "Dear Theodosia," sung by the character of Aaron Burr in the musical *Hamilton*. But the real-life Theodosia was a beloved child that grew into a very intelligent, complicated adult whose own story would likely be worthy of another Broadway smash.

Theodosia Burr was born in Albany, New York, on June 21, 1783. Her mother, also named Theodosia, was a cultured woman of great intelligence who had

Theodosia Burr

scandalized New England society by falling in love with an equally brilliant, much younger man named Aaron Burr. She was married at the time and a mother of five. After her first husband died, the two were married and Theodosia, the couple's only child to survive, became of the center of her parents' —– especially her father's —– world.

Father and daughter were particularly close and Burr's plans for his pretty, dark-haired child, who was already displaying an extraordinary intellect and wit, were very ambitious and, for the times, highly progressive. He wanted his daughter to be educated, just as any many would be, and for her to choose the way that she wanted to live her life, which was something not usually available to women in those days.

In 1800, Theodosia fell in love with Joseph Alston, a wealthy planter from South Carolina. The couple were married on February 2, 18901, in Albany. Little more than a month afterward, she and her new husband watched as her father was sworn in as Vice -President of the United States, under President Thomas Jefferson. The couple was further blessed nine months later when their son, Aaron Burr Alston, was born.

But the birth of her only child was a nightmare for Theodosia. She was severely injured during the lengthy and traumatic birth, and the prolapsed uterus that she suffered left her in terrible pain and made intercourse impossible. Although she adored her husband and family, she also had a hard time adjusting to the isolated life of Joseph's plantation, the Oaks, located on the Waccamaw River in South Carolina, and began spending half the year in New York with her father.

On July 10, 1804, Aaron Burr sat down at his desk and wrote a letter of goodbye to his beloved daughter. "I am indebted to you, my dearest Theodosia, for a very great portion of the happiness which I have enjoyed in this life. You have completely satisfied all that my heart and affections had hoped for or even wished."

The following day, Burr killed Alexander Hamilton in a duel in Weehawken, New Jersey.

Rumors swirled about the reason for the duel. Burr had been incensed by a comment that Hamilton made about "still more despicable acts" committed by Burr. Some believe that he may have been referring to Aaron and Theodosia's "morbid affection" for each other, which led to whispers of incest.

Whatever the reason for the incident, Hamilton was dead, and Burr was on the run, even though he was never tried for murder. After serving out his term as Vice President, Burr headed west to establish a new country comprised of North American territory and Mexico. His plan was to become the emperor of the new country, with Theodosia succeeding him as the next ruler. He had the full support of his daughter and son-in-law, who supplied him with much-needed funds. Theodosia and Joseph even went west to help Burr in his quest. Theodosia wrote to her half-brother excitedly about, "the new settlement which I am about to establish."

Obviously, the Burr dynasty did not work out. The plot was discovered, and Burr was arrested. In 1807, he was tried for treason in Richmond with the always-loyal Theodosia by his side. Amazingly, Burr was acquitted but his life and career were ruined. With help from Theodosia, he was smuggled out of the country and was on his way to Europe.

With her father gone, Theodosia's health —– she is believed to have been suffering from uterine cancer —– deteriorated further. She wrote to her doctor of her condition, describing, "Hysteric fits, various colors and flashes of light before her eyes, figures passing around her bed, strange noises, low spirits and worse."

She also missed her father desperately. Since he had left the United States, Theodosia had been campaigning for his return. Eventually, she was successful, and he returned to New York. Things seemed to be brighter, despite Theodosia's poor health; , but then, her son, Aaron, died of malaria in South Carolina, and her world became darker. "There is no more joy for me," she wrote. "The world is blank. I have lost my boy."

On December 10, 1812, Joseph Alston was elected governor of South Carolina. But all his wife wanted was to go and be with her father at home. Joseph's position made it impossible for him to accompany Theodosia, and with the War of 1812 raging in the Atlantic, he was worried about his frail wife making the dangerous trip on her own. Hoping to ensure his daughter's safety, Burr sent his friend, Dr. Timothy Green, to secure passage for Theodosia on a ship and escort her home.

On December 31, Theodosia, Dr. Green, a maid, and a skeleton crew, boarded a small schooner called *Patriot* at the port of Georgetown. One week passed, then two, then three—with no word from *Patriot*, its small crew or passengers. "In three weeks, I have not yet had one line from her," Joseph Alston wrote to his father-in-law. "My mind is tortured—after 30 days—my wife is either captured or lost!" By February 24, he had given up all hope. "My boy and—-my wife—- gone both! This, then is the end of all the hopes we had formed," he wrote to his Burr. "You may well observe that you feel severed from the human race. She was the last thing that bound us to the species."

Theodosia was never seen again.

Joseph died, still a young man, in 1816. His life had been destroyed. Burr lived for another 23 years, long enough to hear all the conspiracy theories that emerged about his daughter's fate. They had started to spread within weeks of the *Patriot's* disappearance. Burr refused to believe she was still alive. He stated firmly, "She is dead. She perished in the miserable little pilot boat in which she left. Were she alive, all the prisons in the world could not keep her from her father."

One of the most likely suggestions as to Theodosia's fate was that the *Patriot* fell victim to some sort of military action related to the war. Perhaps the passenger ship was mistaken for a war vessel and was sunk by a British enemy ship.

Many suggested that the *Patriot* had been captured by one of the pirate ships that sailed along the Outer Banks. Over the years, numerous "death-bed confessions" from various aged or imprisoned pirates were reported in papers all over the country.

The first to gain traction was the case of Jean DeFarges and Robert Johnson, who were executed in 1819 for other crimes. An 1820 article in the *New York Advertiser* claimed that the two had confessed to having been crew members on *Patriot*. They claimed to have led a mutiny, and scuttled the ship, killing all on board.

In 1833, the *Mobile Commercial Register* reported that another man had confessed to raiding the *Patriot* with other pirates, killing everyone on board.

Perhaps the most oft-repeated "confession" was that of Benjamin F. Burdick, a "hard, rough old salt" of a sailor known as "Old Frank," whose account appeared in an 1878 edition of the *New York Times*. On his death bed at a poor-house in Michigan, he is said to have confessed to a minister's wife that he had been on the pirate ship that overtook *Patriot* and Theodosia had been forced to walk the plank. Even though "walking the plank" was more pirate fiction than fact, there were other problems with the authenticity of Burdick's account. He said she was clutching a Bible before she descended into the sea "without a murmur." But Theodosia, like her father, had no interest in religion.

Another unverified story that is undoubtedly more legend than fact involved a locket engraved with "Theodosia" that was found in the possession of a Karankawa Indian chief. The chief claimed he had rescued a young woman from a wrecked ship, and she gave him the locket before dying.

Other stories claimed that she had become the wife of an American Indian in Texas, been taken as a pirate's mistress to Bermuda, or that she had killed herself after resisting the advances of the pirate Octave Chauvet. Yet another fanciful story had her writing farewell letters to her father and husband and stuffing them, along with her wedding ring, into a champagne bottle and throwing it into the Carolina sea before being executed.

And then there are the considerably more eerie accounts.

One of them is the curious grave of the "female stranger" that can be found in St. Paul's Episcopal Cemetery in Alexandria, Virginia. It is said that a "veiled lady" arrived in the city in 1816, with a man claiming to be her husband. The woman was very sick and when a doctor was summoned, the couple refused to answer any questions about their identity. The woman died a short time later. Legend has it that this was Theodosia and Dr. Green, recently returned from captivity in the islands.

But the most mysterious account is the story behind the Nags Portrait.

It may be the only clue that exists as to what really happened to Theodosia. Anna Pool told the story of the painting after she and her father discovered it in 1869. According to Anna, Polly Mann told them that her dead husband, Joseph Tillet, had been a "wrecker" who scavenged the ships that washed up on the shores of the Outer Banks. Polly claimed that, decades before, he and his friends had come upon a scuttled, empty schooner near Kitty Hawk. In one cabin they found many fine items, including the portrait and dresses, which were now in Polly's possession. In fact, Anna stated that she showed them "a vase of wax flowers under a glass globe and a shell beautifully carved in the shape of a nautilus."

Polly gave the portrait to Dr. Pool in lieu of payment and he took it home with him. Over the years, he attempted to get the portrait authenticated by someone in the Burr or Alston families, but no one was able to agree as to whether it was Theodosia. By then, almost everyone who had known her was dead and, of course, photography had not been invented when she had died, so there was nothing to compare it with.

Those who believe in the painting's authenticity think it proves that Theodosia died off the coast of the North Carolina shore —-- one way or another. There were fierce storms on the Outer Banks in early January 1813, which caused damage to other ships along *Patriot's* planned route. It's possible that the small ship was overpowered by the storm, but who knows? Perhaps pirates, rogue wreckers, the British, or something else caused the boat's destruction. Or perhaps Theodosia was taken captive to some exotic land and lived a long life — though with her precarious health that seems very unlikely.

Today the legend of Theodosia lives on.

The Nags Head Portrait now hangs in the Lewis Walpole Library at Yale. Her ghost is said to haunt her plantation The Oaks, as well as the Outer Banks, Richmond Hill, and Bald Head Island. In the late nineteenth and early twentieth centuries, the mystery was the source of several novels and countless magazine articles. Many little girls were named after her — including Theodosia Burr Goodman, who would become famous as the silent screen vamp Theda Bara. Her story was a favorite of poets, including Robert Frost, whose poem *Kitty Hawk* includes the line: "Did I recollect how the wreckers wrecked Theodosia Burr off this very shore? Twas to punish her, but her father more."

We will never know the eventual fate of a young woman whose father had helped to shape the country in which we now live. Her life made a mark, but her death, will always remain a mystery.

1855: The Mystery of James B. Chester

The mystery of Theodosia Burr Alston is not the only maritime tragedy of the nineteenth century. There are many others. There are vessels that vanished completely with all hands on board, for reasons that cannot be explained. There are supernatural mysteries of phantom ships, manned by spectral crews, which come and go like mist on the water.

And there are strange tales of ships from which the crew disappears, leaving only an abandoned vessel behind. One such account is that of *Mary Celeste* in 1872, which has become perhaps the most famous of all "ghost ships." In fact, it has become so well known that the case has overshadowed other similar ——- and just as tragic — -- stories.

One haunting tale concerns a three-masted ship called *James B. Chester* ——- which left behind a mystery that remains unsolved to this day.

In late February 1855, the British vessel *Marathon* was on course about 600 miles southwest of the Azores when it came across another ship nearby. In those days, ocean crossings by sail consumed huge amounts of time and even a passing encounter with another vessel on the lonely expanse of the sea was a pleasant, however brief, interruption of boredom. However, the encounter with this particular passing ship would turn out to be anything but boring.

The three-masted bark, *James B. Chester*, seemed perfectly ordinary until *Marathon* drew closer and the crew noticed something very odd about her ——- there was no one at the *James B. Chester's* helm.

When the two ships drew close together, the bark was hailed, but the cry failed to elicit any response. No one could be seen on her deck, although somehow, the ship had remained on course. The master of *Marathon* was intrigued. In addition to his natural curiosity, he knew that if the ship was abandoned, he would have the right to salvage her. With this in mind, he sent a boarding party over to the other vessel.

James B. Chester was searched thoroughly and found to be completely devoid of human life, on deck or below, living or dead. Her cargo was undisturbed, but something strange had certainly happened on board. The ship showed signs of frenzied activity. The cabins were a mess — clothing and personal items were scattered about, drawers and chests ransacked, and tables and chairs overturned. And yet, there were no signs of a fight or a struggle, such as might have been provoked by a mutiny or pirates. The boarding party could only conclude that the ship had been abandoned in haste, but they could not explain why. The ship was in excellent condition and carried more than enough food and water for the voyage. There was simply no one on board, although all the lifeboats were securely tied in place. All had vanished, taking the ship's compass and log with them —– wherever they had gone.

With no evidence of blood or violence on board, and the cargo intact, mutiny was ruled out, as was piracy. Furthermore, pirates would have likely scuttled the ship to destroy any evidence. There had been no fire and no explosion. *James B. Chester* was perfectly sound and the lack of damage to her decks and sails also ruled out a storm. The sailors would not have normally abandoned the ship unless it was in imminent danger of going down, in which case they would not have wasted the time to create such disarray in the cabins.

Only a truly drastic situation would have forced seasoned mariners to abandon a vessel in the middle of the ocean. But with all those reasons ruled out, what could have caused the crew to abandon the ship —– seemingly in terror and panic? And perhaps stranger yet, how had they managed to leave her?

The derelict was brought into Liverpool as a salvage prize by the crew of *Marathon*. There, she was treated as a curiosity for a time but eventually she vanished into the shadows of history. The eventual fate of *James B. Chester* has long been forgotten.

For several months, though, many pondered the fate of the men who had been on board her, all of whom were never heard from again. They had simply vanished — –impossibly —– without a trace, into the pages of history.

1872: "Ghost Ship"
The Mystery of Mary Celeste

Is the ship accursed? Was there ever a voyage which began
so fairly, and which changed so disastrously?
Sir Arthur Conan Doyle – "J. Habakuk Jephson's
Statement."

History is filled with many mysteries of ships and the sea. But of all
the ships in history, none has a more haunting reputation that the
infamous *Mary Celeste*, a vessel from which the entire crew
inexplicably vanished and was never seen again. Discovered
floundering in the waters of the North Atlantic in December 1872, the
ship soon became an enigma, a much-talked-about puzzle that still
intrigues historians and sailors a century-and-a-half later.

It is, without question, the greatest nautical disappearance of all
time.

On the chilly afternoon of December 4, 1872, the British brigantine
Dei Gratia cut through the waters of the North Atlantic. She was on
course from New York to Gibraltar and the weather promised smooth
sailing with sunny skies and a good wind. Suddenly, across the bow, a
two-masted square-rigger appeared over the horizon. The ship's
course was unsteady and as the wind veered, the vessel shifted
aimlessly. The strange ship was under short canvas in the brisk wind,
yawing heavily while lurching along at only two knots. Two of her sails
were missing and the lower fore topsail hung slackly at the corners.

The captain of *Dei Gratia*, David Reed Morehouse, could see no
one at the helm. He ran up a signal, but there was no reply. Captain

The infamous Mary Celeste

Morehouse, along with First Mate Oliver Deveau, raised their telescopes for a look. He recognized the ship as the *Mary Celeste* but could see no one on board. Morehouse was stunned. He knew the captain of this ship, Benjamin Spooner Briggs, and in fact, had a passing friendship with him. The two men had dined together less than a month before when their ships had been loading cargo at neighboring piers in New York. *Mary Celeste* had set sail for Genoa on November 5, 10 days before *Dei Gratia* had left port.

Deveau pointed out that there seemed to be no distress signal. As the two ships approached within hailing range, Captain Morehouse broke out his speaking trumpet.

"*Celeste* ahoy!" he called out. "Can you hear me?"

There was no reply from the other ship, only the creaking and flapping of plank and canvas. Morehouse called again but nothing stirred on the ship. The captain could see that *Mary Celeste* was on a starboard tack, but the jib sail was set to port. To the experienced seaman, he knew this meant only one thing: the ship was out of control, and or the crew was either incapacitated or dead. He ordered his first mate to take two men with him and board the ship. "Find out what's amiss," he instructed Deveau.

A boat was lowered, and the first mate and two crewmen cast off toward the silent ship. The dinghy was tied up to the larger ship and the three men climbed aboard.

What they found on the ship has remained a mystery ever since.

The deck was empty. No crew member came forward to meet them. They shouted, but no one answered. The wheel stood unattended, spinning idly as the waves slapped at the rudder. The only sound aboard the ship was the groan of wood and rope. The silence was eerie.

They searched the ship from stem to stern, but there was no one on board. The vessel was absolutely deserted but if the crew had abandoned her, they had left everything behind.

The hull, masts, and remaining sails of *Mary Celeste* were all sound. The cargo, which consisted of barrels of crude alcohol, was all intact —- except for one barrel, which had been opened. There was plenty of food and water. Sea chests and clothing lay dry and undisturbed. In the galley, a meal was being prepared and still hung over a dead fire. The bed was unmade in the captain's quarters and the table had been set for breakfast and then abandoned. There was porridge on one of the plates and the remains of eggs on another. Next to one plate was an open bottle of cough medicine with its cork and a spoon lying beside it. In the deck cabins, the skylight stood wide open and rain and sea water had soaked the bedding and clothing and formed large pools on the floor.

The ship itself was seaworthy and most things were in their proper place. It looked as though the entire crew had suddenly winked out of existence. Whatever had occurred, the searchers realized, had taken place a short time before. None of the food had rotted and nothing metal had rusted in the sea air. Everything on the ship, including money and valuables, was intact. The only things that seemed to be missing were the ship's chronometer and the lifeboat. Deveau knew that *Mary Celeste* had carried a boat lashed to the main hatch and now that spot was empty. A piece of railing parallel to it had been removed, apparently in order to launch the craft.

The crew, it seemed, had managed to leave the ship in a single lifeboat and they must have done so in a feverish hurry. Not only had they left behind their personal belongings, including their pipes and tobacco, which most sailors did not abandon unless in fear of death, but the ship had a disturbed look about it that suggested possible violence. Rope and canvas were scattered about on the deck. The ship's compass had been smashed into pieces. In one cabin, they found a cutlass that was smeared with what could have been blood. They found similar stains on the starboard deck rail, near a cut that looked as though it had been made with an ax. On each side of the bow were strips of wood that had been cut from the deck. The strips were six feet long, but why they had been cut was anyone's guess. The windows in the captain's cabin had been boarded up with canvas and heavy planks.

Had the crew abandoned ship in fear of an attack or some other great calamity? If so, how had they escaped? It was unlikely that everyone on board could have fit into the single lifeboat. There had been a crew of seven on the ship, along with Captain Briggs, his wife, Sarah, and their two-year-old daughter, Sarah Matilda.

Deveau checked the ship's log and found the last entry was dated for November 24, 10 days before. At that point, *Mary Celeste* was passing north of St. Mary's Island in the Azores, which was more than 700 miles away. If she had been abandoned after the entry, then the ship had sailed itself, unmanned and unsteered, for more than a week and a half. Such a feat seemed impossible. Deveau believed that someone had to have been on the ship for at least several days after the final log entry. But who had it been? And where had everyone gone? Were they stricken with disease, madness, or something far more sinister?

Deveau returned to *Dei Gratia* and made his report to Captain Morehouse. Although saddened by the disappearance of his acquaintance and his family, Morehouse saw an opportunity and money to be made. He ordered Deveau to return to *Mary Celeste* with two crewmen and then follow *Dei Gratia* to Gibraltar. He would claim the ship as salvage, which would bring him a sizable reward.

Both ships arrived in the Gibraltar harbor one week later. Instead of salvage money, though, Morehouse was met with an official order from the British Admiralty's office to seize the *Mary Celeste* for an immediate investigation.

As it turned out, the *Mary Celeste* had always been known as an unlucky ship. Originally called *Amazon*, her first captain died just 48 hours after his appointment. On her maiden voyage, she collided with a fishing boat off the coast of Maine and damaged her hull. During the repairs, a fire broke out below decks. Her third captain managed to run into another ship off the Straits of Dover. Her fourth captain ran the ship aground on Cape Breton Island and she was wrecked, nearly beyond repair. After all of that, *Amazon* was salvaged and repaired. She was given a new name and an experienced captain in Benjamin Briggs and was put back into service.

And we all know how that turned out.

The investigation in Gibraltar uncovered little more than theories as to what had become of *Mary Celeste's* crew. They considered the abandonment to have been perhaps some plot by the American crew to steal the ship's cargo or to sink the ship and collect the insurance. Finally, mutiny was thought to be the solution. The Admiralty believed that the crew had murdered the captain and his family and then had escaped in the single lifeboat. There was no explanation as to why valuables, including jewelry and an expensive Italian sword, were left behind on the ship.

The American merchant navy was angry over the finding of mutiny. Captain Briggs was not only a fair and decent man, but he was well-liked by all the men who served with him. He also ran a "dry" ship. The only alcohol that was aboard *Mary Celeste* was the cargo, but and it was crude alcohol and impossible to drink. To do so would cause severe stomach cramps and even blindness.

Finally, in March 1873, the British Admiralty admitted that they had no solution to the mystery. It was the first time in history that the court had failed to come to a definite conclusion over maritime law. The owners of *Dei Gratia* were awarded one-fifth of the value of *Mary Celeste* as a salvage fee and the ship was returned to her owner. He wasted no time in selling the cursed ship.

Over the next decade, no new evidence was unearthed about the abandonment of the ship. No one from the crew was ever seen again and, in time, interest in the story began to fade.

Then, in 1882, the strange story of *Mary Celeste* took an unusual turn.

The events that led to the sudden surge of new interest in the "ghost ship" began with a seemingly unrelated incident in the small town of Southsea, in England. The incident was simply that a newly licensed doctor named Arthur Conan Doyle put up a nameplate on the wall outside of his office door.

If Doyle had suddenly found himself with more patients than he could handle, the tale of the *Mary Celeste* might be as forgotten now as the *James B. Chester*, another vessel whose crew vanished without a trace.

But that wasn't what happened. After hanging his name outside his door, Doyle spent days and weeks waiting for patients and prosperity, only to find neither. Instead, he discovered a love of writing and he chased away the boredom of his lackluster medical practice by penning stories. Doyle would go on to become a prolific writer of mystery and horror novels, the creator of the legendary detective Sherlock Holmes, and an outspoken proponent of the Spiritualist movement. In those days, though, he was simply a penniless doctor with a taste for weird tales.

In the fall of 1882, he would write one of these strange stories and it would go on to not only create a sensation but would also earn a unique place in history. In fact, Doyle's harmless story would jumble the facts of the *Mary Celeste* mystery so badly that many believe that the blame for the case never being solved rests squarely on Conan Doyle's shoulders.

The story, titled "J. Habakuk Jephson's Statement," appeared in the *Cornhill Magazine* of January 1884. The tale was not only one of Doyle's best early tales, but he used a fictional setting to create a theory about what happened to the crew of the real-life *Mary Celeste*. To do this, he created an entirely different scenario. In the first sentence alone, he changed the location of where the ship was found, the circumstances behind her discovery, and even the name of the ship itself from *"Mary Celeste"* to *"Marie Celeste."* Doyle was obviously trying to get the story noticed and in that, he succeeded marvelously.

The public and the popular press immediately seized upon the story. It was published anonymously and accepted as truth with the fictional Jephson claiming to be on board the *"Marie Celeste"* when she is taken over by a black radical leader with a hatred for whites. No one seemed to notice the obvious changes that Doyle had written into the story. It was taken very seriously and debated by people as the true story of the real *Mary Celeste*.

The adventures of Jephson created a storm of controversy for the British Admiralty. The chief investigator in Gibraltar, Solly Flood, was so outraged by the story that he sent a flurry of public telegrams denouncing Jephson's "true account" as an outrageous lie. He followed these rather embarrassing telegrams with an official report to the Admiralty pinpointing each of the mistakes in the account. Needless to say, when the real details of the fictional story were learned, the press was delighted, as was Conan Doyle. The story launched his literary career.

The story was also the catalyst for a new wave of interest in the *Mary Celeste* mystery. In the years that followed, many other hoax accounts of the last days of the ship —-- although none as successful as the first —-- emerged. Nothing was ever heard from any known member of the ship's crew again, but there was a steady surfacing of *Mary Celeste* survivors whose names, somehow, had been left off the ship's register. They popped up all over the world, with stories that ranged from the impossible to the ridiculous.

Writer of the strange Charles Fort suggested that the missing passengers and crew could have been whisked off the ship by what he called a "selective force," which left the ship itself untouched. In 1926, Adam Bushey claimed that *Mary Celeste* had been "dematerialized" en route but when it returned to solid form, the crew did not return with it. Other weird stories emerged of strange accidents, giant squids, krakens, time warps, abductions by aliens, and the mythical "Bermuda Triangle."

Countless serious theories were also expressed as to the fate of the ship's crew.

Even though the Admiralty in Gibraltar eventually ruled out theories of murder and conspiracy, the suspicion of foul play has always lingered. Insurance fraud on the part of the ship's owner, James Winchester, was briefly suspected, largely because some newspapers claimed that *Mary Celeste* was heavily over insured. Winchester was able to refute these allegations, though.

In 1931, an article in the *Quarterly Review* suggested that Captain Morehouse could have lain in wait for *Mary Celeste*, then lured Briggs and his crew aboard *Dei Gratia* and killed them there. This theory ignores undisputed facts, though —- *Dei Gratia* left New York eight days after *Mary Celeste*, was a slower ship, and would not have caught up to *Mary Celeste* before she reached Gibraltar.

Another theory suggested that Briggs and Morehouse were partners in a conspiracy to share in the salvage money. The two men had been friends but little else about the theory makes sense. If Briggs and Morehouse had been planning such a scam, they would not have devised such an attention-drawing mystery. In addition, if Briggs planned to permanently disappear, why would he leave his son, Arthur, behind?

In 1925, historian John Gilbert Lockhart surmised in a book that Briggs, in a fit of religious mania, had slaughtered everyone on board and then killed himself. In a later edition of his book, Lockhart, who had by then spoken to Briggs's descendants, apologized and withdrew this theory.

What most could agree on was that, to precipitate the abandonment of an apparently sound and seaworthy ship, with ample provisions, that some extraordinary and alarming circumstance must have taken place.

James Briggs, the brother of the ship's captain, was convinced that the solution to the mystery lay in the ship's last log entry. It stated that the wind had dropped after a night of heavy ocean squalls. If this is correct; it could have meant that the ship lost speed and drifted toward the rocks of Santa Maria Island. The hull of the ship may have been breached, explaining a few pools of water that *Dei Gratia* First Mate Deveau found below decks. The crew may have believed the *Mary Celeste* was sinking and abandoned the ship.

During the inquiry into the ship's fate, Deveau suggested an explanation based on a sounding rod found on the derelict's deck. A sounding rod was a piece of iron used to ascertain the depth of water in a ship's hold. He surmised that Briggs might have abandoned ship after a sounding that, because of a malfunction of the pumps or other mishap, had given a false impression that the vessel was taking on water rapidly.

Another explanation claimed that the ship was struck by a waterspout. This would explain the damage done to the sails and the water found below decks. The low barometric pressure generated by the spout could have driven water from the bilges up into the pumps, leading the crew to assume the ship had taken on more water than she had, and was in danger of sinking.

There is also a theory about a displaced iceberg that Briggs could have feared running into with the ship. It's unlikely that an iceberg would have drifted that far south, though. If it had done so, other ships would have reported seeing it.

It's also possible that *Mary Celeste*, while becalmed, could have drifted toward nearby reefs. The theory supposes that Briggs, fearing his ship would run aground, launched the lifeboat in the hope of reaching land. The wind could then have picked up and blown *Mary Celeste* away from the reef, while the rising seas swamped and sank the smaller escape boat. The weakness of this theory is that if the ship had been becalmed, all sails would have been set to catch any available breeze, yet the ship was found with many of its sails furled.

There is one feasible explanation for what happened to the ship that takes into account everything that was discovered by the *Dei Gratia's* crew. There was no structural damage done to the ship, and yet it had apparently been abandoned in great haste. For this reason, it seems that the evacuation was not carried out because of something that had already happened —- but because of something they were afraid was going to happen. The only danger potential danger on board the *Mary Celeste* was her cargo.

Captain Briggs had never carried crude alcohol before and was likely unfamiliar with its chemical reactions. He had come from the cold weather of New York to the much warmer region of the Azores and the barrels, shaken by stormy weather, may have started to leak fumes into the hold. It's possible that Briggs feared that the vapors could either poison his family and the crew, or that the barrels might explode. One of the barrels, it will be remembered, was opened, probably during an inspection. If the inspection had taken place by candlelight, the open flame could have caused the fumes to burst into flame —- which convinced the captain that the entire ship was in danger of exploding.

Terrified for the safety of his men, not to mention his wife and daughter, he may have ordered everyone into the lifeboat. In all likelihood, Briggs intended to stick close to the ship so that they could get back on if no further explosion occurred, but it would not have taken much wind to send the *Mary Celeste* sailing away from the lifeboat —- thus, abandoning the crew at sea. The crew almost certainly would have tried to catch up with the ship, but rough seas may have prevented them from doing so, and the crew and passengers of the *Mary Celeste* were lost forever.

This theory was first offered by James Winchester, the ship's owner, and it has since been considered by several authors. Somehow, though, it's never been generally accepted, perhaps because pirates, sea monsters, and time warps are much more exciting than an ordinary, yet fatal, accident.

That's not quite the end of the story.

After the Court of Inquiry was finished with her, James sold the ship as soon as he arrived back in New York, some say at a great loss. But perhaps the unluckiest person in the deal was the man who bought her. *Mary Celeste* was rumored to be jinxed from the beginning and the events that followed the vanishing of her crew continued her run of terrible luck.

The new owner loaded the ship with a cargo of lumber and sent her to Montevideo. During a storm that occurred while en route, the deck cargo, and a good amount of the ship's rigging, was lost. The voyage turned out to be a total loss. On the return trip, carrying a load of horses and mules, most of the animals died in the hold and a few days later, the new owner followed suit.

From that point on, the *Mary Celeste* changed hands so quickly and so frequently that it became almost impossible to keep track of who owned her and when. She continued to sail up and down the American coastline, slowly falling apart.

Then, in 1884, she was purchased by an old seaman from Massachusetts named Gilman C. Parker. For most of his 61 years, Parker had dabbled in almost every kind of illegal activity on the sea, except for outright piracy. He and some of his friends concocted a scheme to make some money off the notoriously unprofitable *Mary Celeste*. They loaded her with a cargo of junk, worth nothing more than a few hundred dollars, but insured the cargo as being worth nearly $27,000. After that, Captain Parker took the ship on her death voyage to the Caribbean.

In Haiti's Gulf of Gonave is a coral reef called Rochelois Bank, which had proven fatal to scores of ships over the years. Parker set a course for the reef and the brigantine was grounded on the razor-like coral. With waves crashing around her, the ship began to settle. There was no immediate danger and the crew had plenty of time to row the cargo ashore. When everything worthwhile had been salvaged, Parker ordered kerosene poured onto the decks and then he lit a torch. The *Mary Celeste* burst into flames and by evening, was nothing but a charred skeleton.

Back in Boston, Parker and his associates filed their insurance claim. The company was suspicious and dispatched detectives to question the crew. The sailors, who were not getting a share of the money, freely talked about what they had seen. Soon after, Parker and his partners were in federal court, facing a charge of barratry —— an act of gross misconduct committed by a master or crew of a vessel which damages the vessel or its cargo. In those days, this was a hanging offense.

The jury was unable to reach a verdict in the case, however, and Parker and the other conspirators were set free. They never collected their claim and the notoriety of the case killed their reputations. Eight months later, Parker died in disrepute and poverty. One of his friends was confined to an insane asylum and another committed suicide.

Even after she was destroyed, *Mary Celeste*, the most famous cursed ship in history, was still bringing bad luck to anyone connected to her.

1874: Little Boy Lost

During the first half of the nineteenth century, the United States could hardly be thought of as a crime-conscious nation. There is no question that American cities and towns certainly saw more than their share of murder, thievery, mayhem, and assorted violence. But in the absence of telegraph and telephone communication, these crimes remained localized. By this I mean that most towns and cities were largely ignorant of sensational events —— criminal or otherwise —— in other parts of the country.

But by the middle of the century, that would all change. When President Abraham Lincoln was assassinated in 1865, the entire country united in a single bond of horror, stunned by the horrible deed that had been done. Crime had become a part of the American consciousness.

Then, in 1874, nine years after the president was slain, the country was again shocked by another terrible event. It was not the death of a leader, but the disappearance of a previously unknown four-year-old boy named Charles Brewster Ross. Little Charlie Ross —– as Americans would come to know him —– was stolen away in what became the first instance of kidnapping for ransom in the United States.

Even worse, Charlie Ross was never found.

Charlie Brewster Ross

Charlie, a serious, blond-haired, blue-eyed boy, was the son of Christian K. Ross, the head of Ross, Shott & Company, a well-established Philadelphia grocery business. The company was a prosperous one and the Ross family lived in a well-appointed home on Washington Lane in the affluent Germantown neighborhood. Surrounded by other handsome homes in a well-to-do area, the Ross mansion was about 200 yards from the Germantown railroad depot. The sounds of the passenger trains were the only noises to disturb this quiet community. Boys and girls were free to run and play wherever they wanted, and the chief danger to children in Germantown in 1874 was they might wander too far from home and get lost in the woods.

Christian and his wife had seven children, of whom Charlie was the youngest. Mrs. Ross suffered from occasional health problems and in mid-June of 1874, her doctor advised her to take a trip for some rest. Her husband readily agreed to a vacation for his wife, and with a capable staff to watch over the needs of the household, Mrs. Ross and her five daughters journeyed to Atlantic City for a month.

On the afternoon of June 27, Charlie and his brother Walter, age six, were playing in a lane behind the Ross home. It was a fine sunny day and the boys were enjoying the afternoon. But their play was suddenly interrupted by the approach of a horse-drawn buggy. Two men were inside it, both large, rough-looking, and poorly dressed. One sported a black mustache and a full, chest-length beard. His companion had a sandy-colored mustache and while he wore no beard, he was sporting a pair of smoked goggles, which were used as sunglasses in those days. Presumably, they were worn as a disguise.

The shabby-looking men stopped in the road and one of them leaned over to ask the boys their names and where they lived. Charlie and Walter, with no reason to fear anyone, didn't shy away from the two men. Walter spoke up and told the men his name, along with that of his brother. He indicated the large Ross mansion behind them and told the men that they lived there.

The men exchanged a glance and then invited the boys into their buggy for a ride. At the invitation, caution, or shyness, took over and Walter refused. The men chuckled and then one of them reached into his pocket and pulled out a large handful of candy. He dumped it into the outstretched hands of the two little boys. The driver of the buggy cracked the reins across the back of the horse, and they drove away.

When Christian Ross arrived home that evening, he asked the boys where they had gotten the candy. Informed of the two strangers in the buggy, Ross smiled indulgently and uttered what became one of the heart-breaking statements in the case —-- "Those men must love children," he said.

Over the next five days, the two men in the buggy became a familiar sight on and around Washington Lane. They drove past where the Ross boys were playing every day, passing out liberal amounts of candy and making pleasant conversation. By 4:00 p.m. on July 1, Walter and Charlie considered them friends. On that day, the strangers told the boys that they were on their way to downtown Philadelphia to buy fireworks for the Fourth of July. They invited the boys to go along with them. Without hesitation, the boys climbed into the buggy. Walter seated himself between the two men and Charlie trustingly sat himself on one of the men's laps.

For an hour, the buggy traveled along through the countryside and when Charlie complained of being hungry, the men stopped at a roadside tavern and bought the boys some cakes. Soon, the buggy arrived at the corner of Palmer and Richmond streets in Philadelphia, where there was a store that offered a dazzling array of fireworks in the window. One of the men handed Walter a quarter and told him to spend it inside. The boy climbed happily from the buggy and disappeared into the store. He spent 10 minutes inside, happily buying everything that he wanted, and then he ran outside to show his purchases to his brother and his friends.

But the buggy containing his brother and the two men was gone.

Walter panicked and began running up and down the street looking for them. He was in such of state of terror that passersby stopped and questioned him. One of them, a Germantown resident named Peacock, recognized him as one of Christian Ross' sons. He took the weeping boy by the hand and led him to the railroad station. Walter protested that his brother Charlie was still in Philadelphia with two strange men. Peacock concluded that the men in the buggy got tired of waiting for Walter in the store and had decided to drive Charlie home.

At 8:00 p.m., still clutching an armload of fireworks, Walter entered the Ross home on Washington Lane. Christian Ross had been worried about his sons, although foul play had never crossed his mind. Yet Walter's story of the men in the buggy sent a chill through his heart. After Walter had eaten dinner and was on his way to bed, Ross returned to Philadelphia and went directly to the police.

Unfortunately, the role of the police in the disappearance of Charlie Ross is hardly an inspiring one. History places most of the blame for their failures on the fact that this was an unprecedented situation. Officers who had spent most of their time dealing with mundane crimes, murders, and theft, were suddenly forced to handle something completely beyond their understanding. There were no police procedures to handle something like this. In fact, when Christian Ross appeared at the police station and respectfully told the story of Charlie and the two men, the officers were incredulous. Who would want to steal a boy —— and why? The police at headquarters agreed to alert patrolmen throughout the city to watch for the buggy and its three occupants.

No one saw Charlie that night and he did not return home. The next day, the police instructed Ross to place an advertisement in the *Philadelphia Public Ledger* newspaper for July 3. It read:

LOST, on July 1, a small boy, about four years of age, light complexion, and light curly hair. A suitable reward will be paid on return to E.L. Joyce, Central Station, corner of Fifth and Chestnut Streets.

The name of E.L. Joyce was used because Mrs. Ross was still vacationing in Atlantic City. Undoubtedly, she read the *Public Ledger* —– everyone in Philadelphia did, even on vacation. Her husband did not want her to become upset by the disappearance of her youngest child.

While the newspaper advertisement was running, the police were preparing a circular of their own. It described the two rough-looking men as accurately as Walter Ross could remember them and gave a more detailed description of Charlie and his clothing —– "a brown linen kilt-suit with short skirt, a broad-brimmed unbleached Panama hat with a black band, laced shoes, and blue and white striped stockings. The boy has long flaxen curly hair, hazel eyes, clear skin, round full face, and no marks except those made by vaccination on arm."

Nothing was heard about Charlie until the morning of July 5. The morning mail made it clear that the boy was not merely lost —– he had been kidnapped. Dated and posted in Philadelphia the day before, a letter to Christian Ross stated that Charlie was in good health and safely hidden. The letter emphasized that there was no sense in searching for him. Most important, the police should not be called into the search. The note ended by saying Ross would hear more in a few days. Until then, he must do nothing. The letter was signed only with the name "John."

The letter itself was strange. It was crudely lettered in rough pencil, had no capital letters, and was inconsistent with misspellings. It seemed that the writer was trying to make himself appear more ignorant than he was.

Ross rushed the letter to the police, who still had trouble believing that a kidnapping had actually taken place. They assured Ross that they would do everything possible to quickly apprehend the abductors — and then did nothing.

Two days later, on July 7, Christian Ross received the first ransom demand in American history. Using the same crude phrases and spelling, the letter demanded $20,000 in exchange for the safe return of Charlie Ross. "If you are willing to part with your money," the letter said, "why you can have your child, otherwise he must die." Ross was instructed to place an ad in the newspaper if he was willing to pay the ransom.

With the threat against his son's life in hand, Ross again hurried to police headquarters. Finally, the police seemed willing to take a serious view of the kidnapping. It was seven days after the abduction and detectives were just now being ordered to search trains and boats and stop all of those leaving the city by horse and buggy. A house-to-house search for Charlie was instituted and known criminals were rounded up.

It was impossible to hide the police activity that was taking place and, at last, the story of Charlie Ross broke in the newspapers, sending a panic throughout the city. Parents were terrified that something might happen to their own children. On numerous occasions, little boys who looked like Charlie Ross were hauled to the nearest police station. The police added to the general frenzy by stating that the kidnappers might dye Charlie's hair and dress him like a girl. Thus, any child, regardless of coloring or sex, was suspected of being the lost boy.

Time passed and Christian Ross received daily letters from the kidnappers. On July 8, one note asked if he was prepared to pay "4,000 pounds for the return of your son?" The police dismissed this as a ploy to make the kidnappers seem British, but customs officials at Atlantic ports were nonetheless alerted to watch for Charlie. English authorities were contacted and asked to inspect any small boys seen disembarking from American ships.

Ross also received other letters from all over the country, each telling him of seeing a golden-haired boy in the company of suspicious characters. One letter, from Goshen, New York, told of a blond child who was seen traveling with a band of gypsies. Ross made the first of several long trips to investigate, but the boy was not Charlie.

Oddly, it seemed the kidnappers were belatedly discovering that Christian Ross was not a wealthy man. He was well-off, but far from rich. Earlier in his career, he had gone bankrupt and it had been his brother-in-law who set him up in the grocery business. The size of the Ross mansion had convinced the kidnappers that he was a man of wealth, but as the entire city hunted them, they discovered that he was not. In one of the letters, they wrote. "We know you are not worth much money, but we are aware that you have rich friends from whom you can borrow. If you love money better than your child, its blood will be on your head."

Although Ross made no real effort to raise the $20,000, he placed ads in the newspaper that indicated that he was doing so. The kidnappers warned him that no amount less than what they demanded would be accepted. Ross replied, "Have not got it; am doing my best to raise it."

Five more days passed and the city of Philadelphia, as well as people all over the country, waited anxiously to see what would happen next in the case. Accounts of the kidnapping were now being featured in newspapers and magazines all over America, including *Harper's Weekly* and *Leslie's Weekly*, the two most popular periodicals of the time.

More days passed with Christian Ross promising the ransom but not delivering it. The police, meanwhile, were scouring the city and the surrounding area for the kidnappers. Late in July, the mayor of Philadelphia ended his vacation in New Jersey and returned to his official desk. There, he presided over a meeting of police chiefs and prominent citizens at which it was decided to offer a reward of $20,000 for information leading to the arrest of Charlie's abductors. The elaborate proclamation accompanying this announcement apparently drove the kidnappers out of the city. The next letter that Ross received was postmarked from New York and warned him to produce the ransom money —- or accept the consequences.

He was to collect the cash in bank notes of small denominations and place them in a leather bag that would be painted white so that it would be clearly visible at night. With the money in the bag, he was to board the New York train on the night of July 30. He must come alone, without the police or any witnesses. During the trip, he was to stand on the back platform of the train. When he saw a bright light, with a white flag waving beside it, he was to toss the bag down onto the railroad tracks. The train was not to stop, nor was Ross to end his journey at New York City. He was directed to remain on board as far as Albany. Before this date, he was to place an ad in the *New York Herald* indicating his willingness to go along with the plan.

Ross showed the letter to the police, who convinced him to stall. He was told to place the newspaper ad and purchase a leather bag, which could be painted white. But instead of money, he was to place a letter in the bag that stated that he would not pay the ransom until he could see Charlie alive. He insisted —- or the police instructed him to insist —- that the exchange of money and the child take place at the same time. He was also told to ask for a better means of communication than the personals column of the newspaper.

On the night of July 30, white bag firmly gripped in his hand, Ross took up his position on the rear platform of the New York train. Hidden inside the car was a contingent of Philadelphia police officers. Presumably, the train could be stopped when the light and waving flag were seen and the kidnappers could be captured. Ross waited patiently as the train steamed toward New York, ready to toss the bag as soon as the signal was spotted —- but it never happened.

No one knows why the kidnappers failed to go through with the ransom drop that they had themselves devised, but Ross and the police officers arrived in New York red-faced and angry. Since the kidnappers were now in another city, Ross and the Philadelphia police arranged for a conference with New York City Police Chief George Walling. He took an interest in the case and asked to see the ransom notes that had been mailed from New York. The veteran policeman took a careful look at the letters and announced that they appeared to be in the handwriting of a man named William Mosher, who also went by the name of William Johnson.

Mosher was a small-time criminal with a long arrest record in the city. He frequented the city's notorious Five Points neighborhood, especially along Mott Street. He was well-known to the New York police, but no one seemed to be able to find him now. Walling personally led the search for Mosher and repeatedly questioned William Westervelt, Mosher's brother-in-law. Westervelt, until recently, had been a New York City policeman but he had been kicked off the force for accepting bribes from gamblers. Walling offered to give Westervelt his job back if he could lead them to Mosher. Westervelt stalled, asking for a higher price. He demanded complete exoneration, back pay, and a promotion. Walling refused and the two men met several times, arguing heatedly. The deal fell through and Westervelt refused to provide any information. Strangely, Walling never thought to have Westervelt followed so that he might lead the police to Mosher and to Charlie Ross. Walling's carelessness in this regard made him as ineffectual as the Philadelphia authorities had been.

In Philadelphia, Christian Ross continued receiving letters from the kidnappers. He also got an increasing number of letters from around the country, reporting that Charlie had been found. Blond-haired children seen wandering the streets, abandoned by their parents, or even playing close to their own homes, were hysterically identified as Charlie Ross. His father took a number of trips to see these lost children but returned home disappointed every time.

In mid-November, a letter from the kidnappers arrived and ordered Ross to stand in the lobby of the Fifth Avenue Hotel in New York on November 18. He was to carry $20,000 with him, wrapped as an ordinary package. He must remain in the lobby all day and at some point, a messenger would arrive for the money. If he agreed to this plan, he was again supposed to insert an ad in the *New York Herald*. It was to read "Saul of Tarsus, Fifth Avenue Hotel – instant."

Christian Ross placed the advertisement. By now, he was a beaten and downtrodden man. His wife was heartbroken, and Ross was fed up with the clumsiness of the police. He had hired the Pinkertons and on their advice, had raised most of the $20,000. He wrapped the money in a plain brown package, but he himself did not wait in the hotel lobby. He delegated his brother and nephew to take his place. They waited all day, but the messenger never came.

After that, the kidnappers fell silent.

One month later, a seemingly unrelated crime occurred in the Bay Ridge section of Brooklyn. There, Judge Charles Van Brunt, presiding judge of the appellate division of the New York Supreme Court, owned a splendid home overlooking New York Harbor. The judge spent many happy summers at the house and as much time during the winter season as he could. Frequently, however, judicial duties kept him in New York and Albany, and he closed up the Bay Ridge house. Fearing robbery in his absence, he arranged for an elaborate burglar alarm system that sounded in the nearby home of his brother.

On the night of December 14, the sound of the alarm broke the silence of his brother's home. The weather outside was cold, wet, and miserable, and Van Brunt and his oldest son looked out at the judge's house. They spotted a flickering light moving in the darkness behind the windows. Van Brunt roused two hired men and the four of them ran out into the night with guns and rain gear. They converged on the judge's home and stationed themselves at each corner of the house.

A few minutes later, the cellar door opened, and two men emerged, pulling a heavy bag behind them. Van Brunt shouted at the robbers to drop the bag and raise their hands. The men let go of the bag, and then one of them ran straight for one of Van Brunt's hired men, who shot him dead. The other robber opened fire, but a bullet from Van Brunt's own gun dropped him where he stood. With a cry, the burglar fell to the ground.

The men converged on the fallen robber and as he lay dying, he gasped out his final words. His name, he said, was Joseph Douglas. His companion was William Mosher. Then, he croaked out more words, "We kidnapped Charlie Ross. We did it to make money."

Van Brunt dropped to his knees beside the man and begged him to tell where Charlie could be found. "I don't know," Douglas whispered, "but Mosher does."

Van Brunt's son dragged over Mosher's dead body so that his companion could see that his partner was incapable of ever telling anyone anything. It made no difference. Douglas only shook his head weakly. He assured Van Brunt that Charlie Ross would be returned safely in a few days. "Chief Walling knows all about us," he added. "He was after us and now he has us." With those words, he died.

The next day, Walter Ross, now age seven, was brought to New York to view the bodies of the two dead men in the morgue. Without hesitation, he identified them as the two men in the buggy who had taken Charlie.

The police rushed to question Mrs. Lillian Mosher, the kidnapper's wife and the sister of former police officer, William Westervelt. She first stated for the record that Mosher, a father of four, had been a fine husband and parent. Moments later, she admitted that he had planned the Charlie Ross kidnapping. She had no idea where the boy might be and had never known where he was hidden. Yet, like the dying Douglas, she stated with conviction that the child would soon be safely returned.

Westervelt was arrested for conspiring with the kidnappers but as much as they tried, the police were unable to tie him directly to the abduction. Police informants came forward and testified to Westervelt being drunk in a Mott Street bar and boasting that he knew the identities of Charlie's kidnappers. He also claimed that he thought up the secret signals, like Saul of Tarsus, by which Ross and the kidnappers communicated. The police, stung by the fact that Westervelt had once been one of their own, tried desperately to get him to talk. In the end, he was charged only as an accessory to the kidnapping.

He was brought to trial in Philadelphia on August 30, 1875. At the trial, both the judge and the prosecutor hammered at Westervelt to tell whether Charlie was alive, and if so, where he might possibly be. Westervelt, denying everything, sullenly repeated that he did not know the boy's whereabouts. At the same time, he, too, stated that he was all right and would be returned home soon.

On September 30, 14 months after the kidnapping, the jury found him guilty as an accomplice. The judge sentenced him to seven years of solitary confinement at Eastern State Penitentiary in Philadelphia. He served his time and was never heard of again.

Tragically, the same thing could be said for little Charlie Ross.

He was never found. Christian Ross spent 20 years looking for his son. He spent more than $60,000 in advertisements, Pinkerton fees, and lengthy trips in search of Charlie, traveling to the West Coast, Mexico, and Europe in his quest. After looking at as many as 273 children who were not his son, he finally gave up.

As the Westervelt trial ended, newspapers speculated that Charlie might have died of grief, malnutrition, or mistreatment. Some believed that he was murdered, and his body buried in a secret location, and others surmised that he had been adopted by some unknowing family. Of these alternatives, death by murder or neglect seem the most likely. Why else would Westervelt have remained silent, preferring long years in prison to telling what he knew? Had he told the truth, Westervelt might have been tried for Charlie's murder.

Chances are that Charlie died soon after the abduction. During the long correspondence from the kidnappers, no clue was ever given as to Charlie's health, his state of mind, or general welfare. No proof was ever offered that he was still alive. Many have speculated that Westervelt transported Charlie to New York immediately after the kidnapping, leaving Mosher and Douglas in Philadelphia to write the first series of ransom notes. Westervelt may have become alarmed by the fact that he was holding America's first kidnapped child and killed him, or neglected him, and, as rumor had it, dropped his body into the East River.

Even though he was likely dead, Charlie Ross remained very much alive in legend, rumor, and in the hearts and minds of those who remembered him. Well into the 1900s, mothers warned their children that they might be kidnapped like Charlie Ross if they did not behave. In the 1920s and 1930s, a rash of elderly men on their deathbeds claimed to be Charlie Ross but none of them were.

We'll never know what happened to Charlie. He will always remain the original "little boy lost."

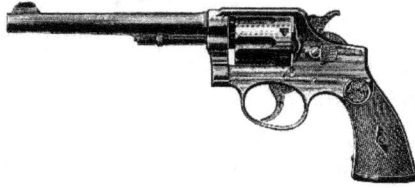

1896: The Case of Colonel Fountain

When Colonel Albert Jennings Fountain and his son, Henry, climbed into their wagon on a cold January day in 1896, they had no idea that within a few days they would become a part of one of the greatest unsolved disappearances in the history of the American West. Fountain and his son vanished without a trace that day and were never seen again. They were presumed dead but to this day, no one knows if they were murdered and, if they were, who might have taken their lives.

They simply disappeared and no trace of them was ever found.

Colonel Albert Fountain was an important figure in New Mexico history. He was a member of the original California Column that marched to New Mexico during the Civil War. After serving in the military, he organized a civilian militia to protect settlers from raiding Apache and Navajo Indians and to guard against outlaws and others who terrorized the citizens of the state. He achieved the rank of colonel during this time and earned the respect of the New Mexican people.

During one of the battles with Navajos, he was wounded and while recuperating in an El Paso hospital, developed an interest in politics. As he nurtured those ambitions, he founded a newspaper in Mesilla, New Mexico, which dealt with many governmental issues. Despite how well-liked he was, his pointed and often critical editorials angered many. He was often accused of taking the wrong side in arguments where he saw others' rights being infringed upon, such as when he took up the defense of Billy the Kid during Billy's murder trial in Mesilla.

Colonel Albert Jennings Fountain, who vanished with his son, Henry, in 1896. His story remains one of the great unsolved mysteries of the West.

Fountain lost the case and the Kid was sentenced to hang, although he later escaped from custody.

In 1888, Fountain, running as a Republican, won a seat in the New Mexico legislature, badly beating his opponent, an aggressive Democrat named Albert Bacon Fall. While serving in Santa Fe, Fountain was elected Speaker of the House. In 1892, Fountain was defeated by Fall after a hotly contested campaign that was rife was accusations of voter fraud, bribery, and voter intimidation. Each man harbored an intense and deepening dislike for one another.

Fountain spent his life as a soldier of fortune, legislator, judge, frontier lawyer, newspaper editor, miner, and military man, and at the time he disappeared in 1896, he was the nemesis of New Mexico's cattle thieves. He had taken on the role of a special prosecutor for the Southeastern New Mexico Livestock Association and had, just 30 days earlier, secured grand jury indictments against 32 men for cattle theft. Among those indicted were a number of prominent ranchers including

William McNew, Jim Gilliland, and Oliver Lee. McNew was a business partner and close friend of Albert Bacon Fall. Not surprisingly, this aggravated the tension between Fountain and Fall. By this time, their hatred for one another had become the stuff of legend throughout the region.

As word leaked out about the indictments, Fountain began receiving threats on his life. In fact, on the morning that he and Henry were preparing for a trip from Las Cruces to Lincoln -- located about 150 miles to the northeast — he was handed a note that warned him that he would be killed within a week if he did not drop the charges against the ranchers. Fountain treated the note as he had all the other threats against him: he ignored it and refused to change his plans.

He wrapped Henry in a warm blanket on the buckboard seat next to him, snapped the reins across the backs of his team of horses, and set off down the road toward Mesilla. It is believed that Fountain took Henry with him on his business trips at the urging of his wife, Mariana, who was convinced that no one would harm the prosecutor if he was accompanied by his nine-year-old child. Mariana came to regret this belief.

The two-day trip proved uneventful, but the streets and saloons of Lincoln were buzzing with news about Fountain's indictments. He knew the grand jury indictments were but a small step toward a trial. This realization exhausted him, and he was not in a celebratory mood when he collected Henry from the home of friends and departed from Lincoln on January 30.

The first day of travel was quiet. The Fountains spent the night at Blazer's Mill, located on the west side of the Mescalero Apache reservation. The next morning, Colonel Fountain and Henry got off to an early start and were on the road shortly after dawn. They had not traveled far before they were stopped by a Mescalero Apache man who was leading a pinto pony. The Apache owed money to Fountain and he offered the pony as payment. The two men spoke briefly, and Fountain eventually took the horse, mostly because of the other man's insistence. He tied the animal to the back of the wagon and continued down the road.

Around noon, they stopped in the town of Tularosa, arriving at a general store that belonged to Fountain's friend, Albert Dieter, who offered them lunch. Fountain declined but fed oats to the horses before continuing with the journey. They drove on for a few more hours before finally stopping at the La Luz settlement, where they spent the night at the home of a man named Sutherland.

The next morning, after stowing gear, his satchel filled with legal work and indictments, and a Winchester rifle into the buckboard, Fountain tucked Henry into the seat and started off again. They faced a long, arduous ride across the open basin between La Luz and Las Cruces. Earlier that morning, Fountain had agreed to transport a young woman named Fannie Stevenson to Las Cruces that day, but because the weather was so cold, she had declined to leave with them.

As he was leaving La Luz, Fountain stopped for a few minutes to speak with a man named Hill, who was on his way into town. Hill later recalled that Fountain mentioned that he had seen three men on horseback riding along the trail ahead of him.

Around lunchtime, Fountain halted the wagon at a place called Pellman's Well, near what is now White Sands National Monument. The Colonel fed and watered the horses and then had a quiet lunch with Henry before continuing with the trip.

After another two hours on the road, Fountain met a mail carrier named Santos Alvarado, who had completed a journey to Luna's Well and was on his way back to Tularosa. After the two men visited for a few minutes, Fountain asked Alvarado if he had seen three riders on the road ahead. The mail carrier agreed that he had but stated that they had turned off the main road and had traveled east in the direction of the Sacramento Mountains. The two spoke about other things, said farewell, and moved on in opposite directions.

A short distance later, Colonel Fountain encountered five more riders traveling toward Tularosa. Among them was another mail rider and friend, Saturnino Barela. During a brief conversation, Fountain told him about the three men that he had seen riding ahead of him. Barela told Fountain that he and his companions had apparently encountered the same men on the trail some distance back, but when the strangers spotted the travelers, they quickly left the trail and rode away. Concerned that these men might pose a threat to the Fountains, Barela advised him to return to Luna's Well and remain for the night. In the morning, Barela promised, he would accompany them to Las Cruces.

Fountain thanked his friend for the offer but told him that he was determined to reach home by midnight. He waved and continued down the road. Saturnino Barela became one of the last people to see Albert and Henry Fountain alive.

On February 2, Barela was on his way to Mesilla down the same road that he had traveled the previous day. About three miles beyond the point where he had visited with Colonel Fountain, he spotted the ridge of Chalk Hill and noticed some unusual disturbances in the trail. It was apparent to him that something terrible had occurred there. He hurried to Mesilla and when he arrived, he contacted Fountain's son, Albert, Jr., and explained what he saw. The younger Fountain, already concerned over the whereabouts of his father and brother, hastily assembled some friends to ride out to Chalk Hill with him. It was dark by the time they arrived, and they couldn't make out much of anything from the trail.

The next morning, they were joined by other men, including some experienced trackers. After studying the area, they found the tracks of three horses, spent cartridges, and a spot where Fountain's wagon was either driven or led off the main road to the south. A short distance away, it had stopped and then continued on. There were heavy splashes of blood on the ground near this site. The men in the search party believed the Fountains were ambushed at Chalk Hill, led off the road, and then possibly killed at that spot. The buckboard was found later that afternoon, abandoned about a dozen miles from Chalk Hill. Blood was spattered all over it and lying on the floor was Henry's hat, Fountain's tie, and a number of other items that were apparently pulled from the Colonel's satchel, inspected, and then tossed away.

Tracks showed that three riders had accompanied the wagon to that point, unhitched the horses, and rode away to the east. The pinto pony that had been tied to the back of the buckboard had either broken loose or had been cut away. It ran off to the north. The trackers followed a trail to an empty camp and later in the day, found one of the horses from Fountain's team at St. Nicholas Spring. The hair on its back was coated in blood, as though a dead or wounded person had been placed on it.

Three miles from the camp, the tracks diverged and two riders, leading Fountain's horse, rode through a northern pass in the Jarilla Mountains. Their trail led to Dog Canyon Ranch, which was owned by Oliver Lee. The remaining rider turned to the southeast and rode through a pass that was located south of the first. The trackers separated into two groups and continued their pursuit. When the party following the first group was within three miles of Lee's ranch, they found the tracks had been wiped out by a passing herd of cattle.

The other group followed a trail to Wildy Well, which was also part of Lee's ranch. In addition to a well, a couple of low stone buildings occupied the site. When they arrived, the trackers found Lee and some of his men at work there. Lee claimed to have no information but allowed the men to water the horses and then sent them on their way.

The search for the Fountains continued until Wednesday, when the trackers ran out of supplies and were forced to turn back to Mesilla. During the weeks that followed, other search parties scoured the desert for the Colonel and his son, but no trace was found of either of them.

News of the Fountains' disappearance spread quickly. Those working for New Mexico statehood at the time feared the image of the rough and dangerous frontier might destroy its chances and so it was decided that something must be done for public relations in regard to the Fountains. The authorities contacted former lawman Pat Garrett to investigate the whereabouts of Colonel Fountain. As the time, Garrett had been out of law enforcement for some time and was living in Texas. However, state officials believed that his high profile and reputation as the lawman who allegedly killed Billy the Kid would generate positive newspaper headlines and convince everyone that New Mexico was doing everything that it could to bring criminals to justice.

Garrett was joined by Pinkerton Detective agents and, working with Judge Frank Parker, he obtained warrants for Bill Carr, Jim Gilliland, Oliver Lee, and William McNew. Based on the evidence, Garrett expressed confidence that these four men could be prosecuted for the kidnapping and murder of Colonel Fountain and his son. Carr

Famous western lawman, Pat Garrett

and McNew were arrested within hours, but Carr was soon released for lack of evidence. Gilliland and Lee proved more difficult to locate.

Three months after the initial arrests, Garrett received information that the other two suspects were hiding out at Wildy Well. Accompanied by four deputies, Garrett went after them. As they searched one of the buildings near the well, the lawmen discovered the two suspects hiding on the roof. Gilliland and Lee opened fire and a fierce gun battle erupted. By the time it was over, one of the deputies was seriously wounded. He died two days later. Garrett and his men were forced to surrender and were disarmed by Lee, who made them ride away, leaving the wounded man behind. The fugitives vanished once again.

The two men remained on the run for the next several weeks, hiding out with friends and sympathizers. When they tired of the chase, they offered to surrender, but not to Garrett. They would only turn themselves in to Sheriff George Curry of Otero County, a long-time friend of Oliver Lee. Lee told several acquaintances that if he surrendered to Garrett, that the former lawman would shoot him in the back at the first opportunity.

Otero County, which had only been formed a few weeks earlier, did not have a courthouse for a trial so hearings were held in Hillsboro, the county seat of Sierra County. The small mining community had one hotel and very few rooms to rent, so it was ill-prepared for the hundreds of people that descended on it. The defendants, prosecutors, witnesses, and court officials were forced to live in tents that were set up at opposite ends of the town.

The prosecution was represented by Silver City District Attorney R.R. Barnes and attorneys Thomas B. Catron of Santa Fe and W.B.

Childers of Albuquerque. The defendants were aided by attorneys H.H. Daugherty and Harvey Ferguson of Albuquerque and Albert Bacon Fall, Fountain's old enemy and an increasingly powerful figure in New Mexico politics.

For strategic reasons, the prosecution withdrew the charges against McNew, but the strategy ultimately back-fired. The charges pertaining to the murder of Colonel Fountain against Gilliland and Lee were also dropped and the prosecution believed their best case against the two men was for the murder of young Henry Fountain.

The prosecution began to suffer difficulties from the beginning of the case. Before the trial, one of the principal witnesses, Jack Maxwell, told lawyers Barnes and Catron that he had seen Gilliland, Lee, and McNew arriving at Lee's Dog Canyon Ranch only hours after the Fountains disappeared. It was clear, he said, from the condition of their horses that the three men had ridden hard over a long distance. On May 29, 1899, the day that witnesses were scheduled to testify, Maxwell was nowhere to be found. He was eventually located in Alamogordo and finally escorted to the courthouse by an Otero County deputy. After he was sworn in, though, he backtracked on his original testimony, damaging the prosecution's case.

In the end, the most effective argument offered by the defense was the lack of bodies. Until they could be located, no one could prove that a murder had been committed. After 18 days of testimony and arguments, the jury returned with a verdict of not guilty.

No matter what the defense attorneys wanted everyone to believe, the Fountains were almost certainly dead. It seemed beyond question that they had been murdered, more than likely at dusk on February 1, 1896, just off the rise of Chalk Hill. Searches for their bodies have continued periodically for more than a century. There was even speculation that Pat Garrett bought a ranch in the San Andres Mountains, only 20 miles from Chalk Hill, because he refused to give up on the case.

But no remains of the Fountains, father or son, have ever been found.

Who killed them? The Fountain family believed that Gilliland, Lee, McNew, and possibly others, conspired to kill the Colonel and his son. Otero County Sheriff George Curry suspected a small-time rancher and former Billy the Kid compatriot named Jose Chavez y Chavez of the murders. He had expressed a hatred of Fountain after the Colonel prosecuted him as a rustler. He was acquitted but told Curry, "I will get that scoundrel Fountain if I have to hang for it." Rumor had it that Chavez was spotted at Luna's Well on the night of the disappearances, but he was never questioned about it. Curry never saw him again.

In 1949, the *Albuquerque Tribune* named train robber "Black Jack" Ketchum as Fountain's killer. The story was sensational for a moment, but quickly passed.

There were other culprits named but serious suspicion always came back to Oliver, Lee, Gilliland, Bill McNew, and Albert Bacon Fall as a sort of aloof, but deeply involved mastermind. Fall's career continued upward after the Hillsboro trial. He bought a fine, established ranch at Three Rivers in Lincoln County, and while keeping his New Mexico residency, built a splendid brick home in downtown El Paso and opened a law office. His rich clients soon made him wealthy. He quit the Democratic party in 1902, sensing that the Republicans were on the rise and might send him to Washington. He waited, serving as territorial attorney general, and, in 1912, became one of the first United States Senators representing New Mexico. He served nine years in the Senate, until 1921, when President Warren Harding appointed him as Secretary of the Interior.

After two years, Fall resigned from the office, citing failing health and reverses in his finances as the reasons for returning to private life. But Washington wasn't done with him. He was brought back to the capital under subpoena when a congressional investigation revealed that he had leased government oil lands at Teapot Dome, Wyoming, and Elk Hills, California, to two business associates and accepted a $100,000 payoff from one of them. He was found guilty at his bribery trial but permitted to serve his sentence in Santa Fe. He spent six months behind bars, most of it in the prison hospital, and was released in May 1932. He lost his beloved ranch and spent the rest of his life as an invalid, moving from one hospital to another. He died in November 1944.

George Curry, friendly with Oliver Lee, was convinced that Lee did not take part in the murders. Lee eventually owned and ran a considerable ranching empire and was elected to the New Mexico State Senate in 1922 and again in 1924. He died in Alamogordo in 1941.

Others were not so sure about Jim Gilliland. New Mexico historian William Keleher once wrote, "Polite, courteous and responsive up to a point, Gilliland skirted and evaded all efforts on the author's part to get him to talk about pivotal points in the case. Jim's secret knowledge passed away with him." In 1903, Gilliland and his wife Adelia built a successful cattle ranch in the San Andres Mountains and operated it for 37 years before retiring to Hot Springs, where he died in August 1946.

William McNew died after a stroke in June 1937. He was a minor player in the Fountain case, although Pat Garrett considered him to be "the meanest and the most vicious of the three." McNew, just like the other men, never spoke publicly of the Fountain case.

But who killed the Fountains is only part of the mystery. There remains the puzzle of what happened to the bodies. Western historian C.L. Sonnichsen heard all sorts of stories about the fate of the Fountains' remains. One woman told him that they had been burned in the firebox of a steam boiler that was located on Lee's ranch. Another man said they were buried beside a water tank and covered with concrete.

In 1909, a letter was mailed from Texas and arrived at the Masonic lodge in Las Cruces that asked if a reward was still being offered for the location of the bodies. When word was sent that the reward was still available, the letter writer wrote back, providing directions to the bodies that he claimed were buried in a section of the Jarilla Mountains. A search party was assembled and Albert Fountain, Jr. was invited to participate. As the party approached the region identified by the letter writer, Albert grew agitated and upset, finally breaking down, and stating that he could not continue. He told members of the party that the discovery of the skeletons "would kill my mother." The search was called off.

In 1950, a man who claimed to be involved in the murders told a friend where the remains were buried ——- at a high spot in the San Andres Mountains, the site marked by a pile of stones. A search party, which included three Fountain grandsons, went to the location in November 1950 and found the pile of stones, but no bodies.

To this day, the disappearance of the Colonel and Henry Fountain still intrigues and mystifies Western history buffs and crime enthusiasts. It is one of the strangest cases in American history and unfortunately, is riddled with missing facts, lost pieces of evidence, and entire pages of information that will never be known.

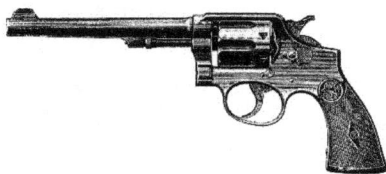

1900: The Lighthouse Keepers of Eilean Mor

One of the strangest unsolved disappearances of all time involved the vanishing of three lighthouse keepers from Eilean Mor, the largest of the seven Flannan Islands, off the west coast of Scotland.

It was on Eilean Mor (which means "big island" in Gaelic) that a lighthouse was constructed and lit for the first time on December 7, 1899, to guide ships around Cape Wrath and safely to Pentland Firth.

And it was on this island one year later that three keepers assigned to operate and maintain the light vanished without a trace. After more than a century, the fate of the Eilean Mor lighthouse keepers remains one of history's most enduring mysteries.

Scotland's Flannan Islands were named for St. Flannan, an Irish saint and the one-time bishop of Killaloe and Kilfenora, who was said

to have performed miracles on the sea. It was claimed, for example, that when he set out for Rome to meet Pope John, he sailed there on a floating stone. Another legend credits him with attracting vast schools of fish to the shores to feed his people.

The sturdy lighthouse on the Flannans' main island, Eilean Mor, was designed in 1899 by engineer Alan Stevenson. George Lawson carried out the actual work, which cost nearly £7,000, a very large sum in those days. The lighthouse was 74-feet tall and flashed a white beam out to sea every 30 seconds. It could be seen for more than 24 nautical miles. The construction work including landing docks and steps leading up to them, as well as homes for the lighthouse keepers and their families at Breasclete on the Isle of Lewis, cost an additional £3,500. Breasclete was chosen because of its proximity to Loch Roag, where there was safe anchorage for the boat that carried the lighthouse keepers back and forth from Eilean Mor.

When the light was established on the island, there was no radio communication available, so Roderick MacKenzie, a gamekeeper, was paid £8 per year to keep watch on the Eilean Mor lighthouse in case the keepers signaled for help, or the light went out. MacKenzie's observation post was Gallan Head on the Isle of Lewis, just southeast of Eilean Mor.

There were four keepers who manned the lighthouse: Joseph Moore —--- who was on leave when the disappearances occurred —--- James Ducat, Thomas Marshall, and Donald MacArthur, who was a part-time assistant.

The first inkling that something was wrong on Eilean Mor came on the night of December 15, 1900. When Captain Holman of the steamer *Archtor* passed the Flannans that night, he was certain that he was close enough to the islands to see the light if it had been on. He saw nothing, though, and noted in his log that the light was not burning.

On December 26, Captain Harvie, who was in charge of the lighthouse supply tender *Hesperus*, sailed to Eilean Mor and arrived there at noon. To his surprise and that of his second mate, McCormack, no preparations had been made to receive the supplies that the ship was carrying. They sounded the siren and steam whistle of the *Hesperus* but there was no response from the lighthouse keepers. Finally, a signal rocket was fired from the ship's deck. There seemed to be no one stirring on the island. *Hesperus* then sent a boat to the east landing dock of Eilean Mor, but there was no sign of the three lighthouse keepers.

Joseph Moore was also on board. He had been on leave and returned with *Hesperus* to the island. He quickly began to grow worried about the safety of his friends and colleagues. He scrambled ashore with some difficulty and went to explore the scene. Moore found the entrance gate and the outside door were closed. When he got inside, he found that the clock had stopped, and the fire had gone out. He quickly examined the bedrooms to see if his companions had fallen ill, but their beds were empty. Moore than ran back to the boat for help.

Second Mate McCormack and one of the sailors went ashore and the three men made a thorough search of the lighthouse. There was no sign of the three missing men nor any clue as to what had happened to them. Captain Harvie asked Moore to stay on at Eilean Mor to tend to the vitally important light. Two sailors named Campbell and Lamont volunteered to stay and help him, and Buoymaster MacDonald, also on board *Hesperus*, volunteered to stay with them until proper replacements could be found. The four men managed to get the light started again, while Captain Harvie sailed back to Breasclete and sent a report to the Lighthouse Headquarters.

A portion of Harvie's message read:

A dreadful accident has occurred at the Flannans. The three keepers, Ducat, Marshall, and the occasional have disappeared...

The men who had stayed behind on Eilean Mor made another search of the lighthouse and the surrounding island, desperately hoping for any sign of the missing men. Everything that they found confused them about the situation even more. The oil tanks and storage vessels were all properly filled. The lenses of the light were clear and all the mechanisms for the device were properly cleaned and lubricated. The last entry in the lighthouse logbook had been December 15, 1900. If a meal had been prepared that day, everything had been cleared away and put into its place. All appeared to be normal at the start of that afternoon. In fact, everything was as it should be — --- except for the vanished men.

The two landing docks, one at the east end of the island and one at the west, had been built so there would always be a secure place for men and supplies to land, no matter which way a wind or a storm might be blowing. When the search party went around to the west landing place, however, things were far from normal. A toolbox containing ropes and other essential equipment, which was usually stored on a ledge about 20 feet up the cliff, had been smashed open and some of the ropes stored in it were found draped around an iron crane on the platform below. The platform had sturdy iron railings around it, which were now curiously twisted and bent. Furthermore, a large block of stone had been dislodged by something and had fallen to the pathway below. The damage appeared to have been caused by some sort of freak storm, which led to perhaps the most popular theory about the missing men on Eilean Mor —- that they had literally been washed off the island.

When the protective clothing of the men was examined, it was discovered that Ducat had been wearing his waterproof gear and sea boots when he vanished. Marshall's boots and oilskin were also gone. According to the theory, they had put on their protective clothing to go down and work on the landing docks, probably to make sure that everything was stored away before the worst of the storm hit Eilean Mor. It was deduced by the missing oilskins that Donald McArthur may have lost his life trying to save the other men. It was believed that he had prepared lunch that day and had stayed at the lighthouse to clean up while his partners went down to the landing. With a higher observation point than the other men, McArthur may have seen large waves bearing down on the island and ran down to warn his companions. But as the waves hit the western side of Eilean Mor, they shattered the toolbox, hurled its contents onto the platform below, twisted the iron railing, and swept the three lighthouse keepers to their deaths.

This was the only logical explanation in the case, and it was filed in an official report by Superintendent Robert Muirhead during his investigation. As he looked for answers, he spoke with Roderick Mackenzie, the observer on the Isle of Lewis, and his two sons. Mackenzie had noted his observations in a report and added that Eilean Mor had not been visible from Lewis from December 7 to December 29, thanks to fog and poor weather conditions. Whatever occurred on Eilean Mor on December 15 took place out of the sight of any living person.

What really happened to the lighthouse keepers on Eilean Mor?

No one will ever know for sure. Logic insists that the men died in a storm, even though they were experienced seamen and had grown up around the often-dangerous shores of western Scotland.

Others insisted that supernatural forces were at work in this mysterious disappearance. Eilean Mor had long been known as a strange, and some said, evil place, haunted by the spirits of the rock's ancient inhabitants, who left behind only traces of an old dwelling and chapel on the island.

Although rational evidence points toward a natural marine disaster, the hint of the supernatural has never quite left this case. What really happened was —- and will always remain —- a mystery.

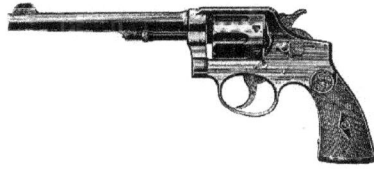

1910: The Vanished Heiress

On the cold morning of December 12, 1910, a young woman named Dorothy Arnold left her parent's home in Manhattan to go shopping for a dress to wear to her younger sister's "coming out" party. It was the holiday season in New York and a time for festivities, galas, and balls, and this particular party was a much-anticipated one for Dorothy, a young and beautiful graduate of Bryn Mawr and the daughter of a prosperous and socially prominent couple.

She left the house that day for a dress and vanished without a trace.

The mystery of the Dorothy Arnold disappearance is as great today as it was more than a century ago. No clue has ever been discovered as to where she went and, at the time, a newspaper wrote: "She disappeared from one of the busiest streets on earth, at the sunniest hours of a brilliant afternoon, with thousands within sight and reach, men and women who knew her on every side, and officers of the law thickly strewn in her path."

But she was never seen again.

Dorothy Harriet Camille Arnold, society girl and niece of United States Supreme Court Justice Rufus L. Peckham, was last seen at 2:00 p.m. on the afternoon of December 12. She was, at that moment, 25-years-old, stood five-feet, four-inches tall and weighed about 135 pounds, which was perfect for a fashionable young lady of the time. She was a quiet, pretty, and studious girl. She had graduated cum laude from Bryn Mawr five years before and had the manner of a serene and serious young woman. Her hair, swept up in the high style of the day, was dark brown and her eyes were blue-gray in color.

Vanished heiress Dorothy Arnold, who went missing in 1910

On the day of her disappearance, she was well-dressed in the height of fashion in a tailor-made jacket of blue serge that was fitted at the waist, a matching ankle-length hobble skirt, and high-button shoes. Dorothy carried with her a silver-fox muff and a satin handbag and wore a black velvet hat.

When Dorothy descended the stairs of her family home at 108 East Seventy-Ninth Street on the fashionable East Side of Manhattan, she found her mother waiting. She informed Mrs. Arnold that she planned to spend the rest of the day shopping for an evening dress for her sister Marjorie's coming-out party, a long-anticipated event that was scheduled for December 17.

The Arnold home was presided over by Dorothy's father, Francis W. Arnold, a wealthy businessman who could trace his family lineage back to the *Mayflower.* His sister had married Supreme Court Justice Rufus Peckham. In addition to two daughters, Arnold also had two sons, John and D. Hinckley. The family was a proud one, known for its propriety, and was well-respected in the city.

When Dorothy met with her mother that morning, Mrs. Arnold offered to accompany her on her shopping trip. Although a semi-invalid, she was perfectly willing to go with her daughter that morning, but Dorothy refused. She knew her mother did not feel well and didn't want her to go out into the chilly air.

We can only wonder if history would have been different if Dorothy had not been so concerned about her mother's health and allowed the older woman to come along.

When she left home, Dorothy had about $25 of her $100 monthly allowance with her. She had withdrawn $36 from her accounts to take a girlfriend to lunch and to see a film. As she left the house, several acquaintances stopped and spoke with her as she walked west along Fifth Avenue and others saw her going toward a bookstore on Twenty-Seventh Street. They all said that she seemed cheerful. A clerk who sold Dorothy a box of chocolates said that she was "very carefree."

Dorothy walked more than 52 blocks that day but no one, police or family, thought there was anything unusual in this lengthy trek. Dorothy was a healthy young woman and walking was her only exercise. She was not athletically, but artistically, inclined. She loved literature and hoped to be a writer someday. It was this aspiration that had led to a recent disagreement with her domineering father.

Only two months before, after a vacation to the family's home in Maine, Dorothy requested her father's permission to take an apartment in the artist's and writer's enclave of Greenwich Village. Mr. Arnold exploded in anger and refused the request, telling his daughter that "a good writer can write anywhere." Always the dutiful daughter, Dorothy did not pursue the matter any further. Instead, she took her father's advice and over the next few weeks, wrote a short story called "Poinsettia Flames," which she then sent for consideration to *McClure's* magazine. Unfortunately, Dorothy told her family about the story and all of them began teasing her about her literary pretensions. The teasing became worse after the story was rejected a short time later. After days of this, she took the daring step of renting her own postal box so that any future correspondence about her stories could be kept private.

By the time she disappeared, Dorothy had written another story called "Lotus Leaves" but it's unknown whether she ever submitted it anywhere.

On that day, Dorothy was apparently more concerned about other people's writings than her own. During her trip, she entered Brentano's bookstore at Fifth Avenue and Twenty-Seventh Street, where she looked at a number of books. She then purchased a humorous volume called *An Engaged Girl's Sketches* by Emily Calvin Blake, which had recently been featured in the *Ladies Home Journal*. She charged the book to the family account and walked back out into the cold.

Outside Brentano's, she ran into a friend, Gladys King, who was also going to be attending Marjorie Arnold's debut party. Gladys had a note of acceptance with her in response to the party invitation and she handed it to Dorothy, making a joke about the postage saved. Dorothy laughed and the two chatted for several minutes. Their conversation ended when Gladys remembered that she was supposed to meet her mother for lunch. She said goodbye and hurried away, turning at the corner of Twenty-Seventh Street to wave to Dorothy one last time.

She was the last person who knew Dorothy Arnold to admit to seeing her alive.

When Dorothy did not return home for dinner that evening, her family reluctantly ate without her. It was very unusual for her to miss a meal, especially since she had not told anyone that she wouldn't be home. After a few hours passed, the Arnolds began to worry. Later that night, they began to make discreet telephone calls to Dorothy's close friends, asking if she had dropped in on them. Told that she had not, the Arnolds begged that no mention be made of the telephone call. It was all about the avoidance of scandal and, later, they asked the same girls not to speak with reporters. None of them ever did.

On this first night, a friend named Elsie Henry, one of the people who had been called, telephoned back around midnight to see if Dorothy had returned home. Mrs. Arnold answered the call and again, hoping to avoid any sort of impropriety, lied and claimed that Dorothy had come home with a terrible headache and had gone to bed.

Over breakfast the next morning, the distracted family made another strange decision -- they agreed not to call the police. Instead, Dorothy's brother, John, telephoned a friend named John S. Keith, a junior partner in the law firm of Garvan & Anderson. Keith was only a year older than Dorothy and occasionally escorted her to social functions, dances, and society gatherings. John refused to tell Keith what was wrong on the telephone and insisted that he come to the Arnold home that morning. When Keith arrived, he was told about the young woman's disappearance and his help was enlisted in the search for her. He was taken directly to Dorothy's room, where everything seemed to be in perfect order. Mrs. Arnold assured him that none of her dresses were missing, except for the one that she had been wearing the previous day.

Keith searched the room and found a pile of personal letters, some with foreign postmarks. On the desk, he found two Trans-Atlantic steamship brochures. Getting down on his knees, he peered into the fireplace and discovered a small bundle of burned papers. He poked at them but saw no writing on the charred remains. John Arnold suggested that the burned papers might be the manuscript for Dorothy's rejected story, "Poinsettia Flames."

Keith went to work for the Arnold family, one of his firm's most important clients, and for weeks, he searched hospitals, morgues, and jails in New York, Boston, and Philadelphia. He inspected patients, inmates, and corpses before finally giving up in despair. He was forced to suggest that the family call upon the Pinkerton Detective Agency, which was more suited to handle such an investigation. Pinkerton officials listened to the story of the disappearance and immediately mailed a descriptive circular about Dorothy to police departments throughout the country. In addition to describing the young woman and her attire, the letters offered a $5,000 reward for information leading to her return.

Presumably, the New York City Police Department received one of the flyers, but standing on protocol, the department refused to get involved until they were directly appealed upon to do so. The investigations of John Keith and the Pinkertons lasted for almost six weeks but no trace of Dorothy was found. On January 24, 1911, Francis Arnold was finally forced to contact the police. Accompanied by Pinkerton detectives and John Keith, he called upon New York Deputy Commissioner William J. Flynn.

Already familiar with the general facts in the case, Flynn, who would later become head of the United States Secret Service, advised an immediate conference with the press. This would bring the most attention to Dorothy's disappearance, but it was a tactic that filled Francis Arnold with distaste. Up to this point, very few people knew that Dorothy was missing, and he preferred it that way. He abhorred the notoriety that was sure to come, and he argued for two days before finally giving in and contacting the newspapers. Arnold summoned reporters to his office and announced his belief that Dorothy had been "attacked in Central Park" on her way home and that her body had been thrown into the reservoir. As grim and hopeless as this sounded, the rigid and proper Arnold would rather his daughter be dead than the alternative --: that she had run away with a man with whom she had spent a clandestine week several months before.

That man's name was George Griscom, Jr. He was a plump, balding, 40-year-old who lived quietly with his elderly parents on the Philadelphia Main Line. Griscom was firmly under his mother's thumb —– she still bought all his shirts and ties for him —– but he did have moments of independence, as did Dorothy. The newspapers soon revealed that she and Griscom, whom she had met at Bryn Mawr, had at one time called themselves engaged. During the summer of 1910, Dorothy had dutifully accompanied her family to the Arnold summer home at York Harbor in Maine but left for a week, telling her parents that she was going to Cambridge to visit her friend, Theodora Bates.

In truth, Dorothy had gone to Boston to meet Griscom. He arrived in the city the day before she did and reserved a room at the Hotel Essex. On the morning of her arrival, he had reserved a room for her at the nearby Hotel Lenox. The two spent the entire week together and those who remembered them said that they were animated and happy. They did nothing to hide their identities and Dorothy was registered at the Lenox under her own name and with the correct New York address. Two days before leaving Boston, she entered a pawn shop and obtained $60 for an assortment of personal jewelry. Again, she used her correct name and address. The pawnbroker later revealed the news about Dorothy's visit to the newspapers and the police.

Dorothy rejoined her family in Maine and Griscom returned to Philadelphia, where he prepared for a trip to Europe with his parents. The Arnolds returned to New York at the end of the summer and it was at this time that Dorothy made her request for an apartment in Greenwich Village, wrote her two stories, and rented a private post office box.

At Thanksgiving, Dorothy drew her friend Theodora Bates into her secret life. She decided to visit her friend in Washington for the holiday. On Thanksgiving morning, Dorothy expressed a desire to remain in bed, which was so unlike her that Theodora assumed that she was having her menstrual period. Far more remarkable was the package that was delivered for Dorothy at Theodora's home later that same morning, especially because no mail deliveries were taking place on the holiday. Whatever was in the bulky envelope, Dorothy did not open it or even comment on it. She tossed it indifferently on her bed and Theodora, who was deeply curious, asked no questions for fear of hurting her friend's feelings.

On Friday, Dorothy, already a puzzling guest, astounded Theodora by coming downstairs for breakfast fully dressed to travel, carrying her bag. Her friend was dismayed because she had believed that Dorothy had planned to stay until Monday. Her parents were equally surprised when she returned home later that evening. They were also convinced that she would be away until Monday, but Dorothy insisted this was not the case.

She spent the rest of the Thanksgiving weekend at home, reading and sewing. On Monday, she visited her downtown postal box, extracting several letters with foreign postmarks, probably from Griscom, who was in Italy with his parents. At home, she retired to her room and answered Griscom with a letter that he saved and later turned over to the police. For the most part, the correspondence was chatty and cheerful, but at the close of it was an intriguing paragraph:

Well, it has come back. *McClure's* has turned me down. All I can see ahead is a long road with no turning. Mother will always think an accident has happened.

Dorothy's mention of her mother, the supposed semi-invalid overwhelmed by her domineering husband, was partially explained in the six silent weeks following Dorothy's disappearance. Mrs. Arnold, as it turned out, was not only capable of doing things on her own but had the courage to do them.

At the press conference on January 26, Francis Arnold stated that his wife, her bad health worsened by shock, had retired to a rest home in Lakewood, New Jersey. Newspapermen were asked not to bother her and, out of deference to her health, age, and social standing, left her alone. Instead, they cabled European correspondents to locate Griscom. He was quickly found in Florence, where he admitted to receiving a cable from attorney John Keith on December 16. It read:

Dorothy Arnold missing. Family prostrated. Cable if you know anything about her whereabouts.

Guests at Griscom's hotel reported him acting agitated as he read the telegram. He quickly responded that he had no idea where Dorothy might be. In the weeks that followed, he received other messages inquiring whether Dorothy had appeared in Florence. He answered all of them in the negative. Then, on January 16, a young man and a heavily veiled woman came to visit him. After two hours, they departed and took with them a packet of letters.

The young man turned out to be Dorothy's brother, John Arnold, who traveled to Europe before the story of his sister's disappearance appeared in the newspapers. He returned to New York alone at the end of January and refused to talk about his veiled companion. With this new mystery, newspaper writers applied themselves to learning her identity and discovered that it was Mrs. Arnold, whose privacy was still being honored by reporters. She and John had sailed from New York on January 6, and she remained in Europe in hopes that Dorothy might still turn up near Griscom. She had not been in a rest home after all.

John Arnold's arrival in New York added still another angle to the baffling case. Reporters on board the ship, who got the news about Dorothy's disappearance on January 26, peppered John with questions. He professed to be totally unaware that anything had happened to her, claiming to have been away from New York since November. The reporters had no idea that he was lying. When he arrived in the city, he went straight to the offices of Garvan & Anderson, where he expressed his anger over his father's press conference. He still believed that the story should not have become public knowledge and still believed that Dorothy would be found.

John refused to answer any questions, but rumors swirled, including one that he had actually attacked George Griscom in Florence. Griscom denied any knowledge of Dorothy's whereabouts but John was allegedly so suspicious of the rich bachelor that he throttled him and threatened to kill him if he didn't reveal where Dorothy was hiding. Griscom insisted that he had nothing to do with her disappearance, but he did turn over the letter that she had recently written to him concerning her depression over the story she had written that had been rejected by a magazine. Griscom feared that she had been so distraught over this that she had taken her own life. Or so he said. A few friends believed that if Dorothy had committed suicide, she had done so because Griscom refused to marry her.

Griscom returned to America in February and inserted personal ads in New York newspapers, begging Dorothy to communicate with him. There was no response.

Some theorized that Dorothy had been murdered or that she simply ran away to escape from her oppressive home life. Others insisted that she had been kidnapped from the street and pressed into involuntary service as a prostitute, for this was the era when fear of "white slavery" rackets ran rampant. Another theory was that Dorothy was in a hospital somewhere, suffering from amnesia. It was thought that perhaps she had slipped an icy sidewalk that chilly afternoon and had fallen, striking her head on the pavement. A thorough check of the hospitals never revealed anyone matching her description, however.

The nation's police, chasing leads that hinted at suicide, elopement, amnesia, and personal rebellion, found nothing but dead ends. As the publicity spread, "Dorothy sightings" began coming in from all over the country. She was "recognized" in hundreds of cities, but all the reports turned out to be false. On one occasion, a headline that read "DOROTHY ARNOLD FOUND" spread across the country but it proved to be a hoax.

After this incident, Francis Arnold reduced the reward from $5,000 to $1,000, at the same time repeating his stubborn belief that Dorothy had been murdered in Central Park. Arnold spent more than $100,000 trying to recover his daughter, but it all amounted to nothing. He died in 1922 and his wife passed away in 1928, never knowing what became of the young woman. In Arnold's will, though, a provision stated that he had left nothing for Dorothy "for I am satisfied that she is not alive."

George Griscom also continued to search, spending huge sums of money on "Come Home Dorothy" ads in major newspapers. But could this have been an act to throw off a trail that may have led to his own door? Six years after the heiress disappeared, a Rhode Island convict released a story to the press that claimed he had been paid $150 to dig a grave for the murdered woman. The description that he gave of the man who he claimed paid him was strikingly close to that of Griscom; however, he said he never learned the man's name. The convict stated that Dorothy had died after a botched abortion and that she had been buried in the cellar of a house near West Point. Police unearthed cellars all over the area, but they found no sign of a corpse.

More than a century later, no trace of Dorothy has ever been found. Her body was not discovered in some forgotten grave, there were no death-bed confessions of identity, and she did not return from some life of shame. Dorothy Arnold, the girl who seemed to have everything, never returned from her seemingly innocent shopping trip.

She simply walked off down the street one day and was never heard from again.

1912: The Mystery of Bobby Dunbar

There is no question that one of the worst nightmares that a parent can experience is the disappearance of a child. Could anything be worse than that? Perhaps...

On a late summer day in 1912, a young boy disappeared while on a family trip. Eight months later, though, the authorities announced that the boy had been found. But instead of solving a mystery, the return of the child began a new puzzle that endured for decades.

On August 23, 1912, a four-year-old boy named Bobby Dunbar vanished while on a fishing trip to Swayze Lake in St. Landry Parish, Louisiana. When Mrs. Lessie Dunbar realized that her son was gone, she contacted the police, who began a massive search for the boy. Bobby's father, Percy, who had been away on business, rushed to the scene. He was followed by numerous volunteers who also joined the search. The woods were combed for any trace of the boy. The lake was dredged up and alligators were killed to see if Bobby's remains might be found in their stomachs. But nothing was found, and the authorities began to assume the worst.

The trail went cold and the family returned to their home in Opelousas, Louisiana, to wait for news. Since the Dunbars were a fairly prosperous family, they held out hope that Bobby had been kidnapped for ransom. Newspapers began promoting the kidnapping theory. Pictures of Bobby, along with his grieving parents and his two-year-old brother, Alonzo, began appearing in papers in New Orleans and across the region. Thanks to the $6,000 reward that was offered for information, the police received numerous tips from people hoping to cash in. While members of the Dunbar family personally checked out every lead, the tips led nowhere.

Eight months passed before the family's hopes for Bobby's return were finally realized —- or at least that's how it seemed.

In April 1913, investigators located a child in neighboring Mississippi who seemed to match Bobby's description. The boy was living in the home of William Walters, a handyman who specialized in repairing pianos and organs. When interviewed by the police, Walters readily admitted that the boy was not his son, but he did state that he knew the boy's mother. The child was not the missing Bobby Dunbar, he said, his name was Charles Bruce Anderson —- who went by the name of Bruce. He was the son of Julia Anderson, a young woman who worked for the Walters family. Strangely, thanks to the publicity surrounding Bobby's disappearance, the police had already questioned Walters several times. In fact, Bobby's uncle had personally spoken to

Bruce and concluded the boy was not his nephew. However, people in the area —- likely enticed by the promise of the reward —- kept contacting the police and insisting that Bruce was the missing child. Finally, investigators had to act. Walters was arrested for kidnapping and the boy was taken into state custody.

Meanwhile, Percy and Lessie Dunbar, hurried to the town of Hub, Mississippi, to claim their child. The case soon became mired in controversy. While some newspapers claimed that the boy cried out and ran into the arms of Lessie Dunbar, other sources claimed that he wept frightened tears, and that Mrs. Dunbar expressed doubts about whether he was actually her son. Reports about Bobby's reunion with his brother, Alonzo, were also mixed. Some claimed the boy was happy to see his brother, while others said the boys appeared to be strangers.

Despite the obvious difference in appearance between Bobby and Bruce —— not to mention the absence of a prominent scar on one foot —— Percy Dunbar openly concluded that the boy was Bobby. The difference in their hair color was explained away by Walters using hair bleach, while other physical differences were dismissed as the rough life he had been living with the handyman. As for Walters' motive in kidnapping Bobby, Percy insisted that he had taken the boy to be used as a shill for begging, despite the fact that Walters was not a beggar, homeless, or even unemployed.

Lessie Dunbar, though, was not so sure. She didn't say anything on the first evening. In fact, it was not until the next day, after Lessie said she had given the little boy a bath and found what she claimed were familiar marks and moles on his body, that she was convinced. With her husband's urging, she told reporters that the boy was definitely her lost son, Bobby.

People who knew William Walters came to his defense, including some who pointed out that Bruce had been seen with him long before Bobby had gone missing. But Percy Dunbar had the money and influence to override the objections and to make sure that Walters stayed in jail. As for Bruce himself, he was thoroughly frightened about being separated from the only father he knew but the townspeople who hoped to get the reward were thrilled by the turn of events. Percy

The boy raised as "Bobby" with the Dunbar family

Dunbar never bothered to tell them that the reward offer had expired months earlier.

Percy was anxious to get his wife and son home. He presented a letter to the local sheriff formally recognizing the boy as his son and the boy was released into his custody. When the Dunbars returned home to Opelousas, a parade was held in their honor, celebrating little Bobby's return.

In the meantime, the media coverage of Bobby's story continued to grow. The Hippodrome Theater in New Orleans contacted Percy Dunbar for the right to put the little boy on display, something to which he immediately agreed. Percy also made a number of public statements during which he announced that Bobby had all the identifying marks needed to prove his identity. He also created a lot of animosity toward Walters by announcing that Bobby had recognized his mother —- he hadn't —- and that the boy had been whipped into submission by his kidnapper, something that forced the sheriff to increase security at the jail where Walters was being held. There were concerns that he might be lynched.

At this point, no one knew what to do about Bobby's alleged kidnapper, the thoroughly confused William Walters. Not only was he facing kidnapping charges in the town where he lived, but details of the case were being reported all over the country. Given the public anger surrounding the supposed kidnapping, he was quickly becoming one of the most hated men in America.

But there were many troubling questions about how Walters, who walked with a visible limp, could have kidnapped Bobby Dunbar in the first place. Many people knew Walters and were willing to speak up for him, while others —– including the sheriff —– just hoped to get a piece of the reward money. The entire town of Hub was basically split over the question of whether the boy was really Bobby Dunbar.

After the Dunbars took the boy in question back to Louisiana, the case had lost its prime witness. Luckily for Walters, he had a lawyer who took pity on him and stepped in to try and help. Hollis C. Rawls, working on Walters' behalf, began collecting formal depositions in support of his new client, including one from a woman who swore that the boy had been sitting on her lap when she read a newspaper story about Bobby's disappearance.

Unfortunately, public opinion —– helped along by Percy Dunbar —– was very much against Walters. The possibility of a fair trial seemed increasingly remote, and, with kidnapping being a capital offense in Louisiana, it meant Walters could be hanged if he was convicted. Hollis Rawls was doing everything that he could to make sure that his client was not extradited from Mississippi to the state where the crime occurred. This was not an easy task. Dozens of newspaper stories were printed in Louisiana, each showing photographs of Bobby with his loving parents. It didn't matter who had doubts about Bobby's identity. The Dunbars were publicly claiming the boy was their son and this proved to the public that Walters was guilty as charged. Nothing his defenders said or did could change that.

The case was becoming a political hot potato, too. Louisiana's governor was leaning on Mississippi's Governor Earl Hall to agree to Walters' extradition. But Hall didn't appreciate the pressure. He went as far as to hire a private detective to look into the matter, who found that the Dunbars were mistaken —– the boy was not their son, he stated. But Percy Dunbar fought back by arranging for his family physician to examine Bobby and write a letter to bolster the case for extradition. The doctor agreed to write anything that Percy Dunbar wanted him to write.

The deck seemed stacked against William Walters — until Julia Anderson showed up.

The young woman had been working as a field hand in North Carolina when she heard that her son had been taken from Walters' home in Mississippi. Scraping together what little money she had, she traveled to Louisiana, claiming that her son, Bruce, had been unlawfully kidnapped. But little attention was paid to her. The Dunbars ignored her and the police thought little of her story. The public was just as skeptical. Julia was regarded as "morally unstable." She wasn't even sure who Bruce's father was, although the most likely candidate was William Walters' brother, Bunt, who had skipped town after he learned she was pregnant. She went on to have another child, a daughter named Bernice, whose father was also unknown. Realizing that she couldn't care for her children on her own, she arranged to have Bernice adopted and entrusted Bruce to William since they had already become close.

When she learned that William had been arrested and Bruce had been effectively kidnapped, she had rushed home with hopes of settling the matter. Percy Dunbar, after hearing that Julia was on her way, did everything he could to keep the boy from being taken away. He arranged a "line-up" of sorts in which Julia was expected to choose which of three similar-looking boys was her son. The room was kept dark and worst of all, Bobby/Bruce was not even in the room.

Julia did her best. She had not seen her son in over a year and when faced with three unfamiliar children in a dimly lit room, she announced that none of the boys was her son. She had passed the test —– but no one listened to her after Percy Dunbar triumphantly announced to reporters that she had failed. Even when she managed to see Bruce and had correctly identified him, she was publicly dismissed as a fraud. County officials —– who should have been conducting the test —– objected to how things were done, but they were overruled. Finally, facing threats of being arrested for her role in Bobby Dunbar's kidnapping, and with no money to pursue the case in court, Julia Anderson left town in despair.

Despite the controversy over how the identification test had been conducted, the last barrier to William Walters' extradition was out of the way. He was finally transferred to Louisiana to stand trial for kidnapping. In order to cover the costs of the trial and legal experts that Hollis Rawls needed, Walters was forced to put up his share of the family farm as collateral and borrowed heavily to get the rest.

The trial began almost immediately and was covered each day in the newspapers. Despite the evidence presented by Rawls in William's defense, public support was against them. The Dunbars had invested considerable time and resources by hiring detectives to dig into William's life and find anything they could to discredit him. Simply put, the Dunbars were wealthy and people like William Walters and Julia Anderson were not. They used the newspapers to play up the difference in their social status and to keep Bobby on display as often as possible. To add to the confusion, Bobby himself had spent weeks with the Dunbar family, treated as their son. As memories of his earlier life began to fade, the little boy accepted his new name and life with a privileged family became much easier to accept.

The trial lasted for two weeks. The prosecutor presented the unique theory that Walters had somehow exchanged Bruce Anderson for Bobby Dunbar and likely had both boys in his possession for a time. Although what supposedly became of the real Bruce Anderson was never mentioned in court. Though defense witnesses testified that Walters had been in Mississippi when the kidnapping occurred, prosecution witnesses swore they'd seen him in Louisiana. Julia Anderson also testified on William's behalf, but her status as a "loose" woman worked against her. The newspapers never failed to refer to Bruce as her "illegitimate child."

William never had a chance of winning. The case went to jury and on April 28, 1914, he was found guilty of kidnapping. The jury spared him the death penalty, but he was still sentenced to life in prison. Later that same evening, someone managed to enter his cell and beat him severely, likely giving him an idea of how he could expect the rest of his years in prison to be.

Attorney Hollis Rawls filed for an immediate appeal, but the request was rejected. Julia, devastated by the verdict, collapsed outside the courtroom and spent weeks in a New Orleans charity hospital recovering.

William was sent to a federal penitentiary to serve out his sentence. His supporters continued to rally for his release and Julia, after being released from the hospital, moved back to Mississippi to help with the effort. Finally, after two years of legal pressure, William's sentence was overturned on a technicality and he was released. Even so, the stigma of his conviction and the ordeal of his incarceration would traumatize him for the rest of his life. His time in prison had shattered his health. He left the penitentiary on a stretcher and had to be treated in a hospital before he could return home. When he returned to Mississippi, he found little of his old life was left. While Hollis Rawls and many of his friends stood by him, he had still been publicly branded as a kidnapper. The cost of his defense had depleted his life savings and he was in desperate need of money. For a time, he joined a touring company and did shows where he talked about his ordeal and the truth behind his conviction. Once public interest in the case faded, his stage career came to an end and he became a drifter. No one knows what became of him after 1920. His death and final resting place were never recorded.

William Walters was freed from prison but any possibility of getting the Dunbars to admit their mistake and return Bruce to his mother seemed remote at best. Even though Julia remained determined to get her child back, her lawyers had largely given up trying since public opinion was so firmly set against them. It didn't help that the Dunbars continued to parade Bobby around in every venue they could find, trying to ensure that public sentiment would never turn against them.

Julia remained in Mississippi and eventually married a cousin of Hollis Rawls. She went on to have eight more children, although she never gave up hope of being reunited with Bruce. Her children all grew up hearing stories about their "missing" brother.

Some would say that fate had a hand in how things turned out for the Dunbar family. In the years that followed William Walters' conviction, public opinion slowly turned against them. Perhaps people were tired of the entire spectacle, especially since Percy continued to milk the publicity, even going as far as to use it to advance a political career, or maybe they had finally started to doubt his story. Lessie Dunbar, for reasons that she never shared publicly, later abandoned her family and moved to California. After she and Percy divorced, following a public scandal related to one of Percy's many affairs, she returned to Louisiana, remarried, and had other children. Strangely —– or not, I suppose —– she had no relationship with Bobby, who was supposedly her oldest son.

As for Bobby himself, he had learned to regurgitate the details of his kidnapping ordeal on command and, over time, came to accept the memories that had been given to him as the truth. Regardless, the doubt about his identity followed him for many years afterward. Percy later shipped both his sons off to live with their grandparents, and Bobby was enrolled in military school. Whenever the story of his kidnapping resurfaced, as it did on occasion, he continued to insist that he was a Dunbar. In one news story from 1948, he expressed the wish to meet William Walters to learn more about the story of his kidnapping. He even traveled to Mississippi as an adult and met Hollis Rawls to learn more about the case. What was said between them is unknown. There is also no indication that he ever met Julia Anderson, even though she was living nearby at the time.

When Percy Dunbar died, Bobby was left nothing in his father's will. Alonzo Dunbar inherited everything. By all accounts, he was largely estranged from the Dunbar family by the time he reached adulthood. He became a certified electrician and moved to Houston, Texas, where he and his wife, Marjorie, raised four children.

Bobby Dunbar died of a massive heart attack on March 8, 1966, at the age of 57. His obituary mentioned that he was survived by his wife, children, and six grandchildren but made no mention of the mystery that once held the attention of the nation.

But the mystery of Bobby Dunbar's disappearance lived on.

In 1999, his granddaughter, Margaret Dunbar Cutright, started her own investigation into the case. She had initially started her investigation hoping to prove that she was a Dunbar. The results, however, told a different story. After considerable research and numerous interviews, she came to believe that her grandfather was not Bobby Dunbar —– he had been Bruce Anderson all along. Margaret's investigation divided the family, many of whom wished she had left the past alone. Then, in 2006, Robert Dunbar, Jr., Margaret's father and the son of the man known as Bobby Dunbar, participated in a DNA test with his cousin, the son of Alonzo Dunbar.

The test proved that they were not related.

While many members of the family were angry about the results, the DNA tests brought closure to the story. The boy that the Dunbars had claimed was their son was Bruce Anderson —– there was no question about it.

But was this really the end? Hadn't the tests raised even more questions —– namely, what happened to little Bobby Dunbar? In a case that was filled with tragedy —– from the taking of Julia Anderson's son to the two years that William Walters wrongfully spent in prison —– the greatest horror was the unsolved disappearance of the boy that was never found.

To this day, no additional clues have been discovered as to the 1912 vanishing of the real Bobby Dunbar. The case was closed many years ago when, sadly, everyone just stopped looking for him.

1913: "Can Such Things Be?"
The Disappearance of Ambrose Bierce

On the cold evening of November 8, 1878, a 16-year-old boy named Charles Ashmore walked out of the back door of his family's farmhouse near Quincy, Illinois. He carried with him a bucket with which to fetch fresh water from a spring a short distance away. When he did not return, his family became uneasy and his father, Christian Ashmore, accompanied by his oldest daughter, Martha, took a lantern and went in search of the boy. A new snow had just fallen, and Charles' footprints were plainly visible in a straight line across the yard. His father and sister followed his path, traveling about 75 yards toward the spring and then the footprints abruptly ended. Beyond the last one was nothing other than smooth, unbroken snow.

The boy's footprints simply came to an end.

Ashmore and his daughter made a wide circle around the tracks, careful not to disturb them, and went on to the spring. They found the water covered with a layer of unbroken ice and it became apparent that Charles had gotten no closer to the spring than his tracks had indicated. The boy had vanished without explanation.

But the story does not end there. Four days later, the grief-stricken mother of the young man went to the spring for water and insisted that she heard the voice of her son calling to her when she passed the spot where his footprints had ended. She wandered the area, thinking that the voice was coming from one direction and then another. Later, when questioned about the voice, she said that the words were very clear —-- the voice was definitely that of her son —--- and yet she could make not understand that they were saying.

For months afterward, the voice was heard every few days by one family member or another, or sometimes many of them. It seemed to come from a great distance and none of them could determine its message or repeat its words. Soon, the intervals of silence grew longer, and the voice much fainter, and by mid-summer of 1879, it was heard no more.

Those with an interest in the strange and the unusual have likely heard this story before. Or perhaps the reader has run across a slightly different variation of it, with the name of Charles Ashmore replaced by that of David Lang and the location being moved from Illinois to Gallatin, Tennessee. Or the reader may have heard yet another version —-- enhanced by the young man crying for help before vanishing —-- in which the boy's name was Oliver Larch and the location was South Bend, Indiana. All these accounts have appeared in various books of true stories about ghosts, unsolved mysteries, and the unexplained over the years.

The problem is that not even one of them is true.

The story of Charles Ashmore first appeared in the writings of journalist Ambrose Bierce, who penned not only newspaper articles, but several books, scores of stories about ghosts and the Civil War, and a number of acerbic and cutting essays over the course of his career. Bierce's style and journalistic background gave his stories of war and strange disappearances such an uneasy realism that many mistook them for being true. Such was the case of the story of Charles Ashmore and many others that he wrote and, as time has passed, the stories have often been presented as being real disappearances that took place years ago.

Critics often scoff at writers who mistake these literary creations for true stories, often because it seems obvious that one cannot simply walk out the door one day and vanish into thin air.

Such a thing cannot possibly happen. Or can it?

Ambrose Bierce believed that it was possible for people to simply "disappear" and in fact, his fictional stories of Charles Ashmore and others were based on a real-life experience that intrigued Bierce at the start of his journalistic career. And ironically, the author of stories like that of Charles Ashmore and the chilling tale called "The Spook House," in which two travelers enter a house in Kentucky but only one emerges, himself vanished without a trace in 1913.

No clue has ever been found to explain what may have become of the one of the most famous American writers of the early twentieth century. But it cannot be denied that Bierce was a strange, unusual and eccentric man and his life was riddled with many mysteries.

In the San Francisco of 1900, Ambrose Bierce reigned as the unchallenged literary king of the city and was considered the best-known writer west of the Rocky Mountains. Along with Jack London, there is no question that he was one of the best writers of the period but there was a long road from the beginning of his career to his mysterious disappearance. And there were many who weren't unhappy to see "Bitter Bierce," as he came to be called, vanish without a trace.

Legendary curmudgeon, Ambrose "Bitter" Bierce

Ambrose Gwinnett Bierce was born in Meigs County, Ohio, on June 24, 1842. In his family were nine brothers and sisters, all christened with names that started with the letter "A" – Abigail, Addison, Aurelius, Amelia, Ann, Augustus, Andrew, Almeda, Albert, and Ambrose. It might be expected that parents who named their children so whimsically would be warm and devoted but, according to Bierce, they were not. In fact, Bierce grew into a child who saw no good in either parent. In time, he wrote five short stories, which he collected under the title of *Parenticide* —– the killing of one's own parents. One story, "An Imperfect Conflagration," began, "Early one June morning in 1872, I murdered my father —– an act which made a deep impression on me at the time."

Whatever his upbringing was like, though, Bierce's father was an avid reader and had accumulated a large personal library, which Bierce explored as a boy. Through his voracious reading of books and newspapers, he became an ardent abolitionist as a young man and went to work for an anti-slavery newspaper in northern Indiana. As he began writing, he realized his life's work and spent the next number of years as a journalist. He briefly attended the Kentucky Military Institute but left in 1859 without a degree. This lack of education would dog him through his critics for the rest of his life as they complained of his poor grammatical skills. Bierce never let this stop him, and as a born storyteller, he was able to achieve success with those who mattered —--- his readers.

Bierce was always considered cynical and aloof. He reveled in the unknown and his life was marked by adventure. Both his writings of war and his writings of ghosts and horror were separately influenced by events in Bierce's life. It's possible that his interest in weird happenings and strange disappearances stemmed from an event about which he wrote, which took place in 1854.

One hot day in July of that year, a planter named Orion Williamson from Selma, Alabama, was sitting on the veranda of his home with his wife and child. As he squinted out into the bright sunshine, his gaze fell on the 10-acre pasture where his horses were grazing. Williamson stood up and announced to his wife, "I forgot to tell Andrew about those horses." Andrew was his overseer. Mrs. Williamson later remembered her husband stepping down from the porch and walking out into the field. He picked up a small stick in his hands and he absent-mindedly swished it back and forth as he walked through the ankle-high grass.

At that same time, a neighboring farmer, Armour Wren, and his son, James, were returning from Selma in a buggy, passing by the field on a road that ran along the far side. They stopped when they saw Williamson approaching and Wren stood and waved to him. At that split second, with four sets of eyes upon him, Williamson abruptly disappeared. A moment earlier, he had been walking away from his family and waving at friends —--- and the next moment, he had vanished into thin air.

Stunned, Wren and his son jumped from their wagon and ran into the field, where they soon met Mrs. Williamson and her child. They breathlessly searched the area where Williamson had vanished but saw nothing but bare ground and sparse grass. It seemed impossible, but the man was gone.

For two hours, the Wrens and the Williamsons searched the field. They found nothing, and as the realization of what had happened occurred to her, Mrs. Williamson collapsed in shock. She was taken to

Selma and hospitalized. When news spread of what had occurred, 300 men from town gathered at the field. They formed three hand-to-hand ranks and moved across the field inches at a time, stopping every few feet to kneel down and examine the ground for openings or holes. They searched the field dozens of times and when night fell, they used torches and lanterns to light up the area. Bloodhounds were brought in, but no trace of the farmer could be found.

The following morning, hundreds of additional volunteers arrived from nearby communities, along with a team of geologists. They began digging at the point where Williamson disappeared but, a few feet below the surface, they hit solid bedrock. There were no caves, crevices, or holes to explain where he had gone. He had simply vanished.

The sensational word of Williamson's disappearance attracted the attention of journalists from around the South and Midwest. Later, one of those was Ambrose Bierce, whose own fascination with the unknown caused him to investigate the case and to write a short story about it entitled "The Difficulty of Crossing a Field." The unexplained aspects of this particular story inspired him to pen many other variations on the theme.

And while what happened to Orion Williamson was certainly strange, it did not prepare anyone for what happened next. The following spring revealed an odd circle that appeared in the field at the exact spot where Williamson was last seen. The grass within the circle died and this curious event was pointed out to Mrs. Williamson by investigators who were still interested in the mystery. By this time, Mrs. Williamson was still so traumatized by the vanishing that she was reluctant to mention her husband's name or to consider what had become of him. Her strange behavior brought many questions from volunteers and the authorities alike. Why was the woman still in such a state of shock? True, the disappearance of her husband was undoubtedly bizarre, but why did she refuse to talk about him?

In a quavering and fearful voice, Mrs. Williamson finally explained. She told the searchers that in the days following her husband's disappearance, she and her child distinctly heard Williamson's voice calling for help from the spot where he had vanished. They had run to the spot each time they heard him, but there was no one and nothing there. The calling continued for almost two weeks and Williamson's voice becoming weaker and weaker as the days passed. On the last night he was heard, the family slept at the edge of the spot where he vanished. They heard Williamson's whispers and then he was heard no more.

Ambrose Bierce would interview not only the searchers in the Williamson affair, but also "experts" who claimed to have theories as to where the farmer had gone. One of them, Dr. Maximilian Hern, was a scientist who had written a book called *Disappearance and Theory Thereof.* He stated that Williamson had walked into "void spot of universal ether." These spots, he explained, only lasted for a few seconds but were capable of destroying any and all material elements that happened into them. Other scientists stepped forward with theories, as well. One of them said that he believed Williamson walked into a periodic "magnetic field" that disintegrated his atomic structure and sent him into another dimension.

None of these theories helped to discover the missing Orion Williamson, though, and while he was immortalized in Bierce's writings, he now seemed to be gone for good. His story refused to die, however. Not only did he appear in a story by Ambrose Bierce, but he would also provide the inspiration for other stories by the writer. In addition, his story would be plagiarized numerous times over the years, starting in 1889.

In that year, a traveling salesman from Cincinnati named McHatten was trapped by a snowstorm in Gallatin, Tennessee. With nothing to do but sleep, eat, and drink, McHatten decided to rewrite the Orion Williamson story and sell it to a newspaper as an original report. He changed Williamson's name to David Lang and the site of his disappearance to Gallatin. He also altered the date of the occurrence from 1854 to 1880. McHatten's story, except for the basic facts, was a complete fabrication and has since been accepted and rewritten to appear in many reputable journals and books. Research has revealed that no one named David Lang ever lived in Gallatin.

Orion Williamson, however, was a real person and was not the figment of anyone's imagination. According to census records, he was a resident of Selma, Alabama, in 1854 — – although his residence in that city tragically came to an end one hot afternoon in July.

The accounts of Orion Williamson that Bierce discovered almost surely provided the inspiration for the writer's works on the unknown, but it would be his service during the Civil War that would provide inspiration for his gritty tales of death and adventure. Bierce always considered the war to be his finest hour. He originally enlisted at age 18 with the Ninth Indiana Infantry and through the bloody battles of Shiloh, Murfreesboro, Kennesaw Mountain, Franklin, and Nashville, he rose through the ranks to first lieutenant. At the time of his final discharge in 1865, he was a major.

He enlisted three times and the war took a physical toll on him. He was wounded twice, once quite seriously in the head, but he always returned to the battlefield after he had recovered. He seemed to love the war, but his brother, Albert, always believed that it changed him in terrible ways. He stated that Bierce was never the same after he was wounded in the head. "Some of the iron of the shell seemed to stick to his brain," he said, "and he became bitter and suspicious."

Following the war, Bierce joined a military expedition that fought its way through Indians to reach the Pacific. He settled in wild San Francisco, among the miners, gamblers, and prostitutes. Times were changing in the West and a good newspaperman was needed. Bierce was determined to provide that service, and he soon became a popular writer. He earned a reputation for his wit but was considered as unpredictable and as odd as many of the people he wrote about.

He was strikingly handsome, though, and stood six feet tall and carried himself with the erect manner of military life. His eyes, under reddish-blond brows, were blue and piercing. His flowing hair and luxuriant mustache were blond, with red streaks running through the gold. And if his looks were not enough, Bierce had a commanding vitality. Women swooned at the sight of him and according to one account, "Young ladies claimed that they could feel him when he stood ten feet away."

Despite his good looks, though, Bierce was a failure with women. He simply worshipped them too much, placing them on a pedestal from which they were guaranteed to fall. When he discovered their flesh and blood failings, his love turned to dislike and hatred. His tirades against women were infamous and they became even worse after he destroyed his marriage to lovely society belle Ellen Day. He was married to her long enough to father two sons and a daughter, but never stopped hating his wife for having failed to meet his impossible standards. He never had much contact with his sons, both of whom died young, and yet he maintained a loving relationship and voluminous correspondence with his daughter, Helen.

Bierce's bitterness was not only directed at his wife. He made many enemies in San Francisco. His writings contained a level of viciousness and brutality that was unrivaled in journalism of the day and he received scores of threats. Bets were placed on how long he might live, and he took to always carrying a pistol with him on the streets. He was not subtle in his criticisms, but he was impartial about how he handed out the abuse. In other words, Bierce hated just about everyone.

With his marriage on the rocks, Bierce took a long trip to London, where his reputation as a bitter curmudgeon took hold. His writings became even more acidic, perhaps because of his dislike for England, and yet people seemed to love what he published. He was writing seriously for the first time and ironically, he sold his first efforts to a magazine called *Fun!* They were gloomy, cynical pieces that were amazingly well received. In 1871, they were collected into a book called *Cobwebs from an Empty Skull*.

Bierce's work attracted so much attention that he was hired to write and edit a magazine called *The Lantern*. It was financed by none other than the dazzling Empress Eugenie of France, who was anxious to have the British take a friendly view toward her frivolous activities. Bierce was not above enhancing the truth when needed and he turned out to be a superb creator of propaganda. British opinion swung strongly to the Empress, who decided to show her appreciation to Bierce by commanding him to appear in her presence. It was a costly error. Ambrose Bierce had not allowed himself to be commanded by anyone since he left the Army — - and certainly not by a woman. He never showed up to the scheduled meeting and he sent no regrets. The outraged Empress fired him.

In 1874, Bierce returned to San Francisco and found that he was now a celebrity, largely because he had lived and published a book in England. He returned to writing in San Francisco, working with two different local newspapers. There was no reconciliation with his wife. Instead, Bierce began to test his mettle as a drinker. He boasted proudly that no matter how much he drank, he always remained on his feet to order, and pay for, the last round of drinks. However, alcohol managed to alter the course of Bierce's life. One night after a long drinking bout, he took a long walk and then stumbled into a graveyard to sleep off the effects of the liquor. While he slept on a flat gravestone, he was enveloped by a damp San Francisco fog. The chill that resulted gave him acute attacks of asthma, which plagued him for the rest of his life.

Because of this, he moved to the hills around San Francisco and rarely appeared in the city. He sent his writings to the newspapers by messenger and managed to become the most popular writer west of the Rockies.

Soon, Bierce became one of the star writers in the spreading editorial empire of William Randolph Hearst. Their partnership became an arrangement that would last for more than 20 years, despite frequent arguments and resignations. Bierce and Hearst eventually came to hate one another. "Working for Hearst has all of the satisfactions of masturbation," Bierce once wrote to the delight of his audience.

But Hearst, who had no love for his famous writer, cared more about sensationalism and a rising circulation than he did about being insulted. Bierce's writings appeared in the *New York Journal*, the *New York American* and the *San Francisco Chronicle*, as well as in Hearst's tremendously popular magazine, *Cosmopolitan*. His name became a household word and between his sharp attacks on everyone from clergymen to politicians, he wrote short stories of the Civil War and of the bizarre and the curious. Collections such as *Fantastic Fables* and *Can Such Things Be?* began to appear. Many of the stories were based on real-life happenings, or claimed to be, and Bierce's mixing of fact with fiction continues to thrill readers today. In many of his stories, he wrote about unsolved disappearances and seemed obsessed by them.

On several occasions, he conducted interviews at the sites where people had vanished, and while many of them expressed skepticism as to the supernatural nature of the vanishing, they did draw attention to the events.

Oddly, Bierce began to joke about the possibility of his own disappearance, which would no longer be a jest in 1913.

In the rustic surroundings of the California hills, Bierce lived alone. Occasionally, a woman joined him, but it never lasted for long. Bierce never had a satisfactory relationship with a woman and he never stopped hating his wife. He seemed to despise the women who were attracted to him and while he used them, he considered them damaged because they were willing to give themselves to a married man.

Bierce found all the companionship that he needed with animals. He loved cats, and other assorted creatures, except for dogs, which he never liked. He kept a lizard as a pet for many years and the animal perched on his shoulder each day as he wrote. When the lizard died, he found a humble garden toad to serve as his new writing companion. He grew so fond of the toad that he let it hop around on the table when he ate his meals.

With the publication of the stories "The Damned Thing and The Monk" and the "Hangman's Daughter," Bierce truly became famous. He was never a best-selling author like Mark Twain, but a devout cult of followers sprang up. Bierce's writings, which were riddled with tales of death and the supernatural, influenced his fans. Two fellow writers who admired Bierce met particularly violent ends. Author George Serling committed suicide and Herman Scheffauer killed his wife and then himself. That both men idolized Bierce was well known, and their deaths managed to add to Bierce's dark allure for his readers.

Bierce was pleased by this, although the misfortunes and tragedies of his life kept him from enjoying any true happiness. His greatest tragedy stemmed from the passing of his two sons. Although they had never been close to their father, both men died young. One of them died of acute alcoholism and the other was stabbed to death in a saloon fight.

In 1909, Hearst sent Bierce to Washington, D.C., to cover a story involving the California millionaire Collis P. Huntington. The

Washington climate – humid and hot in the summer and bitingly cold in the winter – was disliked by most of the residents of the nation's capital, but Bierce loved it. He claimed that his asthma actually improved in Washington and he decided to settle there, write for the Hearst papers in New York and San Francisco, and retire to edit his collected works. He labored over the 12 volumes with the help of his devoted secretary, Carrie Christiansen, the only woman besides his daughter that he could stand to be around. His other published works were selling steadily, and Bierce was assured of a good income. With Carrie's help, he was able to take his time and rework every story and poem that he had ever written. This kept him occupied until 1912 and then, apparently, Bierce decided to examine the prospects for the last years of his life.

At the age of 70, Bierce made two important decisions about the rest of his life. One of them was that he would retrace the paths that he had taken on battlefields of the Civil War, and the second was that he would travel to Mexico, where revolutionary forces were fighting to overthrow the federal troops of dictator Victoriano Huerta.

In 1913, no one could foresee that the Great War would break out in Europe just one year later. But in Mexico, there was fighting. Just below the border, the forces of Pancho Villa had risen to challenge the dictatorship of President Huerta. The United States, much concerned, had adopted a policy of watchful waiting. American troops were stationed at Laredo, Texas, but anyone who stepped over the border would find themselves in the midst of Villa's ragged, yet spirited, troops. Bierce became determined to see what was taking place in Mexico. The Civil War had been one of the greatest experiences of his life and he wanted to see combat one last time before he died.

Bierce first wanted to make a sojourn to the battlefields of his youth, and in October 1913, he retraced his steps through Shiloh, Chickamauga, Murfreesboro, Kennesaw Mountain, Franklin, and Nashville. After that, he stayed in New Orleans for a short time. While he was there, a reporter managed to land an interview with him, and Bierce made the claim that he had never amounted to much after the Civil War. Then he told the reporter, "I'm on my way to Mexico because I like the game. I like fighting. I want to see it."

During his travels, Bierce had written long, almost daily letters to Carrie Christiansen in Washington and, less frequently, to his daughter, Helen, in Detroit. The letters continued until mid-December, when Bierce reached Laredo, Texas. His last letter to Carrie, dated December 16, 1913, was full of information, detailing the local color and his excitement about seeing the Mexican Revolution. It also contained a cryptic message: "I am going into Mexico with a pretty definite purpose which is not at present disclosable."

From there, Bierce crossed the border into Juarez, which had recently been liberated by Pancho Villa. The bandit, now turned general, issued Bierce credentials that would allow him to accompany Villa's army. By this time, Bierce had not ridden a horse in almost 30 years. The fact that he managed to keep up with the soldiers was a remarkable accomplishment for him.

He sent a last letter to his daughter dated December 26. He said that he had ridden four miles to mail the letter and that he had been given a sombrero as a reward for "picking off" one of the enemy with a rifle at long range. He also told her that he was leaving with the army for Ojinaga, a city under siege, the following day.

In his closing lines, he wrote, "As to me, I leave here tomorrow for an unknown destination."

After that, the facts behind the disappearance of Ambrose Bierce end and the speculation begins.

Lack of word from Bierce bothered Carrie greatly. Helen, who did not hear from her father as often, was not as concerned. Both assumed that Bierce was too busy to write and was doing exactly what he wanted to be doing. Daily, they expected him to return to Texas, or to at least to get another colorful message from him in the mail. But the letters never came.

Finally, 10 months after he crossed the border into Mexico, in September 1914, Helen appealed to the state department for help in finding her famous father. The commander of American troops in Texas was ordered to conduct as much of a search was possible under the circumstances. He, in turn, appealed to American consular officials in Mexico. The only information they could find was that Bierce was with Pancho Villa, acting as a military advisor.

But, if this were true, why had he not written to his daughter or to Carrie Christiansen? There were a number of American military correspondents traveling with Villa's army. Bierce could have asked any one of them to send back word that he was safe. Or Bierce himself could have found ways of slipping messages back across the border, just as he had done with the letter to his daughter in late December 1913.

The mystery of Ambrose Bierce began to capture the public's attention. In April 1915, an astounding rumor claimed that Bierce was alive and well and not in Mexico at all. By that time, Europe was also at war, and several American newspapers printed a story that Bierce was attached to the staff of England's Lord Kitchener as a major specializing in recruitment. Helen immediately requested Washington to verify this and word came back from London that the story was completely false. There was no doubt that the cantankerous Bierce would have been pleased to learn that he was considered important enough to be the subject of an international hoax.

By 1919, with both European and Mexican wars ended, reporters, writers and friends were about to investigate Bierce's disappearance.

George F. Weeks, a friend of Bierce's from California, set out on a personal search for the author in February 1919. No word had come from his old friend since the last days of 1913 and while most assumed that he had long since died, answers were still being sought about his final destination. In Mexico City, Weeks managed to track down an officer who told him that Bierce had been killed during a campaign in January 1914. He had collapsed during the attack on Ojinaga and had died from hardship and exposure. There was no proof of this and no one else could verify it; however, Pancho Villa, fearing world opinion, did have a policy of keeping names of foreigners off the casualty lists.

Other rumors, clues and leads suggested that Bierce was killed by a firing squad, conducted by federal soldiers. He was also said to have been killed by the volatile Pancho Villa himself after the two of them had quarreled. Or that he was killed by guides or by Villa's men after one too many insults from his sharp tongue. Some have suggested that

Bierce did not go to Mexico at all, and instead committed suicide over his failing health. One story claimed that he had blown his own brains out on the edge of the Grand Canyon. There were also rumors that he had been poisoned in El Paso and secretly buried in someone's backyard.

Others theorized that Bierce had crossed back into the United States to live and die in obscurity and have a last laugh at those who puzzled over his mysterious disappearance. While this sounds like something Bierce might have done, most would agree that the lure of war would have been too strong for him to be able to resist going to Mexico. Odo B. Slade, a former member of Pancho Villa's staff, recalled an elderly American with gray hair who served as a military advisor to Villa. The American called himself "Jack Robinson" and he criticized the Mexican's battle strategies with the eye of a military expert. Slade later stated that "Robinson" quarreled violently with Villa and was shot to death when he announced his intention to leave and ally himself with the enemy.

But what really happened to Bierce remains a mystery and will, without a doubt, remain that way forever. He vanished, as he wrote in his own words, into a space "through which animate and inanimate objects may fall into the invisible world and be seen and heard no more."

And that's just the way that Ambrose Bierce would have wanted it.

1921: Mystery of Carroll A. Deering

On January 29, 1921, a ship was discovered grounded on Diamond Shoals, off the coast of Cape Hatteras, North Carolina. It had been

The mysterious Carroll A. Deering ghost ship

spotted, adrift in the waves, on the previous day and attempts had been made to hail the crew —-- but something strange seemed to be happening on board. When she threw herself onto the shoals the following morning, her name could be seen, painted on the hull —--- *Carroll A. Deering.*

Every attempt to signal the men on board her failed. There were no lights and no movement on board the vessel. Where had they gone? That was a question in 1921 and remains a question to this day. The mystery of the *Carroll A. Deering* has never been solved.

The *Deering* was not some derelict vessel, abandoned at sea. She was almost brand new, built in Bath, Maine, in 1919 as the last ship of the G.G. Deering Company. She was 255 feet long and 45 feet wide with 5 masts and 3 decks. She was more luxurious than normal for a cargo ship. She had been outfitted in oak, mahogany, and ash, with a functioning lavatory, steam heat, and electricity.

In September of 1920, Captain W. B. Wormell, a retired seaman with years of experience, was assigned to the Maine schooner *Carroll A. Deering* after its captain, William H. Merritt, took ill. The ship had a 10-man crew of Danish sailors with orders to deliver a shipment of coal to Rio de Janeiro. The journey was without incident, although Captain Wormell didn't think much of his crew. While the coal was being unloaded at Rio de Janeiro, the captain granted them leave and met with a friend and the captain of another cargo, Captain Goodwin, to discuss his problems with discipline. He had little good to say about the *Deering's* current crew, aside from the engineer, Herbert Bates.

The *Deering* set sail —– with the same crew on board —– in late 1920. During the return journey, they stopped for supplies in Barbados. While in port, First Mate Charles B. McLellan, got drunk at the Continental Café and was overheard complaining about Captain Wormell's competence and making a threat against the Captain's life. McLellan was arrested and jailed but was released on Wormell's orders, and they sailed onwards to Hampton Roads, Virginia.

There is no record of what happened in the weeks that followed. The ship was next seen by the Cape Lookout Lightship in North Carolina on January 28, 1921. The *Deering* attempted to hail the lightship's keeper, Captain Jacobson, who reported that a man with ginger hair and an accent told him the *Deering* had lost its anchors. Jacobson acknowledged the information, but his radio was not working, and he was not able to report to authorities. He noticed that the crew seemed to be wandering about on the foredeck, which seemed very unusual.

On January 29, 1921, the *Deering* was seen grounded on Diamond Shoals off the coast of Cape Hatteras. She seemed silent and empty. The men who had been seen on the previous day seemed to have vanished. Rescue ships were dispatched but inclement weather caused a delay, and the ship was not boarded until February 4th.

The rescuers found a very strange scene on the ship.

The ship's log and navigation equipment, the crew's possessions, and the lifeboats were gone. The galley was set up for a meal with food still in a frying pan and coffee on the stove, but there was no one on the ship. There were several different footprints in the captain's quarters indicating activity there, but the captain —– along with the rest of the men —– was missing. A map and logbook were found, in the captain's handwriting, chronicling the ship's route until January 23. After that, the records were written in a different hand —– and they revealed nothing of the crew's fate.

The Coast Guard attempted to salvage the ship so that the investigation could continue, but it could not be dragged off the rocks. Finally, they were forced to dynamite the ship so it would not interfere with other shipping traffic.

The investigation – demanded by the wife of Captain Wormell – continued and eventually involved the United States Commerce Department, the Treasury, the Justice Department, the Navy, and the state of North Carolina. Secretary of Commerce and future President Herbert Hoover and his assistant, Lawrence Ritchey, were placed in charge of the investigation. They had a lot on their hands at that moment. It was not the only ship to be lost in the area, but all the other vessels had been sailing near large hurricanes. This situation was much different. Ritchey tried to trace the *Deering's* route from its last sighting at Cape Lookout to running aground at Diamond Shoals using logs of the Coast Guard lightships and determined that the *Deering* must have been sailing away from the area of the storms.

But this didn't explain the missing crew.

An FBI agent went to Dare County in July 1921 and asked local Coast Guardsmen if they believed the crew had mutinied and abandoned ship. Captain Ballance of the Cape Hatteras station said the coastline was too jagged for lifeboats to land. "I believe they abandoned her after taking everything of value," he said, "and ran her up on the Shoals intentionally."

Wormell's problems with First Mate McLellan were well-documented at their stop in Rio de Janeiro, and Captain Jacobson at Cape Lookout knew the man who hailed his ship was not Captain Wormell, nor was he an officer. The investigation was closed in late 1922 with no answers ever discovered, but either mutiny or bootleggers who operated in the area were assumed to be the cause.

More recently, the speculation has become much wilder —— including aliens. The *Deering* has also become a favorite victim of the so-called "Bermuda Triangle" (see the last section of this book for details about this myth, cooked up by conspiracy theorists) but, like so many other ships connected to that particular story, was nowhere near it when the crew vanished. Men had been seen on board near Cape Lookout the day before she was grounded, which is nowhere near the "Bermuda Triangle."

But it is a mystery that remains unsolved. Although in this case, I believe the mystery was caused by the murderous acts of men, rather than the supernatural.

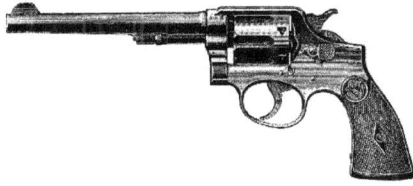

1921: The Man They Never Hanged

On December 11, 1921, "Terrible" Tommy O'Connor became a Chicago legend.

It certainly wasn't because of any great fame he achieved. In fact, he was a lowlife, small-time crook who never would have made a mark in history except for the fact that the old Chicago gallows were kept waiting for him for more than 50 years after he was sentenced to hang. The rotting timbers remained in storage in the Cook County Jail — just in case O'Connor was ever captured.

Tommy O'Connor became a mythical figure in Chicago history, and a portrait of him still hangs in the atrium of the old Criminal Courts building. But how did a petty thug, universally disliked by police officers and fellow criminals alike, become of the most unusual characters in Windy City crime?

He did it by vanishing without a trace.

Tommy was born in Ireland but moved to Chicago with his family when he was only two-years-old. He grew up in the West Side Maxwell Street neighborhood, a notoriously bad area that was so riddled with crime that reporters had dubbed it "Bloody Maxwell." His immigrant father worked hard, putting in enough long hours to be able to move his family to a small house near 13th Street and Paulina Avenue. But even in these better surroundings, Tommy still managed to fall in with a bad crowd. He and his best friend, Jimmy Cherin, began hanging out in local saloons and it wasn't long before they were committing minor hold-ups and robberies.

"Terrible" Tommy O'Connor

Tommy loved being a criminal —– even a small-time one. He earned a nasty reputation as a man quick with a gun. During one hold-up, Tommy was told by the leader of the gang that there would be no shooting. Tommy shot the robbery victim anyway and told the leader that he did it because he felt like it and he would shoot the boss too if he didn't like it. When Chicago Police Sergeant Herman Otten killed a bandit friend of his named Jimmy Higgins, Tommy sent a letter to Otten, promising to kill him. Luckily for the cop, he never followed through on the threat.

Tommy continued his sordid career for about two years and then was arrested for the first time. He was indicted for the murder of a robbery victim, and even though one of the members of his own gang testified against him, the prosecution was unable to make to make the charges stick and O'Connor was set free.

After being released, Tommy was bitter towards the man who testified against him, another lowlife named Emerson. After stewing about it for several days, he went to see his old friend, Jimmy Cherin.

The two had spent their youth committing crimes and dreaming of becoming important criminals and now, O'Connor asked Cherin to help him kill Emerson. But Jimmy refused. He had since gone straight and was now married with a newborn child. No one knows what words were exchanged between the two men, but it has been surmised that Cherin not only turned Tommy down but may have threatened to tell what he knew to the police.

Jimmy's refusal sealed his fate. Tommy shot his longtime friend five times, killing him in his own home. He was indicted for murder but, once again, was never brought to trial. The murder also claimed two more victims. A short time later, Jimmy's wife, insane with grief, killed herself and her baby.

By March 1920, Tommy had killed at least five men. Late one night, a squad of police detectives raided the home of O'Connor's brother-in-law, where Tommy was lying low after a string of robberies. The police had a warrant. He'd skipped out on his bail bond after the murder of Jimmy Cherin.

When the police burst into the home, Tommy grabbed his gun and began firing wildly. Five shots rang out and a bullet struck Chicago Detective Sergeant Patrick "Paddy" O'Neill in the chest. O'Neill died half an hour later. In the melee, O'Connor escaped, managing to slip past uniformed policemen who were looking for him less than 50 feet away.

For the next four months, the police hunted for Tommy all over the United States in what was said to be the most extensive manhunt in the history of the Chicago police. They followed numerous false leads until finally tracking him down aboard a train to Omaha. He was drunk and held up the porter who sold him the beer. The train was stopped in St. Paul, Minnesota, and O'Connor escaped. As he jumped down onto the tracks, he pulled out a gun and tried to board the switch engine of another train, only to be kept off the train by a fireman who swung an ax at him. He ran alongside the tracks on foot for a while before being captured by a switch foreman on the Chicago--Great Western passenger line. He was only arrested for being drunk and disorderly, but then made the mistake of telling the St. Paul police who he was.

Within days, he was back in Chicago, where he claimed his innocence in the shooting of the police officer. "It wasn't my revolver that killed (O'Neill)," he said. "(he) was shot by his own pals. A mistake, of course, but they shot him. And after that mistake they ran away and put the blame on me. What chance had I with every policeman in the city out to get me dead or alive?"

Not surprisingly, no one believed his story. He was tried, convicted, sentenced to hang, and sent to jail to await his execution.

But on December 11, 1921, a few days before O'Connor was to be hanged, he escaped.

While talking with a prison guard about getting a pass to go to the hospital, Tommy and three others overpowered guard David Straus with a pistol that had been smuggled in by an accommodating prison cook. They beat Straus, tied him up, and took his key. As they made their way through the jail, they were surprised by another guard, but managed to subdue him also. The escapees made their way to the roof, where they jumped nine feet down into an alley. The jump was too much for one of the prisoners. He broke both his ankles when he landed on the ground and made it no further.

The other three men ran north up the alley to Illinois Street, where they jumped onto the running boards of an automobile and ordered the owner to keep driving. A guard from the jail chased after them, almost snagging O'Connor's shirt with an outstretched hand. But O'Connor pistol-whipped him, knocking him away and the car sped away.

It was the last the law would see of "Terrible" Tommy O'Connor.

Huge rewards for his capture were offered. At one point, offers were made to a newspaper from underworld characters to secure an interview with Tommy in exchange for a large sum of money and immunity. The newspaper took the deal but hastily backed out of it. They worried that any reporter who gained information on Tommy O'Connor wasn't likely to live long.

Tommy O'Connor was never found. Rumors circulated for years that he was somewhere on the South Side, under the protection of friends. Others say that he had fled the country and gone to Ireland.

Many reports from the 1930s stated that he became a part of the Touhy Gang, a group of Chicago toughs and kidnappers led by Roger Touhy.

For decades, rumors about O'Connor's whereabouts came to the attention of the police every couple of months. Practically every year, the newspapers would run stories about the legendary escape. All the while, the gallows were kept in the basement of the prison, just in case. When the prison was torn down, and the prisoners moved to a facility on 26th Street and California Avenue, the gallows went with them.

As more years passed, the chances that Tommy would ever be captured began to fade. Some still believed that there was a chance that he would actually be hanged, and that when he was captured, the gallows would be brought back to the vicinity of the old jail — , which was a parking lot by then — , and set up, with canvas walls around it, and there, Tommy would swing at last.

But fewer and fewer people believed that would happen. Even if O'Connor were caught, there would surely be appeals. After all, many years had passed since his escape. Judge Kickham Scanlan who had sentenced him was long dead. Harry Stanton, the jail plumber who had built the scaffolds for 65 men, had retired in 1927 after 29 years. And in 1964, the warden said that the gallows had rotted, and would be impossible to use for a hanging. If O'Connor were alive at all, he had outlived the very gallows themselves.

But the gallows, decayed or not, remained in storage until 1977, when workers clearing out the basement of the court building came upon the beams and bolts, piled high in a corner. They asked Chief Criminal Court Judge Richard J. Fitzgerald if they could dispose of them once and for all. After all, Tommy was surely dead by then. The judge said he'd sign a court order to have them destroyed. "Heck," he said, "under present laws we couldn't execute the guy even if he surrendered tomorrow." But he suggested setting the gallows up one last time just to see what they looked like.

Workers managed to assemble the gallows, and they added a fresh rope to them, along with a sign that read "Tired of waiting, Tommy." After that, the gallows were dismantled for the final time.

Tommy O'Connor, if he managed to survive, had officially escaped the noose.

1925: The Lost Explorer of the Amazon

In the first decades of the twentieth century, before air travel was commonplace, the faraway jungles of the Amazon basin were largely unknown to what we refer to as "civilized" man. Although much of Brazil had been mapped and explored by that time, the Amazon region and the Matto Grosso lay undisturbed, shrouded in mystery and legend.

And they were strange legends indeed. They were tales of ancient stone towers with lights that never went out, and stories of barbaric white Indians with blue eyes and blond hair called the "Bat People," who lived in caves during the daylight and went out at night and attacked the nearby tribes while they slept. And, of course, the legend of the fabulous lost city that was built in Greco-Roman style, half buried in the undergrowth of centuries, yet glittering like gold in the equatorial sun.

The lost lands of the Matto Grosso haunted writers and explorers for decades. Sir Arthur Conan Doyle wrote one of his famous novels, *The Lost World*, about an expedition to these unknown lands and he was not alone in his fascination for the mysteries they offered.

Adventurers dreamed of venturing into the dark Brazilian jungles. One of them was a man named Colonel Percy Harrison Fawcett, who obsessed about this uncharted region for nearly 20 years before he vanished into it without a trace, lured to his death by visions of riches and a fabulous lost city.

The story of Colonel Fawcett is a tale of one of the last great explorers in history and it remains one of the great unsolved mysteries of all time.

Over the centuries, far too many men and women have followed the promise of gold and riches to their doom, but Percy Fawcett was no wide-eyed treasure hunter, who was only motivated by greed. He was a cautious, deliberate explorer whose goal was cultural discovery. Exploration and adventure were literally in his blood.

Percy Fawcett

Fawcett was born in 1867 in Torquay, Devon, England, to Edward and Myra Fawcett. His father was the child of colonist parents in India and was a Fellow of the Royal Geographic Society, the gentleman explorers of the day. Percy's older brother, Edward, was a mountain climber, Eastern Occultist, and popular writer of adventure novels. It's no surprise that Percy followed in the family tradition.

In 1886, he received a commission in the Royal Artillery and served in Trincomalee, Ceylon, (now Sri Lanka) where he also met his wife. While in Ceylon, he spent much of his free time searching for tombs and hidden treasure. Later, he worked for the British secret service in North Africa and learned the surveyor's craft. He was a friend of authors H. Rider Haggard and Arthur Conan Doyle, who used Fawcett's Amazonian field reports as an inspiration for *The Lost World*.

Fawcett's first expedition to South America was in 1906 when he travelled to the continent to map a jungle area at the border of Brazil and Bolivia at the behest of the Royal Geographic Society. The society had been commissioned to map the area as a third party, unbiased by local or national interests. During the expedition ——— an arduous journey that dragged on for three years ——— Fawcett claimed to have seen a giant anaconda, for which he was widely ridiculed by the scientific community. It would be many years later when science finally conceded that such animals did exist.

Fawcett made seven expeditions in the Brazilian jungles between 1906 and 1924. He mostly got along with the locals through gifts, patience, and courteous behavior. During these years, he became fascinated by the mysterious secrets of the Brazilian interior, especially the seemingly endless and unknown jungle plateau known as the Matto Grosso. Somewhere in that forbidding jungle, he believed, was a great and ancient city whose artifacts and treasure would prove it to be the true cradle of civilization, pre-dating the cities of Egypt by thousands of years.

Fawcett was convinced the city existed and he referred to it as "Z," thanks to a rare document that he unearthed in 1901 in Rio de Janeiro. The incredible lost city, which purportedly rested on the side of a cliff, had been allegedly discovered by a Portuguese expedition that went into the Matto Grosso in 1743. The expedition had been in search of the gold, silver, and diamond mines of adventurer Melchior Dias-Moreya, a half-Indian, half-Portuguese soldier of fortune who was known to the natives as "Moribeca." Legend had it that he had discovered the mines in 1610. Moribeca was imprisoned when he would not reveal the location of the mines and he died in 1622, his secret intact. The Portuguese expedition of 1743, searching for the fabulous mines, went off course and ended up wandering through the Matto Grosso. By accident, they stumbled into a steep crevice and then climbed through an artificial breach in the cliff wall, following ancient paved steps.

Once they entered the passageway, the explorers walked into a giant city that lay in ruins — - wide streets, huge temples, and elaborate courtyards surrounded by massive buildings. Mysterious inscriptions, which were copied down by the amazed adventurers and remain undeciphered to this day, decorated the temples, walls, and buildings. In addition to a wealth of archaeological treasure, a nearby river was said to glitter with massive gold deposits.

The Portuguese were stunned and overwhelmed by their accidental discovery, but lack of food and depleted supplies forced them to abandon the city and search for a way to get home. Only three members of the expedition survived and stumbled, lost and bedraggled, to the coastal state of Bahia, where they told their weird tale in 1754. The 11-year journey was eventually forgotten, except for a detailed report that was filed away in the Bibliotheca Nacional in Rio. Colonel Fawcett found the report there and became determined to find the city himself.

The Great War interrupted Fawcett's plans and he returned to Britain for active service in the Army. After the war ended, he went back to Brazil and launched his first expedition to look for the "Lost City of Z" in 1920. The exploration ended when one of the colonel's companions suffered a nervous collapse. Fawcett had to all but drag his men back to civilization, complaining that the explorer of the modern day was soft in comparison to the Portuguese adventurers who had none of the luxuries of the 1920s. It was Fawcett's habit to travel fast and with little equipment, living off the land and getting assistance from any friendly natives who could be found. Unfortunately, the native population of central Brazil was sparse. The Indians that did live in the Matto Grosso were hostile and superstitious and were more apt to kill intruders than to accept their gifts and trinkets.

Fawcett refused to give up his dream of finding the lost city and, in 1924, submitted a new plan to the Royal Geographical Society. On this expedition, he would be accompanied by his son, Jack, and another young Englishman, Raleigh Rimmel. The expedition would leave civilization at Cuyaba and travel north to the Paranatinga, moving downriver by canoe and then moving east on foot, crossing the Xingu River, then the Araguaya River, making for Port Imperial on the Tocantins, and then emerging from the Matto Grosso at Barra de Rio Grande on the Sao Francisco.

The three men would travel light, which most explorers thought was a terrible mistake. Fawcett was mad, they said, to enter the area without heavy supplies —--- one earlier expedition had entered the Matto Grosso with 1,400 men and a large amount of food and equipment, and all but three of the men had starved to death. Fawcett explained to the society, which would fund the exploration, that "no expedition could carry food for more than three weeks, for animal transport is impossible owing to lack of pasture and blood-sucking bats." Porters were out of the question because most of the tribes hated and feared their neighbors and would rarely accompany anyone beyond the limits of their own territory. Food was also a problem for a large group. Wild game was not plentiful and while there was enough to feed a small party, a larger one would starve.

Some members of the society questioned the reason for the expedition. Fawcett could not be sure of the exact location of "Z," or if he knew, he wasn't telling anyone. They also knew that Fawcett faced unknown jungle trails, vicious attacks by swarms of lethal insects, snakes and other dangerous animals, jungle sicknesses, the fear of falling asleep in the wrong spot where swarms of vampire bats might attack —- and worse. Fawcett was, as usual, undaunted and only looked at the positive side of the near-impossible journey, "Science will, I hope, be greatly benefitted, geography can scarcely fail to gain a good deal, and I am confident that we shall find the key to much lost history."

The three explorers walked into the wilderness at Cuyaba on April 20, 1925. By May 29, they reached the point where Fawcett had turned back in 1920 —- Dead Horse Camp, now called Camp Fawcett. It was from this point, at the dark edge of the Matto Grosso, that Colonel Fawcett's last words were recorded:

Here we are at Dead Horse Camp, the spot where my horse died in 1920. Only his white bones remain. My calculations anticipate contact with the Indians in about a week or ten days, when we should be able to reach the waterfall so much talked about... our journey has been no bed of roses. We have cut our way through miles of cerraba, a forest of dry scrub; we have crossed innumerable small streams by swimming and fording; we have climbed rocky hills of forbidding aspect; we have been eaten by bugs... Our two guides go back from here. They are more and more nervous as we push further into Indian country... We shall not get into interesting country for another two weeks. I shall continue to prepare dispatches from time to time, in hopes of being able to get them out eventually through some friendly tribe of Indians. But I doubt if this will be possible.

Fawcett, his son, Jack, and their friend, Raleigh Rimmel, entered the jungle and were never heard from again.

The Royal Geographical Society held out hope for two years, the length of time that it was estimated it would take for Fawcett's party to reach "Z," but by 1927, things were looking grim. Even the most stalwart believers -- with the exception of Fawcett's wife, who never gave up hope of seeing her husband and son again ---- were resigned to the fact that they would never return.

Dr. Hogarth of the Royal Geographical Society released a public statement: "We hold ourselves in readiness to help any competent and well-accredited volunteer party, which may propose to proceed on a reasonable plan to the interior of Brazil in order to try for news of Colonel P.H. Fawcett... I am forecasting a mission of inquiry alone, not one of relief. The latter is out of the question, as Colonel Fawcett himself stated emphatically, when he proposed to go where none, but he, could hope to penetrate and pass."

Hogarth's announcement was interpreted as an appeal for a search party and thousands of adventurers, from experts to crackpots, immediately volunteered to cut their way through the jungle in search of Fawcett and his companions. The Brazilian government believed that the Fawcett party, exhausted and starving, was killed by one of the various tribes that lived along the Xingu River. They saw no reason to send out a search party.

But reports from the Brazilian jungle claimed that Fawcett still lived. A Sergeant Roger Couturon, retired from the French Army, reported in the pages of a Rio newspaper in November 1927 that he had been hunting alligators near Cuyaba and had met a white man in the jungle. Couturon said, "He was a man of fifty to sixty years old with luxuriant grayish hair and a pepper and salt beard. He was wearing khaki shorts, like those worn by scouts, with a wide-brimmed hat." Couturon approached the man and saw that his bare legs were covered with mosquito bites, although the old man seemed not to care. He was standing silently, watching as the insects continued to devour his legs. He assumed the old man was a foreigner and addressed him in English.

"I say, man, the mosquitoes seem to be taking care of you," the Frenchman said.

The old man looked up at him. His face showed obvious signs of fatigue and the general weakness brought on by fever. But his eyes were straight and forceful and Couturon got the impression that the man had been a soldier. Finally, he replied, "Those poor animals are hungry, too."

Couturon went on his way that day, but he told several stories about the old man, whom he believed to be Fawcett. He said the explorer was living in a luxurious ranch in Brazil's interior and that he had given up on the civilized world and had become a jungle recluse. He also claimed that he had gone mad in the jungle and that some Indians that found him had made a white god of him. In Peru, some months later, the inventive Couturon insisted that he had met Jack Fawcett, who was living a life of ease and begged him not to inform the British government. Since the Fawcett party had been declared dead, Couturon said, Mrs. Fawcett was receiving a handsome pension and Jack didn't want her to lose this. (Mrs. Fawcett never received a pension.) Such fanciful reports further confused the Fawcett disappearance.

The first official expedition in search of Colonel Fawcett was led by Commander George Dyott, a fellow of the Royal Geographical Society. He led a party into the Matto Grosso in May 1928. Dyott's party was large and well-equipped and carefully followed Fawcett's three-year-old trail from Dead Horse Camp down the Rio Kuliseu. Along the river, Dyott questioned the chief of the Anauqua Indians, who told him that Fawcett had reached the dangerous Kuluene River sometime in 1925. Both Jack Fawcett and Rimmel were physical wrecks by that time and almost unable to speak. Fawcett, obsessed with finding the lost city, practically carried the younger men across the river and into the unknown jungles to the east. For five days, the Anauqua and Kalapolo Indians, who inhabited both sides of the river, watched the campfires of the white men. On the sixth day, Fawcett's fires went out and the Anauqua believed that they had been murdered by a fierce inland tribe called the Suya. A short time later, Dyott spoke with a chief of the Kalapolo, who told him that the Anauqua were lying and that they had killed Fawcett and his companions.

Dyott never found the Fawcett party's remains and after spending more time with the Anauqua, he became suspicious of them and his expedition slipped away under the cover of darkness, abandoning much of their equipment. Upon his return to civilization, he announced that Fawcett was, in all probability, dead.

But was he really? Not everyone believed this to be the case.

In 1931, a Swiss trapper named Stephen Rattin was in the Matto Grosso and reported seeing a "tall man, advanced in years, with blue eyes and a long beard" living with an unknown tribe north-northwest of Cuyaba, along the Iguassu Ximary, a tributary of the Sao Manuel River. Rattin spoke with the white man, who was dressed in animal skins, in English while the Indians occupied themselves with getting drunk. The man did not identify himself as Colonel Fawcett but explained that he was a captive and had formerly held the rank of colonel in the British Army. He asked that Rattin contact Major T.B. Paget, a friend of his who lived in Sao Paolo, and inform him that he was alive, but his son was "asleep." Paget had been the man who had helped to fund Fawcett's last expedition. Before being taken away by the Indians, the white man showed Rattin a signet ring that Mrs. Fawcett later identified as belonging to her husband.

When he returned to civilization, Rattin, whose story sounded authentic to many, mounted his own expedition to search for the captive man when he was told that it may have been Colonel Fawcett. The expedition, however, ended in failure.

Other expeditions followed, including one led by Vincenzo Petrullo, who, like Dyott, believed that Fawcett's party had been murdered. In 1932, another expedition was led by Robert Churchward. Peter Fleming, a member of the Churchward party (which was actually more of a hunting trip than a search party), later wrote about the expedition, which reached the conclusion that Fawcett's party, near death from fatigue and starvation, was murdered by the Kalapolo Indians as an act of mercy. Fleming added, however, "there still remains an infinitesimal, a million to one, chance that Fawcett is still alive. If he is, we must assume that he is in some way mentally deranged."

Throughout the 1930s, Fawcett legends multiplied. He was reportedly seen all over the Matto Grosso and it seemed that almost every adventurer who traveled north of Cuyaba returned with a story about having seen Fawcett alive. No less than 50 depositions were recorded by a Cuyaba notary public, all attesting to Fawcett's whereabouts. Many of the stories were contradictory. One gold miner saw three skeletons in a cave and believed they were the Fawcett party. A trapper said that he had run across the colonel alive and urged him to return to civilization, but he refused to face public admission of his failure to find the lost city. One man saw him on the Tocantins River married to four native women and worshipped as a god. Another swore that he had seen his dried and shrunken head hanging from a string in an Indian's hut.

In 1934, an American newspaper reporter, Albert de Winton, went to find Fawcett and he, too, disappeared in the Matto Grosso. In 1937, a missionary, Martha L. Moennich, came out of the Brazilian interior with a story about a half-breed "white" Indian boy called Dulipe. Found in 1926 at an Indian village by Reverend Emilio Halverson, Dulipe was believed to be the son of Jack Fawcett and a local Indian woman. Moennich had seen Dulipe in 1926 and again in 1937. The Fawcett family refused to accept this story. If Dulipe had a white father, they said, it was not Jack Fawcett.

In 1943, a Brazilian newspaper organized a research expedition that was headed by a reporter named Edmar Morel. It concluded that the explorers had been killed by Indians.

In April 1951, Orlando Vilas-Boas of the Central Brazil Foundation said that he had discovered the bleached bones of Colonel Fawcett after traveling into Kalapolo country. The bones were sent to England, where they were tested, and it was discovered that they did not belong to Fawcett. The teeth, as well as the dead man's stature, were not correct. Even as late as 1955, Edward Weyer, Jr., a writer and adventurer, claimed that he met an aged white man in the Matto Grosso who might have been Fawcett.

In January 1952, the last formal expedition was launched in search of clues of the fate of the Fawcett party. Members of the expedition included Orlando Vilas-Boas and Brian Fawcett, the colonel's youngest son. They talked to many Indians and visited a site that was purported to be the Fawcett party's grave — – but Brian was not convinced that the remains discovered there belonged to his father and brother.

Strange stories still come from Brazil about this famous missing explorer, but Colonel Percy Fawcett's disappearance remains a mystery. We will never know what really happened to him, but one can dream that this real-life "Indiana Jones" really did find the lost city of his quest. Perhaps he remained there, never to return to civilization. Who knows?

The mystery will undoubtedly never be solved, and Colonel Fawcett will always remain as lost today in the wilds of the Matto Grosso as the legendary city that he so diligently sought.

1928: Down the River
The Vanishing of Glen and Bessie Hyde

The magnificent and breathtaking Grand Canyon has been a place of wonder and mystery since the first Spanish explorers gazed down from the rim at the Colorado River far below. The canyon was conquered first by John Wesley Powell in the 1860s and has been the scene of both triumph and tragedy ever since. Perhaps the most famous unsolved disappearance in the Grand Canyon is that of a young couple named Glen and Bessie Hyde, who vanished without a trace while journeying through the canyon in 1928.

But they were not the only ones to do so.

In the early 1800s, the Grand Canyon was an enigma so deep and wide that it was commonly believed that no bird smaller than an eagle could fly across it. It was also believed that no one could possibly ride through the canyon in a boat and survive the journey. The canyon was awe-inspiring and intimidating, but the rampaging river that coursed through it was simply terrifying. There were rumors of deadly waterfalls and whirlpools that could swallow a boat of any size. There were even claims that the river went underground at one point and came rushing back up again several miles downstream. It was certain that no one in his right mind would dare to challenge the mighty Colorado River. Even running the river today, with maps and knowledge of what dangers lay ahead, can be death-defying, but a century and a half ago, it was tantamount to suicide and certainly not something to be dared for pure thrills.

Lieutenant Joseph C. Ives was the first to attempt it in the spring of 1858. He had been ordered to do so by his superiors at the War Department in Washington, who had organized and authorized an expedition to determine if the river was navigable. If it was, it would be of great value for transporting supplies to various military posts in New Mexico and Utah. These bureaucrats, having never been west of the Mississippi, believed the best type of craft to make the voyage up the Colorado was an iron-hulled paddlewheel steamer.

Ives was not impressed with the canyon. He told a group of surveyors, geologists, and artists, while standing on the rim, "This region is altogether valueless. Ours will doubtless be the last party of whites to visit this profitless locality. It seems intended by nature that the Colorado River, along the greater part of its lonely and majestic way, shall be forever unvisited and undisturbed. There is nothing to do but leave, and probably none will follow us." Not only was Lieutenant Ives wrong about the Grand Canyon being unvisited in the future, he also picked the losing side in the upcoming Civil War. He resigned his commission in the U.S. Army, signed on with the Confederate forces, became an aide to Jefferson Davis, and was killed in battle.

A few years before that, however, faced with the prospect of navigating the river, he supervised the construction of the steamer —-- a bright red, 54-foot craft that he tested on the peaceful Delaware River. He christened the boat *Explorer* and had it shipped in sections to Panama. The crated sections were then sent by rail to the Pacific Ocean and then around the southern tip of Baja California until they reached the muddy delta of the Colorado. By December 1, 1857, *Explorer* had traveled more than 8,000 miles without ever touching water.

With considerable difficulty, Ives and his men assembled and launched the fragile boat. The first leg of the journey, from Fort Yuma to the mouth of the canyon, was arduous and slow, but they followed a route that had been used before. On January 30, 1858, the vessel passed the previous points of exploration and paddled into the unknown —- for only 24 hours. The expedition came to a halt at the juncture of Black Canyon and the Grand Canyon when the *Explorer's* bow was split by a huge submerged rock. The collision was so strong that everyone on deck was thrown into the water, the wheelhouse was ripped off, and the boiler came loose from its support bolts and caused the smokestack to pitch sideways.

Although his boat was badly damaged and taking on water, Ives refused to give up. He had already gone deeper into the canyon than anyone ever had before, and he was determined to continue. But that determination didn't last for long. He nursed the craft upstream until he reached what he believed was the Virgin River and there, he abandoned the *Explorer* on a sandbar. He and his men climbed up out of the canyon, never knowing that death would have surely awaited them if they had tried to take the unwieldy vessel any further into the rapids ahead.

A decade passed before another expedition was established to try and explore the Colorado River through the canyon. The man who headed this excursion was a stubborn, tenacious, and brilliant explorer named John Wesley Powell. He had been born the son of a Methodist minister, who was also an avowed abolitionist. Powell was never afraid to settle arguments with his fists as a young man and was constantly called upon to defend his family's views against slavery. His fighting eventually led to his being thrown out of public school, and so he had to be privately tutored. At the age of 18, he became a teacher and a few years later, married his cousin, Emma Dean, against the objections of both families.

The wedding took place in 1861, when Powell was serving as a second lieutenant under General Ulysses S. Grant during the Civil War. During the battle of Shiloh, Powell's right arm was shattered by a bullet and it had to be amputated just below the shoulder. Such an injury would have ended the military career of a lesser man, but Powell returned to combat and rose to the rank of major. He commanded an artillery battalion until the end of the war.

After the smoke of war had settled, the discharged veteran found that he had too much idle time and found teaching to be too boring for his restless nature. The West beckoned to him and in the summer of 1867, with the equally adventurous Emma at his side, he led an expedition into the Rocky Mountains to collect geological and botanical specimens for universities in the East. It was there that Powell first encountered the waters of the Colorado River —- and when a plan began to grow in his mind that would assure him a place in history next to the other great explorers of the American West. He became determined to be the first to take an expedition down the river, from the headwaters to the Gulf of California, making it the grandest river run of all time.

Powell spent the better part of the next year seeking financial backing for the expedition and with the help of his friend, fellow officer, and now chief executive, President Ulysses S. Grant, he managed to outfit the journey. On May 24, 1869, he and a crew of nine men launched four, specially-built boats at Green River, Wyoming. As the local folks cheered, the sturdy, round-bottomed boats started off downstream. Each of the vessels had been double-ribbed with cured oak and each was loaded with two tons of supplies and equipment in waterproof bulkheads. Powell led the group in the first boat, *Emma Dean*, scouting the way and giving names to the side canyons and mountains they passed.

The expedition hit the first rough water at Ladore Canyon in Utah. The peaceful Green River became a raging torrent and Powell, from his vantage point, signaled the other boats to go into shore. But the boat called *No Name* responded too slowly and spun like a top before exploding into shards and kindling against the rocks. All three of the crew members were washed away but managed to make it to a tiny island, where they were rescued. The accident was a sobering experience, and as the men were going to find out, the river was unforgiving to those who made mistakes. Powell named the rapids "Disaster Falls" and they moved on.

The flotilla reached the confluence of the Colorado and the Green rivers on June 16 and from there, raced through 64 rapids in Cataract Canyon, passed Lee's Ferry, and entered the Grand Canyon. Powell's journals eloquently described the expedition's plunge through the "Great Unknown" and spoke of the deep river, narrow canyons, and the steady flow of a waterway that rolled, boiled, and dragged the boats into rapids and whirlpools. The breakers often washed over them, capsizing the boats, and making it impossible for them to steer or make it to land. About halfway through the wild and unpredictable canyon, three of the crewmen decided that they'd reached the limits of their endurance. They bid goodbye to Powell and hiked out of the canyon — – only to die in the empty country to the south.

The rest of the expedition plunged ahead, riding the rapids and then coasting through the calm stretches, singing loud tunes that echoed back at them from the towering cliffs. At the end of August, they reached the Mormon town of Callville, where Lake Mead is now located, and came ashore in triumph. Powell became a national hero as newspapers across the land told of the one-armed man who was the first to successfully take a boat through the Grand Canyon.

Almost immediately, though, his claim was challenged.

Many stated that Powell was not the first. There had been another before him. This man – alone -- had survived a run through the canyon. The people of Callville remembered a day back in September 1867 when a crude raft was sighted coming out of the canyon. The pathetic figure clinging to it was half-naked, starved, and delirious from exposure to the sun and water. Several days passed before he could tell his rescuers what he had been through. His name was James White, and what he told them would be argued about for years to come.

White was an unsuccessful prospector who was working the wild and unexplored country between the San Juan Mountains and the Colorado River. With two companions, Captain Baker and George Strole, he had followed the San Juan River for what he thought was about 200 miles over a period of three weeks. When they reached the Colorado, they made camp at the top of a side canyon, which most believe today was in the Glen Canyon area. While encamped, the men were attacked by Indians and Baker was killed. The remaining prospectors managed to escape into the night with their horses and a few supplies, but fearful that they were being pursued, they built a small raft by tying three cottonwood trees together and pushed off into the rushing waters of the river. The raft was about 10 feet long and two feet wide and the men soon ran into trouble. Strole was washed off during a series of rapids, leaving White alone. He tied a rope around his waist and then tied the other end to the raft, hoping that he would survive any other calamities as he plunged down into the Grand Canyon.

The raft turned over several times each day, and White was so afraid of losing his makeshift craft and being stranded at the bottom of the canyon, that he tied it to the rocks each night and slept on it. His supplies were soon gone, save for a few beans, but he managed to survive on a few small lizards that he was able to kill and eat. By the end of the first week, he was so hungry that he cut his leather knife scabbard into pieces and ate it. During a run through some violent rapids, the raft broke apart but White managed to hold onto the logs until he was washed onto a sandbar. He somehow managed to untangle the ropes, tie them together again, and continue down the river.

Two weeks into his journey, White met up with some Indians and he traded his pistols for food. He then continued down the river to Callville, where he was assisted by the Mormons before resuming his life as a drifting prospector. His story was often told around Callville, but it did not attract much attention outside of the region until Powell's expedition made its successful run through the canyon. When the newspapers heralded Powell's accomplishment, White's brother took a letter that the prospector had written to him, describing his ordeal, to the press. It was published in several newspapers and a journalist from Denver managed to track down White and conduct an interview with him. White stuck to his original story but admitted that he didn't know precisely where he had entered the canyon, or how many days that he traveled down the Colorado River.

Powell scoffed at the story when he heard it, knowing from personal experience that no one could survive a journey through the canyon in the manner that White described. According to Powell, the prospector was "a monumental prevaricator, the biggest liar that ever told a tale about the Colorado River."

And perhaps he was, but he had been seen coming out of the canyon and he had obviously been in it for many days. The real question seemed to be whether he had traveled the full length of the Grand Canyon or just a portion of it. Powell insisted that, under no circumstances, could the journey take only two weeks. It had taken his expedition 27 days and they had been experienced and well-equipped. White's defenders countered by pointing out that White had plummeted down the river, hanging on for dear life, and that he had not been exploring side canyons and collecting scientific data.

The controversy refused to be resolved because White's account could neither be verified nor disproved. However, it was an undisputed fact that Powell did make it down the canyon, and the vast majority of the public accepted him as the conqueror of the Grand Canyon. After the canyon was granted national park status in 1919, a monument was erected to honor him on the west rim and to commemorate his achievement. By then, James White had long since died in obscurity.

Other adventurers followed in Powell's wake. In 1937, Haldane Holdstrom made the first officially acknowledged solo run of the river, following Powell's route from Green River, Wyoming, to the Boulder Dam.

At that time, it was firmly believed that running the Grand Canyon was strictly an undertaking for a man. If a stout-hearted man could barely survive the experience, it was certainly well beyond the capabilities of a woman. Then in 1938, Dr. Elzada Clover and Lois Jotter destroyed this misconception when they became the first women to successfully raft down the canyon.

Journeys through the Grand Canyon, until recently, stood a very good chance of being fatal encounters with the merciless river. A disturbing number of people have entered the canyon over the years and have never come out the other end. A death in the Grand Canyon would be a lonely one, vanishing under circumstances that would remain forever mysterious.

One of the most horrific of these deaths was discovered by an expedition in June 1889. A skeleton was found crushed inside the wreckage of a wooden wagon, more than 150 miles downstream from the closest river crossing. It was surmised that someone had misjudged the depth of the river and had tried to cross it, only to be swept downstream and crushed by the Colorado's fury.

Even veteran river runners of the early days were sometimes lost to the river. The disappearance of Albert "Bert" Loper was a perfect example of this. Loper was born on July 31, 1869, the exact day that Powell and his crew found their way out of the rapids of Cataract Canyon, which seemed to make him, some believed, destined to live and die on the Colorado River.

In the early 1890s, Loper frequently ran the San Juan River as a prospector but it was not until 1907 that he decided to try the Colorado. That summer, he and three companions set out in three steel boats. The first boat was lost at Cataract Canyon, the second was wrecked by the Hance Rapid, and the third was damaged so badly at Hermit Rapid that it was a miracle that it made it the rest of the way down. Loper's friends thought the trip was miserable and terrifying, but Loper considered it the most exciting experience of his life. He became hooked on river running.

He ran the river again and again, later becoming a guide and boatman for several scientific expeditions. Over a period of 40 years, he earned the title of the "Grand Old Man of the Colorado." In 1949, with his eightieth birthday approaching, he decided to celebrate by going down the river one last time. He pushed off from Lee's Ferry on July 7 and planned to emerge from the canyon on July 31, his birthday and the anniversary of the Powell Expedition. Loper was accompanied by a passenger, Wayne Nichol, two other boats, and a neoprene raft. Tragically, the boat capsized at Unnamed Rapid the following day and Loper was last seen swirling into the water ahead of it. Wayne Nichol managed to make it to shore and joined others in a desperate search for the old man. The boat was found jammed into the rocks 17 miles from where it capsized but Bert Loper seemed gone for good.

Then, in 1975, a hiker stumbled across a few of his bones that had washed ashore just below Lava Falls Rapid. After the bones were positively identified, Loper's remains were buried beside his wife's grave in Sandy, Utah. Bert's remains are gone from the Grand Canyon, but many believe that his spirit is still there. They swear that they have seen him in his boat on the river at night, and whenever a camper's coffee pot overturns, or a piece of gear is mysteriously lost, Bert always gets the blame.

Of all the accidents, disasters, and disappearances in the Grand Canyon, though, the most mysterious remains the one that occurred in 1928 —-- when honeymooners Glen and Bessie Hyde came to the canyon with plans to run the Colorado River.

Glen Hyde was born in Spokane, Washington, in 1888, the middle child of Rollin and Mary Hyde. He was raised in Washington, California, Canada, and Idaho and after attending college, he worked with his father on their family farm in Hansen, Idaho, in the southern part of the state. In 1928, he married Bessie Haley in Twin Falls.

Bessie had been born in 1905 in Takoma Park, Maryland, just north of Washington, D.C., and had attended Marshall College in West Virginia. She left school after a brief marriage to Earl Helmick, a high school classmate, and then went west to San Francisco, where she studied art in 1926 and 1927.

Glen and Bessie met aboard a steamship from San Francisco to Los Angeles in 1927 and the day after Bessie's divorce from Helmick became final, the two were married. They worked the Hyde farms together through the summer of 1928 and that fall, set off on their honeymoon. They planned an adventure of a lifetime —– running the rapids of the Grand Canyon in a homemade boat. Several newspapers even carried the story of Bessie being the first woman to attempt to ride the river.

One day in November, they hiked up from the river on the Bright Angel Trail and knocked on the door of the Kolb brothers' photographic studio, which at that time, was located at the top of the trail. Emory and Ellsworth Kolb were the foremost photographers of the Grand Canyon in the early twentieth century. Between 1901 and 1941, they captured the magnificence of the canyon in a way that no one else had done, before or since.

Glen and Bessie Hyde

The Kolbs literally moved onto the rim of the canyon, constructing a combination home and studio at the edge of a cliff. They posted a sign outside that read, "Bright Angel Toll Road. Riding Animals. Pack Animals. Loose Animals. $1 each."

By 1928, a steady stream of tourists was handing dollar bills to the Kolbs for the privilege of straddling a burro from a nearby stable and heading down into the canyon. They kept a pretty close eye on everyone who came and went on the canyon trail, so they were surprised on the day when the Hydes hiked in from the canyon down below. They introduced themselves to the Kolbs and explained that they were honeymooners who had spent the past 26 days rafting on the treacherous river. They expected to conclude their journey within another week or two. They asked the Kolbs to take their photograph standing on the rim of the canyon. They would come back to get the photo after their trip.

After taking the photograph, Emory Kolb asked them about their boat, and they explained that they had built it themselves in Idaho and they planned to navigate the canyon with it. Despite the rapids, they did not have life preservers. Kolb was shocked and warned against such foolhardiness. Glen Hyde laughed off the warnings, but Kolb could see that Bessie was nervous about the journey ahead. He told himself that the girl did not want to go back on the river. He later stated that he saw a look of fear in her eyes.

As Glen and Bessie prepared to depart, Kolb's daughter, Emily, came out of the studio to greet the young couple. Emily was very neatly dressed, and Bessie Hyde took one look at her own wrinkled and sun-faded clothing and then smiled sadly at Emily and said, "I wonder if I shall ever wear pretty shoes again." Then, she turned and followed her husband down Bright Angel Trail.

That night, November 16, none of the Kolbs slept well, worried about the haunted young woman named Bessie Hyde. Both Emory and Emily kept thinking about the diminutive girl's parting words. At barely five feet tall and slender, her brown hair cut fashionably short, she seemed much too fragile to be attempting to run the river. By early December, there was still no sign of the Hydes. Finally, Emory Kolb initiated a search of the area, even recruiting a pilot to fly his small plane through the inner gorge of the canyon. This was the first time that such a flight had been attempted. The pilot spotted the Hydes' boat snagged in the rocks of the river.

Emory Kolb joined the rescue party and hiked down from the rim. When they reached the boat, they found everything packed and secure. The food, clothing, and even the couple's books were neatly packed in place. All that was missing was Glen and Bessie. The search party combed the area, but they were nowhere to be found. If they had made it down the river, Bessie would have been the first woman to successfully navigate the canyon. As it was, she and her husband had vanished without a trace.

When the news of their disappearance reached their families, both of their fathers launched search party after search party into the canyon. Glen's father, William Hyde, kept searching sporadically for another year but no trace of the couple was ever found. William died in Twin Falls after being hit by a potato truck, going to his grave without learning the fate of his son and daughter-in-law.

He wasn't the only one – no trace of Glen or Bessie has ever been found.

But that hasn't stopped the stories, and often wild rumors, from being circulated about their fates. Several theories have emerged as to what happened to Glen and Bessie. The most likely scenario is that the couple drowned and that their boat managed to remain intact when it was scuttled. Given their lack of experience with rivers like the Colorado, this seems quite possible.

There is another story that suggests that Bessie may have murdered Glen and then left the canyon to start a new life. This theory was first proposed back in 1971 when an elderly woman named Liz Cutler "confessed" to a group in the Grand Canyon that she was Bessie Hyde and that she had stabbed Glen after a disagreement. Cutler later recanted her story, but it did get some people thinking. Glen had been described as controlling and domineering and it was said that Bessie was afraid of him.

In 1976, after the death of Emory Kolb, friends going through his belongings discovered a skeleton inside a skiff in his garage. Rumors abounded that the body might belong to Glen Hyde. The victim apparently died as the result of a bullet wound to the head. Laboratory tests conducted in 1985 concluded that the remains were not Glen's. The man had been much too young, and a belt buckle found with the body did not match one that Glen was known to wear.

Of course, this created yet another unsolved mystery — – who did the skeleton belong to and why did Emory Kolb have it? That also remains a mystery.

Georgie White Clark, the whitewater adventurer who some believe was Bessie Hyde

One of the most intriguing theories about the lost couple was that the famous river runner, Georgie White Clark, was actually Bessie Hyde. Clark was an unconventional river guide and her penchant for leopard-print swimsuits, canned food cookouts, and amazing daring made her the stuff of legend at the Grand Canyon. She and her "Royal River Rats" raft trips were featured in magazines such as *Life*, on television shows like the *Tonight Show with Johnny Carson,* and in countless newspaper stories. She became the first woman to swim the Grand Canyon and the first woman outfitter to run expeditions for tourists.

Georgie's story was a fascinating one. After her 15-year-old daughter was killed in an accident in 1944, Clark began hiking in Arizona and Utah with a friend, Harry Aleson, to ease her grief. Donning life jackets, the pair swam and floated the lower portion of the canyon in 1945. The next year, they floated the river on a driftwood raft and then, in 1947, became the first to navigate the rapids of the Green and Colorado rivers in war-surplus inflatable rafts. Clark began tying two and three rafts together to make a floating island for passengers in the 1950s and eventually invented the "g-rig," a raft of three pontoons lashed together and powered by an outboard motor. These "thrill rigs," as she called them, helped to create the modern-day river outfitting business. But Clark paid little attention to the pampering that other outfitters were known to provide for their customers. She told guests, "If you want to eat, go to a restaurant; if you want to see the canyon, come with me." Meals on her raft trips usually consisted of canned goods that Georgie dropped into a pot of boiling water. The labels would come off and no one would ever know what they were opening.

Clark died from cancer at age 81 in 1992 and soon after, her already larger-than-life legend took another turn. Evidence discovered at her home in Las Vegas on the day of her funeral raised the possibility that Clark fabricated portions of her past and led many to believe that she was Bessie Hyde. The speculations began when friends started going through her personal effects. Those who had known her for decades, and even those who considered themselves close friends, had never been invited into her home.

Bill George, of Salt Lake City, whose Western River Expeditions bought Clark's company at her request when she became too ill to run raft trips, conducted her funeral. Afterward, he got a call from Clark's good friend and nurse, Lee McCurry, who told him, "Bill, we don't know who we are burying today." She told him that she had gone over to Georgie's trailer and that he would never believe the stuff that she found there.

To start with, Clark's birth certificate showed that her real name was Bessie DeRoss, not Georgie. The name Clark, as well as another surname she sometimes used – White -- were the last names of two divorced husbands. In her 1977 autobiography, she had written about her childhood in Chicago, but she was born in Oklahoma and raised in Colorado. Lee also presented Bill with a marriage certificate, which was notarized, for Glen R. Hyde and Bessie Haley, and showed him a pistol that Georgie kept in her lingerie drawer. "If you match it up to one of the pictures of Glen and Bessie Hyde in the canyon, it looks like the same pistol," Bill George said. "I'm not saying that Georgie was Bessie Hyde, but the whole thing is a little spooky."

Once this information started to get around, others began to point out additional oddities. Georgie had developed the triple rig —- an assemblage of three rafts tied to each other and run with one oar downstream and one upstream —– similar to the manner that Glen and Bessie had operated their boat. She also claimed to hate Emory Kolb when he was alive, and if she would go into a meeting and he was there, she would turn around and leave. It was later speculated that perhaps she did not hate Kolb at all —––– she avoided him because he was one of the few people who might have recognized her as Bessie.

While many have been willing to entertain the fact that Bessie and Georgie were one and the same person, there are just as many others who dispute the idea. They maintain that while some of the connections are "inexplicable," they believe that photographs of the two women show marked differences. Clark's biographer, Richard Westwood, added that he found little to substantiate the theory that Georgie was Bessie Hyde, but he wouldn't put it past her to leave behind the Hyde clues just to keep people guessing.

Georgie, he said, always loved a good story.

So, if Georgie White Clark was not Bessie Hyde, then what happened to Bessie and her unlucky husband? Did she really kill him and then vanish to start a new life? Or did they both perish in the furious waters of the canyon? And if they did, what became of their bodies?

These questions will never be answered and only the Grand Canyon, and the ferocious Colorado River, will ever know what befell the ill-fated young couple.

1928: The Boy Who Vanished

The tragic case of Melvin Horst, a little boy who disappeared in Orrville, Ohio in 1928, remains one of the region's most baffling unsolved mysteries. The investigation into the case yielded little in the way of clues —-- only a pint whiskey bottle and a frozen orange with a bite taken out of it. These pathetic artifacts led nowhere, and investigators ended up with little to show for their efforts when they finally put two men on trial for the crime. Hundreds of witnesses had been interviewed, thousands of dollars had been spent, and every square foot within a 10-mile radius of Orrville had been examined. But it was the questionable testimony of a young boy that finally got five people arrested and landed two of them in prison for eight months.

Even after that, however, the police were no closer to a resolution in the case in the 1920s than investigators are today.

Melvin Charles Horst was only four-years-old when he vanished in 1928.

He was the middle child of Raymond Horst, a roofing artisan employed by an Orrville factory, and his wife, Zora. Melvin had an older brother, Ralph, age nine, and a younger sister, Dora Elgie, who was two. Tall for his age at just over three-feet-tall, and stocky at 49 pounds, Melvin was a good-looking boy with blue eyes, light brown hair, and an eager smile. He was well-known by many of the residents of the small town of Orrville and was a familiar sight in the yard of his parents' home at the corner of South Vine Street and Paradise Avenue. Not old enough for school, he spent most of his time playing outdoors. This was exactly what he was doing on the afternoon of December 27, 1928 —- the last time that he was ever seen in Orrville.

Melvin went outside after lunch, around 1:00 p.m., with a new toy truck that he had received as a Christmas gift from his parents. He soon met up with a friend, Bobbie Evans, age seven, and they went looking for another neighborhood boy, Bobbie Ellsworth. Unfortunately, Ellsworth was sick with the flu that was going around Orrville and was unable to come out and play with them. The other two boys wandered around town for a while, playing with other children, and paying special attention to such small-town excitements as a street bonfire and a passing manure wagon.

Melvin went home to drop off his truck and retrieve his red wagon and he re-joined his friend around 4:00 p.m. This brief visit to the Horst home was the last time that his mother ever saw him alive.

He and Bobbie Evans played for a while longer but at around 5:30 p.m., Melvin told his friend that it was time for him to go home. When Bobbie last saw him, Melvin was walking north on McGill Street, headed toward home. He was wearing a brown stocking cap, a brown overcoat, and a checkered sweater. He was last seen in front of the home of a local man named Elias Arnold.

Melvin Horst

When Melvin did not return home for supper, Zora Horst went outside and called for him. When that failed to bring the boy home, as it normally did, she sent older brother Ralph to check the houses of the boys that Melvin normally played with. He wasn't at any of them. When Raymond Horst returned home from work at 6:00 p.m., Zora sent him out to look for the missing boy. Two hours later, after a fruitless search, the anxious parents notified Raymond's brother, the Orrville city marshal, Roy Horst, who set off the town's fire siren.

As many as 500 residents of Orrville turned out that night —- and over the next 48 hours —- to look for Melvin. In the weeks that followed, they were joined by thousands of people from all over Ohio, who searched hundreds of locations throughout Wayne County and across the state. Every empty lot, field, pond, well, thicket, and forest within an area of 100 square miles was painstakingly checked and house-to-house searches were carried out in the area where Melvin was last seen. A reward for information about the boy reached as high as $16,000 and schools all over Wayne County were dismissed so that students could assist in the search. Nothing valid was turned up then or later, although bogus tips and wild rumors sent lawmen on wild goose chases throughout Ohio and other states.

Somehow, Melvin Horst had vanished without a trace.

Like many other rural American counties in the 1920s, Wayne County, Ohio, did not boast an impressive law enforcement staff. History would later tend to be very critical towards the men who investigated Melvin's disappearance. Led by Wayne County Prosecutor Walter J. Mougey and Sheriff Albert Jacot, the investigation soon gained the services of prominent private detectives John Stevens and Ora Slater, the latter already famous for his work on a 1926 murder of a crusading newspaper publisher in Canton, Ohio. But the detective's investigation was hampered from the beginning because there seemed to be no motive for a kidnapping, much less any evidence as to how, or why, Melvin Horst had vanished.

The initial theory was that it was an accident. Investigators believed that he had fallen down a well or drowned in a pond that no one thought to search. But when another thorough search of such sites failed to turn up his body after three days, investigators began to explore other, darker theories. One, briefly considered, was that Melvin had been hit by an automobile and that the panicked driver had concealed his body. But when no evidence of such an accident could be found, they focused on revenge as the only plausible explanation for Melvin's disappearance. They began to look for someone who might have a grievance against the Horst family.

Raymond Horst was a man of modest means and little property. He was quiet but well-liked and no one could imagine that he had an enemy who disliked him enough to want to hurt his child. But the Prohibition era of the 1920s had created animosities and corruption, even in little towns like Orrville. Roy Horst, Raymond's brother, was surrounded by such unpleasantness. Horst was known for being a vigorous enforcer of the Prohibition laws and had sent a number of local bootleggers to jail. This was said to have angered the more prominent liquor racketeers in Cleveland and Columbus. Mougey and Stevens wondered if perhaps Melvin had been kidnapped to get back at Roy Horst. It was true that he was not the boy's father, but he had lived with the family until recently and was known to be especially fond of Melvin. He might have even been mistakenly identified as Melvin's father by his gangster enemies.

Mougey and Stevens didn't have to look far for someone who disliked Roy enough to want to hurt him. He'd arrested a lot of people during his one year in office, but none of them as often as Horst neighbor Elias Arnold, who owned the house where Melvin had last been seen. Arnold had spent a good part of 1928 in the Orrville jail on various liquor charges, as had several members of his extended family. It was no secret in town that Arnold had a grudge against Roy and had stated a number of times that he planned to get even with him. So, with all the other theories and leads at dead ends, the authorities directed their attentions toward Arnold and his family.

That investigation quickly produced results. In addition to his indiscreet threats of revenge, the officers also discovered two eyewitnesses who claimed to have seen Melvin being kidnapped. On January 2, 1929, Mougey announced the arrest of five suspects in the case and revealed the identity of his important mystery witnesses to excited reporters.

The five arrested – and held on a $10,000 bond for each – included Elias Arnold; his son, William, of Akron; his son, Arthur, who lived with him; his daughter, Dorothy, who was married to Bascom McHenry of Orrville; and Bascom McHenry, Arnold's son-in-law. They were an easy bunch to prosecute. All of them were chronically unemployed, linked with criminal activities, and were generally maligned by the better class of people in town. In addition, their chief accuser was a relative —-- Charles "Junior" Hannah, the eight-year-old son of Charles Hannah, a brother-in-law of Elias Arnold. After hearing the evidence accumulated by Mougey and Stevens, a Wayne County grand jury indicted the five suspects for child stealing on January 9.

Young Junior Hannah seemed to be a great eyewitness. His calm, detailed memories seemed to improve as the March trial date for the accused approached. According to Junior, he had been playing near the Arnold house on the day that Melvin disappeared. Just before 5:30 p.m., Arthur Arnold approached him and asked him to bring Melvin into the Arnold house. Minutes later, Junior brought Melvin to the alley adjacent to the house, and he heard someone say, "Wait a minute, I want to give you something." That was the last time that Junior remembered seeing Melvin, although his memory would later improve a great deal.

Besides Junior, Mougey had found another witness —-- Tommy Johnson, age nine, who corroborated Junior's story that he had been in the alley with Melvin around 5:30 p.m.

There was other evidence, too, although it was mostly circumstantial. It appeared on January 7, when an orange with one bite out of it and a pint whiskey bottle were found in the alley. After being told about the orange, Junior conveniently remembered that someone in the house had passed something over the porch railing to Arthur. Junior thought that perhaps it was the orange. The whiskey bottle, which had nothing to do with Melvin's disappearance, merely reinforced the immoral image of the Arnold clan.

A.D. Metz, a federal bankruptcy attorney, agreed to defend the Arnolds. He was joined by attorney Clarence May of Akron. The two lawyers, inexperienced when it came to criminal defense, were out of their depth at trial. All five defendants vigorously protested their innocence and denied knowing anything about Melvin's disappearance.

Everyone knew that Mougey's case against the Arnolds depended almost entirely on Junior Hannah's testimony and the young boy did not disappoint the prosecutor when the trial opened on March 12. By that time, the whiskey bottle had been deemed irrelevant and the orange had become suspect after a reporter announced that it had appeared in the alley long after it had been searched. In truth, there was little hard evidence against the Arnolds. Except for a few minutes between 4:00 p.m. and 5:30 p.m. on December 27 that were unaccounted for by alibis —-- and Elias Arnold's unspecific threats against Roy Horst —-- there was little to connect the family to Melvin's disappearance. In fact, Mougey exposed the weakness of his case before the trial opened when he dismissed the indictments against William Arnold and the McHenrys.

This meant that all eyes were on Junior Hannah when he took the stand. It would only be his testimony that could convict the remaining defendants. But Junior's memory had greatly improved since his recollections in January. He answered all the prosecutor's questions in a calm, deliberate manner, and now distinctly remembered Arthur Arnold offering an orange to Melvin in the alley and then seizing him and dragging him into the house. Then, as Melvin cried for help, he watched as all the lights in the house ominously went out. Minutes later, as he watched from a hiding place down the street, he saw Arthur carry Melvin out of the house, put him in an automobile, and drive away.

Defense attorney Metz cross-examined Junior, but it was a feeble attempt to shake the boy's story. The attorney did little to press the boy on the improbable aspects of his story. When Metz asked Junior why he had not revealed his knowledge of the kidnapping for several days, the boy retorted, "That's my business!" The judge did not make him answer the question. When pressed a bit toward the end of his testimony, he resorted to tears and was given time to recover himself in his mother's arms.

Thanks to the way that Junior Hannah was coddled on the stand by the prosecution, the judge, and even the defense, it was an impossible task for the surly Elias Arnold to make a good impression on the jury. He did the best that he could, even admitting his bootlegging activities, and denied that Melvin Horst was ever in his house. He stated that Junior Hannah's story was "an unmitigated lie."

In his closing statement, Prosecutor Mougey appealed to the kind of public sentimentality towards children that had shielded Junior Hannah from closer scrutiny on the stand. Calling Junior and the other child witnesses —-- none of whom had directly corroborated Junior's story —- "messengers of God," he condemned Arnold as a man "burning with hate" and with a "desire for vengeance." He stated that he had proved beyond a reasonable doubt that the Arnolds had committed a dastardly crime.

Thanks to the ugly public mood toward the Arnolds, and their lackluster defense, the jury agreed. They returned a guilty verdict after just over seven hours of deliberation on March 16, 1929. It wasn't long, though, before the entire case against the Arnolds unraveled.

As the judge was sending Elias Arnold to the state penitentiary for 20 years and dispatching Arthur to the Mansfield Reformatory for an indefinite stay, new searches for the still-missing Melvin Horst began. Rumors of startling new evidence appeared in the newspapers. A.D. Metz filed a motion for a new trial on behalf of the Arnolds, based on new information that damaged the credibility of Junior Hannah's testimony. The Court of Appeals agreed with his motion on June 24 and ordered a new trial.

The new information that had come to light was presented by Dan Gallagher, a reporter for the *Cleveland News*, who printed a shocking article on March 29. Using detailed photos of the alleged kidnapping site next to the Arnold house, Gallagher proved that Junior Hannah could not, from where he was standing, have seen what he testified to about the alleged abduction. The Ohio Supreme Court agreed with the defense's demand for a new trial on October 16, 1929, ruling that the jury in the Arnold case shouldn't have given such weight to the testimony of a witness so young.

The Arnolds' second trial in December 1929 was an entirely different affair. The state's case was again handled by Wayne County prosecutor Walter Mougey and his colleague, Marion Graven. But this time, the Arnolds were represented by well-known Cleveland defense attorneys Nathan E. Cook and William F. Marsteller. They aggressively pointed out the discrepancies in Junior Hannah's five different kidnap stories and forced him into admitting that he had changed his story many times. The boy's credibility deteriorated further when the defense succeeded in having several of his conflicting statements read into record. There was little left of Junior's story when the case finally went before a jury on December 7. It took them only a few hours to find both Elias and Arthur Arnold not guilty.

Junior Hannah was disgraced by the trial ——- *Cleveland Press* reporters called him a "little skunk" ——- and his subsequent behavior only served to confirm the negative opinions of him. A month after the Arnolds were acquitted, he recanted his accusations against them and then turned around and accused his father, Charles, and an Orrville neighbor, Earl Conold, of having been involved in Melvin's death. On February 20, 1930, Charles Hannah signed a confession, admitting to helping Earl Conold kidnap Melvin at the behest of out-of-town bootleggers who held a grudge against Roy Horst. Earl had murdered the little boy by accident, he said, but then he convinced his son to accuse the Arnolds for the crime. Meanwhile, Earl was putting all the blame on Charles Hannah, saying that the kidnapping had been his idea and that he was the one who accidentally killed Melvin. The finger-pointing dragged on for two months with each man making wilder and more improbable charges against the other.

Finally, in April, Prosecutor Marion Graven, fed up and disillusioned with the whole thing, dismissed the child-stealing and first-degree murder indictments against Hannah and Conold. He didn't believe that either of them had anything to do with the disappearance. At the same time, without comment, Graven also accepted the resignation of Walter Mougey.

Years passed and Orrville returned to its previous calm. After Christmas 1930, Raymond and Zora Horst took down the dried-out Christmas tree that they had been keeping in their living room in the hope that Melvin would return to see his toys under the tree. A number of cruel hoaxes promising Melvin's safe return were perpetrated on the Horsts, the worst of which resulted in a large part of Orrville's population showing up at their house for the promised return of the boy on December 12, 1929. Needless to say, he didn't show up.

Mrs. Horst bravely kept her hopes alive for as long as she could. In 1938, she admitted to a reporter, "I like to think that he is still alive, but I am resigned to the probability that he is not." Ohio governor John W. Bricker briefly re-opened the case in March 1940, on the basis of supposed new information from California, but the investigation led to nothing.

By 1943, Charles Hannah's whereabouts were unknown, as were those of Earl Conold. When last heard from in 1953, Melvin's parents had moved to Eustis, Florida, where Raymond started his own roofing business. He died there in 1961, never learning the fate of his son. Melvin's brother and sister remained in Orrville, had families of their own, and retained only faded memories of the brother they once had.

What really happened to Melvin Horst?

No one knows, or at least no one ever said. Most believed the boy to be dead, likely killed in retaliation for Roy Horst's crackdown on illegal liquor in the area. But *Cleveland Press* crime reporter Bob

Larkin proposed another, more intriguing theory. Based on information that he gained from contacts in the criminal underworld, he agreed that Melvin had been kidnapped to get back at Roy Horst, but that the boy had not been killed. Instead, he was placed with a farm family near Toledo and eventually forgot his family and his real identity. However, attempts to find such a family led nowhere.

Melvin Horst vanished and was never seen again.

1930: "The Missingest Man in New York"

Perhaps no disappearance in American history has created as much speculation as that of New York Supreme Court Associate Justice Joseph F. Crater. For many years, he was known simply as "the most missingest man in New York."

He was last seen on the evening of August 6, 1930, walking out of a New York restaurant. Crater was a tall, heavyset man and an avowed clothes horse. He was especially dapper that evening as he stepped out of the restaurant, waved goodbye to a couple of friends, and then climbed into a taxicab. His friends would remember his double-breasted brown suit, gray spats, and a straw Panama hat over his smoothed-down iron grey hair because it was the last outfit they ever saw him wear. After that final glimpse, Crater was never seen again.

How was it possible for a man as powerful and prominent as a Supreme Court judge to disappear forever?

Judge Crater's career was unquestionably successful. He was born and raised in Easton, Pennsylvania, and later graduated from Lafayette College and Columbia University Law School. In 1913, he began practicing law in New York and got involved in local politics. He soon became president of the Democratic Party Club in Manhattan and saw his law practice flourish thanks to his connections to the corrupt Democratic leadership at Tammany Hall. In April 1930, he was appointed to the New York Supreme Court. He had withdrawn $20,000 from the bank just days before his appointment. The sum was close to a year's salary but, rumor

Judge Joseph Crater, who became the "most missingest man in New York"

had it, that was the standard Tammany payoff for the lucrative post. It was not a poor investment, according to investigators who later looked into his role as a receiver of a bankrupt hotel. Crater sold it to a bond and mortgage firm for $75,000 and, two months later, the city agreed to buy it back for a planned street widening at a condemned property price of almost $3 million.

Crater did just as well in his private life. In 1916, a woman named Stella Wheeler had retained him as her divorce attorney and the next year, right after her divorce became final, Crater married her. By all accounts, they appeared to be a happy and devoted couple.

In the summer of 1930, 41-year-old Crater and his wife were vacationing at their summer cabin at Belgrade Lakes, Maine. In late July, he received a telephone call. He offered no information to his wife about the content of the call, other than to say that he had to return to the city "to straighten those fellows out." The following day, he was back in the city and was seen by the doorman at his Fifth Avenue apartment. Instead of dealing with business, though, he made a trip to Atlantic City in the company of a showgirl. On August 3, he was back in New York and on the morning of August 6, he spent two hours going through his files in his courthouse chambers. He then had his assistant, Joseph Mara, cash two checks for him that amounted to $5,150. At noon, he and Mara carried two locked briefcases to his apartment, and he let Mara take the rest of the day off.

Later that evening, Crater went to a Broadway ticket agency and purchased one seat for a comedy that was playing that night called *Dancing Partners* at the Belasco Theater. He then went to Billy Haas' chophouse on West 45th Street for dinner. There, he ran into two friends, a fellow attorney and his showgirl date, and he joined them for dinner. The lawyer later told investigators that Crater was in a good mood that evening and gave no indication that anything was bothering him. The dinner ended a little after 9:00 p.m., a short time after the curtain had opened for the show that Crater had a ticket for. The group went outside and as Crater stepped into the taxi that he hailed, he waved goodbye to his friends.

His next -- and likely final – destination of the night remains a mystery.

Strangely, there was no immediate reaction to Judge Crater's disappearance. When he did not return to Maine as scheduled on August 9, Mrs. Crater grew concerned. Nevertheless, she waited six days before dispatching Kohler, the family driver, to New York to see if he could learn anything. When Kohler arrived at the Fifth Avenue apartment, the maid told him that Judge Crater's bed had not been slept in since August 8.

Kohler began telephoning Crater's friends. They were all excessively reassuring about the welfare of the judge, believing that no harm could have come to him. All his friends were acutely aware that any hint of a mysterious disappearance might hurt Crater's chances for re-election in November. They were anxious that any odd behavior on Crater's part be kept hidden from the voting public.

In addition, they wanted to make sure his extramarital sex life was carefully hidden. Crater had always confined his interest to night club parties, one-night stands, and prostitutes, there was private talk that perhaps he had taken a young woman away for an extended trip. If that was the case, his cronies were anxious to keep that quiet.

Kohler returned to Maine on August 20, relieved that no harm had come to the judge. He informed Mrs. Crater that her husband must surely be safe, though no one seemed to have any idea where he might be. He was sure that he would return on August 28, when he was scheduled to preside over the first session of the special term.

But when Crater didn't make an appearance for this important session, word began to circulate that something was amiss. Stella Crater, her worst fears apparently justified, hurried to New York. She began calling her husband's friends, including Martin J. Healy, who was summering on Long Island. Healy later stated that Mrs. Crater became hysterical when he could not tell her anything. Healy, along with others, strongly advised her to return to Maine. Against her better judgment, she did.

An unofficial search was started for Crater, led by a city detective named Leo Lowenthal, who often acted as a bodyguard for one of Crater's political friends. He visited the judge's chambers and learned about the two briefcases -- believed to be filled with personal papers, -- that the judge and his assistant had carried out of the office. Lowenthal went to the judge's apartment on Fifth Avenue but found no trace of the papers, nor any charred remains to indicate that they had been burned. He found nothing out of place and nothing to suggest that Crater had been taken away against his will. Regardless, the judge was still missing.

Lowenthal advised Crater's friend that it was time to involve the police. On September 3, the police commissioner was finally noticed of the disappearance. A month had already passed since the last time that Judge Crater had been seen.

The missing judge became front-page news. The story captivated the nation and a massive investigation was launched. Had Crater been killed, or had he simply disappeared on his own? Those were the questions that everyone wanted answered, from police detectives to shady business partners to the average man on the street. The official investigations started off in a hurry, but quickly slowed down. Detectives discovered that the judge's safe-deposit box had been cleaned out and the two briefcases that Crater and Mara had taken to his apartment were missing. These promising leads were quickly bogged down by the thousands of false reports that were coming in from people who claimed to have seen the missing man.

The District Attorney centered his investigation on Mrs. Crater while the police began delving into his financial and sexual affairs. It was found that he had another safe deposit box at the Empire Trust Company, but it turned out to be empty.

Detectives looking into Crater's love life were far more successful and they found that for years, Crater had been on friendly terms with Constance Braemer Marcus, a raven-haired woman in her middle thirties. Lovely and vivacious, she had been a worker for the Cayuga Democratic Club in 1922, when she had met Crater during an election campaign. She liked him and later retained him —– as Mrs. Crater had done —– during her divorce. They became involved in a long-time affair.

Over the years, Crater visited Connie Marcus several times a week and paid her rent at the Hotel Mayflower on Central Park West. In the daytime, Connie Marcus worked as a salesgirl at Milgrim's and at other upscale shops along Fifty-Seventh Street.

When news of Crater's disappearance went public, Marcus added to the chaos by disappearing herself. It seemed a logical assumption that Crater and his mistress had run off together and the police investigation stalled. Then Connie returned to the city alone, explaining that she had left town merely to avoid the publicity. She was questioned closely by investigators, but they became convinced that Marcus knew nothing of the judge's whereabouts.

The police also learned that Crater frequented a Broadway nightclub and speakeasy called the Club Abbey. The Abbey was owned by gangland figure Owney Madden and was frequented by mobsters like Jack "Legs" Diamond, Dutch Schultz, Vincent "Mad Dog" Coll, and others. Several murders had occurred on the premises, and it was definitely not the sort of spot that should have been a favorite hangout for a New York Supreme Court Justice. But this is where Crater went in search of a diversion, although he tried to convince patrons that his name was "Joe Crane." However, since so many other politicians frequented this unsavory nightspot, false names were a waste of time.

At the Abbey, the judge had been especially friendly with a chorus girl named Elaine Dawn. Police questioned her, along with Sally-Lou Ritz, who had been at Crater's table for dinner on the night he disappeared. They also talked to Marie Miller, his Atlantic City party girl date. None of these lovely ladies were able to offer a clue as to his whereabouts.

The search for Judge Crater ground to a halt, even though he was still being reported in Canada, the Adirondacks, Nova Scotia, Cuba, California, Mexico City, and even Africa. Most assumed that the judge had ducked out just one step ahead of someone who was looking for him, but no one could say for sure. Over time, his disappearance became a cultural touchstone and a major event of the early 1930s. His name became a slang term for dodging one's responsibilities —- "pulling a Crater" meant that you slipped out of town, just ahead of the law, your wife, or people to whom you owed money. In 1947, a movie that was loosely based on Judge Crater was released. It was called *The Judge Steps Out* and starred Alexander Knox. It followed the lighthearted exploits of a judge who becomes weary of his responsibilities and leaves his family to become a short-order cook.

Back in the real world, the search for Judge Crater was continuing. In October 1930, a grand jury convened to investigate the disappearance. Mrs. Crater refused to come to New York and participate in the hearings. Nevertheless, the grand jury called 95 witnesses and amassed 975 pages of testimony. After all of that, the conclusion was: "The evidence is insufficient to warrant any expression of opinion as to whether Crater is alive or dead, or as to whether he has absented himself voluntarily, or is the sufferer from disease in the nature of amnesia, or is the victim of crime."

In late January 1931, Mrs. Crater finally returned to New York. From the apartment on Fifth Avenue, she announced an amazing discovery. In a bureau drawer often used by the judge, she found a large manila envelope containing $6,690 in an assortment of denominations, along with three small checks that had been made out to Crater and signed by him. There was also a second envelope that contained stocks and bonds and a binder with three insurance policies. A memo in Crater's handwriting listed the names of men who owed him money, along with the amounts owed by each man. The note was signed with the words, "I am very whary --- Joe." It is believed the misspelled word was likely meant to be "weary."

The discovery caused an uproar. Detectives had searched the apartment four times and never would have missed the bulky envelopes and the insurance binder. Detective Leo Lowenthal, who had made the first unofficial search, maintained that the envelopes had not been in the drawer in August. Had someone —--- perhaps Crater himself —-- placed them there? Had his killers —-- if he had been murdered —-- felt compassion for his widow and placed there in the bureau? Or had Mrs. Crater brought them back with her from Maine?

No one knows, but this was the last dramatic development in the case. The search continued throughout 1931 but no trace of the judge was ever found.

There have been many theories put forward, trying to solve the mystery of Judge Crater. Mrs. Crater and many of his close friends believed that he was the victim of foul play. Stella Crater stated that he was murdered "because of something sinister connected to politics." And she may have been right given his involvement in bribery, back-door dealing with Tammany Hall politics, and questionable real estate deals. She also did not believe that the judge would have voluntarily vanished, insisting, "Joe Crater would not run away from anybody but would meet his problems directly, whatever they were."

In 1937, Mrs. Crater sued the three insurance companies for double indemnity on her husband's life insurance policies. During the trial, her attorney, Emil K. Ellis, advanced her murder theory, but left politics out of the mix. He claimed that Judge Crater had been blackmailed by a Broadway showgirl and he had paid her off. When she demanded more money and Crater refused to pay, a gangster friend of the showgirl had killed him, perhaps accidentally. The attorney's theories did not impress the court and they denied the double indemnity claims.

On June 6, 1939, Judge Crater was officially declared dead, but sightings continued for years, as did the theories as to what happened to him. Possible exits of the judge have included his murder by political cronies just before he could testify against them in a graft investigation, and a cover-up of his death in the arms of his mistress or a prostitute. Some believe he was killed in a dispute over a payoff or that he decided to drop out and start a new life in Canada, Europe, or the Caribbean.

Stella Crater remarried in 1939 but the marriage didn't last. In 1961 she wrote a book entitled, *The Empty Robe: The Story of the Disappearance of Judge Crater.* Although her book concludes she didn't know her second husband very well at all, she seemed to retain fond memories of him —-- either that or she had an ironic sense of humor. Every year on the August 6 anniversary of her husband's disappearance until her death in 1969, Mrs. Crater visited a Greenwich Village bar and ordered two drinks. After downing one, she would raise the other glass and toast, "Good luck, Joe, wherever you are."

Crater's case —-- Missing Person's File 13595 —- was officially closed in 1979, but his story was not yet over.

A possible answer to the fate of "Good-Time Joe" Crater came to light in April 2005, when Stella Ferrucci-Good died in Bellerose, Queens, leaving behind what may be a key to the mystery. While going through Mrs. Ferrucci-Good's possessions, her granddaughter, Barbara O'Brien, discovered a metal box that contained handwritten letter in an envelope marked, "Do not open until my death." In the letter, Mrs. Ferrucci-Good claimed that her late husband, Robert Good, told her that a New York City cop named Charles Burns, and the cop's brother, a cab driver named Frank Burns, were responsible for Crater's death. Robert Good had been a New York City Parks Department supervisor and lifeguard and had died in 1975.

In her account, Mrs. Ferrucci-Good wrote that her husband told her that he learned over drinks with one of the Burns brothers that they, along with several other men, killed the judge and buried him on Coney Island, under the boardwalk at West Eighth Street. That location is the current site of the New York Aquarium.

According to Mrs. Ferrucci-Good's account, her husband told her that when Crater stepped into the cab on West Forty-Second Street that night, the driver was Frank Burns, a Syndicate hitman employed by Jack "Legs" Diamond. Diamond was allegedly angry at Crater's refusal to reverse some lower court decisions that hurt the mob boss. Burns picked Crater up in his cab and then drove a few blocks to where his two accomplices jumped in the vehicle. They drove to Coney Island, where they were joined by two more men. Their intent was to rough Crater up a little and scare him into playing ball with Diamond, but in the judge's struggles to escape the cab, he was accidentally killed.

In her letter, Mrs. Ferrucci-Good said that Officer Burns was one of the cops guarding notorious Murder Inc. hitman Abe "Kid Twist" Reles when the gangster and mob informant somehow plummeted to his death from a sixth-floor Coney Island hotel window in 1941. Reles' death came hours before he was to testify against mob boss Albert Anastasia. Reles became immortalized in New York tabloids as "the canary who could sing but couldn't fly."

Barbara O'Brien also found that the metal box contained yellowed newspaper clippings about Crater's disappearance with written notations in the margins.

Police sources confirmed that a man named Charles Burns served with the NYPD from 1926 to 1946 and that he spent part of his career assigned to the 60th Precinct in Coney Island. Police also confirmed that several skeletal remains were found at the location named by Mrs. Ferrucci-Good in 1956, when the foundation for the aquarium was being dug. Decades prior to the advent of DNA technology, the remains could not be identified. They were reburied in pine coffins made by inmates at Rikers Island prison in an unmarked mass grave in New York City's Potters Field on Hart Island.

Barbara stated that her grandmother never mentioned the Crater case to her or anyone else in the family. She was baffled by the contents of the letter but turned it over to the police —--- just to be sure. Police were unable to verify or disprove the letter, leaving the fate of "the missingest man in New York" a mystery that will likely never be solved.

1934: "NEMO"
The Disappearance of
Everett Ruess

When I go, I leave no trace.
Everett Ruess

I will never forget the first time that I heard about Chris McCandless. It was in an article written by Jon Krakauer. He later turned it into a book called *Into the Wild*. You may have read it, or even seen the movie that was made from it.

It tells the story of a young man named Christopher McCandless who died a tragic death in the wilds of Alaska. He had left his life behind and wandered the American West, working when he needed money to support his simple lifestyle and exploring the world outside of the normalcy of everyday life. In April 1992, he headed off into the Alaskan wilderness, determined to live off the land. It turned out to be Chris's final journey.

Four months after he left civilization, hunters found his painfully thin body huddled in a sleeping bag inside an abandoned bus that had been used for shelter, just outside Denali National Park. It's likely that Chris died of starvation. His journal entries for this time tell of him getting weaker and weaker —– possibly after eating the poisonous seeds of a wild sweet pea —– and finally, becoming too sick to look for food. It remains a mystery as to what really happened to McCandless. Was he simply lacking the knowledge to survive in the woods, or did he have some sort of death wish? No one knows. "If this adventure proves fatal and you don't hear from me again," he wrote to a friend before he departed for Alaska, "I want you to know that you're a great man. I now walk into the wild."

Christ had walked off "into the wild" and he'd never come back. He was, of course, not the first person to do so. He was repeating the actions of another young man, a 20-year-old adventurer named Everett Ruess, who vanished into the vast canyonlands of Utah in 1934.

For many years, Ruess lived on as a legend —- a Western myth that was the embodiment of seeking beauty and freedom in nature. Little remained of him, save for an inscription on a wall of stone in southern Utah's David Gulch. It read "Nemo 1934," an enigmatic reminder from Ruess that we are "no one" in the greater scheme of things.

Everett Ruess was born in Oakland, California, in 1914, the younger of two sons raised by Christopher and Stella Ruess. Christopher was a graduate of Harvard Divinity School and was a poet, philosopher, and Unitarian minister. To feed his family, though, he worked as a bureaucrat in the California penal system. Stella was a headstrong woman with artistic ambitions for both herself and her family. She published a literary journal, the *Ruess Quartette*, with the family motto emblazoned on the cover: "Glorify the Hour." They were a close-knit and nomadic family. They moved across the country, living in Oakland, Fresno, Los Angeles, Boston, Brooklyn, New Jersey, and Indiana, finally settling in southern California when Everett was 14. It was no surprise that Everett also became a wanderer.

Living in Los Angeles, he attended the Otis Art School and Hollywood High School. He embarked on his first solo journey at age 16, spending the summer of 1930 hitchhiking and roaming through Yosemite and Big Sur, eventually winding up in Carmel. Two days after he arrived, he knocked on the door of Edward Weston, the famous nature photographer, who was charmed by the young man and agreed to teach him about art. Over the next two months, he encouraged Everett's uneven but promising efforts at painting and block printing and permitted him to hang around the studio with Weston's sons, Neil and Cole.

At the end of the summer, he returned home long enough to earn a high school diploma, which he received in January 1931. Less than a month later, he was on the road again, tramping alone through the sparsely populated desert lands of Utah, Arizona, and New Mexico. Except for a single semester at UCLA, two extended visits with his parents, a winter in San Francisco — - which he managed to spend in the company of photographers Dorothea Lange and Ansel Adams and painter Maynard Dixon —- Everett spent the rest of his life constantly on the move. He lived on little money, right out of his backpack, sleeping on the ground and going hungry for days at a time. He could not have been happier.

Everett Ruess

Ruess kept a diary and wrote numerous letters to his friends and family, telling them of his "serene and tempestuous days" scaling cliffs, wandering through canyons, and walking across the desert. He befriended many of those he met. He learned to speak Navajo and once sang with a medicine man at the bed side of a sick girl. Hopi Indians painted Ruess and allowed him to participate in their traditional Antelope Dance, which was a high honor.

One day in June 1931, Randolph "Pat" Jenks and Tad Nichols were driving from Cameron, Arizona, to Flagstaff when they came upon Everett and his burro, Pegasus. Ruess was badly sunburned, half-starved, and dehydrated. They stopped and asked him if he wanted a drink. But Everett, thinking that they had asked him for water, started to unleash one of the two canteens that he had strapped to the side of the burro. "He had only a small amount of water left, but was immediately willing to share it," Nichols recalled many years later.

Jenks and Nichols drove Everett to Flagstaff, and the young artist stayed at Jenks' ranch under the San Francisco Peaks for several weeks, painting the aspens. They became close friends and then, just as suddenly as he had appeared on the side of the road, he vanished.

For a time, Everett reportedly worked with archaeologists from the University of California who were excavating ruins near Kayenta, Arizona. His lack of regard for his own safety frightened some of them. "One time in camp, he stood on the edge of a 400-foot cliff in a rainstorm and did a watercolor sketch of a waterfall," archaeologist H.C. Lockett told *Desert Magazine* in 1939. "I remember this clearly because I personally was scared to death just watching him perched on the edge of the cliff."

Ruess financed his wanderings by selling prints and paintings, but he never stayed in the same place for long. He once wrote, "There is always an undercurrent of restlessness and wild longing. The wind is in my hair, there is a fire in my heels, and I shall always be a rover, I know."

According to records, Everett continued to roam the southwest until the age of 20, when he disappeared for good. The last letters anyone received from him were posted from the Mormon settlement of Escalante —--- 57 miles north of a place called Davis Gulch —--- on November 11, 1934. The letters were addressed to his parents and brother, Waldo, and he advised them that he would be incommunicado for "a month or two." Eight days after mailing the letters, Ruess encountered two sheepherders about a mile from the gulch and spent two nights at their camp. These men were the last people known to have seen Everett alive. He did leave one last marker in his wake, however. Later, discovered carved into the sandstone walls of the gulch, Everett twice etched the name "Nemo" —– Latin for "nobody" —– and then vanished.

Some three months after Ruess departed Escalante, his parents received a bundle of unopened mail that had been forwarded from the postmaster at Marble Canyon, Arizona, where Everett was long overdue. Worried, Christopher and Stella contacted the authorities in Escalante, who organized a search party in March 1935. Starting from the sheep camp where he was last seen, they began combing the surrounding region and soon found Everett's two burros at the bottom of Davis Gulch, peacefully grazing behind a makeshift corral that had been fashioned from brush and tree branches. The burros were confined in the upper canyon and nearby, under a large natural arch, they found Everett's "Nemo 1934" inscription. Four pieces of Anasazi pottery, which Everett had likely discovered, were neatly arranged a few feet away.

Three months later, searchers came across another "Nemo" inscription a little deeper into the gulch, although both have long since disappeared under the waters of Lake Powell. Except for the burros and their tack, none of Everett's possessions, including his camping gear, journals, and paintings, were found. Everett was simply gone and the question of what happened to him has produced many theories, but no answers.

Given the rough area where he was camping, it was conjectured that Everett may have fallen to his death while scrambling up or down one of the canyon walls, but no search ever turned up human remains. His parents came to believe that he was murdered for his belongings and likely based their belief on the confession of an outlaw Navajo named Jack Crank. His story was inconsistent, and no corpse was discovered where he said that it would be, despite several intense searches.

If he was not killed, there remains a mystery as to why Everett would have left the gulch with a heavy load of gear, but without his pack animals. This bewildering puzzle has led some to conclude that he was murdered by a band of cattle rustlers known to have been in the area. It was thought that they may have stolen his belongings and buried his remains or threw them into the Colorado River.

Many of the people that Everett met on his wilderness sojourns were so taken with the young man that they contacted his parents with offers to help in the search. Reporters from Los Angeles, San Francisco, and Salt Lake City covered the searches and their dispatches provoked interest and leads from around the country. In the first few months after he vanished, Ruess was "spotted" in all sorts of places, from a transient camp in Florida to a mine in Moab, Utah, and even hitchhiking on a Mexican highway. None of these false leads panned out, though, and the search continued.

In early 1935, a California placer miner named Neil Johnson heard about Everett's disappearance, and he offered to help look for him. He was accompanied on the search by John Terrell, a reporter from the *Salt Lake Tribune*. In August, Douglas and Terrell journeyed through miles of wild country. They swam the Colorado and then continued north to Davis Gulch. At this point, their Indian guide became puzzled and spent two days thoroughly searching the area for any sign of Everett. He finally concluded that the boy had gone into the canyon but had not come out.

Interest in the fate of Everett Ruess continued and, in the summer of 1941, two Paiute Indians told Toney Richardson, a trading post owner at Tonalea, Arizona, that a white man had been found "sleeping" in the sand across the Colorado River in Utah. At the same time, Richardson heard wild rumors from the Navajo reservation about medicine men holding squaw dances using the scalp of a white man. A tiny piece of it was sliced off for each dance and afterwards, it was buried to kill his spirit. The scalp was said to be from a "sleeping" man, who was blond. Everett had been fair-skinned but not quite blond. The identity of the dead man was never determined.

Most of Everett's friends, and the members of the search parties, reached the conclusion that Everett had been murdered, either by criminals or the local Indians. Pat Jenks, who owned the ranch where Everett lived for a time, believed that he stumbled upon a group of Paiute Indians who were on their way to Escalante for winter supplies, and they killed him and stole his gear. Tad Nichols, though, disagreed. "I don't believe he was killed by Indians," he said in 1997. "He got along well with them. Maybe they didn't like him poking into caves, and through their ceremonial material, but I don't think they were responsible." He believed that Everett likely died in a flash flood or fell off a cliff.

Stories of Everett continued to make the rounds and enigmatic discoveries were sometimes still made. Nearly 30 years after he was last seen, archaeologists digging at what it now Arizona's Lake Powell found his canteen and some other gear, including dried-up tubes of paint and a box of razor blades from the Owl Drug Company of Los Angeles. They were Everett's brand.

In 1976, when Colorado River boatman and Grand Canyon legend Emory Kolb died, friends searching through his belongings found a human skeleton inside a skiff in his garage. The skull had a hole behind the right ear and rattling around inside of it was a .32-caliber slug. Some speculated that it had belonged to Everett Ruess. Coconino County sent the remains to University of Arizona's human identification lab and Forensic Anthropologist Walter Birkby stated that the cause of death was certainly murder. However, the bones had belonged to a man well over six feet tall and Everett had only stood five foot, eight inches.

So, that mystery still hasn't been solved —– although both Glen Hyde and Everett Ruess have been ruled out as the enigmatic victim.

In 1983, another "Nemo" inscription turned up on a canyon wall along the San Juan River and rumors persisted that Navajo medicine men were continuing to have visions of Everett – alive and well. Some believe that Everett Ruess never died at all, but simply vanished. One man told author Jon Krakauer that he knew a man who had "definitely bumped into Ruess" in the late 1960s at a remote hogan on a Navajo Indian reservation. According to the man, Everett had married a Navajo woman, with whom he had raised at least one child.

Finally, in 2008, the riddle of Everett Ruess was declared solved.

In May of that year, Daisy Johnson visited her younger brother, Denny Bellson, who lived on a Navajo Indian Reservation, and told him a story about their family that he had never heard before —– a story about their grandfather, Aneth Nez, which took place in the 1930s. According to the account, Nez had been sitting on the rim of Comb Ridge (a sandstone uplift that crosses the Utah-Arizona border). For several days, he watched a young white man riding up and down the canyon below him. He had two mules, one that he rode and one that he used as a pack animal. He acted like he was looking for something.

One day, Nez saw the young man down in the riverbed, only this time he was yelling and riding fast. Nez saw that three Ute Indians were chasing the man. They caught up with him, hit him in the head, and knocked him off his mule. They stole everything and left the man there to die.

As the scene below unfolded, Nez stayed out of view. The Utes and the Navajos had been enemies for centuries, and as late as the 1930s, tensions between the two groups had erupted into violence. He waited until the Utes were gone and then descended Comb Ridge into the bed of the Chinle Wash. The young man was dead by the time that Nez got to him. Rather than looking for a burial site in the open wash, the Navajo hauled the body up onto the ridge and buried him in a crevice.

For more than three decades, Aneth Nez kept quiet about this horrible incident. In the 1930s, the murder of a white man would have brought an invading force of law enforcement officials onto the reservation and would have stirred up a great amount of trouble. Nez felt that he should keep his story to himself. Then, in 1971, at the age of 72, he fell ill with cancer and went to a medicine man to seek traditional treatment. He revealed to the healer the story of the murder and his subsequent movement of the body —--- a close encounter with death that the Navajo believe can cause sickness. The medicine man told him that the only cure for his cancer was to retrieve a lock of hair from the head of the young man that he had buried years before. The hair would then be used in a five-day healing ceremony.

Daisy Johnson, who was then 19-years-old, took her grandfather out to the white man's grave. He retrieved the lock of hair and, after the ceremony, lived for another 10 years. It was a healing that gave Johnson hope. She had been diagnosed with ovarian cancer in 2007 but after chemotherapy, which had made her violently ill and caused her hair to fall out, the cancer had gone into remission. A year later, it came back and this time, Johnson went to see a medicine man. He told her that her sickness had come about because of her grandfather and a darkness that became attached to their family after his handling of the young man's corpse.

As he listened to the story, Denny Bellson realized that the grave of the white man must lie not far from the house that he built in 1993. He became obsessed with finding the grave that his grandfather had dug. Over the course of the next few weeks, Bellson, a carpenter and craftsman, spent his free time hiking on Comb Ridge, looking into every crack and crevice along the rim. Then, one day, in a shadowy crevice just under the crest of the Comb, he found the grave. The bones had clearly been placed there in great haste – and likely, with great fear. Bellson, also a traditional Navajo, did not touch anything. He called his sister and then he brought his friend, Vaughn Hadenfeldt, out to the grave. Hadenfeldt knew the story of Everett Ruess, although Denny Bellson had never heard of him before.

Hadenfeldt wasn't convinced at first that this could be the grave of Everett Ruess —– or any white man. He knew that the Navajo commonly practiced burials of human remains, along with certain personal possessions, in natural fissures in the rocks. He thought that this could be a Navajo crevice burial, but then reconsidered. Something was not right about it. The body was only partially buried, and the top of the skull, intact but fragile, was protruding from the dirt, as if the victim was in a sitting position. There was a dent in the back of the cranium, as if from a mortal blow. Outside of the crevice was a wooden stirrup, tattered strips of leather, and the frame of a saddle with a rusted iron pommel. Also, lying on the ground was a black leather belt, decorated with iron studs. Curiously, the belt was buckled, so it was closed in an empty loop.

A short time later, Bellson contacted the FBI about the body. Agents were skeptical about whether the grave was that of a white man. It was not uncommon to find scattered Indian graves, and, on those occasions, they were covered back up and left alone. A team from the FBI did come out to the site and left it in great disarray. One of the investigators attempted to pick up the skull and it broke into pieces. They left with the impression that it was nothing more than a Navajo burial, piled some rocks on top of the grave and left.

Others were not so sure, including David Roberts from *National Geographic Adventure* magazine. He was instrumental in bringing archaeologist Ron Maldonado to the site, arranging for a computer reconstruction of the skull to be carried out by the University of Colorado at Boulder, and launching a DNA analysis of the remains that could be compared to surviving members of the Ruess family.

The initial analysis was inconclusive. There were also other problems. Witness accounts conflicted with Aneth Nez's story. For the burial site on Comb Ridge to belong to Ruess, a couple of logistical problems had to be resolved. The most troublesome had to do with Everett's mules. In March 1935, searchers claimed that they had found his animals in Davis Gulch, abandoned in a makeshift pen. Why would the Utes have stolen the two burros in Chinle Wash, only to leave them 60 miles away in a side canyon near the Escalante River?

But what if the animals found in Davis Gulch were not Everett's? Many believed that the account of finding the mules was unreliable. According to the official account, after the search team recovered the animals, one man, Gail Bailey, had led them back to Escalante and had pastured them nearby. But when writer David Roberts spoke to old-timers in the region years later, he was told again and again that Bailey had found them on his own, before the search for Ruess had even been organized. Bailey, who died in 1997, may have lied about the mules belonging to Everett or he might have found them somewhere other than where he claimed.

A lie could help resolve the second mystery —--- the fact that Everett Ruess would have had to cover more than 60 miles (or even 90 miles on foot) between Davis Gulch and the Comb Ridge. In four years of exploring the harsh desert regions, Ruess had never been known to stray far from his pack animals. But if he took the burros with him, there's nothing improbable about the trip.

After the first DNA test failed to come up with any clear-cut answers, a second test, this time comparing a molar from the grave with saliva samples from Ruess' two nieces and two nephews, was underway. In late April, it was announced that the results revealed a match —-- the remains did belong to Everett Ruess. However, that announcement was quickly reversed. In October, a new press release announced that the second test had been wrong. Everett's nephew, Brian Ruess, stated that the remains found in southern Utah were not those of his uncle. "After further DNA testing, the Ruess family is now convinced that the remains found last year and reported to be those of Everett Ruess are in fact the remains of someone else," he said.

The new tests were done by the Armed Forces DNA Identification Laboratory (AFDIL) in Rockville, Maryland. The lab is part of the Office of the Armed Forces Medical Examiner of the Armed Forces Institute of Pathology. Technicians there performed an additional round of DNA extraction and analysis from samples taken from the same skeleton used in the earlier tests.

Brian Ruess expressed his sympathy for the family of the unknown victim but was clear that the bones were not those of his uncle. He told reporters, "As a result of the AFDIL findings and the reanalysis, the Ruess family has accepted that the skeletal remains are not those of Everett Ruess. The bones and associated artifacts will be returned to the Navajo Nation Archaeologist for disposition."

The vanishing remains unsolved and thanks to this, Everett's legend lives on.

Only a handful of American adventurers have ever stirred as much passion and speculation as Everett Ruess has over the years. His wandering spirit still refuses to rest.

Author Wallace Stegner described Everett as an artistic athlete, a callow romantic, and an atavistic wanderer of the wastelands, "But one who died – if he died – with the dream intact."

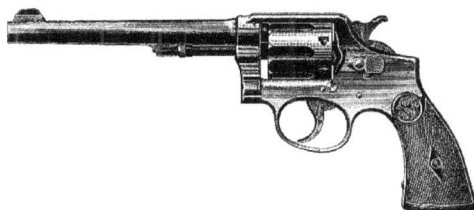

1937: Into the Air
Searching for Amelia Earhart

At the age of ten, I saw my first airplane. It was sitting in a slightly enclosed area at the Iowa State Fair in Des Moines. It was a thing of rusty wire and wood and looked not at all interesting. One of the grown-ups who happened to be around pointed it out to me and said, "Look dear, it flies." I looked as directed but confess I was much more interested in an absurd hat made of an inverted peach-basket which I had just purchased for fifteen cents.

This was written by Amelia Earhart in 1937, a half-remembered little anecdote about the first time she saw what would become the love of her life. Her first airplane deserved little more than a cursory glance but her passion for flying soon became an all-encompassing one. That love was one that first beckoned with adventure, then obsessed her with ambition, and finally swallowed her completely.

Amelia Earhart was one of the greatest figures of the twentieth century. She was a female adventurer at a time when most men believed that women shouldn't work —– they belonged in the kitchen —– and certainly not making newspaper headlines by flying all over the world. She was an American icon, and unfortunately, her story turned to tragedy when she disappeared under mysterious circumstances on the eve of World War II in the vast expanse of the South Pacific Ocean.

What happened to Amelia Earhart? Was her disappearance a terrible mistake? Was it a problem with her aircraft? Did she miscalculate and run out of fuel? Was her disappearance arranged by enemies of the United States in retaliation for her work as a spy? The enigma of her last days are as puzzling as the mystery of what really happened to the aviator during her final flight —– when she vanished completely, as if she had never existed at all.

Amelia Mary Earhart was born in Atchison, Kansas, on July 24, 1898. Her early life was dominated by her grandfather, a wealthy Kansas judge. Her father, Edwin Earhart, who married Amy Otis, Amelia's mother, in 1895, was a ruined man early in life. As a young lawyer, he had dreamed of becoming a judge himself one day, but his attempt to provide the sort of lavish lifestyle that his new wife had enjoyed growing up created enormous financial pressures. Initially, Earhart found lucrative employment settling claims for the railroads, but the crumbling of his early ambitions drove him to drink. By the time his second daughter, Muriel, was born, he was a hopeless

Amelia Earhart

alcoholic. The family moved from city to city —— from Des Moines to St. Paul and Chicago —— as his fortunes disintegrated.

For the most part, Amelia's childhood was rooted in the stable home of her grandfather. His white antebellum mansion stood on a bluff over the Missouri River, and Amelia was able to lose herself in his care, spending hours reading in the library and enjoying the fine things and stable environment that he was able to offer. Later in life, she thought of herself as a spoiled, horrid little girl. Only her love of books, she said, made her endurable.

After attending six schools, Amelia graduated from Chicago's Hyde Park High School in 1916. As was the tradition of her family, she then entered the Ogontz finishing school in Philadelphia, where she was trained in the etiquette of pleasing some future husband, caring for his home, and raising his children. Amelia escaped from the tedium of the school at every opportunity and during one brief escape, traveled to Toronto, where her sister Muriel was stuck in her own finishing school.

In Canada, Amelia saw for the first time the tragedy of the Great War, which was raging in Europe. By that time, Canadians had been embroiled in the war for three years and young wounded men were highly visible limping on the Toronto streets with canes and crutches. Amelia was shocked by what she saw, and she left school to go to work as a nurse's aide for the Canadian Red Cross.

It was in Toronto that Amelia first became enamored of airplanes. She attended a fair one afternoon that featured stunt pilots, all of them former war aces. She was swept away with the romanticism of flight and the attention the pilots received. "These men were the heroes of the hour," she later wrote. "They were in demand at social teas, and to entertain crowds by giving stunting exhibitions. The airplanes they rode so gallantly to fame were as singular as they were."

In 1919, Amelia returned to America and enrolled in medical courses at Columbia University. Regardless, she was unable to give up her dreams of taking to the skies. She traveled to California the following year to visit her father, who was fighting his drinking problem with steady work and participation in an early Alcoholics Anonymous program, an effort that prompted Amelia's mother to join her husband in a last attempt to salvage their marriage. Edwin Earhart was thrilled to see his daughter and took Amelia to an air show, where she watched barnstormers race their flimsy planes across the sky.

A dashing flier named Frank Hawks was the first to take Amelia into the air. As she rose just a few hundred feet above the earth, she realized that flying was the only thing that she wanted to do with her life, and she became resolved to raise the $500 that was needed to enroll in a 12-hour flying course. With her father's help, she enrolled as a student with pioneering female pilot Neta Snook. Amelia took her advanced training with John Montijo, a former instructor with the Army, and under his guidance, she soloed in 1921. Amelia took great pride in her ability to pilot an airplane and even greater pride in her swaggering appearance, dressing like the wartime pilots who first captured her imagination a few years before. No matter how she dressed, though, there was nothing boastful about her skill as a pilot. She was cool under pressure and experienced male pilots marveled at her nerve. She worked hard to master one plane after another and flying became her life.

But there were few jobs for male pilots in those days of early aviation, let alone female fliers. Even men like the celebrated Charles Lindbergh had a hard time finding employment in the air, grabbing anything they could find, from stunt flying to mail delivery. Amelia took several secretarial jobs and even worked in a darkroom, where she became an excellent photographer.

With her savings, along with money from her supportive father, Amelia purchased her first airplane, a sport biplane that was built by William Kinner and called the "Kinner Canary." Amelia performed every conceivable test on the airplane with her expert piloting skills, performing spins, stalls, and forced landings. Soon after, she crashed for the first of three times in her career. The motor failed in a borrowed plane and she cut the engines and landed hard in a cabbage field. She also set the first of her records that same year, ascending to 14,000 feet, the highest altitude ever achieved by a female flier.

But Amelia's dreams of the sky were interrupted when her parents separated once more. Edwin had started drinking again and this time, Amy Earhart decided that she'd had enough. The couple divorced in 1924. Amelia sold her plane and used the money to purchase a yellow Kissel sports car in which she and her mother motored to Medford, Massachusetts, to live with Muriel.

Amelia tried to resume her medical studies, but this proved to be a failure. She dropped out of Columbia University in 1925, and through the Massachusetts University extension program, the would-be aviator settled down to teach English to immigrants in the Boston area.

Amelia Earhart never expected to fly again.

In the spring of 1928, a British socialite, Mrs. Frederick Guest, whose husband had been in the Air Ministry in England, bought a tri-motored Fokker airplane from Commander Richard E. Byrd. Mrs. Guest intended to be the first woman to fly across the Atlantic Ocean —- as a passenger, not a pilot. The dangers of flying in those days were pointed out to the adventurous Mrs. Guest, however, and she was persuaded to allow another woman to take her place. Since Charles Lindbergh, an American, had been the first to cross the Atlantic a year earlier, it was only fitting, thought Mrs. Guest, that an American female make the trip.

A sort of talent hunt got underway, with George Palmer Putnam, of the G.P. Putnam Sons publishing company, leading the search. While in Boston, Putnam was told of an amazing lady pilot named Amelia Earhart, who had already logged more than 500 hours in the air, broken several records, and was the first woman to be granted an F.A.I. pilot's license from the World Air Sports Federation, which had been founded in 1906. Amelia was tracked down and asked if she wanted to be the first woman to fly the Atlantic. Needless to say, she happily accepted.

George Putnam was no fool. Beyond Amelia's flying skills, he knew that she was a marketable commodity. She even bore a resemblance to the dashing Charles Lindbergh. He envisioned her as a "Lady Lindy" and he not only set Amelia up for the Atlantic flight, but signed her to a book contract, too. Putnam had already made a fortune with Lindbergh's book about his solo flight to Paris and he was sure that Amelia could be just as popular.

The pilot of the Atlantic flight was Wilmer L. Stultz and the flight mechanic was Louis "Slim" Gordon. Amelia was the only passenger. Stultz, known as "Bull" to his friends, was an air veteran and received $20,000 for his work. Gordon got $5,000 and Amelia got the glory.

The plane took off on the morning of June 3, 1928, soaring into the air above Boston, headed for Newfoundland. They landed in Trespassy and then sat on the ground for three weeks, due to bad weather. Stultz, who was a raging alcoholic, drank more than a fifth of brandy every day and was once so drunk that he fell from a pier and nearly drowned. Amelia's experience with her alcoholic father provided her with the patience to deal with the drunken pilot and a sober Stultz finally lifted the plane out of the Newfoundland fog on June 17.

During the flight, Amelia busied herself taking copious amounts of notes, which later appeared in her book *20 Hours, 40 Minutes*. She was thrilled to be on the flight, despite the dangers involved. Stultz fought one storm after another as they crossed the Atlantic but managed to set the plane down gently at Burry Port, Wales. Cheering crowds greeted the crew in England and when they returned to the United States, but most of them came to see Amelia, who was now famous all over the globe. She discarded her usual men's attire to slip into a dress that was loaned to her by a local Welsh woman before newsmen snapped her photo. When she came home to America, she moved into a cottage on the Putnam estate while she finished her book, which was published in 1929. Ironically, the book was dedicated to Putnam's wife, Dorothy, but within two years, the Putnams were divorced and George was spending almost every waking moment with Amelia.

Amelia refused to marry Putnam six times but eventually, his money, flattery, famous friends, social position, and adoration finally wore her down. They were married on February 8, 1931. The "aviatrix," as women flyers were then called, handed him a note just before the wedding in which she stipulated the rules of their strange relationship. Among her directives, she stated that she would not hold him to "any medieval code of faithfulness to me" and she would not be faithful to him either. If they were honest with each other, she said, no difficulties would arise. They would also agree not to interfere in one another's work and Putnam would not be allowed to tell her what to do or where to go. There were times, she said, when she needed to be alone and could not "endure the confinements of even an attractive cage."

Putnam, who was 12 years older than Amelia, agreed to abide by her terms. There were rumors of many affairs over the years, including with her navigator Fred Noonan, Hollywood stunt pilot Paul Mantz, and others, but all were kept quiet and Amelia never embarrassed her husband. Putnam, meanwhile, spent the next six years promoting his wife in one scheme after another. He sold his interest in the publishing house to a relative and began marketing all manner of items in Amelia's name, from luggage to aviator-style clothing for women.

Amelia busied herself with flying. With Putnam backing her financially, she purchased the best planes available and in one of them, a Lockheed Vega monoplane, she took off from Harbor Grace, Newfoundland, on May 20, 1932, and landed in a meadow in Londonderry, Ireland, 14 hours and 56 minutes later. She was the first woman to fly solo across the Atlantic. Only months later, she established a record in transcontinental flight for women, traveling non-stop from Los Angeles to Newark, New Jersey, in 19 hours and five minutes. In 1933, she beat her own record by two hours. Thousands turned out to greet her in January 1935 after she flew from Hawaii to Oakland's Bay Farm Airport in 18 hours and 15 minutes. She became the first to solo from Los Angeles to Mexico City a few months later. Hours after landing, she was again in the air, soloing from Mexico City to Newark.

Amelia Earhart had become one of the most famous people in the world. Politicians, scientists, educators, and movie stars clamored to meet her. She dined at the White House with President Roosevelt and even took Eleanor Roosevelt for a moonlight flight.

But one final challenge remained —-- to fly around the world. On March 20, 1936, she purchased a plane from Lockheed for $50,000. The twin-engine, 10-passenger 10-E Electra airliner was the most powerful non-military plane of the day. Amelia had it stripped and larger gas tanks installed so that it would have a range of 4,500 miles. A complete navigation room, with all the latest instruments, was installed aft of the main cabin. She called the plane "my flying laboratory," but what Amelia planned to study during her around-the-world jaunt continues to be debated today.

Amelia's legendary flight began on May 29, 1937. Her Electra flew across the United States and then departed from Miami for Puerto Rico, Venezuela, Brazil, then across the Atlantic to Africa, landing at Senegal. She flew across Africa to Karachi, India, then Burma, the Dutch East Indies, the island of Timor, then Port Darwin, Australia. From there, Amelia and her navigator, Fred Noonan, flew to Lae, New Guinea. By July 1, more than 7,000 miles remained in her journey with the most difficult leg of the trip being the non-stop flight to tiny Howland Island, which was 2,556 miles across open ocean.

On the night before she departed from New Guinea, Amelia wrote in her pilot's log, "Not much more than a month ago I was on the other shore of the Pacific, looking westward. This evening, I looked eastward over the Pacific. In those fast-moving days which have intervened, the whole width of the world has passed behind us — - except this broad ocean. I shall be glad when we have the hazards of its navigation behind us."

Amelia had every reason to be worried. The last sweep of the journey was an arduous one, over a stretch of water that no one had ever before flown. Outside of the normal shipping lanes, Howland Island was seldom visited by ships and was considered one of the loneliest, most desolate places on the planet. It was an almost impossible place to find on a map, let alone from the air. Howland Island, a United States possession, was a mere half-mile wide and only two miles long. At high tide, its elevation was only 15 feet above the sea. A lesser pilot would have been terrified to know that his or her life depended on finding this tiny speck in the vast expanse of the South Pacific.

But there was no one better to make this dangerous journey than Amelia. In July 1937, she was 39-years-old. Her good-natured face was amazingly unwrinkled, her gray eyes sparkled, and her bright, toothy grin made her look like everyone's fun-loving, albeit a little wild, kid sister. She was a skilled pilot with a navigator who was second to none.

Fred Noonan had no qualms about the flight to Howland Island. He had many years of experience in the Pacific, guiding Pan American's China Clipper during her maiden flight from San Francisco to Manila a few years before. Noonan had chronometers to aid him, as well as a direction finder. There would also be radio bearings sent to the Electra from ships and shore stations. The Coast Guard cutter *Itasca* had been stationed at Howland Island to assist Amelia if she needed it. The U.S.S. *Swan* was also standing by, stationed between Howland and Honolulu. The U.S.S. *Ontario* was between New Guinea and Howland Island.

The morning of July 2 was clear, and Amelia was ready to depart. She wanted to be in California by July 4, an apt day of celebration for her around-the-world accomplishment. The Electra was loaded with 800 gallons of gasoline and 70 cans of oil. Wearing her traditional military slacks and a plaid shirt, Amelia climbed aboard the plane, followed by Noonan. They cheerfully waved goodbye to the Dutch officials and natives who had gathered to see them off.

Behind the controls, Amelia revved the engines and the plane rolled forward and picked up speed. The heavily-laden craft seemed to barely lift itself from the runway and it became airborne just 150 feet before the strip ended abruptly at a cliff that dropped off into the ocean. The plane took off at 10:30 a.m. on July 2, although according to the calendar on the *Itasca*, which was waiting at Howland Island, the international dateline made Amelia's departure at 12:30 p.m. on July 1. There would be plenty of time to make it to America by Independence Day since Amelia and Noonan were technically flying into yesterday.

A few hours after Amelia departed from New Guinea, Commander W.K. Thompson, the skipper of the *Itasca*, received a radio dispatch from San Francisco that she was in the air and on her way toward Howland. Thompson had stationed four men on constant alert for Amelia's signal. The Electra's radio schedule called for Amelia's call letters, KHAQQ, to be broadcast with messages on 3105 kilocycles every 15 and 45 minutes past the hour. Homing signals and weather reports were to be broadcast by the *Itasca* to Amelia every hour and half hour on 3105 and 7500 kilocycles.

For some reason, Commander Thompson was worried about the flight. He made a point of contacting the direction-finder unit ashore at Howland several times to see if anything had been picked up from KHAQQ. Nothing had been heard. At 1:12 a.m., he wired to San Francisco, "Have not heard Earhart's signal but see no cause for concern as plane is still about 10,000 miles away."

At 2:45 a.m., a voice, barely discernible, broke through the static on the 3105 wavelength. The anxious seamen in *Itasca's* radio room quickly adjusted their controls, leaning forward to make out the voice. "Cloudy and overcast," they heard Amelia's voice say over the static, "…headwinds.

Thompson immediately wired San Francisco, "Itasca heard Earhart plane at 0248."

The next expected signal at 3:15 a.m. did not come. At 3:30 a.m., *Itasca* radioed the weather report. Thompson veered from the scheduled routine as he became more concerned. He added to the weather report, "What is your position KHAQQ? *Itasca* heard your phone. Please go ahead on key. Acknowledge this broadcast next schedule."

At 3:45 a.m., another signal came through. Amelia was still using voice transmission and had apparently not heard the last message from Thompson because she gave no acknowledgement of it. Her voice seemed even more distant, "*Itasca* from Earhart... *Itasca* from Earhart... overcast... will listen in on hour and half hour at 3105."

Again, *Itasca* asked for key transmissions, but Amelia remained on voice transmissions, her words faint and garbled. Strangely, the experienced aviator gave no positions or bearings. Later, it was recalled that Noonan was having trouble with his chronometers before leaving New Guinea, something to do with radio interference that prevented exact settings and threw off position fixes from the stars. If Amelia was flying in storms and could receive no ship- or shore-to-plane communication, that left only dead reckoning to fly by. Thompson knew what that meant —– a one-degree deviation from the flight plan could send the plane one mile off course for every 60 miles of headway. Howland Island, that tiny speck in the ocean, could be easily overshot by Amelia and Noonan and they could easily fly into a vast area of ocean and, most likely, into oblivion.

The signals from Amelia's Electra stopped around dawn. Commander Thompson ordered a ground crew to clear the runway at Howland of clustering birds. The skies were bright and clear when the sun came up, but there was no sign of Amelia's plane.

At 7:42 a.m., Amelia's voice finally broke the silence of the radio room. Jittery and high-pitched, she was almost shouting, "KHAQQ calling *Itasca*. We must be on you but cannot see you. Gas is running low. Only about 30 minutes left. Been unable to reach you by radio. We are flying at an altitude of 1,000 feet."

About 15 minutes later, Amelia's voice clearly came through again, "KHAQQ calling *Itasca*. We are circling but cannot see you. Go ahead on 7,500 either now or on schedule."

Thompson ordered a steady stream of signals sent out immediately. For the first time, Amelia acknowledged the broadcast from *Itasca*, "We are receiving your signal but unable to get a minimum [bearing]. Please take a bearing on us and answer with voice on 3105." She sent out her steady signals, but the sound drifted and faded before a bearing could be determined.

According to dead reckoning, Amelia and Noonan would have calculated the distance from New Guinea since their takeoff 18 hours earlier. From Amelia's mention of having only 30 minutes of fuel remaining, Thompson figured the Electra must be within 100 miles of Howland. To the south, about 38 miles away, was Baker Island. If Amelia overshot Howland in that direction, she was bound to see Baker. To the north, there was nothing, and it was there that Thompson charted a block of ocean for a possible search and rescue.

Amelia's final words were heard at 8:43 a.m. She sounded confused, frightened, and desperate —– words that had never been used to describe the confident flyer before. Chief Radioman Leo G. Bellarts in the radio shack aboard *Itasca* saw that her radio signal strength registered as a "5," the highest possible. To him, Amelia's voice sounded so loud that she must be within sight of the ship.

The words came out in a scared babble, "We are in line of position 157-337... will repeat this message. We will repeat this message at 6210 kilocycles, wait. We are running on line, listening on 6210 kilocycles. We are running north and south..." And the signal abruptly ended.

Bellarts later said, "She was so loud that I ran up to the bridge expecting to see her coming in for a landing."

But to his astonishment, the sky was empty.

Bellarts later recalled in his memoirs, "The last time we heard her, her voice was so loud and clear you could hear her outside the radio shack. We heard her quite a few times, but that last time it sounded as if she would have broken into a scream if she hadn't stopped talking. She was just about ready to break into tears and go into hysterics. That's exactly how I'd describe her voice. I'll never forget it."

Commander Thompson was overwhelmed with a feeling of dread. Amelia had overshot the island and was headed into a no-return section of ocean in a plane that was quickly running out of fuel. He ordered the *Itasca* out of Howland harbor and headed northward. He sent out immediate messages to Washington, D.C., and San Francisco, "Earhart unreported at 0900... believe down. Am searching probably area and will continue."

Amelia's husband, George Putnam, was waiting in San Francisco. He tore Thompson's message from the hands of the radio operator and let out an audible sound of dismay. He put on a brave face for reporters, though. He stated, "Even if they are down, they can stay afloat indefinitely. Their empty gas tanks will give them buoyancy. Besides, they have all of the emergency equipment they need —– everything." Putnam was correct in that the Electra carried food and water rations, life belts, a two-man rubber raft, a flare gun, and a signal kit, but if the huge plane was down, it would sink rapidly into the sea, empty tanks or not.

Before *Itasca's* signal was received for a seaplane to be sent from Honolulu to help in the search, the Navy commander in Hawaii had already been instructed by Admiral William D. Leahy, Chief of Naval Operations, to "render whatever help you deem practical in search of Earhart and Noonan."

The seaplane was sent out, along with the battleship *Colorado,* accompanied by several smaller craft. From San Diego, the carrier *Lexington* was dispatched with its scores of planes waiting on deck to help look for the lost flyer.

Millions of people waited and watched for news. As the story of Amelia's disappearance swept across the country, it became one of the most widely reported news stories of the twentieth century. People wept over the fate of their beloved "Lady Lindy."

The seaplane from Hawaii was forced to turn back after hitting a sudden storm, but *Itasca, Colorado,* and her sister ships scoured the ocean north of Howland Island. They found nothing. For more than a week, the U.S. Navy, using ships and planes, searched nearly 263,000 square miles of ocean. *Lexington* and her 76 planes joined the search, but there was still nothing.

On July 12, the Navy finally called it off. Amelia's disappearance officially ended with a terse Navy statement, "Lost at sea."

The Navy report may have been short and to the point, but much more provocative have been the countless stories and legends that have emerged about the vanished aviator, many of which continue to this day.

The most widely accepted version of Amelia's disappearance is usually referred to as the "crash and sink theory." Many researchers believe that the Electra ran out of fuel and Amelia and Noonan ditched at sea. Navigator and aeronautical engineer Elgen Long and his wife, Marie K. Long, devoted 35 years of exhaustive research to this theory. U.S. Navy Captain Laurance F. Safford, who was responsible for the interwar Mid Pacific Strategic Direction Finding Net and decoding of the Japanese PURPLE cipher messages for the attack on Pearl Harbor, began a lengthy analysis of the Earhart flight during the 1970s, including the intricate radio transmission documentation, and came to the conclusion of "poor planning, worse execution." Rear Admiral Richard R. Black, who was in administrative charge of the Howland Island airstrip and was present in the radio room on *Itasca*, asserted in 1982 that the Electra went into the sea not far from Howland, although didn't explain why the search turned up no clues.

There were many who agreed that the plane went down after running out of fuel but didn't agree about where Amelia went down. Many believed the Electra crashed in the Phoenix Islands (now part of Kiribati), some 350 miles southeast of Howland Island.

The Gardner Island theory has been characterized as the "most confirmed" explanation for Amelia's disappearance. The International Group for Historic Aircraft Recovery has suggested Amelia and Noonan may have flown without further radio transmissions for two-and-a-half hours along the line of position Amelia stated in her last transmission received at Howland, arrived at then-uninhabited Gardner Island (now Nikumaroro), landed on an large, flat reef near the wreck of an old freighter, and ultimately died there.

The group's research has produced a range of documented archaeological and anecdotal evidence supporting this idea. For example, in 1940, Gerald Gallagher, a British colonial officer and pilot, radioed his superiors to inform them that he had found a "skeleton... possibly that of a woman," along with an old-fashioned sextant box, under a tree on the island's southeast corner. He was ordered to send the remains to Fiji, where in 1941, British colonial authorities took detailed measurements of the bones and concluded they were from a stocky male.

However, in 1998, an analysis of the measurement data by forensic anthropologists indicated the skeleton had belonged to a "tall white female of northern European ancestry." The bones themselves were misplaced for many years but recently, it's believed they have been found —– at the Te Umwanibong Museum and Cultural Center on an island in Kirabati. The bones were in a large box where several sets of remains had been stored. One of the sets was female and believed to be the bones that disappeared from Fiji years before. In 2019, they were sent for DNA testing and comparison against the DNA of Amelia's one living niece. As of this writing, the test results have not returned, so the mystery of the bones also remains unsolved.

This has not stopped researchers for continuing to search the island. Artifacts that have been discovered there have included improvised tools, an aluminum panel (possibly from an Electra), an oddly cut piece of clear Plexiglas that is the exact thickness and curvature of an Electra window, and a size nine shoe from the 1930s that resembles what Amelia was wearing in several photographs.

In July and August 2007, a 15-member expedition from The International Group for Historic Aircraft Recovery, which included engineers, environmentalists, a land developer, archaeologists, a sailboat designer, a team doctor, and a videographer, searched the island again. They were reported to have found additional artifacts including bronze bearings which may have come from the Electra and a zipper pull that could have come from Amelia's flight suit. The evidence remains circumstantial, but it is intriguing.

Only the DNA from the discovered bones can provide the answers about the island that so many seek.

The stories about Amelia that tend to fascinate most people are the ones that say that she did not die when she disappeared in 1937. This theory was first publicized in 1943 by RKO Studios, which produced a film called *Flight for Freedom*, starring Rosalind Russell. It was the film's contention, and that of several writers' decades later, that Amelia purposely flew off course, heading not for Howland but for the Japanese Mandates, islands that, through agreement, the United States could not inspect. The United States knew that the Japanese were building up their military in the islands they occupied but did not know if airstrips for bombers had been constructed. The RKO movie had Amelia begin the last leg of her around-the-world flight with the intention of "crash landing" on one of the Japanese islands, which would prompt the U.S. Navy to ignore past agreements and hurry to the area and rescue the pilot —– all the while accomplishing their real mission of photographing the massive Japanese military build-up. Rosalind Russell's "Amelia" learned that the Japanese discovered the ruse and intended to pick her up before the rescue mission could get underway. She heroically crashed into the ocean near the island. She was killed during the crash, but the rescue effort was able to take place anyway.

Although the plot of the film was presented as fiction, there is much to support the belief that Amelia Earhart was indeed on a secret mission to photograph the Japanese-occupied islands, especially Saipan. As late as 1949, Amelia's mother stated, "Amelia told me many things, but there were some things she couldn't tell me. I am convinced she was on some sort of government mission, probably on verbal orders."

But orders from whom? It has been claimed that they came directly from the President himself, Amelia's close friend, Franklin D. Roosevelt. He wanted to use Amelia's around-the-world flight and subsequent crash in the Japanese island area as an excuse to examine their hidden war preparations. Many believe this idea is a credible one and also believe that Amelia may not have died when her plane went down but was captured by the Japanese instead. Rumors spread over the years about a young woman who was captured on Saipan in 1937 and was taken to Japan and executed as a spy. Similar stories emanated from the Japanese islands over the years. Natives and Japanese officers who survived the war recalled seeing Amelia as a prisoner and witnessing either her imprisonment or her execution in Japan.

In 2017, a documentary was featured on the *History Channel* that claimed to solve the mystery of Amelia's disappearance —- stating that she was captured by the Japanese and the filmmakers had a photograph that proved it. The photo, taken before World War II, featured a group of people on a dock in Jaluit Atoll, one of the Marshall Islands. In the photo —- the filmmakers stated —- were two Caucasian people: a man standing next to a post and a person of indeterminate sex squatting at the edge of the dock. The photo caused a sensation when it was widely publicized that the two people were Amelia and her navigator, Fred Noonan.

The photograph presented in 2017 as proof that Amelia Earhart had survived her disappearance. She is alleged to be the woman seated on the dock with her back to the camera. The photo was later debunked.

This suggested that not only did they survive their crash, but that they had been taken prisoner by the Japanese, which is why they were never heard from again. Television news shows, radio programs, and podcasts began proclaiming that the mystery of Amelia Earhart had been solved.

It didn't take long, though, before the photograph was debunked. A Japanese military history writer named Kota Yamano produced evidence to show that the photo had been published in a Japanese-language travelogue about the islands of the South Pacific in 1935 — two years before Amelia disappeared.

This discovery did not completely discount the idea that Amelia crashed and was taken prisoner by the Japanese military, but it certainly debunked the photograph.

But being taken prisoner by the Japanese wasn't the wildest story that has been circulated about Amelia's fate. There were other, much wilder, rumors.

One popular story had it that Amelia was forced to make propaganda radio broadcasts as one of the many women compelled to serve as "Tokyo Rose" during World War II. This story was thoroughly investigated by Amelia's husband, George Putnam, but after listening to many recordings of the many women known as "Tokyo Rose," he did not recognize her voice among them.

Perhaps the strangest story about Amelia's disappearance was first started in 1970 in a book called *Amelia Earhart Lives* by Joe Klaas. In the book, the author asserted that Earhart had survived the flight, inexplicably moved to New Jersey, and became Irene Craigmile Bolam. Irene Bolam, who had been a banker in New York during the 1940s, denied being Earhart, filed a lawsuit against the author and publisher, and submitted a lengthy affidavit in which she refuted the claims. The publisher, McGraw-Hill, withdrew the book from the market shortly after it was released and later reached an out of court settlement with Bolam. Research of her life proved that she could not have been Amelia Earhart.

For George Putnam, who waited for seven days in the Coast Guard radio room before giving up hope, Amelia died in 1937. After finally realizing that his wife was not coming home, he opened a letter that she had given him with instructions to only read it if she failed to appear. In tears, he read the final words that she had left him, "Please know that I am quite aware of the hazards. I want to do it – because I want to do it. Women must try to do things as men have tried. When they fail, their failure must be but a challenge to others."

Putnam's heady promotions of Amelia were over, lost in his grief and exhaustion. He told reporters that, "If she's gone, this is the way that she would have wanted it."

And he was likely right. If Amelia Earhart had to die, she would have wanted to leave this world in a plane. Her mischievous personality probably would have also loved the idea that, if she was going to go, her death would remain one of the great unsolved mysteries of the century.

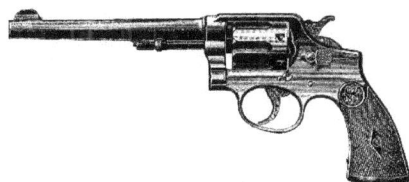

1937: What Happened to Ruth Baumgardner?

In 1937, an attractive young woman named Ruth Baumgardner disappeared.

She vanished without a trace and her shocking disappearance was as mysterious then as it is now —– and was just as unsolvable. Was she kidnapped by a "sex pervert," as the newspapers claimed? Or did she come down with a case of amnesia, an explanation that was deemed more credible in those days than it is today? Or could her disappearance have just been a desperate attempt to start a new life, free from the constraints of her upper-middle-class existence?

We'll likely never know —– but we'll never stop wondering.

Ruth Baumgardner was a 22-year-old coed at Ohio Wesleyan University in Delaware, Ohio, when she vanished in May 1937. Just a few weeks away from graduation, Ruth, a talented art major, was last seen by some of her fellow Tri-Delt (Delta Delta Delta) sorority sisters shortly before 11:00 p.m. in her dormitory, Austin Hall, shortly after she returned from choir practice. Ruth had her hair in curlers and seemed her ordinary, happy self. She didn't appear to be under any kind of strain or stress, the other girls later recalled. A little before midnight, Ruth said goodnight to her friends –— and was never seen again.

Ohio Wesleyan University was a small, very closely-knit campus. When Ruth failed to show up for any of her classes the next day, missing a test that she had been studying for, her sorority sisters alerted the campus police at 10:30 p.m. Organizing themselves into a volunteer search team, the Tri-Delts began checking with local taxi

Ruth Baumgardner

drivers, railroad station and bus personnel, and at all of the campus hangouts. By the next day, May 6, everyone in Ohio and in the neighboring states were on the lookout for Ruth Baumgardner. She was five-feet, five-inches tall, weighed 110 pounds, had blue-gray eyes, and blonde hair with an irregular lighter streak on the left side.

The mystery of Ruth's disappearance only deepened as authorities looked closer into Ruth's last hours before she went missing. Someone, presumably Ruth herself, had carefully left her dorm room key on the back corner of the Austin Hall staircase, between the second and third floors. Her red Dodge convertible, an early graduation present, was found in its regular parking spot, with the key in the ignition. Ruth's single room was left in perfect order —-- which, in itself, was a little unusual, since Ruth was known for being a bit messy —-- with her watch and sorority pin left on top of the dresser. The robe and pajamas she had worn the night before were hanging in the closet. Either she had not slept in her bed or she had made the bed before leaving. Her alarm clock, which had been set for 6:00 a.m., had apparently been turned off that morning, suggesting that Ruth had risen at 6:00 a.m. and had left the dormitory without anyone seeing her. It seemed likely, based on an inventory of the clothing left hanging in her closet, that she was wearing a brown suit and hat and brown lace-up "ghillie" shoes (like ballet shoes, but made from leather) and was carrying a handbag when she left.

The initial theory of her disappearance —-- which was strongly embraced by her frightened parents —- was that Ruth had suffered an attack of amnesia and was wandering somewhere along Ohio's back roads. She had apparently been very stressed lately, one of her friends told the police, about making sure that she had all the college credits needed to graduate. This was echoed in a letter that she had recently written to her father, a wealthy manufacturer, in which she stated, "she had so many things to do she did not know how she was going to do them, and that she was extremely tired."

Unfortunately, though, the amnesia explanation didn't fit with the clues that began to accumulate as the multiple state search for the young woman continued. Mrs. Wilmer Smith, who lived near the Olentangy River, next to the Ohio Wesleyan campus, reported hearing three eerie screams between 2:00 a.m. and 3:00 a.m. on the morning of May 5. She said that they sounded like the cries of a hysterical person.

A barber in Worthington, Ohio, reported seeing a woman that matched Ruth's description about noon on the same day. He said that she was pacing back and forth on Grandview Road and he recalled that she was wearing a brown suit.

Two women reported seeing Ruth in Zanesville that day, shortly before noon. Mrs. Edward Hiehle and Mrs. R.A. Earick said that she was hitchhiking, apparently with a young man whom they described as looking like another college student.

H.B. Matthews, who worked in a signal tower for the Baltimore & Ohio Railroad in Grafton, reported seeing a girl who matched Ruth's description hitchhiking alone on the afternoon of Thursday, May 6.

Several days later, traveling salesman, Joe W. Smith, reported to the authorities that he had given a ride to a young man and a girl who looked like Ruth Baumgardner in Nashville, Tennessee, on May 7. Smith told the police that he had taken the pair to Memphis and the young man had called his companion "Ruth."

Other sightings of Ruth were reported in Ohio, Pennsylvania, New York, Tennessee, California, and New Mexico. They were all followed up but as one clue after another was checked out and then discarded, suspicions began to grow that Ruth had arranged her own disappearance. The alleged sightings of Ruth with a young male companion helped to foster such conclusions. But why would Ruth have done such a thing, and in such a manner, especially so close to her graduation? As far as anyone knew, Ruth was happily engaged to a long-time boyfriend, Harry "Bud" Moore, back home in Lakewood,

Ohio, and none of her friends were aware that she was seeing anyone else. Moreover, it seemed likely that Ruth could not have had more than $5 in her purse when she vanished, which was hardly the sum needed to start a new life and identity.

Alternate theories, like Ruth being the victim of a kidnapping or an accident, had no evidence for or against them, despite what the newspapers suggested. An exhaustive search, especially of the quarries that were popular as swimming holes with local college students, failed to turn up any trace of the young woman. There seemed to be nothing in her personal life to suggest that Ruth had any enemies on campus.

The search continued for many days, eventually stretching out into the summer months. Her heartbroken parents hired the Burns Detective Agency to look into the case, but even these experienced operatives failed to turn up any hard evidence about Ruth's fate. All the attempts to find Ruth Baumgardner eventually came to a halt.

To this day, no one knows what became of the lovely young coed and her story remains one of the most heartbreaking tales in the annals of the unsolved in Ohio —– and in America.

1939: *Sea Dragon*
The Last Adventure of
Richard Halliburton

Today, there are few people who remember the name of Richard Halliburton. But I can assure you that a trip to your local used bookstore will uncover a number of titles that he wrote about his adventures in exotic places in the 1930s.

Halliburton was a true adventurer. Known for his wanderlust and his extraordinary travels that took him to far-flung places, he entranced the American public. They thrilled to his exciting stories, which were published in a syndicated newspaper column and, later, in all those dusty books that you'll find still on the shelves of the many old bookshops. The public was invited to travel along with him as he braved the air, land, and ocean.

Halliburton was a beloved character during his lifetime, but it would be his disappearance in 1939 that would make him a legend.

Richard was born in Brownsville, Texas, in 1900. His father, Wesley, a civil engineer and real estate speculator, and his mother, Nelle, had a second son, Wesley, Jr. in 1903. The family moved to Memphis, where the brothers, who were not close, spent their childhood. Richard's favorite subjects in school were history and geography and he showed an aptitude for the violin, as well as for golf and tennis. In 1915, though, he developed a rapid heart condition that kept him in bed for almost four months. Two years later, his brother died following an apparent bout of rheumatic fever.

Richard attended Memphis University School for Boys and he later graduated from Lawrenceville School, a New Jersey prep school, where he was chief editor of the newspaper. He also graduated from Princeton University, where he was on the editorial board of *The Daily Princetonian* and chief editor of *The Princetonian Pictorial Magazine*. He excelled in courses in writing and public speaking and considered a career as a lecturer —– but then his thirst for adventure got in the way of those plans.

In 1919, Halliburton left college for a short time and took a position as an ordinary seaman on the freighter *Octorara*, which was bound from New Orleans to England. He toured historic places in London and Paris and then returned to Princeton to finish his education. His travels had inspired a lust for more travel, and he developed a love for bachelorhood, adventure, and the thrill of the unknown. To earn a living, he decided that he would write about his adventures —– a plan that his father greatly disapproved of. He told Richard to get the wanderlust out of his system and then return to Memphis and adjust his life to "an even tenor."

Richard disagreed. He later wrote, "I hate that expression and as far as I am able, I intend to avoid that condition. When impulse and spontaneity fail to make my way uneven then I shall sit up nights inventing means of making my life as conglomerate and vivid as possible…. And when my time comes to die, I'll be able to die happy, for I will have done and seen and heard and experienced all the joy, pain and thrills—any emotion that any human ever had—and I'll be especially happy if I am spared a stupid, common death in bed…"

Halliburton published his first book in 1925. It was called *The Royal Road to Romance* and it became an immediate bestseller. Two years later he published *The Glorious Adventure*, which retraced Ulysses' adventures throughout the Classical Greek world as recounted in Homer's *The Odyssey*. In 1929, Halliburton published *New Worlds to Conquer*, which included tales of his swimming the length of the Panama Canal, his re-tracing of the conquest of Mexico by Cortez, and his role as a cast-away-like Robinson Crusoe on the island of Tobago.

Today's reader will likely not believe me, but I promise you that if you do find a copy of any of Halliburton's books and go to the trouble of buying them, you will not be disappointed. They are a time capsule of the era, but they are also very entertaining.

In 1930, Halliburton hired aviator Moye Stephens with a handshake —– for no pay, but unlimited expenses —– to fly him around the world in an open cockpit biplane. The modified Stearman C-3B was named "The Flying Carpet" and it became the title of his 1932 bestseller. The two men embarked on "one of the most fantastic, extended air journeys ever recorded" taking 18 months to circumnavigate the globe and visit 34 countries.

They took off on Christmas Day 1930, making stops along the way, from Los Angeles to New York. After landing in New York, the *Flying Carpet* was crated up and loaded onto the ocean liner *Majestic* for the trip to England, where their extended journey began. They flew first to France, then Spain, Gibraltar, and on to Morocco. They crossed the Atlas Mountains and flew across the Sahara to Timbuktu, getting permission to use fuel caches that belonged to Standard Oil. The pair then flew eastward and spent several weeks with the French Foreign

Legion in Algeria and then continued to Cairo and Damascus, with a side trip to the stone city of Petra.

In Persia (now Iran), they met the celebrated German aviatrix Elly Beinhorn, whose plane had been forced down because of mechanical problems. They were able to assist her and then worked out shared itineraries. Later, Halliburton wrote a foreword to Beinhorn's book, *Flying Girl,* about these and other adventures in the air.

While in Persia, Crown Princess Mahin Banu climbed into the front cockpit for a ride. In neighboring Iraq, the seat was briefly occupied by the young Crown Prince Ghazi, whom they flew over his school yard.

In India, Halliburton visited the Taj Mahal, and in Nepal, the *Flying Carpet* soared close to the summit of Mt. Everest. Richard stood up in the cockpit, nearly causing the plane to stall, and took his first aerial photograph of the mountain. In Borneo, Halliburton and Stephens were met by Sylvia Brett, wife of the White Rajah of Sarawak. They gave her a ride, making her the first woman to fly in that country. At the Rajang River, they took the chief of the Dyak headhunters for a short flight. In return, he gave them several shrunken human heads, which they couldn't refuse but got rid of as quickly as possible. They were the first Americans to fly to the Philippines, and in Manila; the plane was again loaded onto a ship to cross the ocean. They flew the final leg of the journey from San Francisco to Los Angeles.

The around-the-world trip had cost Halliburton over $50,000, plus fuel, but in the first year, the book he called *The Flying Carpet* earned him royalties of $100,000: a remarkably large sum in those Depression-era days.

Early in 1934, the Bell Syndicate Newspapers contracted with newspapers throughout the country to publish Sunday feature stories of history and adventure that were written by Halliburton. The syndicated newspaper columns brought him even more fame and the following year, he published another book, *Seven League Boots,* which was filled with his latest adventures and was perhaps the last great travel book of the period.

Halliburton became one of the most beloved authors of the era, offering colorful and simply- told adventures that appealed to almost everyone. The main device of his books was to attach himself to a famous historic person, or place, and then, performing some type of stunt, he escorted the readers to a different time and setting. In this way he duplicated Hannibal's elephant crossing of the Alps; he emulated Ulysses' adventures in the Mediterranean; he reenacted Robinson Crusoe's island solitude; he retraced the fateful expedition of Cortez to the heart of the Aztec Empire; he lived among the French Foreign Legion in North Africa; he climbed the Matterhorn and Mt. Fujiyama (its first documented winter ascent); he descended twice into the Mayan Well of Death at Chichen Itza; and so on. Occasionally, his travels resulted in trouble with the authorities, such as when he was arrested for taking photos of the guns at Gibraltar; attempting to enter Mecca, which was forbidden to non-Muslims; and hiding in the grounds of the Taj Mahal to experience the sunset in solitude and to swim in the pool facing the famed tomb by moonlight. He was able to connect with the armchair traveler and make them part of the story, which was why the world was shocked when he disappeared in 1939.

By the time that he celebrated his thirty-eighth birthday, Halliburton had sold millions of books and had become fabulously wealthy. He decided to make his birthday a time to celebrate what would become his last romantic adventure.

Halliburton wanted to sail an authentic Chinese junk from Hong Kong to San Francisco, where the World's Fair would be held that summer. It was a distance of 9,000 miles. Richard believed the journey would make a wonderful first chapter for a new book that dealt with the pre-Columbian discovery of America.

In Hong Kong, Halliburton was disappointed with the quality of vessels available for the voyage. Most of them were broken-down old tubs, unseaworthy and unreliable in any heavy storm. Captain John Wenlock Welch and engineer Henry von Fehren were hired to build a special junk for the journey. More than $50,000 was spent on the construction of the ship and its keel, hull, and rudder were specially reinforced for the trip.

Despite the time and money spent on the junk, nervous friends warned Halliburton that the voyage, which he was planning for midwinter, could easily turn out to be disastrous. No ship of that kind had ever made the voyage and the Pacific was erratic at that time of year.

Richard Halliburton and his recreated Chinese junk, Sea Dragon. They both vanished without a trace

Winter storms were known to quickly form and could damage even the sturdiest of ocean liners. Halliburton scoffed at the warnings and bravely told newspapers that a "storm could carry away our ship's main mast and wreck the junk's auxiliary engines and we could still make 70 miles a day on the open sea." He never explained how he planned to do this.

Even though the junk, which Richard christened *Sea Dragon*, was completed in record time, he spent weeks preparing the vessel to face the ocean's unknowns. Superstitions were honored through elaborate ceremonies at the Hong Kong dock where the ship waited. *Sea Dragon* was painted red with white and gold stripes along her rails. Her three mainmast sails were orange, scarlet, and white. The Chinese god of sailors, Tai Toa Fat, was placated by Halliburton with the assistance of several priests. Halliburton personally helped in nailing two huge black eyes on either side of the prow, in the tradition of the Chinese seafarers who gave their ships eyes to see through the storms and mists of the Pacific. Afterward, the priests washed the black eyes with rice wine and beat on drums and gongs. Paper prayers were affixed to the ship's masts. Firecrackers were religiously exploded on the deck. Halliburton and his crew of 13 were finally ready to depart.

On March 4, 1939, *Sea Dragon* sailed out of Hong Kong harbor with 2,000 gallons of water and two tons of food packed into her hold. Fuel drums, enough for 12 days, occupied every bit of remaining storage space.

For the next week, there was silence. Then the crackle of *Sea Dragon's* radio was heard on March 13: "Twelve hundred miles at sea. All's well." A six-day silence followed but on the evening of March 19, another message was heard: "Half-way Midway… arriving there April 5."

On March 23, a heavy storm rocked the Pacific causing 40-foot waves and dangerous conditions. An American ocean liner, *President Coolidge*, was caught in the storm and suffered damage. Many feared for the safety of those aboard Halliburton's junk. That evening, a message was received aboard the *President Coolidge*. The junk's captain, John Welch, radioed his friend Dale Collins, the executive officer of the ocean liner, which was struggling nearby: "Southerly gales, squalls, lee rail under water… wet bunks… hardtack… bully beef… having wonderful time… wish you were here instead of me." Hardtack is the traditional name for a simple ship's biscuit made from flour, water, and salt. Sailors were known to refer to them as "tooth-dullers." Bully beef is another name for corned beef.

It was the last that anyone ever heard from the *Sea Dragon*, her crew, and Richard Halliburton. The U.S.S. *Astoria*, a cruiser, was dispatched to the area and searched more than 15,000 square miles of ocean, looking for the adventurer and his crew. The search was eventually abandoned when no sign of them was found. Dale Collins later stated at a hearing three months later: "If *Sea Dragon* encountered such weather as we did on the night of March 23, and she undoubtedly did, there is small chance that the little craft survived."

No matter how bad things looked, though, the millions of readers who had thrilled to Halliburton's tales of adventure and wanderlust refused to believe that he could so easily vanish off the face of the earth. It wasn't until October 1939 that a chancery court finally declared

Richard Halliburton officially dead, the victim of a Pacific Ocean storm.

His end seemed almost fitting. The great explorer had sailed off into one of his own adventures and simply never returned.

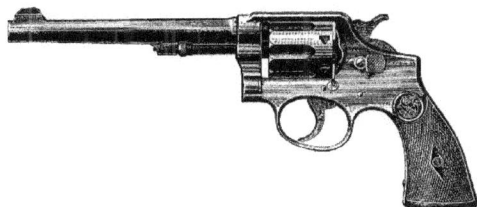

1939: The Girl Genius Who Vanished
The Unsolved Mystery of Barbara Newhall Follett

Nobody may come into this room if the door is shut tight (if it is shut not quite latched it is all right) without knocking. The person in this room if he agrees that one shall come in will say "come in," or something like that and if he does not agree to it he will say "Not yet, please," or something like that. The door may be shut if nobody is in the room but if a person wants to come in, knocks and hears no answer that means there is no one in the room and he must not go in.

Reason: If the door is shut tight and a person is in the room the shut door means that the person in the room wishes to be left alone.

- A 1923 note on the bedroom door of Barbara Newhall Follett, wishing not to be disturbed as she wrote her first novel.

She was 8-years-old at the time.

On December 7, 1939, a young woman who was regarded as a child prodigy after publishing her first novel at the age of 12, walked out of

Barbara Newhall Follett

her house one evening and was never seen again. Like a character from her best-known book —- who disappeared into the woods one day — - Barbara also vanished. She was never seen again, and to this day, her disappearance remains unsolved.

Barbara Newhall Follett was born on March 4, 1914, to critic and editor Wilson Follett and his wife, Helen. She was an exceedingly bright toddler, who was obsessed with words and letters. When she was just three-years-old, she discovered her father's typewriter and, to his delight, became fascinated with the machine. A typewriter, her parents realized, could unleash a flood of thoughts from a gifted child who still lacked the coordination to write in pencil.

By the time she turned five, she was being homeschooled by her mother. This allowed Barbara as much time as she wanted to pursue her creative interests. She began her first book, "The Life of the Spinning Wheel, the Rocking-Horse, and the Rabbit," at the age of eight, brushing aside time with her friends in order to write. While her notes to her family and her close friends were wonderfully warm, she closely guarded her writing time. Neighborhood children who didn't understand this were coldly dismissed. "You don't understand why I have my work to do – because at this particular time, you have none at all," she wrote in a letter to a complaining former playmate.

Her fascination with flowers and butterflies was expressed through stories, poems, and fairy tales. During her childhood years, she also created an imaginary world called "Farksolia," for which she developed a complete language and vocabulary. There was no question —- she was not an ordinary child.

The warning notice quoted at the start of this chapter appeared on her bedroom door the following year and this marked a new project — - young Barbara was attempting a full novel. On some days, she wrote more than 4,000 words. Several years passed and Barbara wrote and rewrote her tale of a girl who ventures into the woods and vanishes into nature.

Finally, in 1926 —- after many drafts, one baby sister, and a manuscript-destroying house fire later —- Barbara had finished her novel. She was now 12-years-old. The book was called *The House Without Windows*. She explained that it was a tale of Eepersip, "a child who ran away from loneliness, to find companions in the woods – animal friends."

It was originally meant to be a vanity publishing project. "Daddy and I are correcting the manuscript," she said, "putting in and taking out, to copy it, and get it all ready to go to the printer."

But Wilson Follett had an idea. He had been working for Knopf in New York and he decided to pass along his daughter's novel to an editor. It was quickly approved for publication, and in February 1927, the glowing reviews began pouring in. *The New York Times* praised the book, as did famed English children's author Eleanor Farjeon, who said, "I don't know what to call this book, except a miracle." The *Saturday Review of Literature* found the book "almost unbearably beautiful." Fame came suddenly for the young girl. She was soon being asked to review the latest A.A. Milne book for the papers. H. L. Mencken wrote to her parents with his congratulations. In his letter, he stated, "you are bringing up the greatest critic we heard of in America."

But one critic was unimpressed.

Anne Carroll Moore wrote in the *New York Herald Tribune*, "I can conceive of no greater handicap for the writer between the ages of nineteen and thirty-nine than to have published a successful book between the age of nine and twelve."

Moore was the creator of the Children's Room at the New York Public Library and one of the most powerful critics of children's literature in America. Her issues were not with Barbara's writing: – "I have only words of praise for the story itself. *The House Without*

Windows is exquisite – but that it was published at all. It is playing with fire. What price will Barbara have to pay for her 'big days' at the typewriter?"

Moore declared that Barbara needed to be outside, playing with children her own age. She should grow up unburdened by early fame. She added, "There are no satisfactions comparable to a free and spacious childhood with a clear title to one's own good name at maturity."

But Barbara was having none of this —— and was angry with Moore's criticisms. She responded in a fiery letter: "It is surely very rash to slam down in the mud a childhood and a system of living that you know nothing about. I am very much amused at the favorable reviews that are being written – I do not take them at all seriously – but I do take seriously an article which distorts into a miserable caricature my living, my education, my whole personality."

To read her book "as I were tyrannized over," Barbara wrote, insulted both her and her parents. "The book," she noted, "is an expression of joy – no more."

Keep in mind, Barbara was 12 when she wrote this reply.

The reviews were still rolling in for her first book when Barbara announced her second —– she was going "to become a pirate" and take to the sea for her next book. She had long dreamed of being a ship's crewman. It didn't matter that she had just turned 13. Her parents found a lumber schooner to take her aboard as a passenger who insisted on doing chores.

Following a journey up to Nova Scotia, Barbara's next book, *The Voyage of the Norman D.*, was written at a frenetic pace. The voyage took place in July, the final manuscript was in Knopf's hands by November, and the book was in stores by the following March. This was the kind of work being completed by an adult in the making, not a child prodigy.

The book's confidence stunned reviewers on both side of the Atlantic. Barbara was no longer a cute "child authoress" —– she was a real writer. *The Saturday Review* featured her book alongside Dorothy Parker's latest, declaring it "a fine, sustained, and vivid piece of writing." And yet, the *New York Times* couldn't resist pointing out,

"Miss Barbara Newhall Follett celebrated her fourteenth birthday just twelve days before the publication."

Regardless, Barbara's future looked bright on the surface. Inside, though, her heart was breaking, and her career was nearly over.

In the week before the publication of Barbara's second book, her father, Wilson, delivered devastating news. In the midst of a mid-life crisis, he had decided to leave his family for a younger woman. Barbara was devastated by her father's betrayal. Barbara pleaded with her father to stay but there was nothing that could change his mind. At the moment of her greatest triumph, she was abandoned by the man who had fostered her ambitions.

Wilson left them with little money. At first, Helen tried to be optimistic and proposed that she and Barbara go on an adventure. They'd take their typewriters to sea, sail to Tahiti, and write books. But by September 1929, Barbara found herself stranded and alone with family friends in Los Angeles. She was so unhappy that she fled to San Francisco, hid out in a hotel, and wrote poetry. But she'd been reported as a runaway, and when the police broke into her room, they narrowly prevented her from escaping out the window.

"I loathe Los Angeles," Barbara told reporters and the story made national news.

Helen and Barbara were eventually reunited in New York, but their financial situation was so drastic in March 1930 that Barbara, now 16, had to find work. There was little to be found. The Wall Street Crash had happened just a few months before and she and her mother were not the only people who were in desperate straits. After a course in shorthand and business typing — - which she called "a decidedly more tawdry use of its magic" —- she began working as a secretary.

She kept writing, though. She got up early every morning before she had to take the subway to work so that she could spend time working on a new book, *Lost Island.*

By 1934, she had finished the book and had written another, a brisk travelogue about the Appalachian Trail called *Travels Without a Donkey.* But worn down by six years without the encouragement of her father, or from an editor, the writing finally stopped. Barbara was burned out and she settled down into an ordinary life.

She found a kindred soul in an outdoorsman named Nickerson Rogers and they eloped. For a while, things were peaceful for her. The couple settled in Brookline, Massachusetts, which seemed to give Barbara too much time to think. The young woman who was once "America's next great novelist" had no high-school degree, no work, and was a teenage bride. She wanted to be happy and was willing to seek out a distraction. She backpacked through Europe, and between secretarial jobs in New York and Boston, she discovered dance classes. She took some summers off to travel west for dances classes at Mills College, which she loved. It was a taste of the college life that she had never been allowed to have.

But the peaceful times wouldn't last. Returning to her husband in Brookline in November 1939, she was shaken even worse than she had been by her father's abandonment —– she discovered her husband had been cheating on her.

She wrote to a friend, "There is somebody else. I had it coming to me, I know." Her despair was so deep that she could only rest with the help of sleeping pills. Soon, her letters grew darker. "On the surface, things are terribly, terribly calm, and wrong... I still think there is a chance that the outcome will be a happy one, but I would have to think that anyway, in order to live, so you can draw any conclusions you like from that."

Barbara's life was once again in chaos and the couple began to argue constantly. After one argument on the evening of December 7, 1939, Barbara walked out of the house with $30 in her wallet.

She never came back.

Nick Rogers waited two weeks before reporting his wife's disappearance to the police, and another four weeks before filing a missing person's report. Hospitals and morgues were contacted, hotels were searched, but there was no sign of her. A public plea was sent out, but because no one recognized the name "Barbara Rogers," as opposed to her more famous maiden name, the call for information went largely unnoticed.

It wasn't until 19636, when Helen co-authored a slim academic essay for *The Atlantic* —– "To A Daughter, One Year Lost" —– that the public realized that Barbara was missing at all.

Helen, belatedly discovering how little that Nick Rogers had looked for Barbara, began pressing the authorities to look for her daughter. By then, however, more than 13 years had passed. "There is always foul play to be considered," she told Brookline's police chief. To Nick, she was blunter: "All this silence on your part looks as if you have something to hide concerning Barbara's disappearance. You cannot believe I shall sit idle during my last few years and not make whatever effort I can to find out whether she is alive or dead, whether, perhaps, she is in some institution suffering from amnesia or a nervous breakdown."

Barbara before she vanished. Her adult life never lived up to the dreams she had as a child

Helen vowed to continue the search and while there was renewed interest in the story for a time —– as well as in Barbara's work —– it quickly faded. There was still no trace of the missing woman.

To this day, she has never been found.

Those who knew her best came to believe that Barbara simply decided to follow the storyline of her books —– in which the characters ran off to the woods, or left on a voyage across the sea, when their troubles became too great. She'd simply had enough of her current reality, they thought, and decided to create a new one from her own imagination.

Her work had always been her escape. Her mysterious disappearance echoed the final words of *The House Without Windows*, when the lonely girl vanished forever into the woods.

She would be invisible forever to all mortals, save those few who have minds to believe, eyes to see. To these she is ever present, the spirit of Nature – a sprite of the meadow, a naiad of the lakes, a nymph of the woods.

We'll probably never know what happened to the young genius who just wanted to write books. We're left with the mystery of whatever happened to her —- and the mystery of what books she might've someday written if her life had not gone awry.

1944: Glenn Miller's Last Moonlight Serenade

On December 15, 1944, Major Glenn Miller, one of the most famous band leaders in the world, climbed into a single-engine Norseman aircraft at a military airstrip near Bedford, England, some 40 miles north of London. He was scheduled to perform with his acclaimed U.S. Army Air Forces Band in a Christmas concert for allied troops the next week in liberated Paris. At the last moment, he asked for a change in his orders so that he could arrive in France before the band. A chance encounter at an officer's club on the night of December 14 had earned Miller a spot on the small plane. The pilots were defying rain and fog to make the short hop across the English Channel.

Always nervous about flying, Miller expressed doubts about the single-engine plane. "Where the hell are the parachutes?" Miller jokingly asked his fellow passenger, Colonel Norman Baesell.

"What's the matter, Miller? You want to live forever?" Baesell laughed in reply.

A few minutes later, the Norseman took off into the dense fog and vanished forever.

Not until December 24 -- after Miller's wife back home in New Jersey had been notified -- was it announced that the famous band leader was missing. Preoccupied with the final days of the war in Europe, the American high command assumed that the Norseman had crashed into the channel when its wings iced over or its engine failed. No search was ever launched, and no inquiry was ever made into the tragedy.

Glenn Miller

Friends and fans of the popular swing musician were not satisfied by the official dismissal. Wild rumors soon circulated that Miller's plane had been shot down by the Germans and that the horribly crippled and disfigured band leader was hidden away in a hospital somewhere.

Or that he had been killed in a Paris brothel.

Or that Miller had been assassinated as a German spy.

And from there, the stories got even wilder.

Absurd stories aside, Glenn Miller's disappearance has never been truly explained and legends and conspiracies about the lost musician continue to thrive today.

Glenn Miller was born in Clarinda, Iowa, on March 1, 1904. He went to grade school in North Platte, Nebraska, and in 1915, his family moved to Grant City, Missouri. Around this time, he was given his first trombone and began performing in the town orchestra. In 1918, the Millers moved again, this time to Fort Morgan, Colorado, where Miller started high school. During his senior year, he became interested in a new style of music called "dance band music," which he enjoyed so much that he encouraged some of his classmates to start a band with him. By the time Miller graduated from high school in 1921, he had decided to become a professional musician.

In 1923, Miller entered the University of Colorado, but spent most of his time away from school, going to auditions and playing any gigs that he could get. He dropped out of school after failing three out of five classes one semester and decided to concentrate on his musical career.

Miller began touring with several musical groups and, in 1926, landed a spot in Ben Pollack's band in Los Angeles. During this time, he had the opportunity to write several musical arrangements of his own. In 1928, when the band arrived in New York, he sent for and married his college sweetheart, Helen Burger. He was a member of Red Nichols' orchestra in 1930 and, thanks to Nichols, also played in the pit bands of two Broadway shows. His band mates included clarinetist Benny Goodman and drummer Gene Krupa. Both of them would go on to earn their place as music legends, along with Glenn Miller.

Miller earned a living as a freelance trombonist in several bands until November 1929, a vocalist named Red McKenzie hired Miller to play on two records that are now considered to be jazz classics: "Hello, Lola" and "If I Could Be With You One Hour Tonight."

In the middle 1930s, Miller worked as a trombonist and arranger for the Dorsey Brothers Orchestra and for several other groups. By 1937, the slender, serious-looking young man with rimless glasses had formed his own band. It failed to distinguish itself, though, and soon broke up. Discouraged, Miller returned to New York. He realized that he needed to develop a unique sound, unlike the other big bands of the day, and got to work putting together a new orchestra.

In the fall of 1939, the new Glenn Miller band went on national radio and before long, young people from coast to coast were dancing to such hit tunes as "In the Mood," "Pennsylvania 6-5000," "Tuxedo Junction," "String of Pearls," and what became Miller's signature song, "Moonlight Serenade." The band became one of the biggest attractions in the music business and in 1941, made the first of two movie appearances in *Sun Valley Serenade*. Miller's recording of the film's hit song "Chattanooga Choo-Choo," sold a million copies and earned him a gold record from RCA Victor.

Eight months after America entered World War II, Miller gave up his phenomenal success and volunteered his services to the military. In the fall of 1942, he was given the commission of captain in the U.S. Army. Seeking out other musicians that had been drafted or were volunteering for service, Miller formed the U.S. Army Air Forces Band, which began by playing for cadets training at Yale University.

When he introduced swing music into marches, a senior officer reminded him that John Phillips Sousa had been good enough for soldiers in World War I. Miller asked him, "Are you still flying the same planes that you flew in the last war, too?"

The military accepted swing.

The band toured the country and raised millions of dollars for war-bond drives, but Miller never felt like he was doing enough. Finally, in June 1944, he got permission to take the band overseas to play for troops stationed in England. Over the next five and a half months, the band played 71 shows —– they were the biggest morale booster for the men, one general said, "next to a letter from home." The shows were broadcast over the Allied Expeditionary Forces Network and were heard by soldiers throughout Britain and Europe. Two of Miller's biggest fans were Princesses Elizabeth and Margaret, who listened to the broadcasts nightly.

In December, he was ordered to take the show to France. On December 15, Miller, who was now a major, took off for Paris, where he would be playing for soldiers in the recently liberated city. The Norseman took off that night and vanished into the sky.

No trace of the aircrew, passengers, or plane has ever been found.

Since Miller's disappearance, there have been many theories about what happened that night. Buddy DeFranco, who was the leader of Miller's band in the 19370s, told biographer George T. Simon that he heard theories about what happened to Glenn all the time. DeFranco said, "If I were to believe all those stories, there would have been about 12, 458 people there at the field in England seeing him off on that last flight!"

Miller's plane may have been bombed accidentally by Royal Air Force aircraft over the English Channel after an abortive air raid on Siegen, Germany. There is a clear record of 138 Lancaster bombers, short on fuel, that jettisoned approximately 100,000 incendiaries in a designated area before landing, per standing orders. It's possible that one of those bombs may have struck Miller's Norseman. The logbooks of Royal Air Force navigator Fred Shaw recorded that he saw a small single-engine plane spiraling out of control and crashing into the water. If this was indeed Miller's plane, the RAF crews were not at fault because the Norseman would have had to have strayed off course and into the designated drop area.

However, a second source, while acknowledging the possibility, casts doubt on this version, citing other RAF crew members flying the same mission who stated the drop area was in the North Sea, a more likely location.

In 1983, the band leader's younger brother, Herb Miller, stated that Glenn did not die in a plane crash over the English Channel, but from lung cancer in a hospital. He said that Glenn did board the Norseman that night but when it landed a half hour later, he was taken to a military hospital where he died the following day. Herb Miller said that he fabricated the story of the plane crash so that his brother would die as a hero and not "in a lousy bed." Because there was no crash, there was no need for a search and inquiry. Both the pilot of the Norseman and Miller's fellow passenger, Colonel Baesell, had died later in battle with the Germans. Supporting this story were rumors that Glenn seemed depressed, irritable, and exhausted in his last few months of life. Some of his band members claimed that he had lost weight and that his tailor-made uniforms no longer fit him correctly.

Herb Miller's version of his brother's death has never been substantiated. For it to have been true, it would have required the cooperation of the military, doctors, numerous flight and medical personnel, and the crew of the Norseman. It seems unlikely that the secret could have been that well-kept for nearly 40 years. Miller's story also couldn't explain the fact that the Norseman vanished and was never listed on any airplane manifest again.

Another theory about Miller's death is more chilling than any of the others. A former member of Eisenhower's personal staff, journalist Lt. Colonel Hunton Downs, also claimed that Miller wasn't killed in a plane accident over the English Channel in 1944. He stated that this was a story made up by the U.S. government because they didn't want the public to know how he really died. Downs suggested that Miller, who spoke German, had been enlisted by Eisenhower to serve as a secret envoy, to try and convince some German officers to end the war early and offer terms of armistice. Hitler allegedly found out about this effort and Miller was captured, and eventually taken to a Nazi-controlled brothel in Paris, where he was interrogated, tortured, and killed. Reportedly, some American soldiers saw Miller's body dumped there. The cover-up was intended to save embarrassment about his body being found in a brothel and the failed nature of the secret allied operation.

The true story of Glenn Miller's disappearance will probably never be known. He vanished during the final days of World War II, but his legacy lives on with audiences who are far too young to remember when his music was at the top of the charts but still love to swing to the smooth sounds of Glenn Miller.

1945-1950: The Mystery of the Long Trail

The historic Green Mountains of Vermont are a part of the most beautiful stretch of wilderness in New England. The warm weather months make this a place of tranquil shade, soaked in a warm array of greens and browns. In the autumn, the hills come alive with a symphony of breath-taking color. But at other times, a darker side emerges from these rugged mountains. It occurs when the shadows grow long and the snow starts to fall, covering the landscape in a monotonous blanket of white.

There are places, like the most eerie corners of these mountains, where the fabric of time and space is stretched a little bit thinner. Places where things that are not supposed to do so, slip through into our world. And where things from our world sometimes slip out —— never to be seen again.

Odd secrets hide in the Green Mountains near Bennington, Vermont. The area has always had a reputation for strangeness. It is a spot that is remote and often inaccessible and since colonial days, it has been plagued with reports of mysterious lights and sounds, Bigfoot sightings, UFOs, ghostly tales and unknown creatures. Master of weird fiction H.P. Lovecraft based his space alien story "The Whisperer in Darkness," near Glastonbury. The local Native Americans shunned the region and according to tradition, used it as a place to bury the dead.

And while stories of spook lights and Indian curses may stretch the limits of credulity, there is no denying that nearby Glastonbury Mountain ——- and its scenic Long Trail ——- has been the site of a great American mystery. This unsolved puzzle involves the disappearance of a number of people who have never been found. Thousands of hours were spent searching for them, but not a single clue was ever discovered.

The string of bizarre disappearances began on November 12, 1945, with the vanishing of Middie Rivers, a 74-year-old hunting and fishing guide. He was reportedly in perfect health and knew the area well, having been a native of the region for most of his life. The day that he disappeared was unusually mild for late fall and Rivers led four hunters up onto the mountain. After spending the day away from camp, they packed up to return with Rivers leading the way. He got a little bit ahead of them, walked around a bend in the trail —— and vanished without a trace. One minute he was there and the next he wasn't. The old man simply disappeared.

The hunters searched frantically and then notified the authorities. State police, soldiers, boy scouts, and local residents combed the woods for hours. They refused to lose hope, knowing that Rivers was an experienced outdoorsman and could survive in the woods, even under icy cold conditions. When no sign of him turned up, efforts were expanded, and the search continued for a month. It was eventually called off, though, and Middie Rivers was never seen again.

Vanished student Paula Welden

Then, on December 1, 1946, Paula Welden —--- a young woman from nearby Bennington College —--- followed Middie Rivers into oblivion. Paula was from Stamford, Connecticut, and was a sophomore at the college. Her father was Archibald Welden, an industrial engineer who was employed by Revere Copper & Brass Co., and she had come to Bennington College because of the excellent reputation that the school had for progressive teaching. Paula was described as blue-eyed, blond, attractive, quiet, soft-spoken, and polite. She was a good student whose favorite subject was botany. Her interest in trees and plants gave her an excuse for solitary walks along the local forest trails.

On the afternoon of Sunday, December 1, she told her roommate, Elizabeth Johnson, that she was going out for a short afternoon hike. Paula changed into outdoor clothing —-- blue jeans, white sneakers, and a red parka with a fur-trimmed hood —-- which was warm, but not particularly suited for the gloomy, rainy day. Elizabeth asked her why she wanted to go out in the mud and cold rain, but Paula was determined, so she didn't argue with her friend.

What happened next is unknown. Against the drab December day, she should have made a conspicuous figure with her bright red coat, but only a handful of people were out to notice her. An attendant at a gas station across Route 67A from the Bennington College gates saw her hitchhiking a short distance from the gas station at around 3:15 in the afternoon.

Paula was picked up on the road by Louis Knapp, a contractor who lived about 15 miles east of the college in the direction of Glastonbury Mountain and the start of the Long Trail, which is where Paula intended to go that day. The trail was always busy in the summer months with tourist cottages and cabins, but in the cold weather, it was deserted. Only four families lived along it in the winter months, which made Paula's choice for her hike that day a strange one. Nevertheless, Knapp agreed to take her up the highway as far as to where he lived in Woodford Hollow, just three miles from the start of the Long Trail. When Knapp stopped the car at his driveway, Paula asked him the distance to the trail and then she got out and started walking. She soon vanished into the mist that had replaced the cold rain of the early afternoon.

About an hour later, she encountered another resident of the area, Ernest Whitman, a night watchman for the *Bennington Banner* newspaper. Whitman was surprised to see a young girl sloshing along the desolate road, especially since it was growing dark. He spoke with Paula for a few minutes and gave her directions. After that, other witnesses spotted her on the trail itself and remembered her distinctly because she had been wearing a bright red parka.

They were the last ones to see her alive.

Paula had a shift waiting tables at the dining hall that night, but she did not show up for it. She also didn't appear at her usual bedtime. Although worried, Elizabeth Johnson decided to wait until morning to report her absence. After a sleepless night, she left her room at dawn and made her way to the Dean's residence. The Dean offered the opinion that Paula might have made a last-minute application to stay away from the college all night, but a quick check of the sign-out records showed that this was not the case. The two of them hurried across campus to the home of Bennington president Lewis Webster Jones. He had no solution to the problem, except to make a careful telephone call to the Welden home in Stamford to see if Paula had unexpectedly turned up there. She hadn't. Jones's next call was to Sheriff Clyde W. Peck, who came straight to the college. He was later joined by veteran Vermont State Police detective Almo Fronzoni.

Fronzoni took charge of the investigation. He searched Paula's dorm room and saw no sign that she had taken any extra clothing or money with her. He checked the local bus and train stations, but with no luck. He questioned Paula's friends and found that she had not told anyone where she was going that day. Aside from Elizabeth Johnson, no one knew that she had left the campus.

By this time, the newspaper was covering the disappearance and night watchman Ernest Whitman contacted the authorities. Fronzoni also heard from driver Louis Knapp, the gas station attendant who had spotted her, as well as witnesses on the Long Trail. A search was immediately started along the trail, led by game wardens, sheriff's deputies, search dogs, and volunteers. They walked the trail, scoured the woods, and searched the empty cabins along the trail.

By Tuesday, December 3, hundreds of additional volunteers had joined the hunt. Classes at Bennington College were suspended and nearly 400 students took part in the effort. Faculty members, students from nearby Williams College, Boy Scouts, trappers, woodsmen, and locals joined deputies and law enforcement officials as they scoured the area. There was also a contingent of volunteers from Revere Copper & Brass, as well as mountain climbers from the National Guard. The U.S. Navy even sent nine Marine search planes from the air base at Squantum and a helicopter was brought in to fly low over isolated areas. The army of searchers sloshed along in long lines through the woods and foothills. The weather was cold and wet, and everyone was soaked to the skin.

The Bennington student body, along with Paula's family and friends, put together a $5,000 reward fund for information. The offer of a reward brought in even more volunteers and the search continued for two full days. On December 5, though, it was called off thanks to overhanging clouds that had grounded the search planes, followed by several inches of snow that covered the landscape —- and concealed any clues that might have been left behind.

By now, everyone was exhausted. They were sure that Paula had not left on her own —- she had been murdered or kidnapped, they believed. Many feared she was already dead, but her family refused to give up hope. Paula's parents insisted that she had been kidnapped. But with no evidence of this, the FBI refused to get involved. When the official refusal became public knowledge, well-known novelist Dorothy Canfield Fisher, a Bennington College trustee, wrote letters to J. Edgar Hoover and several political figures in Washington. "Paula is not in these hills," she stated. "She was taken away against her will."

Many determined appeals were made, but all were turned down. The governor appealed to both New York and Connecticut for skilled investigators to assist them but only Connecticut responded, sending two state detectives who had succeeded with puzzling missing person's cases in the past. Their laborious investigations still failed to produce the missing girl. One of the investigators, Robert Rundle, agreed with Detective Fronzoni when he had declared Paula's case to be the most perplexing of his career. "We have not a single clue," Rundle admitted.

Paula was simply gone. They found not a single clue —- no blood, no clothing, nothing. In the end, helicopters, aircraft, bloodhounds and as many as 1,000 people combed the mountain for the young woman but no evidence was found. She was simply never seen or heard from again.

The strange disappearances in the area weren't over.

On December 1, 1949, three years to the day of Paula Welden's disappearance, an elderly man named James E. Tetford also vanished near Bennington. Tetford had been visiting relatives in northern Vermont, and his family had placed him on a bus in St. Albans for the journey back to Bennington, where he lived at the Vermont Soldiers' Home.

For some reason, though, he never arrived. Where he actually disappeared is just part of the mystery. Witnesses recalled him getting on the bus and several were sure that he was still on board at the stop before Bennington. At some point, though, he apparently got off along the road. He left no clues behind. No one saw him disappear, including the bus driver, but he was never seen again.

Another disappearance took place near Bennington in October 1950. An eight-year-old boy named Paul Jepson vanished from the town dump, where his parents were caretakers. Paul was waiting in the family's truck while his mother relocated some pigs. She was away for only a moment but when she looked up, the boy was gone. It was between 3:00 and 4:00 in the afternoon and was a sunny day. Paul was wearing a bright red jacket and should have been easily spotted —— but he was nowhere to be seen. Mrs. Jepson searched frantically and called for him and after a little while, went for help.

Volunteers assembled to start another search and hundreds of local residents joined police officers in combing through the dump, walking the roads, and hunting in the mountains. They even instituted a "double check" system so that after one group checked an area, another would follow them and check it again. But even with the search parties and aircraft brought in by the Coast Guard, there was no sign of the boy.

The only clues came from a group of bloodhounds that were borrowed from the New Hampshire State Police. The dogs managed to follow Paul's scent, only to lose it at the junction of East and Chapel Roads, just west of Glastonbury Mountain. According to locals, this was the same spot where Paula Welden had last been seen. The search was eventually called off and another person was lost to the mountains.

About two weeks later, on October 28, the mountain claimed another victim.

Her name was Freida Langer and she was on a hike that day with her cousin, Herbert Elsner. The 53-year-old Langer was described as a rugged outdoorswoman with years of experience in the woods and skilled with firearms. She was also very familiar with the region and, like Middie Rivers before her, was an unlikely person to simply get lost or to wander off the trail. Somehow, though, she managed to disappear.

At about 3:45 p.m., Freida slipped and fell into the edge of a stream, soaking her boots and pants. Since she and her cousin were only about a half-mile from camp, she said that she would run back and change clothes and then catch up with him. Elsner sat down to wait but after

Frieda had been gone for a while, he began to grow concerned. After an hour, he started back up the trail to their camp. When he got there, he discovered that no one had seen her come back and from the looks of her gear, she had never returned to change her wet clothing. He immediately contacted the authorities.

Alarmed by another disappearance in the same area, local officials quickly launched another massive search. Again, hundreds of volunteers combed the woods, tracing and re-tracing what should have been Freida's footsteps between the stream where she had fallen and the camp.

On November 1, General Merritt Edson, the state director of public safety, started a second search. He vowed that they would find Freida, dead or alive, and he ordered his men to keep searching around the clock. More helicopters, aircraft, officers, and volunteers were brought in, but once again, they found no clues. Another search was started on November 5 and the volunteers divided up into groups of 30. They lined up and marched side by side along trails and through the forest, scanning every inch of ground. There was still no sign of the missing woman.

On November 11, the largest search so far was organized. Over 300 volunteers joined police officers, fire fighters, and military units as they scoured the woods. A few days later, Frieda's family gave up hope and the search was called off.

Strangely, though, Freida Langer was the only person to go missing on the Long Trail that was later found.

On May 12, 1951, seven months after she had vanished, her body was discovered lying in some tall grass near the flood dam of the Somerset Reservoir. It was nowhere near the spot where she had vanished and impossibly, this site had been thoroughly searched while the hunt for the missing woman was being carried out. The volunteers swore that the body had not been there during the initial search. The site where the corpse was found was an open and clearly visible area and it was simply impossible that the searchers could have missed it. Unfortunately, no clues could be gathered from Frieda's body and no cause of death was ever determined by the medical examiner. Her remains were too decomposed, and the newspaper stated they were in "gruesome condition."

Could someone have placed the body there after the search was concluded? Rumors swirled about a killer who was hiding on Glastonbury Mountain, claiming victims that were chosen from those who vanished into the woods. In those days, the term "serial killer" had not come to public attention and later examinations of the cases do suggest that a killer might have been at work. The disappearances occurred over a limited amount of time and all in one central area —- - around the mountain and the Long Trail. Perhaps the killer was someone who came to Vermont each fall, committed his crimes, and then left. That might explain why no one ever became a suspect in the vanishings but why was no body, save for that of Freida Langer, ever found?

What happened in the mountains near Bennington, Vermont, between 1945 and 1950? Was a madman preying on lone hikers or were darker and more mysterious forces at work? Could these people have simply gotten lost or were they carried off against their will, to a place that none of us can imagine?

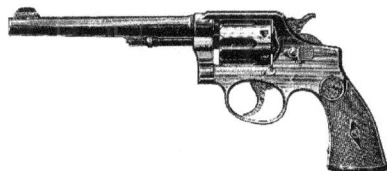

1948: The Vanishing of Virginia Carpenter

On June 1, 1948, a young woman named Virginia Carpenter left her home in Texarkana, Texas, bound for the Texas State College for Women in Denton —- but she never started her classes. To this day, what happened to Virginia remains a baffling mystery and one that will likely never be solved.

Virginia Carpenter, who vanished under mysterious circumstances in 1948

Virginia was only 21-years-old at the time of her disappearance. She was a pretty girl, with lots of friends, a bubbly personality, and ambitions to make something of herself. She had recently enrolled at the Texas State College for Women and planned to become a laboratory technician. She had previously attended Texarkana Junior College and had saved her money to continue her education. She dreamed of pursuing a career in laboratory sciences, but, sadly, those dreams would never come true.

She boarded a train in Texarkana on the afternoon of June 1. She was on her way to the Denton campus to start her summer classes. When she got off the train at the station in Denton, she hailed a taxi, which took her to her college home at Brackenridge Hall. The driver – Edgar Ray "Jack" Zachary – later told police that he arrived at the dorm around 9:30 p.m. When they stopped, Zachary saw two men in a convertible parked in front who called out to the young woman who had just exited his cab. According to the driver, Virginia seemed to know them and replied, "Well, what are y'all doing here?"

Virginia's belongings, packed in a large steamer trunk, had not yet arrived, so she paid Zachary $1 to pick them up from the train station the following morning. Virginia did have suitcases in the taxi, but she told the driver that the two men would assist her with them. She said she knew them. Zachary said the three were talking when he drove away. Virginia gave him a smile and a wave —- and that was the last reported sighting of her.

Virginia never checked into her dormitory that night.

Zachary picked up her trunk at the station the next morning and dropped it off at Breckenridge Hall. The police later found it unopened, sitting by the front door.

The identities of the two men who met her outside the hall remain a mystery. The only information that detectives ever had was a description given by Zachary, who didn't pay much attention to them since Virginia obviously knew them. One was tall, he said, the other was short and stocky. Their car was cream-colored.

On June 4, Virginia's boyfriend, Kenny Branham, contacted Virginia's mother and told her that he had not been able to get in touch with her. Virginia's mother contacted the college and discovered that Virginia had never checked into her dorm and had not attended any of her classes. The following day, she contacted the authorities in Denton and reported that Virginia was missing.

With so little to go on, the police targeted Kenny Branham and Jack Zachary, the cab driver. Branham passed the polygraph tests that were given to him and insisted that Virginia had not run away. She didn't have another boyfriend, no jealous former lovers, and had no reason to run away. She was very excited about starting at the new college. Kenny was also the first to report her missing – why would he have called the police if he had been involved?

The investigation then turned to the cab driver, who was the last person to see Virginia alive. In 1948, Zachary and his wife both claimed that he had arrived at home that night by 10:00 p.m. and that Zachary went back to the hall the next day to drop off the trunk. In 1957, though, the story changed. Zachary's wife —– by then his ex-wife —– told the police that she had lied at the time of the disappearance. She said that he did not actually come home until 2:00 or 3:00 a.m. She had no idea where he had been.

But Zachary was questioned many times during the investigation. Investigators always believed that he was being cooperative. He passed multiple polygraph tests and was never charged. His ex-wife's new statement to the police was never given much weight. He was never really a serious suspect and maintained that he had no idea what happened to Virginia until his death in 1984.

In the weeks and months that followed Virginia's vanishing, alleged sightings of the young woman came in from all parts of South Texas, Louisiana, and Arkansas. One of the few reports that was taken seriously came from a bus ticket agent in DeQueen, Arkansas, who claimed that on the night of June 11, a young woman had gotten off a bus from Texarkana and found a the seat in the station's lobby. She matched Virginia's description. She seemed nervous, walked around, and asked about local hotels. A few minutes later, a man in his mid-twenties with light brown hair came into the station and the two of them left together. A short time later, the agent received a telephone call from an unknown woman.

The caller asked if Miss Virginia Carpenter was in the station.

But this sighting — - along with all the others —- was never confirmed. By late 1948, the case had grown cold. There were simply no clues as to where Virginia could have gone. In 1955, she was legally declared dead.

Over the years, new leads and theories have been few and far between, but the case has not been forgotten altogether. In 1998, the police received a tip from a man in his 70's who claimed to not only know who killed Virginia, but where her body had been buried. He claimed the two men who met her at the dorm that night raped and killed her, then buried her. Police searched the alleged burial site that the man told them about but found no remains. Investigators stated that the two suspects who were named by the informant were both deceased. Their names could not be released to the public.

And there was one other thing —- which may be nothing but a coincidence —- but it's worth mentioning. Virginia grew up in Texarkana, which was the scene of a murder spree in 1946 that has also never been solved. The murderer —- dubbed the "Phantom Killer" —- terrorized the region and has spawned both books and films. And while that case seems to have nothing to do with a young girl's disappearance two years later, there is one intriguing fact about that case that ties it to this one: Virginia Carpenter knew three of the Phantom Killer's victims.

Did it mean anything? Probably not —- but it's those kinds of eerie coincidences that have kept this case alive for nearly 75 years.

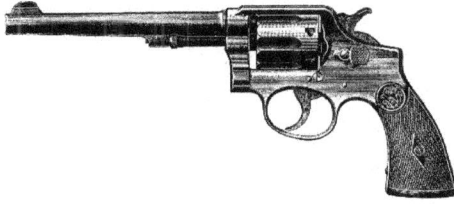

1949: The Vanished Housewife

Many unsolved disappearances are not only mysterious but are also tinged with tragedy and despair. The case of Dorothy Forstein is among the saddest of these stories and is also one of the most unusual in the annals of American crime. To this day, her disappearance has never been solved and, strangely, the case was dropped from newspapers within a week after she vanished. Numerous attempts have been made to remove this case from the history books in recent years, but weird, tantalizing details still remain — – despite the efforts to make sure that her story is forgotten.

Dorothy Forstein vanished from her Philadelphia home in 1949, having been married nine years to her childhood sweetheart, Jules Forstein, who was a clerk for the Philadelphia City Council at the time of their wedding. Dorothy was a happy, outgoing young woman and she became the devoted mother of two children —-- Marcy, an infant, and Merna, age 10, who were children from Jules' first marriage. His wife had died in childbirth not long before he and Dorothy had become reacquainted. Their marriage was a happy one and Forstein's professional life began to prosper when

Dorothy Forstein

he was made a magistrate in 1943. Another child, Edward, was born a short time later.

The Forsteins' idyllic life was shattered on January 25, 1945. Dorothy left the children with neighbors and went out to do some shopping. She reportedly joked with the butcher and chatted with friends as she went about her errands. Later, her neighbor saw her return home and thought that someone was with her, or walking behind her, as she made her way through the late evening shadows to her front door. It was getting dark and the neighbor, Maria Townley, admitted that she didn't look closely at the man who was behind her. It was a safe neighborhood and she never imagined that Dorothy was in trouble.

Just as Dorothy was entering her three-story brick home, the stranger —--- or whomever it might have been that Mrs. Townley saw —--- jumped out of the darkness at her. He began beating her with his fists and some sort of blunt instrument. Dorothy fell to the ground and was pounded into unconsciousness. As she tumbled into the house, her arm dislodged the hall telephone. In those days of live operators, the voice on the other end of the line heard the commotion and quickly summoned the police. The attacker fled at the sound of approaching sirens.

Police officers arrived moments later and found a battered Dorothy on the floor of the hallway. She had suffered a broken jaw, a shattered nose, a fractured shoulder, and a brain concussion. She was rushed to the hospital and when she awakened, she could only weakly explain that, "Someone jumped out at me. I couldn't see who it was. He just hit me and hit me."

Investigators labeled the attack an attempted murder and Captain James A. Kelly of the Philadelphia Detective Bureau began trying to put the pieces together. He concluded that it could only have been someone trying to kill Dorothy since no money, jewelry, or anything else had been taken from the Forstein home. Jules Forstein himself was investigated, but he had an unimpeachable alibi and the children were too young to have been involved. The case was complicated by the fact that Dorothy had no known enemies, and in fact, was one of the most well-liked residents in the neighborhood. The most prevalent theory for the police investigators was that the attacker might have been someone who had appeared in court before Forstein and had assaulted Dorothy for revenge. Every possible lead was investigated but no arrests were ever made.

Dorothy recovered from her injuries but was so shaken by the incident that she was never the same again. Her happy and carefree personality was gone, replaced by an anxious woman who was nervous and upset, jumping at every noise in the house, and checking and rechecking the locks on the doors and windows. She was sure that someone was out to get her —- but who?

Jules Forstein was perplexed. He was sure that no one with whom he had come into contact as a magistrate would bear him enough of a grudge to hurt his wife or his family, and yet he could not explain Dorothy's attack. He seldom left his wife and children alone but on the night of October 18, 1949, he made plans to attend a political banquet. As he was leaving the office, he called his wife to check on her, explaining that he didn't plan to be home too late.

Dorothy replied that everything was fine at home and she joked with him for a moment, finally seeming more like her old self. "Be sure to miss me!" she reportedly said just as she was hanging up.

Tragically, her words would turn out to be prophetic ones.

Around 11:30 p.m., Forstein came home to be greeted by the wails of his two youngest children, Edward and Marcy. They were huddled on the floor, crying and shrieking. Their sister, Merna, was staying at a friend's house, and Dorothy was nowhere to be found. Forstein quickly discovered that the children were crying because their mother was missing.

While surprised that she would have left the children at home by themselves, Forstein assumed that Dorothy was visiting with friends or neighbors. He telephoned for several hours and no one had seen her. Finally, he called Captain Kelly again and the detective soon started his men checking hospitals, morgues, and hotels all over Philadelphia. They worked frantically but no clues were discovered. Kelly went door-to-door in the neighborhood, but no one had seen anything unusual. Wherever she was, Dorothy had left her purse, money, and keys at home. The front door to the house had been locked.

The only lead came from nine-year-old Marcy Forstein, but her story was so wild that detectives at first dismissed it as nothing more than a child's frightened and overactive imagination. She told Captain Kelly that she had been awakened and had left her room to see a man coming up the stairs. He went into her mother's room. The door was cracked open and Marcy stated that she could see Dorothy lying face down on the rug. "She looked sick," the little girl offered.

Then, the man, who she described as wearing a brown hat and brown jacket with something sticking out of the pocket, picked up her mother and put her over his shoulder. Dorothy was wearing red silk pajamas and red slippers at the time. Marcy asked the man what he was doing. He patted her on the head and replied: "Go back to sleep, little one, your mommy has been sick, but she will be all right now."

The man carried Dorothy downstairs and out the front door. He locked the door behind him and vanished. Marcy awakened her brother and they waited together for their father, who arrived home about 15 minutes later. The little girl told the detectives that she had never seen the man before and had no idea who he was.

As bizarre as the story sounded, it was the only possible explanation the police had for Dorothy's disappearance. Nothing was disturbed in the house. There was no sign of a struggle and no indication that anyone else had been there. There was not a single fingerprint in the house that did not belong to the family, and the investigators wondered how a man could have walked down the street with a woman in pajamas over his shoulder without someone noticing. And how had he gotten into the locked house anyway? It seemed impossible that the girl's story could be true and yet it had to be. If no one had spirited the young woman away, then where had she gone? If she had walked away on her own, why had she not taken her purse or keys with her?

Dorothy Forstein was never seen again. There were no leads, no suspects, and no explanations as to who might have taken her or why. Newspapers all over the country, especially in Pennsylvania, carried stories about her disappearance and possible kidnapping, and then, by the end of October, the story largely disappeared, just as Dorothy had done. She simply vanished —- gone without a trace.

For decades, no further word of Dorothy Forstein appeared in print. Then, in 2003, I featured the story of Dorothy Forstein on my website, and soon after, I received a letter from an attorney from representing the Forstein family asking if the story could be removed. The letter was not threatening. It merely made an appeal for the privacy of the family members and asked if I would consider removing it from the internet out of consideration for their grief. I agreed to do so, and I later learned that several sites that had also featured my article on the disappearance had received a similar letter.

Why the secrecy about a 50-year-old disappearance? No one could say and to this day, no one is talking. The recent attention to the case of the missing housewife is almost as mysterious as the original vanishing —– and neither is likely to ever be solved.

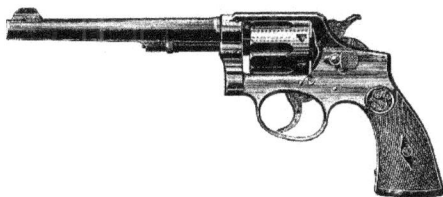

1949: The Missing Starlet
The Disappearance of Jean Spangler

Jean Elizabeth Spangler was one of the many hundreds of pretty, talented girls who came to Hollywood hoping for their big break in the movie business. While she waited for big things to happen, Jean studied, worked hard, and acted regularly in the movies as a bit player and an extra. Jean had been with the Earl Carroll Theatre and Florentine Gardens as a dancer, earning money to support her mother and five-year-old daughter, Christine, who had been born during World War II. Jean's marriage broke up soon after the war ended.

In 1949, Jean was 27-years-old, a tall brunette with an oval-shaped face, large dark eyes, and a wide, sensuous mouth. She had been raised

Hollywood hopeful Jean Spangler

in Los Angeles, attended Franklin High School, and got a job after graduation as a legal secretary, but gave that up to try and make it in the movie business. She was a beautiful young woman but, unfortunately, had little to set her apart from the other beautiful young women who arrived in Hollywood every day —– until the unthinkable happened.

Jean Spangler vanished without a trace one day and the short period of fame that followed turned out to be tragically more than she ever found on the silver screen.

On October 7, 1949, Jean left her home in Los Angeles around 5:00 p.m. Her sister-in-law, Sophie Spangler, lived with Jean and cared for her daughter Christine while working. Before she left, she told Sophie that she was going to meet her former husband to talk about his child support payment that had been due a week before. After that, she was going to work on a movie set. Jean had recently finished a small role in the film *The Petty Girl* and had been in a good mood. She seemed nervous today, though, as she kissed her daughter goodbye and left the house. She was wearing a wool blouse, green slacks, and a white coat.

That was the last time that Jean's family ever saw her alive.

When Jean failed to return home that night, Sophie became worried. Jean had a number of friends and went out a great deal, but she had never before failed to telephone home, much less stay out all night. Jean's mother was visiting family in Kentucky at the time, so Sophie went to the police and filed a missing person report the next morning.

Jean had told Sophie that she was going to work on a movie set after she met with her former husband, but the police checked and found that none of the studios had any work in progress or were even open on the evening of October 7. They next checked into her story about meeting her ex-husband. When the couple of divorced in 1946, Jean's husband, Dexter Benner, had been awarded custody of Christine. A battle ensued and two years later, Christine came to live with Jean. There had been ongoing problems with Benner's child support payments, so meetings between the divorced couple were not uncommon. This time, however, Benner told the police the meeting hadn't happened. Yes, his child support was late, but he told detectives that he hadn't seen his ex-wife in several weeks. His new wife, Lynn, stated that he was with her at the time of Jean's disappearance.

Two days after she vanished, on October 9, Jean's purse was found near the entrance gate to Griffith Park in Los Angeles with both straps on one side torn loose as if it had been ripped from her arm. There was no money inside — -- Sophie told the police that Jean had no money when she left the house, ruling out robbery as a motive in her disappearance --— but it did contain her membership cards in the Screen Actors Guild, the Screen Extras Guild, her driver's license, and a curious note. The note read:

Kirk – can't wait any longer. Going to see Dr. Scott. It will work out best this way while mother is away,

The note ended with a comma and was apparently unfinished. A police handwriting expert was able to determine that the note was in Jean's handwriting.

More than 60 police officers and over 100 volunteers searched the sprawling park, but no other clues were found. Detectives began working to track down any leads they could find about Jean's life and an all-points bulletin was issued. Photographs of the young woman were sent to newspapers and, soon, witnesses began to come forward, disclosing the secrets of the aspiring actress' tangled and complicated life.

One of those witnesses was Hollywood attorney Albert Pearlson, who had employed Jean as a legal secretary for a short time. He told the police that Jean had met Dexter Benner in high school and the mismatched couple became romantically involved. Jean was outgoing and her boyfriend was an introvert. They were married in 1942, shortly after Jean started working at Pearlson's law firm. He told detectives that about six months after the wedding, Jean came to him looking for a divorce. Pearlson tried to talk her out of it, but Jean was insistent. A complaint was filed, but the couple reconciled, and the divorce hearing was removed from the calendar. Benner went into the Army during the war and about six months after he left, Christine was born. Then, after she had broken into the movies as a bit player, Jean began to be seen around the Hollywood nightspots.

In 1944, Benner was discharged from the military and he sent word to Jean that he was coming home. Even though she no longer worked for the attorney, Jean came to Pearlson and pleaded with him for help. She had apparently fallen in love with a first lieutenant in the Air Corps. Benner was under the impression that she had saved the money he had been sending to her, and that she owned a car. However, Jean had spent all the money and had wrecked the car months before. Pearlson agreed to help her and when Benner returned to L.A., Jean met him when he arrived and brought him straight to Pearlson's office to tell him that she wanted a divorce. Benner agreed and custody of Christine was given to him.

Four days later, Jean returned to Pearlson's office with a black eye and a bruised face. She said that her boyfriend had beaten her and threatened to kill her if she ever left him like she had her husband. The lawyer called him and issued him a warning, but he didn't hear from Jean again until a year later. By that time, she had broken off the affair with the Air Corps officer and wanted Pearlson to help her file suit to regain custody of her daughter. She lost the initial suit but sued again in May 1948 and won. Benner decided not to fight the second time after Pearlson convinced him that Jean was a troubled young woman and having Christine might help her.

Other witnesses came forward, including the owner of a store near where Jean lived. A cashier at the store, Lillian Marks, said that Jean had wandered around the place for a few minutes around 5:30 p.m. on October 7, as if waiting, or looking, for someone. She saw no one approach her and she did not notice when Jean left.

The only definite clue that the police had to work with was the mysterious note, but neither Jean's family nor her friends knew anyone by those names. Jean's mother, Florence, returned to Los Angeles and told police that someone named Kirk had picked up Jean at her house twice, but he stayed in his car and didn't come in. Police searched for Kirk and the only person in the Hollywood community that they could think of with that name was Kirk Douglas, who had starred in a recent film, *Young Man With A Horn,* in which Jean had a small part.

Douglas was vacationing in Palm Springs and heard about the disappearance. He called the police and told them he was not the Kirk mentioned in the note. Douglas was interviewed by the head of the investigating team and stated that he had heard the name and that Spangler had been an extra in his new film, but he didn't know her personally. He said that he didn't remember her at all until a friend reminded him that she had been in the film. He told the detectives, "If she's the one I'm thinking about, I remember talking to her. But I never saw her before or since and I never went out with her."

Exhausting their leads in the search for "Kirk," the police turned to finding "Dr. Scott." They contacted and questioned every doctor with the last name Scott in L.A., but none of them had a patient with the last name Spangler or Benner. Attorney Pearlson recalled that Jean had called her Air Corps officer boyfriend "Scotty," but the lawyer said that she not seen him since 1946.

Some of Jean's friends told the police that they suspected that she had been pregnant when she disappeared, and that she had talked to one or two of them about getting an abortion, which was illegal at that time. The police talked with several people who frequented the same nightclubs and bars that Jean did who told them they had heard there was a former medical student known as "Doc," who had said that he would perform abortions for money. Police searched for "Doc" with the idea that Jean had gone to him to have an abortion and died as a result, but they couldn't locate him and no one they questioned would even admit to having met him. The idea of her getting an abortion while her mother was out of town did seem to make sense in conjunction with the note that had been found in her purse, but nothing solid ever came from this line of investigation.

As the investigation was running into dead ends in Los Angeles, tips began coming in from places that kept the investigators busy. Each one of them was checked out over the weeks and months that followed, no matter how flimsy or strange. Rumors had her in Mexico City, the San Fernando Valley, Yuma, Arizona, San Francisco, and Fresno. A psychic contacted the police to and offered her services, and another man claimed that he could locate her body with a radar gadget.

After three weeks, the case seemed to be at a dead end. "The only thing we've been able to find out," one detective wearily told reporters, "is that this girl really got around." Among the many people she "got around" with were a wealthy nightclub owner, a rich playboy, a prominent professor, an assortment of actors and jet-setters, and David "Little Davy" Ogul, a henchman of notorious gang boss Mickey Cohen.

Ogul had last been seen in Palm Springs. Mickey Cohen and his crowd had a long history of vacationing and partying in Palm Springs. Interestingly, Jean was connected to Cohen in other ways, too. She had allegedly once dated Johnny Stompanato, the gangster who would be murdered at movie star Lana Turner's house in 1958. Ogul, who was under indictment for conspiracy, had disappeared two days before Jean did. This led police to investigate the possibility that Jean had left town and met Ogul in Palm Springs, then left California with him. But this was just a guess —- Jean wasn't in Palm Springs and no one admitted to knowing where she'd gone.

Four months later, the case took another turn when a U.S. Customs agent in El Paso, Texas, reported shadowing a woman he thought was Jean Spangler in the company of Davy Ogul and Frank Niccoli, another

Cohen associate who had also been under indictment for conspiracy and who had also vanished a month before Ogul.

An employee at the hotel where the trio stayed also identified Jean Spangler from her photograph. The Customs agent told the Los Angeles cops that they had reason to believe that Jean had left El Paso for Las Vegas.

But was it really her? Who knows?

Eyewitness reports continued to arrive at LAPD headquarters. Jean was still being spotted everywhere —·-- Northern California, Phoenix, Mexico City, and several times in Palm Springs, but all leads led nowhere.

Soon, the case turned ice cold. The police were never able to identify any secret boyfriend, or the mysterious doctor. It seemed likely that at some point, Jean had gotten mixed up in something that probably led to her death. The authorities continued the search and circulated Jean's picture for several years in an unsuccessful attempt to find her, but nothing turned up. Most veteran detectives came to believe that she was dead.

Following Jean's disappearance, a bitter custody battle for Christine began between Dexter Benner and Jean's mother, Florence Spangler. The courts awarded the child to her father, but Florence was given visitation rights, which Benner fought against. He claimed in his suit that Christine had been "abandoned" by her mother and that Florence was a negative influence on her. The case wore on until 1953, when Benner suddenly vanished with his wife and the child. He was never found.

Not every detective gave up on the idea of finding Jean Spangler alive. Nationwide bulletins were still issued for years after she vanished, and Florence Spangler periodically appealed to the press for information about her daughter's fate. She even enlisted the aid of gossip columnist Louella Parsons, who appeared on television with photos of Jean and offered a $1,000 reward for information. But no information ever came and Florence, who hung onto the desperate hope that Jean might still be alive, eventually resigned herself to the fact that her daughter had been murdered.

To this day, Jean Spangler is still listed as a missing person with the Los Angeles Police Department and her case file remains open.

1950: The Vanished Cadet

One of the strangest disappearances of the middle twentieth century was that of a West Point cadet named Richard Colvin Cox. As far as anyone could tell, he vanished without a trace while still on the grounds of the legendary military academy, creating a mystery that remains unsolved to this day.

West Point, America's most esteemed military academy, is located on the banks of the Hudson River, about 50 miles from New York City. It is an impressive gothic-like fortress with slit windows, turrets, and stone walls that give the impression of it being an impregnable place.

The academy has a rich history. During the era of the Revolutionary War, it was a strategic location, with defenses that cost more than $3 million dollars. A huge chain was stretched across the Hudson at West Point, but this and other defensive measures were rendered useless by the treason of its commandant, Major-General Benedict Arnold. He made plans to betray the fortress to the British, but the plot was eventually thwarted.

West Point never again took an active part in a war, but it provided America's armies with its top commanders, as well as a number of notable personalities, including Union and Confederate Civil War officers like Grant, Lee, Hood, Jackson, Longstreet, Sheridan, Sherman, and Stuart, along with George Armstrong Custer, John J.

Pershing, Dwight D. Eisenhower, Douglas MacArthur, and many others.

West Point has become legendary for a reason —- it's not easy, and it's not for the faint of heart. Many of the young men and women who walk through its doors have doubts about that decision during their first year. During that time, the "plebes," as they are known, are the lowest of the low. Hazing by upperclassmen is rough and old-fashioned, as are the scholastic and psychological approaches of the academy. The purpose of West Point has always been to mold young people into field commanders, and the original idea behind the hazing was to blot out a cadet's past personality and turn him or her into a West Pointer.

Every once in a while, a cadet finds himself or herself unable to withstand the pressure and, occasionally, a plebe —- or even an upperclassman —- goes absent without leave from West Point. However, the tradition and honor code of the academy usually brings them back again, ashamed and penitent. Oddly enough, West Point, usually rigid and severe, has always maintained sympathy for such cases and while a punishment is always meted out, cadets are almost always welcome back into the fold.

In 1950, one cadet who successfully weathered the stress of his plebe year at West Point was a young man named Richard Colvin Cox. He was 21-years-old, with blue eyes, a fair complexion, and light brown, close-cropped hair. Instructors and fellow classmates later recalled that Cox was morose during his first year, but not unusually so. His mood hadn't affected his studies and he rated in the upper third of his class. All in all, he seemed to be shaping up into top officer material.

Cox was an exceptional student and a promising young man. Born July 25, 1928, in Mansfield, Ohio, he was the son of Rupert and Minnie Cox and was the youngest of six children. His father died when Richard was 10. There were rumors of suicide, but his death actually resulted from an aggravated diabetic condition. He was a practicing Christian Scientist and received no medical treatment for his illness. Minnie Cox took over her husband's insurance business after his death.

Vanished West Point cadet, Richard Cox

Richard was an exceptional student, president of his senior class, and a member of the National Honor Society, which required good character as well as good grades. While in high school, he told a friend that he no time to participate in sports because he always had an after-school job. During summer vacations, he worked full-time and while on a road crew in Mansfield, he fell and cut his arm badly. Richard went home to get help from his mother, but she refused to call a doctor, due to her religious teachings. The cut became infected and a neighbor finally took Richard to the hospital. He ended up with a prominent scar from the incident.

Although described as "shy," Richard began dating Betty Timmons in high school. By the time that he reached West Point, the two were engaged. Cox spent his 1949 Christmas leave in Mansfield, where he and Betty had been inseparable. They talked constantly of their future together.

Richard had always dreamed of being an Army officer. He was in high school during most of World War II and he enlisted in the Army as soon as he graduated in June 1945. After training in Kentucky, he was assigned to the 27th Constabulary Division, a military police unit in Germany, which had recently surrendered. His unit, located in Coburg, Germany, was assigned to patrol the newly created border between East and West Germany. He took to Army life and spent his free time sightseeing and playing basketball on the Army team. He was an outstanding soldier and rose quickly to the rank of four-stripe sergeant. Cox began thinking of West Point and took the competitive exam for the Point. While he was waiting for the results, he received word from his mother. She had applied for a political appointment for him to West Point and had succeeded in getting it for him. This irritated Cox. He had wanted to get into the academy on his own merits, but as his friends told him, at least he would be able to attend. Cox accepted the appointment and arrived at West Point in September 1948.

Nothing especially remarkable occurred to Richard Cox during his first year at West Point. Already familiar with Army life, he found the regimen at the academy not too difficult. He suffered through his share of hazing, just like the other plebes, and went through a period of depression that was noted by his classmates and instructors, but never seemed to have any thoughts of quitting.

In September 1949, as his second year began, Cox was established in Room 1943 of the North Barracks. He shared the space with Cadets Joseph Urschell and Deane Welch and seemed happy to be back at West Point.

When he returned home to Mansfield for Christmas, he took with him two suits of civilian clothing, as cadets were permitted to do. Free of his uniform for a time, he slipped easily into civilian life. He and Betty Timmons talked of eloping, apparently considering it rather seriously, but if he did it, he'd been expelled from West Point. Cadets weren't allowed to marry. His expulsion could mean the end of his military career. The couple decided to wait until Richard graduated.

Cox returned to West Point on January 2, 1950, and the first week back from vacation passed uneventfully. Then on January 7, the first odd – and still unexplained – event occurred in the case. Peter C. Hains was the Cadet in Charge of Quarters at North Barracks on that Saturday afternoon. At around 4:45 p.m., the B Company telephone rang. Hains answered it and a rough man's voice demanded to know if a fellow named Dick Cox was in the company.

Hains replied that yes, Dick Cox was in B Company and the man said, "Well, look. When he comes in, tell him to come down to the hotel. Tell him George called. We knew each other in Germany. Tell him I'm a friend who wants to buy him dinner."

When questioned later, Hains couldn't remember much about the call, only that the man said his name was "George." He was unsure if it was the man's first name or last name. There was, however, no question about the hotel. It could only be the Hotel Thayer, which was about a half-mile from the West Point grounds. By the academy's rules, this was the only place other than the mess hall where Richard or any other cadet could eat a meal. Cadets who wanted to eat at the hotel needed a special dinner privilege pass to leave the grounds.

Several minutes after Hains took the call, Richard Cox walked past him. Informed of the call, Cox looked bewildered. He had no idea who "George" might be and couldn't remember meeting anyone by that name in Germany. Finally, Richard shrugged off the message and went upstairs to his room.

About 45 minutes after the mysterious telephone call, a man who was about six feet tall, hatless, and wearing a tightly-belted trench coat, walked into Grant Hall and asked to see Richard Cox. Visitors who come to West Point to see a cadet must come through the hall, a large lounge that was decorated with an impressive array of paintings and divisional insignia. Visitors were to give the name of the cadet that they wished to see, and the cadet was informed. If he was free, he reported to greet the visitor at Grant Hall.

Cadet Officer of the Guard Mauro Maresca was on duty that evening, and he remembered the man as having blond hair and a lightly tanned face, which was unusual in New York in January. However, Maresca did not ask the man his name, he merely relayed word to Cox that he had a visitor. A few minutes later, Dick entered Grant Hall. He hung his long gray dress overcoat on a rack, as cadets were required to do, and then presented himself to Maresca. The Officer of the Guard called out Cox's name and the blond visitor stepped forward.

Cox recognized the man and they shook hands. Maresca later remembered that they seemed glad to see each other and after a few minutes, they walked over to the coat rack. While Cox was putting on his coat, the visitor kidded him about how he looked in his uniform. Before leaving Grant Hall, Cox signed out on a dinner pass or DP, which would allow him to dine at the Hotel Thayer. But apparently, he never went there. His DP was signed at 5:30 p.m. and by 7:00 p.m., Cox was back in North Barracks. This would hardly have given him time to reach the Thayer, let alone eat one of the leisurely meals that the hotel's dining room was known for, and return to the barracks.

Nor did anyone recall seeing Cox at the Thayer that night. The hotel had two small dining rooms with about 30 tables in each one. No one, not a staff member or another cadet, saw Cox in the restaurant that night.

There was one thing off about Cox when he returned to the barracks the night ––– he was slightly drunk. He later admitted to his roommates that he and the man didn't eat at the hotel. Instead, they drank from a bottle of whiskey in the man's parked car. This was a foolish and dangerous thing for a West Point cadet to do but Richard managed to get away with it. He went back to his room, changed out of his uniform and into a sweatshirt and running pants, picked up a book, and began to study. When his two roommates came in at about 10:30 p.m., he was asleep with a textbook in his hands.

The curious events of January 7 did not end with the arrival of Cox's roommates.

A few moments after they walked in the door, the bugle sounded for lights out, startling Cox out of his sleep. He leapt hysterically to his feet, not seeming to realize where he was or who was in the room with him. Incoherent, he ran out of the room before his surprised roommates could restrain him. In the hallway, he leaned over the stairwell and shouted words that sounded like, "Is Alice down there?"

Alice? His roommates had never heard him mention a girl with that name. Later, a suggestion was made that Cox actually yelled, "Alles kaput," which translates to "All is over!" This might have made more sense, given the events that were still to come.

Cadet Urschell led Cox back into Room 1943, asking him who Alice was. Cox shook his head, unable to explain his bizarre behavior. He collapsed onto his bed, not turning down the covers or undressing, and was immediately asleep again.

The next morning, Richard didn't speak about anyone named Alice, but he was anxious to tell his friends about the previous night's visitor. He explained that the man had been in his outfit in Germany and before that, was an Army Ranger. They had not been close friends ––– Richard considered the man to be quite morbid ––– and he had had a few drinks the night before, refusing to let Richard out of the car until he had some, too. He told his friends that the man spun terrible stories of his exploits when he was a Ranger, talking of cutting and emasculating Germans and that he'd lived with a girl in Germany, gotten her pregnant and killed her.

Welch and Urschell were as bothered by the stories as Cox seemed to be. He finished the account by expressing his dislike for "George." He was always boasting, bragging all the time, he said, and he hoped that he would not return to visit again.

Unfortunately, George came back again around noon the next day, and once again, Richard went to meet him. He told Urschell and Welch that he would be back in about two hours, all the while complaining bitterly about the time that George was wasting and speaking again of his dislike for the man. He further characterized him as sadistic, strange, and highly strung. He walked away muttering that he hoped to never see the man again.

To Urschell and Welch, Richard didn't seem to fear his visitor. The mysterious George rated no higher than a nuisance. They attributed the fact that Cox went to meet him two times to mid-winter boredom. After enjoying himself during the holidays, Richard was finding it difficult to adjust to the rigid life of the Point again. Even an unwanted visitor like George offered a distraction from day-to-day life.

In the week that followed, Richard continued to make disparaging comments about George. Urschell and Welch could never remember if they asked Cox about Alice again, but they did recall that, back in December, about two weeks before going home to Ohio, Dick had written a letter to a young woman whom he had met in Germany. Without asking him directly, his roommates assumed this girl's name was Alice.

On Saturday, January 14 – a week after George's first appearance – Cox and Welch went together to watch the Army basketball team play against Rutgers. After the game, they walked back to North Barracks. Near the east entrance, Cox told Welch that he wanted to look at his grades, which each Saturday were posted near the company barracks. The two cadets parted ways.

It was later discovered that, just moments later, Richard met with a man who seemed to be waiting for him near the east entrance. It was assumed that this was George, but according to Cadet John Samotis, who witnessed Richard walk up to him, the man was short, had dark hair, and was lighter-skinned than George. He also wore a trench coat, but it hung casually open.

Cox returned to Room 1943 about 20 minutes after Welch and again informed his roommates that he was going to have dinner with a "friend." They assumed that he meant George, although he never stated that. He said that he would be back around 9:30 p.m.

Cox left the room at 5:45 p.m. and he took no money with him. In his room, he left behind $60 in cash, $45 in checks, and two suits of civilian clothes. Over his dress gray uniform, he put on his regulation long gray overcoat, which made him a conspicuous figure and one that would have been remembered if he was seen on the street. Unfortunately, though, no one remembered him, and it was in this recognizable uniform that Cox vanished.

He did not go to the Hotel Thayer, for no one who dined there that night remembered seeing him. He did not return to the barracks that night, as required by regulations, and his bed was empty at 1:00 a.m. during the final check. The next morning, Cadets Urschell and Welch nervously appeared before the Provost Marshal to report their roommate missing. Cadet Richard Cox became permanently absent without leave.

What happened to Richard Cox that night is unknown.

If he left West Point by automobile, then he would have had to have been in the trunk, because cars were inspected when they exited through the gates. A young man in a West Point uniform would have attracted attention, and Cox had to have been in uniform since his two civilian suits were still hanging in his closet. If Cox had been sneaking out, he could have climbed in a car trunk or, worse yet, if George had overpowered him and killed him, he could have hidden Dick's body there. But, considering Richard's physical fitness and dislike for George, this scenario seemed unlikely.

Officials took the disappearance seriously, especially in light of George's strange visits and Cox's reported hostility towards the man. It was concluded that Cox had met either with an accident or with foul play on West Point grounds. A search was made of the academy by a

Special Services regiment stationed at West Point, but no trace of the missing cadet came to light on that Sunday.

In Cox's room, though, an odd discovery was made. On his calendar, the day was circled in red, with the notation "See Kelley," written in Cox's neat hand beside the circle. At first, this was assumed to have been in reference to George, but it turned out that it was James Kelley, a boyhood friend of Dick's from Mansfield and a midshipman at Annapolis, Maryland. Kelley was visiting West Point on February 15 – not January 15 – and Cox had simply made the notation on the wrong calendar month.

On Monday, the Army's Criminal Investigation Command was notified about Cox's disappearance. A circular was drawn up with Richard's description and information was provided to the civilian press the following day. But there was no word from anyone who might have seen Richard Cox. As days became weeks, the hunt for the cadet continued. The Army called in the FBI, and local and state police joined in the search, sending out information throughout the country and to Germany.

At West Point, there was a room-by-room search of all buildings and then the search spread out into the surrounding area. Searchers formed in long lines five or six feet apart and moved slowly up and down the hillsides. When the search of the area yielded no clues, both Delafield Pond and the Lusk Reservoir were drained and dragged. The draining of Delafield Pond alone took two weeks.

In Ohio, the Cox family and Betty Timmons were interrogated by the FBI. They had no idea where Richard might be and had not seen him since Christmas, when his mother said that he was anxious to return to West Point.

Then, another odd thing happened. The letter that Cox had written to the young woman in Germany arrived back at the post and across its face were the German words for "Address Unknown." Investigators who believed this letter had been written to a girl named Alice got a surprise —- Cox had written to a girl named Rosemary Vogel. The contents of the letter were innocent. Cox said that he had been looking through some of his photos of Germany and noticed one of Rosemary and decided to write. Cox's quarters were ransacked in a search for the picture of Rosemary Vogel, but nothing was found. It eventually turned up in Mansfield. Cox had apparently taken the photo, along with the rest of his pictures from Germany, home with him for Christmas.

Although the letter offered no clues of anything other than a young man feeling nostalgic for friends in another country, CID investigators in Germany set out to find Rosemary Vogel. The result was curious. The girl's mother reported that her daughter had married an American sergeant and was living in a small town in New York. FBI men rushed there, only to find a happily married young woman who barely remembered Richard Cox.

Back in Germany, CID investigators questioned every man that Richard had bunked or soldiered with. His daily movements were recreated and yet not a single clue of a double life or any suspicious behavior ever turned up. The FBI search in the United States was just as fruitless.

The hunt for the mysterious George was just as deliberate as the search for Richard Cox himself. Military records in Germany were combed for a man who had transferred from the Rangers to the 27th Constabulary – a man who was blond, a braggart, and perhaps the lover of a girl named Alice. At the Army's dead files center in St. Louis, personnel records of the Rangers and the 27th Constabulary were scrutinized for a man with George as a first or last name and who fit the description of the man who came to West Point. Only one such man was ever found, and he had an airtight alibi for the nights of January 7 and January 14.

At first, the Cox disappearance got little coverage in the newspapers. Then, the actor Robert Montgomery, who also worked as a news commentator, mentioned the story on his show. Soon, reports of Richard Cox began flooding in from around the country. He had been seen in hotels, motels, swimming pools, and nightclubs. A gas station attendant claimed that he had seen Cox in the company of a dazzling blond showgirl. Richard's brother called the report "absolutely preposterous."

Every night for two months, the name Richard Colvin Cox was shouted out in the West Point roll call. There was only silence in reply. Finally, on March 15, Cox was formally dropped from the cadet roster.

Colonel Edwin N. Howell, West Point Provost Marshal, said, "I am convinced there was foul play. I am sure that we will not find Cadet Cox alive."

When the spring thaw arrived, another intensive search of the countryside began. It turned up something interesting – an unusual, Brazilian-made .38 caliber pistol near the West Point firing range. Someone suggested that it was just the sort of exotic weapon that might be used by a Ranger. There was no way to tell how long the gun had been there, since it was so damaged by the rain and snow of the previous winter months.

Richard's birthday was July 25. Every other year that he had been away from home, he had telephoned his family at some point during the day. Now, the family gathered by the telephone early in the morning and prayed that he would call. The phone rang several times, but it was never Richard. At the end of the daylong vigil, his mother sighed, "You just go around in circles and come back to the beginning. There's no end to it!"

At First Army Headquarters in New York, Colonel Robert J. Murphy said almost the same thing: "In view of the fact that the man has not turned up and we have no evidence to prove that he is deceased, we must hold to the belief that he is alive. Apparently, he has no desire to reveal his whereabouts. Therefore, we will search for him until we find a solution of the disappearance."

On the day that Cox's class graduated from West Point, the cadet had been missing for two years, four months, and 24 days. Betty Timmons had decided not to wait for her lost love, and she married a man named William Broad. The case faded from news accounts, but it was not forgotten. When *Life* magazine printed a photograph of a GI in Korea named Cox, hundreds of people wrote in to say that it must be the missing cadet. While it seemed unlikely that the runaway soldier would have used his real name, a CID investigator was sent to question the man. His name was Cox, but he was not the right one, as proven by his fingerprints.

The man named "George" has also never been found. There is nothing to indicate who this mysterious man might have been and whether he had anything to do with the disappearance of Richard Cox.

Dozens of theories about the case have circulated over the years. It has been reported that Richard Cox left West Point on his own and joined the CIA, where he began living a new life as a member of a secret branch of the agency.

In 1966, an author named Harry J. Maihafer published a book called *Oblivion* about the exhaustive search for Richard Cox. His investigation into the disappearance led him to believe that the person named "George" was really an old Army buddy of Richard's from Fort Knox, Kentucky, who arranged for a phony ID for Cox. He believed that Cox, under pressure to marry from his fiancée, was secretly homosexual. Disillusioned with West Point and the Army, Cox decided to disappear and become someone else. Even though Richard was officially declared dead in 1957, he believed that he was still alive at the time of his book, using another name.

In the end, we'll likely never know. The case of Cadet Richard Cox remains open and unsolved to this day. He is the only West Point cadet who ever disappeared without being found, either dead or alive, but what happened to him remains a mystery.

1951: "Home Before Dark"
The Disappearance of Beverly Potts

America in the 1950s was still a place of innocence and hope. Most Americans were concerned with home, children, and work in a time of post-World War II prosperity. In Cleveland, people worried about the performance of the Cleveland Indians baseball team, which was locked in a close race with the New York Yankees during the last hot days of

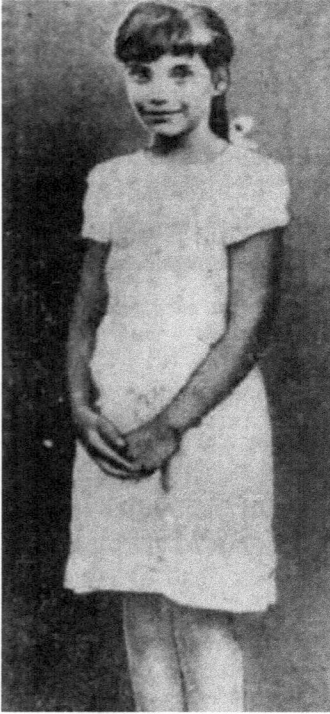
Beverly Potts

August. No one was thinking about little girls being taken off the street by strangers; such things just didn't happen in good neighborhoods.

But, then it did.

The story of Beverly Potts is one of the most legendary, and terrifying, mysteries in Cleveland history and tragically, it remains unsolved to this day.

In the summer of 1951, Beverly Potts was just 10 years old. She was a normal, pleasant, likable girl who stood just under five feet tall. She was known for being a little shy but got along well with her teachers and classmates. She had a close relationship with her family, which rounded out the picture of a normal, happy childhood. Beverly's father, Robert, was a stagehand employed at the Allen Theater on Euclid Avenue in Cleveland. Her mother, Elizabeth, stayed at home and raised Beverly and her older daughter, Anita, 22, who still lived at home.

Late that summer, Beverly was enjoying the last weeks of vacation before starting the fifth grade at Louis Agassiz Elementary School on Cleveland's west side. She spent most of her time playing with her friends, especially her next-door neighbor, Patricia Swing, 11.

On Friday, August 24, Beverly was particularly excited because she knew that tomorrow, she and her sister were going to accompany their parents on an all-day outing to Euclid Beach Park. She was even more ecstatic when she discovered, sometime on Friday afternoon, that the Showagon was coming to nearby Halloran Park that evening.

Sponsored by the recreation league and the *Cleveland Press*, the Showagon had become an annual summer tradition by the 1950s. A troupe of singers, dancers, magicians, and other performers, the

Showagon traveled around Cleveland's neighborhoods during the summer months, offering free performances at parks, playgrounds, and other public venues. It was one of Beverly's favorite summertime diversions, but this time, she was grounded for coming home late. Even so, she begged her mother to go and Elizabeth relented, but only on the condition that she come home right after the show. Beverly knew not to talk to strangers, especially men, and never to go anywhere with them.

After supper, Beverly went next door to get Patricia Swing and the two girls departed for the show at Halloran Park on their bicycles. They arrived around 7:00 p.m. and the show was in full swing. They watched the various acts and by 8:40 p.m., and it was starting to get dark. Patricia told Beverly that she had to go home. Her mother had told her to be home before dark, although Mrs. Potts had given Beverly permission to stay until the show was over. And why not? She was in her own neighborhood, surrounded by hundreds of people, many of whom were her own neighbors.

Beverly stayed, telling Patricia she would follow in a few minutes, and Patricia started for home. Her last memory of Beverly was seeing her standing and watching the show. A "plump, little woman" stood behind her, with one hand on Beverly's shoulder and the other clutching a small child. Patricia walked away down Linnet Avenue and was safely home by 9:00 p.m.

No one can say how many people saw Beverly Potts again that night. A number of witnesses, many of them children and teenagers, later came forward with unlikely stories, some of which proved to be lies told to gain attention. The woman seen standing behind Beverly in the park was never identified, and neither were the two young men who had a green car that a nine-year-old claimed she saw Beverly get into that night. The police also never found the convertible that an out of town visitor stated she saw Beverly riding in at 10:00 p.m. that Friday night. And there were hundreds of other stories like these, of mysterious cars and unknown individuals, none of which could ever be verified.

Around 9:30 p.m., Beverly's family realized that she had not come home, and Anita called the Swing residence. Patricia's parents told her that their daughter had come home alone, and that Beverly stayed to see the rest of the show. Mildly concerned, Robert Potts walked to Halloran Park. After looking around with the help of some neighbors, he returned home at 10:30 p.m. and called the Cleveland Police. Officers arrived a short time later and one of the largest manhunts in Cleveland history got underway.

Within hours, dozens, then hundreds, and then thousands of Cleveland residents began searching for the missing girl. The next morning, every postal carrier in the city was given a description of Beverly, and posters with her picture on them began appearing on utility poles, empty walls, doors, and windows all over Cleveland. Platoons of Boy Scouts, off-duty police officers and firemen, union members, and ordinary volunteers combed the city.

"Beverly sightings" poured in from all over the area, sometimes as many as 1,500 each day. Some of the tips were sincere and had great potential, like a report from a New York Central Railroad engineer who saw a girl matching Beverly's description get into a car with a teenage boy or the witnesses who saw two men in a 1937 black Dodge talking to a girl who might have been Beverly in Halloran Park. Then there were the obvious cranks who inevitably gravitated toward the Potts case. Hundreds of bizarre stories flooded the police department and one veteran newsman said that the case seemed to unleash an unprecedented deluge of "cranks, astrologers, dream interpreters and cultists of every hue."

The Cleveland police did the best that they could, considering there were virtually no clues and no apparent motive for a crime that was still undefined. The FBI declined to get involved with the case since there was no evidence of a kidnapping, but they did eventually distribute 22,000 posters of Beverly across the country.

The city had never seen anything like the hysteria that surrounded Beverly's disappearance. It was kept at a fever pitch by the city's three newspapers and the new local television stations. Every possible theory was investigated, and every corner of Cleveland was searched in the weeks that followed —- but nothing was found. More than 30 suspects —- most of them male deviants with child-molesting records —- were arrested, questioned, forced to submit to polygraph exams, and eventually released. From the moment of her disappearance to this day, no solid evidence as to the fate of Beverly Potts has ever been found.

Eventually, Cleveland began to return to the routine of daily life. The summer ended and the students went back to school. By the middle part of September, the Potts case no longer appeared in the newspapers every day. Grace Michele, Beverly's assigned fifth-grade teacher, kept an empty seat waiting for the girl in her classroom. The little girl was still gone, but she was not forgotten.

There were no developments in the case until a macabre incident occurred in November 1951. On November 9, Robert Potts received a telephone call while working at the Allen Theater. A male voice on the line asked him if he wanted to get his daughter back. The caller said, "If you do, connect your phone tomorrow at 3:30 p.m. and raise $25,000. Don't tell the police or we'll cut the girl's throat. She's out of town."

More calls followed and by the next week, arrangements had been made by Robert Potts — – who was working with the police —– to have Mrs. Potts deliver a ransom to Beverly's captors at 5:30 a.m. on November 15. The delivery point was an address on Prospect Avenue and Mrs. Potts was instructed to turn the money over to a "Negro man."

On the morning of November 15, "Mrs. Potts" —– actually Detective Bernard J. Conley, very unconvincingly disguised in his mother's clothes —– showed up to deliver the ransom, which was actually a bag of newspapers and $5 bills. Whether frightened by the sight of the burly detective in woman's clothing, or something else, the ransom pick-up man panicked before taking delivery of the ransom and began running away. Seconds later, though, 23 Cleveland detectives and police officers had surrounded him and put a shotgun to his head.

It turned out to be a pathetic, simple story of criminal ineptitude. The "kidnapper," Frank Davis, had fallen into debt and decided to extort money from the Potts family by pretending to be Beverly's kidnapper. Davis' cruel hoax turned into a prison term for him, a painful reminder for the little girl's parents of their continued tragedy, and months of teasing for Detective Conley from his colleagues on the police force.

Life continued and Beverly stayed missing. Her sister Anita eventually left home and got a job with the State Department, working for the Point Four Program in Ethiopia. Elizabeth Potts never recovered from the experience, although she tried to forget by giving away Beverly's toys and clothing and storing her pictures. Her health eventually broken, she died from a liver ailment on May 10, 1956. Robert Potts believed that the loss of her daughter had killed the woman in her middle fifties.

More days and months went by with more hoaxes, false leads, and dead ends. Then, in 1955, came what seemed to be a break in the case. Warren J. Tischler, a house painter, father of eight, and convicted child molester, was arrested in Santa Ana, California, on suspicion of Beverly's murder. Tischler, it was learned, had been working at the National Carbon Company plant —- close to Halloran Park —- on the night of Beverly's disappearance and he seemed to know a lot about the case. But the Orange County Sheriff's Department later decided that Tischler had gotten all his information from the newspapers and he was never brought back to Cleveland for interrogation.

Four months later, Harvey Lee Rush, an alcoholic drifter, "confessed" to Los Angeles detectives that he had killed a little girl in Cleveland after luring her from a West Side carnival. Rush was able to pick Beverly's picture out of a group of six photographs, but his description of her appearance, especially what she was wearing that night, was wildly inaccurate. Rush was eventually taken back to Cleveland, where he attempted to find the spot under the Hilliard Road bridge where he said that he buried Beverly's body. Nothing was ever found, and a reporter later got Rush to admit that he had made up the story to evade vagrancy charges and get a free trip to Cleveland. Rush, who had been arrested over one hundred times for public intoxication, was subsequently placed in a state mental hospital.

The following year brought several new oddities to the case, along with the death of Elizabeth Potts. Just five days after she died, a Cuyahoga Falls truck driver and child molester confessed to Cleveland police that he had "killed a girl near a playground" three or four years earlier. But his "memories" of that August night at Halloran Park were filled with inaccuracies and the police dismissed him as another crackpot. In December, a West Side man was arrested for taking lewd pictures, and the charges turned into something more exciting when one of his albums was found to contain a photograph that might be Beverly. But Robert Potts decided that the picture was not that of his daughter, and the search went on.

In 1961, a promising lead developed in New Jersey. The wife of a mental patient at a state hospital became convinced that her husband knew something about Beverly's disappearance. Cleveland police became very interested when it was discovered that the man had accumulated 50 charges of molesting young girls and was accused of exposing himself in Cleveland's Lakewood Park in September 1951. Hopes of solving the Potts case ended, though, after detectives interviewed the man at the Morristown hospital and concluded that he had nothing to do with the murder.

In 1970, Robert Potts passed away, but his death received little attention. In April 1973, Cleveland detectives got a tip from a former playmate of Beverly's that she was buried beneath an abandoned grease pit under Jim's Custom Body Shop on West 52nd Street. The detectives dutifully dug down five feet to the concrete floor, broke it apart, and went down a few feet deeper. Nothing was found, although curiously, Mrs. Amber Ware, a cousin of Beverly's, was living in an apartment in the same building. She had been living there at the time of the disappearance and Beverly had often played with her there.

In 1980, retiring Cleveland Police detective James Fuerst revealed that he and fellow detective James Shankland had "solved" the Potts case six years before. In 1974, Fuerst explained, he received a letter from the brother of a man who fled Cleveland in 1966 after being indicted on a charge of abducting two young girls. The letter writer said that his brother told him many years earlier that he had kidnapped "a girl named Beverly" from Halloran Park. Fuerst and Shankland traced the brother to Maple Heights and confronted him one night in his driveway. Fuerst's recollection was that the man immediately blurted out, "You finally got me, I'm glad it's over."

After the man made other incriminating statements, the two detectives took their information to Cuyahoga County assistant prosecutor Joseph Donahue —- who refused to prosecute because there was not enough evidence. Fuerst was convinced that Beverly's killer got away.

Did he? We'll never know. Strange stories and false clues still emerge on occasion and the city of Cleveland will never be free of the terrible event that blemished its history.

Many who live there today don't know much about the story of this lost little girl, but their parents and grandparents are still reminded of the tragedy with their own memories of the late 1950s —- when it stopped being safe to play outside after dark.

1953: The Babysitter who Vanished
The Disappearance of Evelyn Hartley

On October 24, 1953, Evelyn Hartley, a 15-year-old sophomore from La Crosse, Wisconsin, vanished without a trace while on her way to a babysitting job. It was like something out of a Halloween urban legend, but in this case, the horror was real.

Evelyn was a pretty, well-liked student at Central High School in La Crosse. Her father, Richard, was a biology professor at La Crosse State College and her mother, Ethel, was a homemaker. On the evening of October 24, Evelyn had agreed to babysit the 20-month-old child of

Viggo Rasmussen, a professor, and colleague of her father's. When she left home, she was wearing red jeans, a white blouse, white bobby socks, and glasses.

Evelyn typically checked in with her mother while she was babysitting. When several hours passed with no word from her, Ethel asked her husband to call the Rasmussen home. There was no answer. Worried, he drove over and found the front door locked. He knocked repeatedly, but there was no response. Richard searched until he found an unlocked basement window and entered the house.

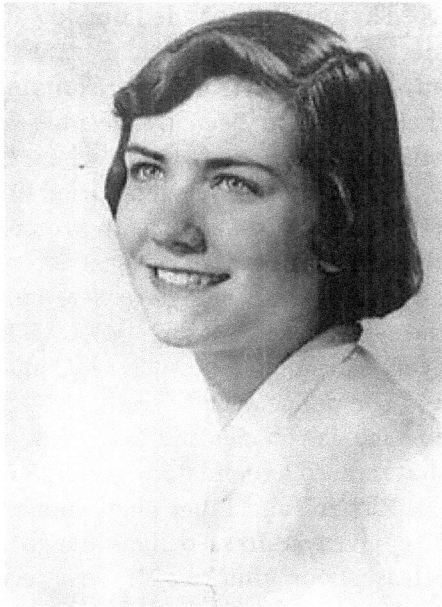

Evelyn Hartley

To his shock, he discovered that the only occupant of the house was the baby, sleeping peacefully in a crib upstairs. Evelyn was nowhere to be found.

Richard immediately called the police. When officers arrived, they also searched the house. They found one of Evelyn's shoes and her glasses, which were broken. Her other shoe was found in a different room in the house. They discovered bloodstains both inside and outside of the residence. There were also bloody footprints on the pavement outside the garage. Search dogs were brought in to follow the scent, which ended at the street. Detectives surmised that Evelyn had been put into a car and driven away.

A massive search began that night. Police officers and volunteers covered the town on foot, while the National Guard, Civil Air Patrol, and the Air Force searched from the sky. Men searched the Mississippi River and walked the banks. College and high school volunteers joined the effort, and within the first few days of her vanishing, there were more than 2,000 people looking for Evelyn.

The search expanded outside of town. Hunters were asked to stay alert while out in the field. Farmers were asked to check their land for any sign of Evelyn and, more ominously, for the suggestion that any of their land had been freshly dug for a grave. This idea sent police officers to local cemeteries, where fresh graves were unearthed to see if Evelyn might have been buried in secret.

Roadblocks were set up around La Crosse so that officers could check the trunks and backseats of every car for fresh blood, or anything out of the ordinary. There were more than 40,000 stickers printed for the search, each reading "MY CAR IS OK." Officers placed a sticker on every car that had been checked and cleared.

The police even "deputized" gas station attendants to report any suspicious vehicles and to provide the license numbers of any drivers that refused a mandatory search.

Richard and Ethel made numerous public pleas for information. They even addressed their daughter's abductor and begged for her release. Soon after, the Hartleys received two telephone calls in which a man offered to trade information about Evelyn for $500. The police set a trap for the caller and captured 20-year-old Jack Duffrin. But he knew nothing about Evelyn's whereabouts. He was charged and convicted of attempted extortion.

Friends, neighbors, local businesses, and civic organizations collected money for a reward fund for any tips that might lead to Evelyn's return. The fund quickly grew to $6,600. Hundreds of tips flooded the police station. Each one was investigated and then promptly dismissed. No one, it seemed, had any idea of what had happened to Evelyn.

The case grew cold, but the authorities didn't give up. A year after Evelyn's disappearance, Sheriff Robert Scullin estimated that his department had questioned 1,200 people. Detective Captain Leo Kihm, who led the initial investigation, placed that number higher, at around 3,500 people. But despite their efforts, no new leads were discovered.

The case was eventually given to A.M. Josephson, an investigator for La Crosse County. He pursued the case for years, focusing primarily on two items of interest that were found early in the investigation — a pair of tennis shoes found on Highway 14 and a bloodstained denim jacket that was found nearby. He believed they were important clues if the case was ever going to be solved.

The shoes had been found about 10 miles southeast of La Crosse, near Shelby, Wisconsin. The tread on the bottom of the shoes had a distinct pattern that detectives believed matched some traces of mud found in the Rasmussen house. Josephson discovered that the soles of the shoes exhibited a distinct wear pattern consistent with operating a Whizzer motorbike. Over the next few months, he poured over sales records and receipts and even tracked down past and present owners of Whizzer bikes, but never found any worthwhile suspects.

The jacket and shoes were photographed and put on display throughout the region, with a plea for information from anyone who might recognize them. Once again, calls flooded the police hotlines but, again, no new leads were found.

As the case got colder, the shoes and bloody jacket were dismissed by most investigators. The shoes were size 11, but the jacket was only a small size 36. Many detectives felt they were unconnected, but not Josephson. He believed that two kidnappers had taken Evelyn. He continued his search, but his efforts ultimately led nowhere.

Years went by without any answers. By 1959, the last remaining efforts fizzled out, and while the Evelyn Hartley case was left open, most believed it would never be solved.

In the years that followed, quite a number of individuals came forward and confessed to the crime. In 1971, a 51-year-old transient named Tommy Thompson was arrested in Casper, Wyoming, for passing bad checks. While locked up, he told police of a rape and murder that he had committed in 1953 and named Evelyn as his victim. Authorities checked Thompson's claims and found that he had been in prison in Minnesota at the time Evelyn disappeared.

There were other confessions, too, but all of them fell apart after being investigated. In 1957, some investigators tried to link Evelyn's disappearance to the crimes of Ed Gein, a Wisconsin man who had recently confessed to murdering two women and fashioning trophies out of human body parts. It was discovered that he had been visiting relatives in La Crosse around the time of Evelyn's disappearance. However, a search of his property and two lie detector tests ruled him out in the kidnapping. Authorities officially declared that Gein was not connected to the case.

Evelyn's parents remained haunted by her disappearance for the rest of their lives. In an interview they gave in 1978, they admitted to losing all hope of finding out what happened to their daughter. It was the last public statement about the case that they ever made.

To this day, the disappearance of Evelyn Hartley remains unsolved.

1955: "The Mary Celeste of the Pacific"

On November 10, 1955, a British ship called *Tuvalu* was traveling about 500 miles southwest of the Territory of Western Samoa when she came upon a badly listing vessel that was wallowing dead in the water. Obviously, a derelict, she could not be identified because she was canting so badly to port that her name could not be read. As the ship rounded the vessel's starboard bow, the letters of her name were clearly seen —– *Joyita*. She had been missing for a month and despite an extensive search, had not been sighted anywhere in the region.

The master of *Tuvalu*, Captain Gerald Douglas, launched a boarding party and a cursory inspection was made. The ship proved to be completely empty. She had taken on water and someone had apparently rigged a tarpaulin over one portion of the deck at some point, either to provide shelter or to protect the ship itself from the elements. There was not a soul on board and few clues pointed to the fate of the crew —– or that of the four tons of cargo that had mysteriously vanished, too. The vessel's logbook, which might have provided some answers, was missing. The crew had apparently abandoned the ship, but why?

News of the discovery was radioed to Suva, the capital of the Fiji Islands, and a tug was sent out to retrieve *Joyita* and bring her some 90 miles to a harbor at Vanua Levu. There, water was pumped out of her hull, but no bodies were found submerged in the lower cabins. The hull was not damaged and had no holes or signs of damage. She was then taken to Suva, where she was pulled from the water for a more thorough examination. During the inspection, it was learned how she had stayed afloat. Considerable amounts of cork filled the hull spaces, making her virtually unsinkable.

A second search was launched, this time for bodies and possible survivors. Nothing was found, and the story of the "ghost ship," dead and deserted, became news all over the world. The mystery appeared in newspapers and magazines and millions of people read the strange account of *Joyita* —– an eerie, modern-day counterpart of the infamous *Mary Celeste.*

Joyita was built as a private yacht in California in 1931 for Roland West, the famous RKO Studios film producer. The 69-foot vessel was constructed with a strong wooden hull and had graceful good looks and a smart interior. West christened her *Joyita*, which meant "little jewel" in Spanish, in honor of his actress sweetheart, Jewel Carmen. The romance fizzled and bad luck began to haunt the yacht even before her launching. On her maiden voyage, the ship had to be towed back into port after an engine room fire.

A few years later, Roland West was considered a suspect in the death of actress Thelma Todd. She was found dead in the garage of her home in December 1935. An autopsy concluded that she died of accidental carbon monoxide poisoning caused by the exhaust of her car, but many believed that she was murdered. Some even suggested that Todd was murdered by West aboard *Joyita* and then later transferred to the car.

Thelma Todd's death brought an end to West's fortunes and in 1936, the yacht was sold. That year began a procession of owners and *Joyita's* days of glamour began to fade. She was used as a pleasure craft until the start of World War II, at which time the U.S. Navy enlisted her as a patrol boat. After the war, she was acquired by a company in Hawaii and converted into a commercial fishing vessel. A new engine was installed, along with refrigerated compartments and the cork flotation that managed to keep her afloat years later.

In 1952, *Joyita* was purchased again, this time by a professor at the University of Hawaii. She apparently bought the former yacht as a business investment for she soon rented it to a friend, Captain Thomas Miller. He, in turn, put the craft back into commercial fishing service. Registered in the port of Honolulu, *Joyita* flew the American flag, although Captain Miller was an Englishman. He would become one of 25 people aboard the ship who later vanished without a trace.

Captain Miller was described as an affable man, a colorful fellow, and a competent sailor. After chartering *Joyita*, he launched a commercial fishing enterprise in Hawaii. He enjoyed a modest success at first, but then began running into problems, complicated by the malfunctioning of *Joyita's* refrigeration equipment, which spoiled several of his catches. When he moved his operation to Pago Pago, the capital of American Samoa, his luck still didn't improve. He sank deeper into debt until he was bankrupt. Authorities in Pago Pago eventually seized *Joyita's* documents to ensure the payment of mounting debts.

Captain Miller didn't let this stop him, and in March 1955, he took *Joyita* from American Samoa to Apia in Western Samoa, which was a territory of New Zealand. There, he made plans to start using the ship to make money again. His luck continued to be bad. He had hoped to work for the Western Samoan government as a supply boat and ferry, but his charter was refused because he did not have ship's papers. They were still being held by the American authorities in Pago Pago. He didn't have enough money to start a commercial fishing business again.

For months, *Joyita* sat idle in Apia, as things went from bad to worse for Captain Miller. He lived on board alone after his crew abandoned him because he was unable to pay them. Miller d barely existed, surviving only with help from friends and from what little money he could earn from jobs on shore.

But then Miller received an unexpected break in September 1955. Pressured by a growing need for food and supplies in the Tokelau Islands, which was the responsibility of the Western Samoan authorities, and by the need for transportation of copra —--- the dried meat of coconuts, the oil of which was used for vegetable margarine, cooking fat, soap, and other products —--- a major Tokelau export, a copra company arranged to charter *Joyita*. This lucky break was engineered by a New Zealander named R.D. Pearless, the newly appointed governor of the Tokelau Islands. He and Miller had become friends on Apia.

Even with his finances in disarray, Captain Miller managed to put together a suitable crew for the ship. They included Chuck Simpson, the ship's mate, an experienced seaman of Native American background who had settled in Western Samoa, and two former crewmen, Gilbert Islanders named Tanini and Tokoka. Both men were reportedly devoted to Captain Miller.

After months of idleness, the ship needed a lot of work and the crew labored long hours to get her into shape. It was later reported that Captain Miller had experienced some sort of trouble with the clutch on the port side's diesel engine but at the time of the charter, did not believe it was serious. He felt that it could be repaired on the way to the Tokelau Islands. After the ship was discovered as a derelict, the port engine's clutch was found to be partially disconnected, indicating that the vessel had gone out to sea with only one engine.

On previous voyages aboard *Joyita*, Miller had been criticized for being lax in maintaining radio contact with Apia. For this Tokelau charter, the ship was assigned call letters and an authority in the island's radio setup urged Miller to test her transmitter before departure, then keep in touch with Apia daily between 10:00 a.m. and 4:00 p.m. For whatever reason, Miller ignored both suggestions. Once *Joyita* departed on that tragic voyage, no one on Apia heard from her again.

Joyita's destination was the port of Fakaofo in the outlying Tokelau Islands to the north of Apia. The voyage was only about 270 miles, which was short by South Seas standards. The ship was loaded with a generous amount of goods needed in the islands, including medical supplies and food.

Miller's friend, R.D. Pearless, came along for the voyage, and in addition, passengers included a physician named Parsons and J. Hodgkinson, a hospital worker from Apia, both of whom accompanied the medical supplies on board. There was also G.K. Williams, a retired executive from New Zealand, and his companion, J. Wallwork. They were on board as representatives of the copra company that had chartered the vessel. Williams reportedly carried a sizable amount of money with which to buy copra in the islands. All the other passengers were native islanders and there were a number of women and children among them.

Joyita sailed on the morning of October 2. An employee who worked for the local government's marine affairs division happened to be watching from the window of his home when the ship sailed from the docks. As he looked on, he saw the vessel belch black smoke from her exhausts, and then drift helplessly until an anchor was dropped. Apprehensive, he telephoned Acting High Commissioner T.R. Smith to report the incident and suggest that government representatives — -- Pearless, Dr. Parsons and Hodgkinson —--- be removed from *Joyita*. Since the ship was at anchor, they decided to wait.

Engine trouble continued. Expecting to sail that evening, some passengers went ashore and found a pub where they could wait out the repairs. It was not until early the next morning that *Joyita* got under way again. By then, the crew was worn out from working on the engines all night and the passengers were unhappy. The government representatives were still on board.

Just after 5:00 a.m., *Joyita* sailed away from Apia. It was five weeks before she was discovered as a derelict. Based on the amount of fuel that was consumed, it was believed that whatever befell her happened on the first night out. Her electrically powered clocks had stopped at 10:53 p.m. and the switches of her navigation lights were in the "on" position. She had more than enough fuel in her tanks to travel 3,000 miles and carried a surplus of food and water for the short trip. Her radio gear was tuned to an emergency frequency, but a later examination revealed a break in the lead to the transmitter antenna,

Joyita, found adrift in the ocean with her cargo and three of her lifeboats missing

which would have prevented her from sending signals that could be heard more than a mile or two away. There was no way to determine if the break occurred before, during, or after the ship's trouble.

When *Joyita* was found, her three life rafts were missing, along with life jackets, compasses, and sextant, which were vital to plotting a course in the vast Pacific, and the vessel's log. For unknown reasons, the captain and crew had decided that abandoning the ship and climbing into the tiny life rafts was preferable to staying on board and waiting for help. The extensive investigation that followed the vessel's discovery failed to yield any survivors or bodies, so there was no clue as to why they left the ship.

Also strange was the disappearance of the cargo. On deck, she had carried about 2,000 board feet of lumber and several large, but empty, oil drums. In an emergency, some of the lumber, and perhaps a few of the drums, could have been fashioned into a raft —--- but it wouldn't account for all the material being missing. If the cargo had been thrown into the sea to lighten the ship, or it had been washed overboard in a storm, there should have been some found floating in the ocean during the search. And yet none of it was ever found.

Even harder to explain was the disappearance of the cargo from *Joyita's* holds. She had been carrying approximately 70 sacks of food staples —– rice, sugar, flour —– for the Tokelau Islanders. The bags weighed between 50- and 150-pounds each, and they were missing from the hold. In another hold had been cases of aluminum strips, used to protect coconut trees from rats. They, too, were gone.

Investigators pursued every possible theory concerning the tragedy. Theories soon appeared from both inside and outside the official inquiry.

Most chilling was the speculation that a "pirate submarine" had attacked *Joyita*, killed or captured everyone on board, and then stole her cargo. This theory was inspired by reports of a mysterious submarine, or submarines, in the general region of the Fiji Islands. The reports were unofficial, and some observers dismissed them as mistaken accounts of whales that were swimming near the surface of the water. However, the pirate submarine idea gained ground when the 60-foot vessel *Arakarimoa* vanished with her passengers and crew on the night of December 28, 1955, while en route from Tarawa to Maiana in the Gilbert Islands. The ship, which had been sailing near her sister vessel, *Aratoba*, was never found.

In Fiji, a major newspaper announced that everyone aboard *Joyita* had been murdered. The story suggested that the vessel had innocently come up on a Japanese fishing fleet known to have been working near the Tokelau Islands. The speculation went on to say that perhaps they had seen something that the Japanese didn't want them to see, and that *Joyita* had been stopped and boarded and her passengers and crew had been either taken prisoner or killed. Although Japanese commercial fishing in their waters was strongly resented by the people of Fiji, officials of the island's government were quick to announce that the newspaper's story was pure speculation.

A plausible, but impossible to verify, theory suggested that *Joyita* was the victim of an undersea earthquake, a natural phenomenon in the Pacific that was often accompanied by catastrophic waves. Earlier that year, a vessel near Fiji had been struck by this kind of disturbance and the sea became so violent that everyone on the ship was thrown overboard. However, a check of other ships in *Joyita's* area at the time of the disappearance brought no report of a seaquake. Even if a localized wave pattern did strike the ship, it is unlikely that all 25 people on board would be jettisoned at once. Even if they had, it seems reasonable to assume that someone would have been able to get back on board.

Another natural theory involved a waterspout, a tornado-like disturbance of water. In support of this conjecture was the fact that *Joyita* was found to have been damaged, possibly by a storm or high waves. Seasoned mariners agreed that the ship could have been damaged by a waterspout, but in this instance, it was not enough to cause everyone to abandon her.

There was no evidence to support mutiny. By all accounts, the crew was dedicated to Captain Miller. Besides, if they had wanted to leave the ship, why wait to do so in the middle of the ocean? They had a perfect opportunity when she was still in Apia harbor with engine trouble.

The investigation of the ship when back in port finally revealed a cause behind the ship's condition when she was found at sea, or at least offered the most sensible explanation. It was discovered that a section of pipe in the port engine's cooling system had deteriorated so badly that sea water had been allowed to leak into the ship. Although the pipe was only one inch in diameter, over a period of time, the leak could have caused serious flooding. Since the leak was hidden under the engine compartment floor, the diesel's rumbling could have masked the sound of incoming water.

The crew had to have been aware of the leak, but the flooding may have already been serious by the time it was discovered. A few mattresses were found in the engine compartment, and this suggested that someone had tried to stem the flood but was unable to find its source. Meanwhile, *Joyita's* pumps were unable to handle the situation. Later inspection showed that they were seriously impaired by the accumulation of dirt and grease in their suction pipes. The crew had improvised an auxiliary pump in a last-ditch effort to assist the regular pumps but this either proved inadequate or didn't work at all. Before long, the water rose high enough to drown the engines and electrical system. Soon, the stricken ship was helplessly adrift in the darkness, unable to radio for help.

After hearing testimony from marine experts who examined *Joyita* on shore, the panel of inquiry officially declared that the cause of the ship's predicament had been a defective pipe in the engine's cooling system.

This was accepted as a plausible, sound reason for *Joyita's* condition when found, but it still offered no evidence about the fate of her passengers and crew. There was nothing that addressed why, or how, they left the vessel.

No one could say why Captain Miller would have abandoned *Joyita*, since he had outspoken confidence in her unsinkability. Furthermore, he knew that it was safer to stay with a large vessel for as long as she could stay afloat, even if her deck was awash. That policy is doubly sound in shark-infested waters, like those of the islands where he was traveling. For the same reasons, the crew would have stayed on *Joyita*, and Captain Miller would have undoubtedly advised his passengers to do the same.

Another problem for investigators was why Captain Miller had not fashioned sea anchors for *Joyita*. They would have been easy to improvise from the cargo of lumber and would have helped stabilize the vessel in rough water.

After the official inquiry was closed, an interesting and possibly significant detail came to light. Because the marine expert involved was never called as a witness, his findings never appeared in the testimony. While searching *Joyita*, he discovered a stethoscope, scalpel, sutures, and bloody bandages among the debris on board. Someone had been injured and treated by Dr. Parsons, but who? Could it have been Captain Miller? If the captain had met with some sort of incapacitating injury, been knocked unconscious, or even killed, the passengers, and perhaps even the crew, might have fled the ship in a panic. The medical instruments and bloody bandages hinted strongly that someone had been seriously injured.

Many believe that Miller was indeed the victim. Badly injured, he might not have been able to abandon the ship, even if he wanted to. In their haste, the others might have left him for dead. At some point, perhaps after everyone else abandoned the boat, someone had rigged a tarpaulin on deck for shelter. This may have been Captain Miller. And since injury might have prevented him from rigging the awning, at least one person may have remained on board with him —- likely Tanini or Tokoka. As for the Simpson, the ship's mate, it seems odd that he would have left, knowing the ship's buoyancy, but he may have been the one who carried off the ship's navigation instruments and logbook. It's possible that as the next in command, he felt a responsibility to the fleeing passengers.

But what happened then? The passengers may have been swallowed by the Pacific, for they were never heard from again. Captain Miller, if he actually stayed behind, might have met a similar fate.

But we'll never know for sure. The story of *Joyita* remains another mystery of the sea —- and one that will never be solved.

1957: The El Paso Vanishing
What Happened to the Pattersons?

On the evening of March 5, 1957, William and Margaret Patterson left their home at 3000 Piedmont Drive in El Paso, Texas, and vanished without a trace, leaving everything they owned behind. To this day, their disappearance has never been solved, although many have tried, suggesting that they were Russian spies or were abducted by aliens.

But, to this day, none of those theories have proven correct. Their vanishing remains just as baffling now as it did more than 60 years ago.

William and Margaret Patterson, an ordinary couple who perhaps weren't as ordinary as they seemed

William and Margaret Patterson were an ordinary couple. They owned Patterson Photo Supply in El Paso and were well-liked by their customers, friends, and neighbors. In addition to their business, they also owned a Cadillac, a boat, stock in a boat company, and property in Guaymas, Mexico. They lived a quiet life, and no one had ever noticed anything unusual about them. A few nights before their disappearance, the Pattersons invited another couple, the Wards —-- owners of the Ward Motor Clinic —-- over for dinner. After the meal, Cecil Ward and William went out to the garage to have a beer and apply some acrylic to William's boat. The Wards later told the police that neither of the Pattersons mentioned any plans to travel. In fact, Cecil added that he and William had plans to get together later in the week.

On the morning of March 6, Cecil opened his auto business and discovered that William Patterson's Cadillac was sitting in the driveway. A man named Doyle Kirkland came into the auto shop a few minutes later. Kirkland managed Duffy Photo Service, and though he and William had competing businesses, they were good friends. When asked why he had the Pattersons' car, Kirkland brushed it off. He told

Cecil that he and William had worked on his boat the previous night, and that the Pattersons were "going on a little vacation." He claimed that William had asked Kirkland to bring the car to Cecil for a tune-up.

But something didn't sit right about the story for Cecil. He called the police. When they arrived at the Patterson house, it was eerily silent. Dishes from the previous night's meal were still in the sink. The newspaper was on the front steps. Mail was in the box. Nothing had been packed. Suitcases were still in the closet. Detectives later learned that clothing, including an expensive fur coat, had been left at the cleaners, waiting to be picked up. None of the utilities had been disconnected, and the newspaper and mail were still scheduled for delivery. Only the family cat, Tommy, stirred in the house and no extra food or water had been left for him. Margaret would have never gone out of town without arranging for the cat's care.

Cecil Ward cooperated fully with the police. He told them everything he knew about the Pattersons. He described William as a boisterous, free-spending, but kind man. But he had his faults. Ward recalled that a month earlier, William had gotten drunk in Juarez, Mexico, and picked a fight with a waiter. It turned out that William had been in town with his 20-year-old mistress, Estefana Arroyo Morfin, and the waiter refused to serve her.

Of course, this led to more questions about the Pattersons' lifestyle, and Cecil suddenly realized how little he really knew about them. Both Margaret and William had been tight-lipped about their respective childhoods, except to say that it had been rough. William was from Chicago and had worked in traveling carnivals. Margaret's parents had not approved of him and demanded that Margaret choose between her family and William. Later, Margaret's friends told investigators that she never told them her birthdate, exactly how she and William had met, or how long they had been married. Everyone seemed to like the couple —– but they really knew very little about them.

To add to the mystery, William's father, Luther Patterson, said that he had always expected William and Margaret to disappear one day, because his son had the free-spirited heart of a carny. Luther added that he was certain that the couple was not dead, and that William had "done things like that before." William's mistress, Estefana, was also questioned and told detectives that William had recently told her that he needed to "disappear soon and do it quickly." She later retracted that statement, however.

The investigation stalled and then, on March 15, Herbert Roth, the Pattersons' accountant, received a telegram. It was sent from the Western Union office in Dallas, where it had been placed from a telephone call near the Love Field Airport. The sender was listed as "W.H. Patterson," which was odd since William's middle name was Durrell. The telegram instructed Roth to act as business manager of the Patterson Photo Supply company. It also asked him to sell a mobile home that was owned by the Patterson, use the proceeds of the sale to support the store, and rent out the Pattersons' home for the next nine months.

And there was one last note. It instructed Roth to hire a new store manager to replace William at the photo company —– Doyle Kirkland.

The telegram seemed to be a new lead, but it deepened the mystery. It had been called in by telephone, which meant that no handwritten original existed. In other words, anyone at all could have placed the call to Western Union. And while the telegram's odd requests certainly cast suspicion on Doyle Kirkland, no further evidence linked him to the Pattersons' disappearance. By the 1960s, Kirkland had left El Paso for parts unknown. The police were unable to trace him.

As time passed, there were regular sightings of the Pattersons. Several people claimed to spot them outside of Mexico City, years after they vanished. Sheriff Bob Bailey tracked down some hotel workers in Valle del Bravo, and after showing them some photographs, they identified the Pattersons as a couple who had stayed with them for several months in 1957. However, no hotel records or signatures in the guest book could be linked to the Pattersons.

William and Margaret Patterson were officially declared dead on March 27, 1964.

The case was cold and stayed that way for the next 20 years. In 1984, though, a man named Reynaldo Nangaray came forward with new, startling information. Nangaray had been the caretaker at the Pattersons' house, and he told a detective that he had found blood in the garage, and a piece of a human scalp on the propeller of the

Pattersons' boat shortly after the couple disappeared. He admitted to having cleaned up at the scene. He also claimed that he had seen a man carry bloody sheets out of the house and throw them into the trunk of a car. He had not gotten a clear look at the man, but it was not William Patterson. When asked why he waited so long to come forward, Nangaray said that he had been an undocumented immigrant in 1957 and feared being deported. Two years after coming forward, Nangaray was killed in an auto accident. None of his information was ever confirmed.

There are many theories about what happened to the Pattersons. Some believe they were murdered —-- although there is no explanation for why the police found no trace of the blood that Nangaray described —-- and others think they were kidnapped. Some feel that the couple went on the run for some reason, or that one of the other of them did, after killing their spouse. Some have pointed fingers at Doyle Kirkland, the only person who seemed to profit from their vanishing. Some even believe they may have been abducted by aliens, although evidence for that seems to be a bit hard to find, as well.

One of the most intriguing theories about the Pattersons is that they disappeared because they had been ordered to do so —- because they were Russian spies. This theory gained attention in 2009, when El Paso County Sheriff Leo Samaniego was interviewed for a retrospective about the lingering case. He told reporter Diana Washington Valdez that he believed the Pattersons had been spies because of how quickly they vanished. The photo supply company had been a cover, he theorized, so that William Patterson could get photographs of nearby Fort Bliss and of military shipments that came in and out by train. There was no evidence to confirm this theory either, but it is a compelling one.

In the end, we'll never know what happened to William and Margaret Patterson. Their case remains just as mysterious now as it was then. Murder? Kidnapping? Aliens? Spies? We'll never know for sure, but the story will remain just as compelling now as it was six decades ago, especially for the people of El Paso.

1959: The Man in the Green Pajamas

One of the most disturbing unsolved disappearances of the last half of the twentieth century occurred in the West Central Illinois town of Jacksonville, when a man named Bruce Nelson Campbell stumbled out of his hotel room one night, dressed only in a pair of green pajamas, and was never seen again.

What happened to the New England stockbroker has never been determined —– he simply vanished without a trace.

In April 1959, Bruce Campbell, age 57, and his wife, Mabelita, drove to Illinois from Northampton, Massachusetts. The reason for their visit was meant to be a happy one. They had traveled to see their newly-born first grandson, son of Bruce, Jr., who was an assistant professor of chemistry at MacMurray College, in Jacksonville.

For some reason, the long drive to Illinois was especially hard on Campbell, and he began feeling sick while he was in the car. The stock investment counselor became confused and disoriented, and when they arrived in Jacksonville, Mrs. Campbell checked them into the Sandman Motel, a small, family-owned establishment that was typical of motor lodges of the day. It was located on the northwest side of town, on Walnut Street. Each room had a door that opened to the outside and parking was located right outside the guest's room. Campbell was put immediately into bed after they checked into the motel. Bruce, Jr. arranged for Dr. E.C. Bone, a local physician, to visit his father. Dr. Bone gave him some medication to help him sleep, but it didn't seem to work. Two days passed before Campbell seemed to show some signs of improvement.

On the evening of April 14, Campbell visited with his family. Bruce, Jr. later recalled that his father was "rational but still disoriented" during his last visit with him. Twice, later that night, Mrs. Campbell said her husband asked her if their station wagon, which was parked outside of their room in the motel's parking lot, was locked. She told him that it was, shortly before going to sleep.

She later woke up at 2:15 a.m. and saw that the other double bed in the room was empty — – her husband was gone. She immediately got out of bed to look for him, and when she realized that he was not in the bathroom, hurried to the door of the room, which was unlatched. There was no sign of him in the parking lot, and the desk clerk on duty said that he had not seen anyone walking past the office. The Campbells' car was still sitting in the lot. The doors were locked, and it was undisturbed.

Because of her husband's weakness and disorientation, Mrs. Campbell quickly called the police. When officers arrived at the motel, she offered a description of the tall, balding man with a slight limp and explained that when he left the motel room, he was wearing only a pair of bright green pajamas, a wrist watch, and a ring with the Delta Upsilon fraternity crest on it. His wallet containing all his money, his shoes, his eyeglasses, and his car keys were still in the motel room.

Police officers searched the surrounding area, the darkened streets, and the Jacksonville downtown area, but there was no sign of Campbell. The next morning, a request was put out for information. Theories of murder, suicide, and amnesia led searchers to local creeks, farm buildings, and wells. Jacksonville Police Chief Ike Flynn and Captain Charles Runkel surveyed the entire area, both in a fixed-wing aircraft, and later, by helicopter. They found nothing.

The next day, local firefighters joined the search, using a boat to dredge nearby Mauvaisterre Creek. About 150 students from MacMurray College joined the search, too. On the third day, the entire 235-member male population of MacMurray —– students and staff —– joined with 50 students from Jacksonville High School to help comb the area.

The *Jacksonville Courier* reported that the massive volunteer search team, broken into smaller groups, covered a six-mile-radius around Jacksonville, including creeks and ponds. It was assumed that, since there were no reports of a barefoot man in green pajamas walking around the city, and, since the Sandman was on the north side, that Campbell must have traveled north into recently planted farm fields.

Unfortunately, this assumption turned out to be overly optimistic. Despite the search, no trace of Campbell was found. Dozens of reports of tall hitchhikers from the surrounding area, including White Hall, Murrayville, Woodson, New Berlin, and Alexander, kept the police busy for days, but the leads went nowhere.

Police Chief Flynn told the newspaper, "We have looked everyplace that has been suggested and have run out of ideas on what to do next. A fortune teller told us that Campbell was seven miles from Jacksonville, either northeast or northwest of the city. We have even looked there."

Whoever this psychic was, they might have been on to something, however. The newspaper reported that the last solid lead —— pretty much the only solid lead —— came in when police were about a week into the search. A farmer who lived several miles northwest of the city told investigators that he had been awakened by shouting on or near his property on the night that Campbell went missing. The police checked the area, but nothing was found. Chief Flynn told the *Courier* that the case was "one of the most baffling mysteries that has occurred here."

The search for Bruce Nelson Campbell —--- the "man in the green pajamas" —--- continued for days and weeks, and then it stretched into years. Mabelita Campbell had reluctantly gone home after two weeks of fruitless searching. But the family refused to give up hope that he would be found alive until 1967, when he was finally declared legally dead. Mrs. Campbell passed away in 2004, never learning what had become of her husband.

After several months of extensive searches by the Jacksonville police, the FBI launched its own investigation into the case. On the first anniversary of Campbell's disappearance, it was revealed that the distraught Campbell family had spent almost all their savings on private investigators who distributed Mr. Campbell's photo and description to police departments around the country. They'd also offered a $5,000 reward for information, which no one ever collected. Unfortunately, this was the only thing that the FBI learned about the disappearance. Like the private investigators who worked the case, the federal agents found no trace of Campbell.

The case of the "man in the green pajamas" turned out to be the last significant case of Jacksonville Police Chief Ike Flynn's career. Just weeks after the vanishing, Flynn retired, and Charles Runkel was promoted to succeed him. Runkel later recalled, even though he was no longer a cop, Flynn never let the case go. He died of cancer several months after he retired, haunted to his grave by the missing man. Until the very end of his life, he never stopped checking in at the department to see if any new clues had surfaced. They had not —— and even today, the case remains unsolved.

What became of Campbell? No one knows. He simply walked away on the dark nighttime streets of a small Illinois town and was never heard from again.

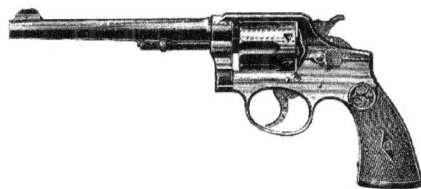

1960: The Murderous Housewife

It was March 19, 1960, and the police were called to a ranch-style house in the town of Independence, Missouri. They were answering a call placed by a young housewife named Sharon Kinne, who claimed that she's heard a gun go off in the bedroom where her husband, James, had been sleeping. When she hurried into the room, she said she'd

*Sharon Kinne, the homicidal
housewife who vanished*

found her young daughter, Danna, holding a smoking .22-caliber pistol.

James Kinne had been shot in the back of the head.

Sirens screaming, the police arrived, followed by an ambulance. James was rushed to the hospital, but he was pronounced dead on arrival.

After an investigation that proved that the toddler could indeed have pulled the trigger on the pistol, the authorities announced that James's death was an accident. Sharon Kinne was cleared of any suspicion —- but she would soon come to the attention of the police again.

Her story wasn't quite over because the death of James Kinne had not been an accident, and Sharon Kinne was just about to vanish without a trace.

A month after James Kinne's "accidental" murder, using money from her husband's insurance policy, Sharon purchased a Ford Thunderbird from an auto salesman named Walter Jones. Even though Walter was married, the two hit it off and began a torrid affair. In May, Sharon asked Walter to go away with her on a trip, but he refused. His wife, Patricia, had become suspicious about this many "late nights at the office." But Sharon didn't appreciate being turned down. She soon announced to Walter that she was pregnant with his child and she expected him to leave his wife. Instead, Walter broke off the relationship.

Not long after that, Patricia Jones went missing.

Walter filed a missing person's report with the police, but he also searched for his wife on his own. He spoke to many of her friends, hoping for a lead. One of the members of a group that Patricia carpooled to work with told him that Patricia had received a mysterious telephone call on the day that she disappeared. The caller was a woman and asked to meet with her after work. Patricia agreed and the carpool driver dropped her off at the meeting place in Independence. A woman was waiting for her at the spot.

Walter confronted Sharon and she admitted that she had met with Patricia that day and told her about the affair. Afterward, she claimed, she had dropped her off near her home. Walter didn't believe her, but Sharon stuck to the story, claiming she had nothing to do with Patricia's disappearance. In fact, she promised, she'd help look for her. Sharon enlisted the help of an old high school friend, John Boldizs, to help with the search and they quickly found Patricia.

Her body, riddled with bullets, had been dumped in a remote spot outside of town.

The police questioned Sharon, Walter, and John Boldizzis, and then arrested Sharon for murder. Her involvement in this crime also caused detectives to take a closer look at the death of her husband, James, and they soon announced that she would be tried for his murder, too. For now, though, since Sharon was pregnant, the trials wouldn't be scheduled until she had delivered her baby.

More than a year passed before Sharon went on trial for James's murder. It turned out to be complicated. The first trial in January 1962 ended in a conviction, but the verdict of life behind bars was overturned due to procedural irregularities. A second trial ended abruptly in a mistrial, while a third trial in July 1964 ended in a hung jury, allowing Sharon to be released on bond.

Plans were made for a fourth trial in October 1964, but before it could happen, Sharon skipped town and headed for Mexico with a boyfriend, Frank Puglise. But she couldn't stay out of trouble. After meeting an American tourist, Francisco Parades Ordoñez, in a bar, Sharon went back to his hotel room. She claimed he tried to rape her, and she shot him, killing him and wounding a hotel employee who entered the room after he heard gunshots. When the ballistics report was examined, it revealed that the gun used to kill Ordoñez was the same gun that had killed Patricia Jones.

Sharon had apparently never thought to get rid of it.

The Mexican authorities didn't believe Sharon's claims of attempted rape and charged her with homicide. After a short trial, she was convicted and received a 10-year prison sentence. She appealed but made things worse for herself. When judges reviewed the case, they thought her sentence was too lenient, so they sentenced her to 13 years instead. Sharon spent the next four years in a Mexican prison.

Then, on December 7, 1969, Sharon didn't show up for the daily roll call in prison. By the next morning —- apparently, things were a little "loose" there —- it was realized that she'd escaped. Some believe she bribed the guards and made her escape during a convenient blackout the night before. Others believe her boyfriend aided in her escape. One lurid theory claimed that the family of her last victim busted her out of jail because they wanted to kill her themselves.

Whatever happened —- she was never seen again.

The FBI, assisting the Mexican authorities, searched for Sharon for a time but believed it was unlikely that she'd return to the United States. Eventually, the search was called off but Sharon's warrant for the murder of her husband is still active today. In fact, it's the longest outstanding arrest warrant in the Kansas City area and one of the longest outstanding felony warrants in American history.

It's been more than 50 years now, but who knows —- maybe Sharon Kinne is still out there somewhere, one step ahead of the law.

1961: The Missing Rockefeller

It's the desire to do something adventurous, at a time when frontiers, in the real sense of the word, are disappearing.
Michael Rockefeller

One of the most celebrated, well-liked, and wealthiest adventurers of modern times, Michael Rockefeller, vanished without a trace in the wilds of New Guinea in November 1961. Although many wondered how such a thing could happen in the modern years of the mid-twentieth century —-- especially with a father who was one of the richest men in the world —-- Michael managed to defy the boundaries that had been created for him and he simply disappeared.

Although rumored sightings of the elusive man continued for decades, no clear evidence has ever been presented about Michael's fate. His vanishing remains one of the most puzzling mysteries of recent times.

Michael Clark Rockefeller was, at 23-years-old, the most adventurous and problematic of the five children of Nelson Rockefeller. He was an heir to one of the greatest fortunes in the world —-- a fortune created by oil. By the late 1800s, John D. Rockefeller controlled 95-percent of the burgeoning oil refining business in America. As the president and founder of Standard Oil, he was perhaps the richest and most powerful industrialist of the age, with vast holdings in oil, lumber, iron ore, manufacturing, transportation, and numerous other enterprises. In the early 1900s, he retired from business and devoted himself to establishing philanthropic endeavors that supported education, medicine, public service, and social welfare.

It is estimated that he gave away as much as $600 million, which was only a fraction of his wealth.

His only son, John D. Rockefeller, Jr., followed in his father's footsteps and not only continued making money, but donating it to various charities. He had five sons, all of whom carried on the family tradition of prominence in public and political affairs as leaders of various Rockefeller enterprises and charitable institutions.

Nelson Rockefeller, the second son, rose to great prominence in United States politics. As the leader of a liberal wing of the Republican party, he served as governor of New York from 1959 to 1973 and launched several construction and modernization projects. However, he failed several times in bids to become president. He was appointed to the office of vice president in 1974 during the Nixon scandals and served for three years. He did not join the GOP national ticket with Gerald Ford in 1976 and, instead, retired from politics when his term as vice president was over. He died in 1979.

Michael was born in 1938 – along with a twin sister, Mary – and was the youngest and favorite son of Nelson Rockefeller. Intelligent and sharp-witted, Michael had a passion for travel and had the money to roam the world. Encouraged by his father, he combined an education at Phillips Andover Academy and at Harvard University with extensive travel and a variety of summer jobs that included ranching in Venezuela and working in a grocery store in Puerto Rico.

He graduated with honors from Harvard in 1960. The handsome, bespectacled, fair-haired, athletic young man had the world at his fingertips and more money than he could ever spend. Born to the best things in life and with a bright future ahead of him in business, he instead chose to join up with the Army Reserve and serve a six-month stint as a soldier. It's possible that his short time in the military was used to prepare him for things to come, because a short time later, he went looking for adventure as part of an anthropological expedition to New Guinea, one of the most remote regions of the world.

Michael had been to New Guinea once before. As a senior at Harvard, he had worked as an audio technician and photographer for a joint Peabody Museum – Harvard University expedition to the Baliem Valley in New Guinea's interior. Accompanied by his best

Michael Rockefeller in New Guinea — before the trip that he never returned from

friend and roommate, Sam Putnam, the trip was meant to be their last adventure together before Michael started Harvard Business School and Sam started Harvard Medical School. The expedition studied the Dani tribe of western New Guinea and produced *Dead Birds*, an ethnographic documentary film produced by expedition leader Robert Gardner, for which Michael was the sound recording engineer.

In 1961, Michael had the chance to return to New Guinea on another expedition into a land that is just as vast and unexplored today as it was then. Located in the South Pacific Ocean, 100 miles north of Australia, New Guinea is a country of jagged mountains, broad rivers, tropical jungles, narrow, nearly impenetrable valleys, active volcanoes, and gigantic swamps. The climate is mostly tropical, though the highlands tend to be cooler and drier and seasonal monsoons drop as much as 300 inches of rain on some parts of the island. Temperatures are usually torrid, and humidity is high, allowing a luxurious rain forest to cover much of the land. Hundreds of species of animals can be found on New Guinea —- most of them dangerous —- including snakes, leeches, crocodiles, and malaria-carrying mosquitoes.

The first white men to visit the island were Spanish and Portuguese sailors in the sixteenth century, and New Guinea has since been claimed by the Dutch, British, and Germans. By the time of Michael's expedition, it was under a divided rule of Indonesia and Australia. Although a semblance of civilization had reached the island by the 1960s, many parts of the interior were virtually untouched, save for remote outposts manned by missionaries.

During Michael's first trip to New Guinea, the Gardner expedition lived among the Dani people. However, in late June, Rockefeller and his friend, Sam Putnam, split off from the other members of the group to make a trip of their own to a southwestern coastal area known as Asmat, an immense mud-covered plain that was covered by tidal swamp and steaming jungles. Crossed by a number of muddy rivers, it was a hostile wilderness called "The Land of Lapping Death" by the local natives, who were also known as the Asmat.

By tradition, the Asmat were headhunters and cannibals. They were also known for being skilled woodcarvers and producing some of the finest primitive art in the world. It was the art that lured Michael to the area and drew him to New Guinea. His main purpose in returning to the island was to study the Asmat people and collect their art for the Museum of Primitive Art in New York, of which he was a trustee. He feared that the pure art of the natives would eventually be corrupted by civilization, and he wanted to collect as many examples of it as he could before that happened.

Michael joined up with a Dutch anthropologist, Dr. Rene Wassing, from the Bureau of Native Affairs in Hollandia, New Guinea, and they planned an expedition to the Asmat people, where they would record their experiences and barter for native art. They equipped themselves with supplies, a native boat called a "proa," which was essentially a platform built over two dugout canoes to which they added an 18-horsepower motor and hired two native boatmen. They took along several cameras and barter goods and set off into the wild.

Two weeks later, they arrived at a small Asmat town in which Dutch anthropologist A.A. Gerbrands and American anthropologist David Eyde were living with the natives. Gerbrands, an expert in Asmat art, had helped Michael during his first trip and agreed to assist him in purchasing, cataloguing, and interpreting the objects during this second journey. They set off again for remote, upstream villages, accompanied by two missionaries from a local Catholic mission. Michael discovered a number of extraordinary objects and sent several letters home, expressing his excitement over the trip. His father later said that he believed the time that he spent in New Guinea was the happiest time of Michael's life.

The expedition spent two weeks in the northwest corner of the Asmat. They visited 13 villages and traveled over two river systems. Despite many hardships —– like terrible heat and humidity, snakes, and swarms of biting insects —– they enjoyed the journey.

On November 12, Michael and Rene arrived in Agats, a town that was large by New Guinea standards, and was used by missionaries and government officials as a headquarters. They planned to take a brief rest, reorganize, and then set off again. Michael wrote his last letter home on November 16.

On the morning of November 18, Michael, Rene, and two boys, Simon and Leo, took off from Agats and were on their way to Ats. To reach it, they had to travel on the Arafura Sea and then traverse the Bets River. The Arafura Sea was known to be treacherous, especially at the mouth of the Siretsj and Bets rivers, where the strong river currents met the heavy ocean swells. Michael was warned that their boat was not sturdy enough to be used on the sea, but he ignored the warnings. Anthropologist David Eyde told him that the boat was not seaworthy, but Michael replied that he had confidence in his "riverboat."

And, sure enough, at the mouth of the Siretsj River, their 40-foot vessel was swamped by a huge wave and the outboard motor died. The men didn't panic, but when the boat began to drift out to sea, Simon and Leo decided to swim to shore and get help. Even though they were less than a mile from shore, a short distance to the strong, native swimmers, it took the boys nearly five hours, fighting against strong currents, to reach land. After that, it took them almost another entire day to walk the 11 miles of mud and jungle to Agats, where they notified the authorities of what had occurred.

Meanwhile, the boat drifted helplessly out to sea. As wave after wave swept over the craft, the canoes began to sink. Finally, they turned over and Michael and Rene were forced to straddle the bottoms of the canoes, using loose boards as paddles, to battle a current that was too strong for them. They spent the night on their bobbing makeshift raft, twice paddling furiously toward the coast, only to be pushed back out to sea again.

At dawn, they could still see land on the horizon, but the boat continued to drift. Unsure about whether Simon and Leo would make it to Agats in time, Michael proposed that their best chance for survival was to swim ashore themselves. Rene argued that it would be best to stay with the overturned boat. The waters in which the boat had overturned were known to be infested with saltwater crocodiles and sharks. The tide was against them, and the current too powerful, and he knew that since he was not as strong of a swimmer as Michael, he would never make it. Rene later said, "We had a very long discussion and I tried very hard to talk that idea out of his head. He listened to me, but I knew in advance that he would go ahead. It was always very difficult to make him change his mind. He was a brave man, but also very unreasonable... His restless nature made it impossible for him to endure our drifting around."

Michael stripped to his shorts, tied his eyeglasses to his head with twine, and lashed two empty gasoline cans to his body to give him some buoyancy in the rough water. "I think I can make it," he told Rene and then jumped into the water. The anthropologist watched him swim in a straight line for almost half an hour until he could only see three dots —- the two gas cans and Michael's head —- and then he vanished from sight in the distance.

Michael Rockefeller was never seen again.

About eight hours after Michael began swimming, a Dutch Neptune patrol boat spotted the capsized boat about 20 miles out to sea and Rene was rescued. Soon after, a massive search was mounted by the Dutch government, and word spread that Michael Rockefeller, heir to a fortune, was missing, perhaps wandering among the forbidding mangrove swamps that lined the southwest coast of the world's second-largest island. Nelson Rockefeller chartered a jet and flew to New Guinea with Michael's twin sister, Mary, and Peabody expedition leader Robert Gardner. "I could never forgive myself," Rockefeller stated, "if I didn't do everything possible to help find my son."

The search took on the scale of a military operation with Dutch and Australian planes, assisted by helicopters, searching by air. Naval boats scoured the lagoons. President Kennedy and the U.S. Pacific fleet offered to send an aircraft carrier, but Governor Rockefeller graciously declined the offer. More than 1,000 natives searched the swamps by canoe and another 5,000 joined the land search, exploring swamps and shoreline. Hundreds of crocodiles were encountered, but there was no trace of Michael.

Nelson Rockefeller refused to give up hope, and for three days, he and his daughter joined the search, flying across the jungles and along the coast in a chartered jet. Gardner explored the area by boat but none of them turned up anything. As the search began to wind down, speculation began that Michael had drowned while trying to swim to shore. If he hadn't, he still had to face sharks and crocodiles. Dutch Resident General Eibrink Jansen was quoted as saying, "It would be a miracle if he is found alive."

On November 24, Governor Rockefeller sadly gave up the search. There was no longer much hope of finding Michael alive and so the search focused on locating the red gasoline cans. If they could be found on land, there was some encouragement that he made it to shore. A single red gasoline can was found in the ocean, although very close to land. Searchers considered it a "good omen." A day later, a wisp of smoke was seen in the forest —– but whoever built the fire was never found.

The Rockefellers returned home on November 28. All official hope of finding Michael had ended. Arriving in New York, the governor expressed the wish that, by some miracle, Michael would be found alive in the jungle but, unless some of the wilder stories could be believed, he never was.

After Michael's disappearance, theories and rumors ran rampant. One speculation was that he was captured by native warriors and carried off as a captive white god. Another asserted that he had wanted to escape from the restrictions of his wealthy life and now was living free and unfettered among the savages. Another claim was that he had brought about his own death by offering high prices for shrunken human heads, stirring up native unrest. None of the rumors offered any real evidence, but they certainly gave people something to talk about.

Perhaps the grisliest of the wild stories that surrounded Michael's disappearance was one that was largely accepted as the "true story" of what happened to him —---- that he was captured and eaten by the Asmat. A Dutch missionary turned out to be the man behind the story. He had heard of a white man who wore eyeglasses, who had been cannibalized by the Asmat. The missionary insisted that he knew of no one in the region who wore eyeglasses at the time other than himself —f – and Michael Rockefeller.

In 1969, journalist Milt Machlin traveled to New Guinea to investigate Rockefeller's disappearance. Machlin's curiosity was piqued by a story from an Australian smuggler who claimed he had seen Rockefeller on one of the small outlying islands. The reporter's search turned up nothing, and he dismissed reports of Rockefeller's living as a captive or as a Kurtz-type character in the jungle (Kurtz was an ivory trader in Joseph Conrad's book, *Heart of Darkness*, who induced natives to worship him as a god). Machlin came to believe that Michael may have survived his swim —– only to be killed on land. Several leaders of Otsjanep village, where Rockefeller likely would have arrived had he made it to shore, were killed by a Dutch patrol in 1958, and thus would have some rationale for revenge against someone from the "white tribe." Neither cannibalism nor headhunting in Asmat were indiscriminate, but rather were part of an "eye for an eye" revenge cycle, and so it is possible that Rockefeller found himself an inadvertent victim of it.

Michael's disappearance was investigated again by adventurer and writer Lorne Blair in 1975. He and a documentary film team retraced Michael's travels in the Asmat and investigated the cannibalism theory, which he found convincing. Several of the natives that he interviewed claimed to have been involved in Michael's death —– and in the gruesome meal that followed.

In 1978, a Canadian geologist visiting the Asmat met a missionary named Otto Konig who showed allegedly showed him Michael's watch and glasses and confirmed that he had been killed and eaten.

In 1979, author Paul Toohey, in his book *Rocky Goes West*, claimed that Michael's mother hired a private investigator to go to New Guinea and try to resolve the mystery of his disappearance. The reliability of the story has been questioned, but Toohey claimed that the investigator swapped a boat engine for the skulls of the three men that a tribe claimed were the only white men they had ever killed. When he returned to New York, he gave the skulls to the family, convinced that one of them was Michael's. If this event did occur, the family has never commented on it.

In 2014, Carl Hoffman published the book *Savage Harvest: A Tale of Cannibals, Colonialism, and Michael Rockefeller's Tragic Quest for Primitive Art*. Hoffman traveled to New Guinea and attempted to follow in Michael's footsteps. During multiple visits to the villages in the area, he heard stories about men from Otsjanep killing Michael after he swam to shore. The stories, which were similar to testimonials collected in the 1960s, center around a handful of men arguing and eventually deciding to kill Michael in revenge for a 1958 confrontation with Dutch officials. Soon after the murder, the villages were swept by a cholera epidemic —– which they believed was retribution from the gods for killing Michael. The natives had kept silent about the murder and cannibalism ever since, fearing what might happen if they talked about it.

Are any of these stories true? No one can say. Many believe that Michael died at sea and never made it to shore at all. But what if he did? Would he have been murdered and eaten by the villagers in revenge for something he'd had no part in? Perhaps other natives that he had managed to befriend and who showed him courtesy and respect in the weeks before he vanished would not have —– but these were a different people, angered simply by the sight of a white man who was alone and vulnerable.

Or could Michael Rockefeller, as some believe, have simply dropped out of sight and "gone native," disappearing into a place where he was the happiest in his life?

The mystery will likely never be solved.

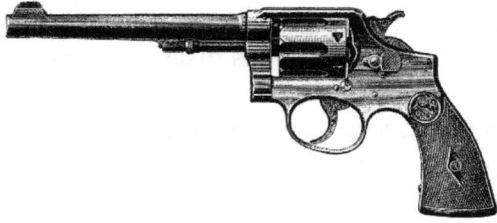

1966: Young Women Lost

On a hot, sunny, summer Saturday, three young women in bathing suits left all their belongings on a crowded beach and climbed aboard a motorboat on Lake Michigan. It was noon on July 2, 1966, at Indiana Dunes State Park, about an hour around the lake from Chicago.

A couple whose beach blanket was next to where the young women had left their blanket, watched as the motorboat glided away, and then waited all day for them to return. They didn't know the girls, but thought it was odd that they would leave their purses unattended on a day when the park was packed with more than 9,000 holiday weekend sunbathers and swimmers. When the couple left at dusk, they pointed out the abandoned blanket to a park ranger. They told him that the young women had left on a boat that was operated by a young man with a headful of dark, curly hair. The ranger bundled up the belongings and stored them away.

A day and a half later, on July 4, Park Superintendent Bill Svetic took a call from a Chicago man inquiring about his daughter, Patty Blough, 19. She had not been heard from since leaving home for Indiana Dunes with two friends on Saturday morning. Svetic opened the blanket bundle that had been left on the beach and found Patty's wallet, keys, and clothing. He also found clothes and purses belonging to her friends, Renee Bruhl, 19, and Ann Miller, 21. Ann's 1955 Buick was still sitting in the beach parking lot. Svetic assured Harold Blough that his daughter would turn up —— she'd probably just had a little bit too much fun over the holiday weekend.

But Patty didn't show up. And neither did her friends. Ann, Patty, and Renee have never been seen again.

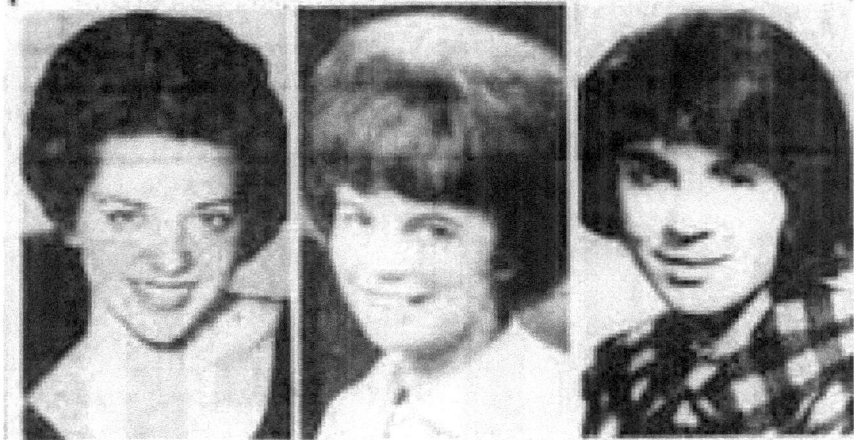

Missing 5th Day at Dunes

The three young women who went missing at Indiana Dunes — Renee Bruhl, Patricia Blough, and Ann Miller

The investigation into the disappearance at Indiana Dunes State Park began belatedly with scuba divers scouring the lake, and searchers on foot and horseback combing the sprawling sand dunes and woods of the park, which stretches along 45 miles of the Indiana coastline.

But no sign of the young women was ever found. In fact, they remain missing more than 50 years later, and their fate remains one of the enduring unsolved mysteries of the region. What happened to the three young women? No one will probably ever know, but it's possible that there are still some clues that might stand out when we trace their movements on the day of their vanishing —– and in the days before their arrival at the beach.

On the morning of July 2, Ann Miller left home in her four-door Buick and picked up Patty Blough from her family's home in Westchester, Illinois, around 8:00 a.m. Patty told her mother that they planned to return home early in the evening since their friend Renee Bruhl was coming with them and she needed to be back in time to make supper for her husband. Ann and Patty picked up Renee from her home on West Fulton Street, on Chicago's West Side, and then stopped at a drugstore to pick up some suntan lotion. The women arrived at the Indiana Dunes State Park at approximately 10:00 a.m. Ann parked in the lot and the women hiked to a spot that was about 100 yards from the Lake Michigan shoreline.

The nearby couple —– who later reported that the girls hadn't returned —--- stated that the girls left their belongings on the beach at noon and they entered the water together. The witnesses then saw them speaking to an unidentified man who was operating a 14- to 16-foot long white boat with a blue interior and outboard motor. They were unsure of the time when this man approached them. The couple described all this to the park ranger around dusk, when they noticed that the women's belongings were still sitting on the beach. The women had gotten on the boat, they said, and had headed west with the driver —– and disappeared.

Renee left behind a large beach towel, shorts, a blouse, cigarettes, suntan lotion, 25 cents, and her purse, which contained about $55 in checks, sitting on the beach. The other women also left clothing, purses, and personal items in the sand. Those belongings were collected by the ranger on the night of their disappearance and stored in the park superintendent's office until July 4, when Patty's father called the park, searching for his daughter and her friends. The park rangers soon learned that missing person's reports had been filed for all three women over the weekend in Illinois by their families. The rangers knew that a Buick had been left in the parking lot, but until that time, didn't know that it belonged to Ann. Her car keys had been left with her purse on the beach, but other items of clothing and personal effects were still inside of the car. The car was still parked in the spot where Ann had left it on July 2 —– no one had moved it.

The park rangers soon got other law enforcement agencies involved, including the U.S. Coast Guard. The search was in full swing by July 5, three days after the girls had vanished. Other witnesses who were in the park that day came forward with conflicting stories, but authorities came to believe that the first witnesses' reports were the most reliable —– the three women were seen boarding a boat and they did not return to the beach.

The search for the three women continued around the clock. It was extended to a six-mile stretch of beach west of the state park, near Ogden Dunes, later in the week. More witnesses came forward that substantiated the initial report that the women got into a boat with an unidentified man. Later accounts claimed that he was in his early twenties with a tanned complexion and dark, wavy hair. He was wearing a beach jacket at the time.

A beach-goer who was taking home movies on July 2 offered his films to investigators. The search was narrowed down to two boats after the detectives watched the footage. One of them was a 16-foot runabout with a three-hulled design, which was operated by a man who fit the description of the man seen with the girls. Three women who matched descriptions of the missing girls were seen aboard the boat in the footage. The second boat was identified as a 26-foot cabin cruiser with three men and three women aboard. The cabin cruiser was seen at around 3:00 p.m., three hours after the women got aboard the smaller boat. After reports came in that Ann, Patty, and Renee were seen walking on the beach and eating after this time, investigators came to believe that they had been dropped off on the beach west of the state park by the driver of the smaller boat while he drove back to retrieve his two male friends and the cabin cruiser.

While on the second beach, the girls were reportedly approached by another unidentified man, who accompanied them to the cabin cruiser. Witnesses stated that this second boat was equipped with a radio / telephone antenna, but apparently did not have a name painted on its stern. This final sighting has never been confirmed, but the authorities did consider it reliable.

The search went on but lead after lead went nowhere. A psychic that was brought into the case claimed to have a vision of a Lake Michigan cabin where the women's bodies were buried. An extensive search of the property believed to be the place seen by the psychic did not uncover any evidence. However, detectives did point out that the shifting sand dunes may have buried any possible evidence deeper under the ground.

Investigators began looking into the backgrounds of the three women, trying to discover if their disappearances could have been voluntary —– and it was there that things got even murkier and stranger.

In Renee Bruhl's purse, the authorities found a letter addressed to her husband, Jeff. The couple had been married for just 15 months in July 1966, but in the letter, she asked for a divorce. She said that she felt her husband spent too much time working on cars with his friends and didn't seem to have time for her. Her husband, though, told the police that he was not aware of any problems in their marriage at the time of his wife's disappearance. Her family agreed with the statement, telling investigators that they believed that Renee had written the note in a moment of anger and never gave it to Jeff because she had changed her mind about the divorce.

But that might not have been all there was to the story.

All three women were friends, drawn together by their love of horses. Patty and Ann met while boarding their horses at the same Illinois stable. Renee was a classmate of Patty's at Proviso West High School in Maywood, Illinois, and she had completed a one-year course in medical technology after graduation. The women often rode together and often met at a tavern in Hodgkins, Illinois, after their outings. According to a theory created by Dick Wylie, a reporter and photographer who chased crime in northwest Indiana for the *Gary Post-Tribune* and the *Chicago Sun-Times* during the 1950s and '60s, the events leading to their disappearance began there.

Both Patty and Ann were single, and Wylie believed they fell for married men they met at the tavern and both got pregnant. Later, statements from some of Ann's friends claim that she was three months pregnant in July 1966 and mentioned going to a home for unwed mothers prior to her disappearance. But did she have plans to end the pregnancy? And what about Patty? Was she pregnant, as well?

Abortion was illegal in Illinois in 1966. According to Dick Wylie, some Chicago women who found themselves in trouble visited a house just across the state line in Gary, Indiana, where a husband-and-wife team, Helen and Frank Largo, performed backroom abortions. Wylie linked the Largos, now dead, to a floating abortion mill that operated on a houseboat offshore in Lake Michigan. He believed Ann and Patty had arranged abortions on that boat on July 2, and they were ferried there by Ralph Largo, Jr., a nephew of Helen and Frank Largo. He was seen at the park that day, and he matched the description of the man last seen with the girls on the beach.

Wylie believed that the women got to the larger boat, but something went wrong with one of the procedures and the other two were killed so that no witnesses would be left behind. The girls had left their belongings on the beach because they expected to be back in 90 minutes, Wylie said. The theory has never been confirmed —– the younger Largo died in 2009 —– but it is plausible. However, unless a body turns up, it's likely to always remain just a theory.

And it's not the only one, of course. There have been many unconfirmed sightings of the three women over the years, but no solid leads have ever surfaced. The boats they were allegedly on in July 1966 have never been located, and the men operating them have never been solidly identified. But people have continued to speculate, especially when it comes to their connection with horses.

Ann, Patty, and Renee often rode at the Tri Color Stables in Palatine, Illinois, which were owned by George Jayne and his brother, Silas, who were involved in fraudulent activities, murders, and worse in the mid-1960s. Cheryl Ann Rude, a young woman associated with the horse market, was killed at the Tri Color Stables in June 1965 by a car bomb that had been meant for George Jayne. George had asked Cheryl to move his Cadillac from the stable entrance and the bomb exploded. Some believe that perhaps Patty, Ann, and Renee (or one or any combination of them) may have witnessed the bomb being planted. However, this does not explain why anyone would have waited an entire year before silencing them. Or does it? In March 1966, Patty received a facial injury that she never explained. One of her friends claimed she made an off-handed remark about it and mentioned trouble with "syndicate people." But no proof of any trouble exists.

There was a connection between the Jaynes and the missing women, though. Both men's telephone numbers were found in their belongings after their disappearance. There is no question that the two men were deeply involved in crime. George was shot to death in 1970, and Silas was later convicted of conspiracy in his brother's murder and sent to prison. He died in 1987. He is also a suspect in the disappearance and probable murder of candy heiress Helen Brach (also featured later in this book). In 1997, a man named James Blottiaux was charged with planting the 1965 car bomb that killed Cheryl Ann Rude at the Jaynes' stables, but neither he, nor the Jaynes, have been positively linked to the disappearances of Ann, Patty, and Renee.

It's hard not to speculate, though, that any of them might have been involved in some way. Silas Jayne reportedly told a sheriff that he had three bodies buried beneath his residence after the 1966 disappearances. Investigators took his claim seriously and planned to search the property, but the sheriff involved was killed in a farming accident before the search took place. For whatever reason, it was not pursued after that, leading some to wonder if the claim was true.

What happened to three pretty young women in July 1966? We'll likely never know. The case is not unsolvable, but without any bodies or any solid new leads, it's unlikely that the truth will ever be known.

1968: The Impossible Disappearance

One of the most baffling disappearances of all time simply couldn't have happened —-- and yet it did. In June 1968, a man named Jerrold Potter vanished from a place that there was seemingly no way out of – the lavatory of an airplane in flight – and disappeared without a trace. Skeptics might maintain that such a thing is impossible, and yet records remain to show that it actually occurred.

I have given into the temptation to end this opening with the famous words – "Believe it, or not!"

On June 29, 1968, a private DC-3 jet took off from Kankakee, Illinois, bound for a Lion's Club convention in Dallas, Texas. The plane had been chartered from the Purdue Aviation Corporation for the trip, and among the 23 passengers on board were Jerrold Potter and his wife, Carrie. They had both been looking forward to the trip for quite some time. Potter, 54, was a successful insurance executive from Pontiac, Illinois. He was also a member of the Lions, belonged to both the Elks and Moose lodges, and was a member of the local Chamber of Commerce. Affable, outgoing, and in the best of health, he had a happy home life, two married daughters, and was not the sort of man whom anyone would suspect of becoming involved in a paranormal mystery that has never been solved.

For an hour after take-off, the Potters, occupying seats toward the rear of the plane, looked down over the rolling foothills of the Ozarks, talking quietly and enjoying the smooth flight. It was a beautiful summer day and the sky was cloudless. The DC-3 was north of Rolla, Missouri, approaching the Camp Leonard Wood area, when Potter decided to use the restroom. His wife saw him start towards the compartment near the rear of the plane and pause along the way to chat with some of his friends, who were also going to the convention. One of his friends was James Schiave, president of the Ottawa, Illinois, Lions Club. Potter stopped briefly to talk with Schiave, and then he continued down the aisle to the lavatory.

A few minutes passed and then, unaccountably, the plane jolted, as if it had bumped over an invisible obstacle in its flight path. It recovered immediately and there was no concern among the passengers. Most of them had flown before and were familiar with the occasional turbulence that was encountered during air travel.

Mrs. Potter, who was not an air travel veteran, was a little unnerved by the bump and looked about for her husband. He had still not returned from the restroom. Failing to see him anywhere, she asked one of the two flight attendants to check the lavatory —– but there was no one inside. The flight attendant quickly checked the plane, but Mr. Potter was nowhere to be found. She hurried up front to speak to the captain.

She told Roy Bacus, the co-pilot, that she believed that Potter was missing. Bacus was skeptical, but she assured him that the man was gone, "He was near the lavatory compartment when the plane quivered. He isn't there now and no one has seen him since."

Bacus hurried back to check for himself and then informed Captain Miguel Raul Cabeza of what had occurred. Bacus believed that Potter may have either been thrown against the rear exit door by the turbulence and fell out, or had gone out the door by mistake, believing that it was the lavatory. Of course, this did not explain how he could have missed the large sign that stated "Do Not Open While in Flight," or how the passengers and crew would have failed to notice that a door had been opened while the plane was in the air.

Cabeza reported by radio that he was changing course, detailed the nature of his emergency, and headed for the nearest airport, which was in Springfield, Missouri. When the plane touched down, it was thoroughly searched for the missing man, but he was simply not on board.

It was difficult to believe that Potter could have accidentally left the plane. The exit door not only bore the large red warning sign, but it was hinged at the top and secured by a safety chain and a large, heavy handle that had to be turned 180-degrees to release two sturdy plunger bolts in order to open it. If Potter had believed that this was the lavatory, then it would have had to have been the most secure restroom that he had ever used.

Grove Webster, the president of Purdue Aviation Corporation, was one of the officials who investigated the incident. He stated, "It would take a monumental effort to open the door during flight. The door was locked securely on takeoff. You can stand in the doorway of a DC-3 in flight and not be sucked out. The plane is not pressurized. And to open the door takes a lot of effort. Crews close the door for our stewardesses and open it. And it is harder to open and close in flight than on the ground. Some of our smaller stewardesses actually have a difficult time opening the door."

Several months later, lawyers for Carrie Potter filed a damage suit against the air charter company, arguing that they were negligent in their maintenance of the aircraft and failed to follow safety procedures. The case was eventually dismissed. There had been 22 other passengers and two flight attendants on board, but there were no eyewitnesses who could state that they had seen Potter open the exit door and fall to his death. The area of the Ozark Mountains where he was presumed to have fallen was carefully searched, but Potter's corpse was never found.

So, what happened to Jerrold Potter? Did he accidentally fall to his death, or did the seemingly happy and untroubled man commit suicide? And if so, how did he open the exit door with no one noticing? Natural explanations for this bizarre case seem to be few and far between.

Could his disappearance be an unnatural one? Did Potter open the lavatory door and step into one of Charles Fort's mysterious "holes in time and space"?

We will never know for sure. Jerrold Potter simply became a man who literally vanished into thin air.

1969: Vanished in the Smoky Mountains

On June 14, 1969, on the day before he would have turned 7, a young boy named Dennis Martin vanished without a trace. His disappearance sparked the largest search in the history of the Great Smoky Mountains National Park but to this day, his vanishing remains unsolved.

It happened on a camping trip over Father's Day weekend when a grinning Dennis, who was playing hide-and-seek with some other children, darted out of sight —– and never returned. Nearly 1,500 searchers combed more than 50 square miles of the nation's most-visited park and came away with nothing. Lessons learned during the field search became textbook training for first responders nationwide, but Dennis was never found. It has become one of the enduring mysteries of the Smokies.

Years later, Bill Martin would remember that there was not a cloud in the sky on the day his son disappeared. Bill, an architect from Knoxville, Tennessee, came to the park's Spence Field that weekend with his father and two sons —– Doug, 9, and Dennis, 6 —– for a weekend of camping and hiking.

Spence Field runs east and west along the Appalachian Trail on the Tennessee-North Carolina line. The area is filled with steep slopes, heavy woods, and jagged ravines where copperheads and rattlesnakes lurked. The forests teemed with bears, bobcats, and wild hogs.

Dennis was a small but strong boy with brown eyes and wavy brown hair, easy to spot that day in his red t-shirt and green shorts. He'd never camped away from home before, but he knew his way in the woods. He often led the way on trails at a pace that adults had a hard time keeping up with. He was a fun-loving boy, which may have led to the terrible events of that day.

Just before 4:30 p.m., Dennis, Doug, and two other boys were playing hide-and-seek in the field. He was last seen by his father going behind a bush to hide, intending on surprising the other children when they walked past. A few minutes later, the other children had appeared, but Bill and the other adults soon realized that something was wrong —- where was Dennis?

Almost at the same moment, a breeze swept across the field, followed by a roll of thunder. A sudden storm broke with a fury.

Dennis Martin, the boy who was never found

It would dump nearly three inches of rain that evening. High winds drowned out the calls for Dennis, but an alarm was raised with the authorities. There was little they could do on that dark and stormy night.

The next morning, more than 250 people converged on Spence Field to help look for the missing boy, including his mother, Violet. Park officials later acknowledged bungling the search with too many overeager volunteers and inexperienced eyes. Green Berets on a training exercise showed up to help. The ranks of volunteers peaked on the seventh day at more than 1,400 people.

Bill called for his son from a helicopter. Searchers questioned whether he could even be heard. On the fourth day, hikers spotted a faint set of child-size tracks about a mile below Spence Field. Park officials dismissed the tracks as prints left by Boy Scouts who had joined the search party. Many years later, Dwight McCarter, a retired Smokies ranger and veteran tracker, wondered about those prints.

"They didn't find tracks from a bunch of kids," he said. "They found tracks from one kid."

Just nine days after what would have been Dennis's seventh birthday on June 20, park officials suspended major search operations. The Martins offered a $5,000 reward for information, but the reward was never claimed, even after a ginseng hunter reported finding a child-sized skeleton near Spence Field in 1985. A follow-up search found nothing.

Over the years, several theories have emerged about what happened to Dennis Martin. Some believe that the boy became lost and died from exposure or some other cause, likely during the first night. Others believe that he was killed by a bear, or some other wild animal, and was carried off.

However, many others, including Bill Martin, believe the boy was abducted and taken out of the park by someone —- or something. On the afternoon that Dennis disappeared, tourist Harold Key and his family, heard an "enormous, sickening scream" and then witnesses saw a "man covered in hair" run away from them while carrying something over his shoulder. While they couldn't completely identify that it was a boy being carried, they said it was possible.

There was a history of such things in the Great Smoky Mountains National Park. A former ranger had been attacked by what was referred to as a "wild mountain man" —- one of several that live in the wilderness of the park. Many suspect that Dennis may have been taken by one of them, too. Others have questioned whether it was a man at all that the witnesses had seen. They believe that it could have been a Sasquatch-type who carried Dennis away.

Weird? Yes, but impossible? I don't think so.

Park Rangers and the FBI investigators concluded that there was insufficient evidence to link the sighting to Dennis's disappearance, particularly given that Key's sighting was approximately five miles away from where the boy disappeared.

Whatever happened that day remains a mystery. Bill Martin died in 2014, never knowing what became of his son. The family has never spoken publicly about the case.

The tragic vanishing of Dennis Martin had an impact on wilderness searches all over the world. Rescue workers still talk about the case, and searchers in the Smokies have failed to find only four missing people since 1969.

Other lives have been saved because of the one that was lost —— although that is probably small comfort to the family of a little boy whose life was cut short on that fateful day.

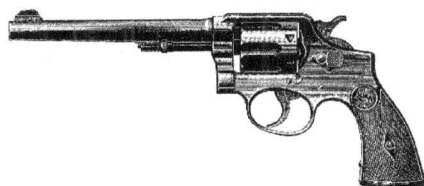

1975: The Missing Teamster

One of the most famous unsolved disappearances of the modern era was that of Jimmy Hoffa, the famed president of the Teamsters Union from 1957 until he went to prison in 1967. There was no question that Hoffa had a lot of enemies in his day, and perhaps none so powerful as Robert F. Kennedy, the president's brother and the United States Attorney General. Hoffa's ties to organized crime landed him in prison, but it would not be until those same gangsters turned against him that those ties would lead to his disappearance and likely murder.

And while Hoffa's body has never been found, there is little question about whether he is dead. One way or another, Hoffa is not coming back.

Jimmy Hoffa was born in Brazil, Indiana, on February 14, 1913, to John and Viola Hoffa. His father was of German ancestry and died in 1920 from lung disease when Jimmy was still a young boy. His Irish-American mother moved him to live with family in Detroit in 1924, where Jimmy lived the rest of his life. He left school at 14 to help support his family, working menial jobs like house painting and bagging groceries.

In 1936, he married Josephine Poszywak, an 18-year-old Polish-American laundry worker. They had met six months earlier during a non-unionized laundry worker's strike. The couple went on to have two children —— a daughter, Barbara, and a son, James. His son would eventually take over the same position as his father as the president of the International Brotherhood of Teamsters.

Hoffa first got involved with union organizing as a teenager, when he worked at a grocery chain. His job paid substandard wages, offered poor working conditions, and had almost no job security. Unhappy with the situation, the workers tried to organize a union. Jimmy was young, but his courage and approachability impressed his fellow workers and soon, he rose to a leadership position. By 1932, after defiantly refusing to work for an abusive shift foreman, he left the grocery chain. He was then invited to become an organizer with the Local 299 of the Teamsters in Detroit.

By that time, the Teamsters Union, founded in 1903, had 75,000 members. As a result of Hoffa's work with other union leaders to consolidate local union trucker groups into regional sections, and then into a national group —– work Hoffa completed over two decades —– membership grew to 170,000 members by 1936. Three years later, there were 420,000 Teamsters in America. The number grew steadily during World War II and during the post-war boom to top 1 million members by 1951.

The Teamsters organized truck drivers and warehousemen, first throughout the Midwest, then nationwide. Hoffa played a major role in the union's skillful use of strikes, boycotts, and other means of leveraging union strength at one company, to then organized the workers, and finally to win contract demands at other companies. This eventually helped to make the Teamsters one of the most powerful unions in the United States.

Trucking unions in that era were heavily influenced by, and in many cases controlled by, elements of organized crime. After Prohibition had ended in 1933, the mob went looking for other sources of money, like gambling, prostitution, racketeering, and skimming

Teamster boss Jimmy Hoffa

from the accounts of unions under their control. For Hoffa to unify and expand trucking unions, he had to make accommodations and arrangements with gangsters, starting in the Detroit area and spreading across the country from there. Organized crime within the union expanded as the Teamsters grew.

Hoffa worked to defend the Teamsters union from raids by other unions and extended the Teamsters' influence across the Midwestern states from the late 1930s to the late 1940s. Although he never actually worked as a truck driver, he came president of the Local 299 in December 1946. His position as head of the Michigan Teamsters was earned a short time later. During World War II, he was given a deferment from military service by making the case that his union leadership skills were valuable to the nation because he could keep freight running smoothly to assist the war effort.

At the 1952 Teamsters convention in Los Angeles, Hoffa was selected as national vice president by incoming president Dave Beck, successor to Daniel J. Tobin, who had been president since 1907. Hoffa had engineered an internal revolt against Tobin by securing support for Beck at the convention. In exchange, Beck made Hoffa the vice president.

After the Teamsters moved their headquarters from Indianapolis to Washington, D.C., Hoffa began spending more of his time away from Detroit. He was either in Washington or traveling around the country for his expanded responsibilities —- which soon included the role of president.

In 1957, Hoffa took over the presidency of the Teamsters. By this time, his predecessor, Beck, was in hot water. He had appeared before the Senate Select Committee on Improper Activities in the Labor or Management Field —-- popularly called the McClellan Committee —- which was investigating mob activities in labor unions, and he took the Fifth Amendment 140 times in response to questions. Beck was under indictment when Hoffa took his place. He was later convicted and sent to prison for fraud.

Hoffa was re-elected in 1961 and began working to further expand the union. It was at this point that he became the target of Robert Kennedy, chief counsel of the McClellan Committee, who later became the U.S. Attorney General. In 1961, Kennedy made Hoffa the top priority of his administration, and his efforts resulted in the labor leader's 1962 trial for extorting illegal payments from a firm that employed Teamsters. The proceedings ended in a hung jury but then Hoffa was arrested for attempting to bribe one of the jurors.

Believe it or not, as this was going on, Hoffa was re-elected, without opposition, to a third five-year term as union president, while his convictions were being appealed. Frank Fitzsimmons, Hoffa's closest crony, was elected as vice president, just in case "Hoffa has to serve a jail term."

In 1964, Hoffa was also convicted of misappropriating $1.7 million in union pension funds but managed to stay out of prison until 1967. He ended up serving 58 months, and his sentence was commuted by President Nixon with the condition that he stayed out of union politics until 1980, which would have been the full term of his prison sentence. Hoffa didn't take this condition seriously and he started legal action to get it set aside. In addition, he went ahead with efforts to regain control of the union from Frank Fitzsimmons. This maneuver did not sit well with mob leaders, as Fitzsimmons was much easier to manipulate than the stubborn Hoffa and could always be counted on to look the other

The Machus Red Fox Restaurant, the last place that Jimmy Hoffa was ever seen alive

way. Fitzsimmons was infinitely more desirable as the head of the union. Hoffa was warned several times by mobsters to stop interfering and trying to regain his position but, not surprisingly, he refused to listen.

On July 30, 1975, Hoffa had a meeting scheduled with Anthony Provenzano and Anthony Giacalone at the Machus Red Fox Restaurant in the Detroit suburb of Bloomfield Township. The Machus Red Fox was well-known to Hoffa. His son James' wedding reception had been held there. He wrote the date in his office calendar, "TG – 2 PM – Red Fox."

He left home at 1:15 p.m. in his green Pontiac Grand Ville. Before heading to the restaurant, he stopped at the office of his close friend, Louis Linteau, a former president of Teamsters Local 614 who now ran a limousine service. The two men, former enemies, had become good friends and by the time Hoffa left prison, Linteau had become his official appointment secretary. He had arranged a July 26 sit down with the Giacalone brothers where the July 30 meeting had been planned.

Linteau was out to lunch when Hoffa stopped by, so he left a message for him before he departed for the Machus Red Fox.

Hoffa arrived at the restaurant first, around 2:00 p.m., but after waiting around for about 15 minutes, he started getting irritated. An annoyed Hoffa called his wife and complained, "Where the hell is Tony Giacalone? I'm being stood up." His wife told him that she had not heard from anyone. This was the last time that she ever spoke to her husband.

Several eyewitnesses saw Hoffa standing by his car and pacing the restaurant's parking lot. Two men on their way out of the restaurant recognized Hoffa and stopped to chat briefly and shake his hand. At 3:27 p.m., Hoffa called Linteau complaining that Giacalone was late. Hoffa said, "That dirty son of a bitch Tony Jocks set this meeting up, and he's an hour and a half late." Linteau told him to calm down, and to stop by his office on the way home. Hoffa said that he would and hung up.

This is Jimmy Hoffa's last known communication.

At 7:00 a.m. the following morning, Hoffa's wife called her son and daughter by telephone, saying that their father had not come home. On her way to the house, Hoffa's daughter, Barbara, claimed to have had a vision of her father, who she was already sure was dead. He was slumped over, wearing a dark-colored, short-sleeved polo shirt.

At 7:20 am, Linteau went to the Machus Red Fox, and found Hoffa's unlocked car in the parking lot, but there was no sign of Hoffa or any indication of what had happened to him. He called the police, who later arrived at the scene. State police were brought in and the FBI was alerted. At suppertime, Hoffa's son, James, filed a missing person's report.

After years of extensive investigation, involving numerous law enforcement agencies including the FBI, officials have not reached a definitive conclusion as to Hoffa's fate and who was involved.

Jimmy's wife, Josephine, died on September 12, 1980. According to her children, she died of a broken heart, brought on by the 1975 disappearance of her husband.

Jimmy Hoffa was declared legally dead on July 30, 1982 —– but his story was far from over.

On the day of his disappearance, Jimmy was seen getting into a car in the Machus Red Fox parking lot with several other men. Investigators are reasonably sure that he never got out of the car alive. Its surmised that Hoffa was brought to the meeting with Provenzano and Giacalone — - which was supposed to occur at the restaurant — and then killed. The two men were just two on the long list of suspects in Hoffa's disappearance, although they had solid alibis at the time when the union leader vanished. In fact, some would say they were too good. Apparently, they were touring several union officials around Hoboken, New Jersey, on July 30. They may not have personally committed Hoffa's murder, but that didn't mean they weren't involved.

The suspect list was overwhelming. The number of possible killers grew as investigators probed their underworld connections and spoke with convicts who were looking for reductions in their prison sentences for giving up the guy who "whacked Hoffa." The main suspects were Provenzano and Giacalone, Russell Bufaliano, and two Hoffa cronies, Thomas Andretta and Gabriel Briguglio. Another suspect, Briguglio's brother, Salvatore, was believed to be offering information on Hoffa's disappearance to the FBI when he was shot to death in March 1978.

As the investigation continued, loose ends began to unravel everywhere. One of the most obvious mysteries was why Provenzano and Giacalone would have linked themselves to a meeting with Hoffa if they planned to kill him. This seemed almost as odd as why the men who were supposed to kill Hoffa showed up 45 minutes late. This was not usual for mob hitmen, who find punctuality certainly makes the job easier. These questions notwithstanding, the authorities were able to track down the car that Hoffa got into, and they did find traces of blood and hair inside. They were convinced that Hoffa got into the car and then was garroted from behind.

But was he really killed? Some insisted that he was not. One union official, after long bouts of questioning by the FBI, swore that Hoffa had skipped off to Brazil with a "black go-go dancer."

Supposedly, this was the inside story among union members but it's unlikely to be the truth.

In the years since Hoffa's disappearance, most of the suspects in the case have died or have gone to prison on other charges. Any convictions for the murder of the vanished union leader would depend on testimony from an inside source, who is unlikely to ever come forward. One unidentified union official stated, "We all know who did it. It was Tony and those guys of his from New Jersey. It's common knowledge. But the cops need a corroborating witness, and it doesn't look like they're about to get one, does it?"

It seems common knowledge that Hoffa is dead, but one of the most intriguing parts of the mystery remains - what happened to his body? Theories — both credible and ridiculous — abound, and some incarcerated felons still seem to be amusing themselves by concocting stories about Hoffa's remains for eager journalists. There are a lot of suppositions and "confessions" floating around about the fate of Jimmy Hoffa, but what the reader cares to believe is their choice in the end.

In his book, *I Heard You Paint Houses*, author Charles Brandt claims that Frank "The Irishman" Sheeran, a professional killer for the mob and longtime friend of Hoffa's, confessed to assassinating him. According to Brandt, O'Brien drove Sheeran, Hoffa, and fellow mobster Sal Briguglio to a house in Detroit. Sheeran and Hoffa went into the house, where Sheeran claims that he shot Hoffa twice behind the right ear, and that he was told that Hoffa was cremated after the murder. But there are problems —- when the bloodstains in the house where Sheeran claimed the murder occurred were tested, they didn't match Hoffa.

In Philip Carlo's book *The Iceman: Confessions of a Mafia Contract Killer*, Richard Kuklinski claimed to know the fate of Hoffa -: his body was placed in a 50-gallon drum and set on fire for "a half hour or so," then the drum was welded shut and buried in a junkyard. Later, according to Kuklinski, an accomplice started to talk to federal authorities. Because of fear that he would use the information to try to get out of trouble, the perpetrators had the drum dug up, placed in the trunk of a car, and compacted. It was sold, along with hundreds of compacted cars, as scrap metal.

In January 2013, reputed gangster Tony Zerilli implied that Hoffa was originally buried in a shallow grave, with the plan to move his remains later to a second location. Zerilli contends that these plans were abandoned. He said that Hoffa's remains lay in a field in northern Oakland County, Michigan, not far from the restaurant where he was last seen. Zerilli denied any responsibility for or association with Hoffa's disappearance. On June 17, 2013, investigation of the Zerilli information led the FBI to a property in Oakland Township owned by Detroit mob boss Jack Tocco. After three days, the FBI called off the dig. No human remains were found.

And there have been lots of other leads that have not panned out, including that Hoffa's body was placed in a 55-gallon drum and carted away in a Gateway Transportation truck to an unknown location.

One prison inmate said that Hoffa's body was mixed in the concrete used to construct the New York Giants' football stadium in East Rutherford, New Jersey. However, the area was scanned with ground penetrating radar, looking for disturbances to indicate that a human body had been buried there. No traces of a burial were found. In 2010, when Giants Stadium was demolished, no human remains were discovered.

Another inmate claimed that he was buried in a gravel pit that was owned by Hoffa's brother, William. Hoffa was also said to be encased in the foundation of a Public Works garage in Cadillac, Michigan, under a swimming pool in Bloomfield Hills, and buried in a field in Waterford Township. Another story had it that he was dumped in a Florida swamp, while others insisted that Hoffa's remains were rendered down at a slaughterhouse, or that he was buried under the helipad of the Sheraton Savannah Resort Hotel, which was owned by the Teamsters at the time of his disappearance.

And the list goes on...

Despite the passage of so many years, Hoffa's case remains open. A special agent at the FBI's Detroit field office remains assigned to it. This ongoing investigation has generated over 25,000 pages of documents gathered from interviews, wiretaps, and surveillance, but no trace of Hoffa has ever been found.

Jimmy Hoffa walked away from a Detroit restaurant one day and vanished into the ether. He was never seen or heard from again. Whether or not his body is hidden away in a landfill or beneath the concrete of a hotel is anyone's guess —- but we'll certainly never see him again.

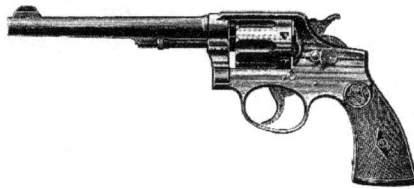

1977: Disappearance of the Candy Heiress

The disappearance of candy heiress Helen Voorhees Brach in February 1977 is a Chicago mystery that remains without an ending. But amidst uncovered plots, alleged conspiracies, and solid convictions in the case, we still don't know what happened to the unfortunate widow after she checked out of the Mayo Clinic and vanished into thin air on the way to her suburban Glenview home.

Helen has simply never been seen again.

Over the years, her disappearance has turned into something more than just a missing person's case. It has become a complicated murder mystery and horse swindle that has involved some of the darkest characters in Chicago criminal history during the mid-twentieth century.

Helen Voorhees was born in the Appalachian hills of southern Ohio and raised under modest circumstances. The red-haired beauty was already divorced by age 21, blaming herself for the failure of her marriage to a philandering playboy. But Helen refused to give up, going

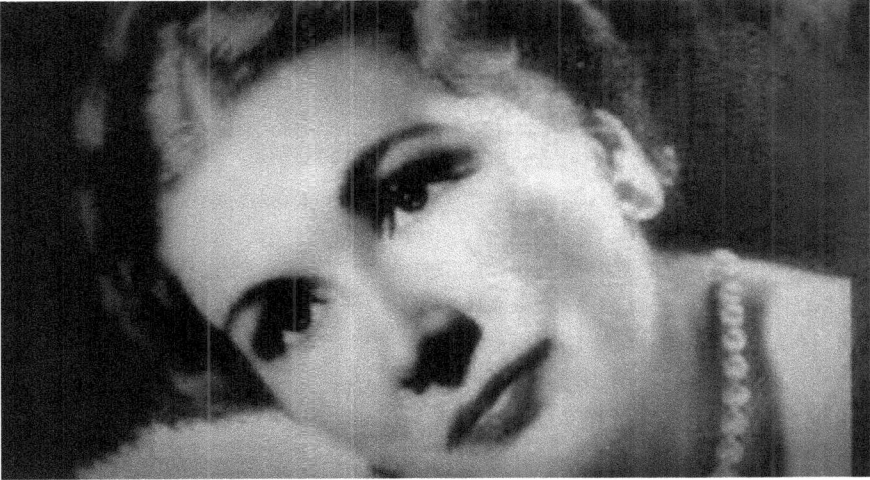

Helen Voorhees Brach

to work in a pottery factory before setting out for Miami in hopes of making it rich or marrying a millionaire —– which she did in 1950 when she met 54-year-old Frank V. Brach, the candy king of Chicago.

Helen was earning a living collecting tips as a hatcheck girl at Miami's Indian Creek Country Club. She had no trouble bewitching Brach, whose marriage to his wife, June, was already on shaky ground. Within a few months, he was actively courting Helen while divorce lawyers were wrangling over the details of a settlement back in Chicago. They were soon married and began their married life together at Brach's wooded seven-acre estate in Glenview.

After the death of his brother, Edwin Brach, control of the candy company went to Frank, but by then he was getting older and losing his passion for the business. He divested himself of his interests in the company in order to stay home and shower Helen with expensive gifts like a lavender Rolls-Royce convertible, a coral-colored Cadillac sedan, and a white-over-pink Lincoln Continental. Then, on January 29, 1970, Frank passed away, leaving Helen with the house, the cars, and about $30 million in assets.

With Frank gone, Helen was effectively cut off from the world. The Brachs had not been part of the Chicago social scene after they were married, and Helen had few local friends. She remained in the rambling house with only her houseman, Jack Matlick, who had been working for Frank since 1959, and her sad memories of her late husband for company. In spite of how she seems to have been portrayed —– as a scheming "gold digger" —– Helen truly loved her husband and she was brokenhearted by his death.

She threw herself into causes, namely animal welfare. She established the Helen Brach Foundation and donated vast sums of money to animal rights causes. Helen showered her love on a collection of stray cats, horses, and two poodles.

She seemed more interested in animals than men, so for the next three years she remained devoted to her causes and to Frank's memory, until, by chance, her Florida landlord introduced her to a handsome, middle-aged man named Richard Bailey, owner of Bailey's Stables and Country Club Stables. Helen had no idea that he was a notorious con artist, always on the lookout for rich widows, when she met him.

Their first meeting occurred at the Morton House, a famous Morton Grove restaurant located at the edge of the Cook County Forest Preserve at Lehigh and Lincoln. In those days, the restaurant was a favorite lunch destination for two-martini-lunch businessmen, their secretaries, and men like Bailey, a professional gigolo who made a fortune seducing older women. Later, federal prosecutors would estimate that Bailey had swindled between 200 and 100 wealthy North Shore women with promises of romance before implementing various schemes to get them to purchase overvalued horses. When he had taken them for as much money as possible, he broke off the relationship, leaving many of them broken and destitute. Helen Brach was simply the next target on Bailey's list.

We will never know what Helen saw in Bailey. Women found him to be sensitive and caring, but Helen could not have been so blind or naïve to think that Bailey was out to steal her heart and not her substantial bank account. Perhaps at this point in her life, she was beyond caring and appreciated whatever flattering attention was paid to her after years of being a widow. She was 62-years-old by this time and Bailey was a dashing 44.

In 1974, Helen confided to Bailey that she was interested in investing in a few good racehorses. Bailey quickly arranged, through his brother, Paul J. Bailey, the sale of three horses – each of them ready for the glue factory. Helen paid $95,000 for the horses, which cost Bailey only $17,500. In addition, Helen was also convinced to buy a group of breeding horses, too.

On New Year's Eve 1976 -- just six weeks before she vanished -- Helen and Bailey

Gigolo, con man, and murder suspect, Richard Bailey

celebrated at the Waldorf-Astoria Hotel in New York before Helen departed for her vacation home on Tappan Lake in Scio, Ohio, where she caught up with old friends. It was around this time that Bailey arranged an elaborate horse showing for Helen, hoping to get her to part with another $150,000 for more worthless horses.

But this time, Helen was suspicious. She hired an appraiser, who recommended that she invest nothing more in the first three horses that she got from Bailey, let alone in new additions to her stable. Furious at Bailey for his scheme, Helen screamed at Bailey and his men, threatening to go to the State's Attorney. She confided this plan to a friend, who promised to introduce her to prosecutors who would be willing to investigate the matter.

After that, things become much more mysterious.

We do know that Helen left a checkup at the Mayo Clinic in Rochester, Minnesota, on February 17, 1977. Her doctors had pronounced her fit and in good health. At a local boutique, Helen charged $41 for cosmetics before proceeding to the airport to fly back to Chicago. Though registered for the flight, she apparently never boarded the plane.

Houseman and chauffeur Jack Matlick, however, told investigators that he had picked Helen up from O'Hare Airport on Thursday, and had taken her back to her house, where she remained alone all weekend, except for a brief meeting with a man that he had never seen before. Helen had plans to leave town on Monday. Matlick insisted that he took Helen to the airport on Monday morning. She was on her way to Florida to handle the details of a condominium purchase that she'd recently made.

But no one other than Matlick had so much as talked to Helen over the course of the weekend, which was highly unusual. Helen spent hours on the telephone with friends in Florida and Ohio, but none of the dozen or so calls answered by Matlick that weekend reached Helen. Callers were told she wasn't feeling well and those who asked were told that she would call them back when she felt up to it.

Matlick waited two weeks to report Helen missing and when he did, his story was filled with inconsistencies. Helen was a late riser and she would not have gone to the airport at 6:50 a.m., as Matlick claimed. Glenview Police Chief William Bartlett checked and discovered there was no 9:00 a.m. flight to Florida, as Matlick had claimed. In addition, it was customary for Helen to ask her Ft. Lauderdale friend, Douglas Stevens, to pick her up at the airport, but he didn't even know she was coming.

Matlick had always carefully guarded Helen's privacy, and despite rumors that he would inherit $50,000 upon her death, there was no evidence that he had done anything wrong —- at least nothing the police could prove. He looked suspicious, though, especially in light of rumors that he had allegedly cashed three forged checks after Helen's disappearance. He also continued to live on a Schaumburg farm owned by Helen until the estate accountant, Everett H. Moore, fired him and forced him to move out. Matlick flatly asserted his innocence but remained a suspect, even though he had not been formally charged of any crime.

Days and weeks dragged by with no new leads. Without a body —- or even any solid clues —- the case was going nowhere. Then, strangely, one year after Helen disappeared, a cryptic message was found spray-painted on the sidewalk near Helen's Glenview home. It read: "Richard Bailey knows where Mrs. Brach's body is! Stop him!" Bailey was questioned but released.

In May 1984, the case was cold, and Helen Brach was declared legally dead by a probate judge. But, strangely, the case would soon start heating up again.

Three years later, in 1987, a Mississippi convict named Maurice Ferguson told an interesting tale to local investigators. He claimed that millionaire horseman Silas Jayne hired him to remove the remains of Helen Brach from a Morton Grove gravesite and transport them to Minneapolis. Jayne —— who was mentioned in the earlier chapter about young women who went missing from the Indiana Dunes in 1966 —-- was a ruthless horse dealer who used worthless animals to carry out frauds on wealthy residents on Chicago's North Side. Jayne was in prison at the time of Helen's disappearance, but he had been partnered with Richard Bailey —-- which turned out to be only one of the possible links that connected Jayne's operation to the crime. Unfortunately, when Ferguson was escorted to Minnesota by the Illinois State Police to help locate the grave, he failed to find it after hours of searching.

Two years later, though, the Helen Brach case was back in the newspapers. In July 1989, federal prosecutors in Chicago returned a 29-count indictment charging Richard Bailey with conspiring, soliciting, and causing Helen's death. Prosecutors argued that he and several others in the horse business hoodwinked wealthy women into paying inflated prices for show horses. There were also charges that Bailey and 22 others bilked insurance carriers into paying off policies on overvalued horses that were destroyed by unscrupulous owners. No one was ever actually charged with carrying out Helen's murder, but U.S. Attorney James R. Burns outlined a likely scenario. Prosecutors verified that, shortly before she disappeared, Helen realized that she had been swindled by Bailey. She was about to blow the whistle on his operation, bringing attention to dozens of questionable transactions over the years. Bailey then allegedly plotted her death.

Bailey, being the con artist that he was, believed that he could skate by with a light sentence. He avoided trial by pleading guilty to racketeering charges, mail fraud, money laundering, and unlawful money transactions. He begged for mercy from the court and counted on the judge to give him a break, claiming that he had an inferiority complex from a debilitating physical condition that caused his reckless behavior. Bailey's gamble failed miserably. With the preponderance of evidence pointing toward the existence of a murder conspiracy, U.S. District Judge Milton Shadur sentenced Bailey to a mandatory term of life imprisonment. The verdict was affirmed on appeal.

Bailey had received a justly deserved punishment, but the mystery of Helen Brach remained largely unexplained.

Then in 2005, former Chicago horseman Joe Plemmons, who had been set to testify against Bailey, confessed to the authorities that he had shot the candy heiress. In Plemmons' version of events, he received a call one night from Kenneth Hansen – who worked for Silas Jayne and was later convicted of the murders of three young Chicago boys in the 1950s -- and was told to come to his stable in Tinley Park. After Plemmons arrived, a Cadillac pulled into the riding ring and the trunk was opened to reveal Helen Brach's battered body. Hansen's brother, Curt, a reputed mob hit man at the time, ordered Plemmons to shoot Helen or be killed himself. Afraid of being murdered, he told detectives, he shot her twice before her body was disposed of at a steel mill.

Some officials at the U.S. Bureau of Alcohol, Tobacco, Firearms and Explosives believed that Plemmons' story solved the case. According to Plemmons, when he lifted Helen's body, a ruby ring fell off her hand. He said that he pocketed the ring and, in 2005, he handed it over to authorities. ATF agents believed the ring to be proof that Plemmons was telling the truth.

Cook County officials, however, were unable to prove through DNA or through Helen's surviving friends or relatives that the ring was actually hers. Edward Donovan, Jr., a Chicago attorney who used to represent Helen's brother on inheritance issues after his sister's disappearance and who long considered Matlick the prime suspect, dismissed the ring. "I don't think the ring has anything at all to do with it," he said. The ring is still in storage at the Glenview Police Department near some of Helen's other possessions, including her former luggage.

In the end, the Cook County State's Attorney's office declined to bring charges on his confession alone.

Plemmons moved to Florida and lived on disability until his death. He was later diagnosed with cancer and had to have portions of his jaw removed. If he did kill Helen Brach, perhaps karma finally caught up with him.

Jack Matlick, who always denied involvement in the disappearance and was never charged, died in 2011. Curt Hansen died in 1993 and his brother, Kenneth, died in 2007. It was the disappearance of Helen Brach that revealed Kenneth Hansen's role in the 1955 murders of 14-year-old Robert Peterson, 13-year-old John Schuessler, and his 11-year-old brother, Anton Schuessler.

Their murders went unsolved for almost 40 years. Then, during the Brach investigation, investigators came across people who accused Hansen of the boys' slayings. In the summer of 1994, sensing the investigation was closing in on him, Hansen attempted to leave town, only to be arrested on an arson charge in a 1972 fire at a suburban Chicago stable. He was charged later the same day with killing the boys. During Hansen's trial, prosecutors contended that the three boys were hitchhiking when they were picked up by Hansen, who took them to the stable — -- owned by Silas Jayne —--- where he worked. He sexually abused at least one of them and strangled them all.

Hansen was convicted in 1995, but the Illinois Appellate Court overturned the conviction five years later after determining that the jury should not have heard evidence that Hansen had cruised the streets, picking up boys for sex. Hansen went on trial again in 2002 and, after deliberating for a little more than two hours, a jury found him guilty again. Hansen was sentenced to 200 to 300 years in prison. He died behind bars five years later.

Richard Bailey, the only person ever convicted in connection with Helen's case, was released from federal prison in July 2019 at the age of 90. Bailey, the known predator of widows and divorcees with hefty bank accounts, admitted in an interview to conning Helen, but denied any role in her disappearance. He claimed his relationship with Helen was different than with others that he'd preyed on, that they were going to be married. "We was [sic] madly in love with each other," he claimed.

Bailey also admitted that he knew about plans for Helen's murder but had no part in them. He claimed that a half dozen people were involved in the planning, including the widow's late butler, Jack Matlick. Matlick had also vehemently denied knowing anything about this former employer's disappearance and death.

Bailey also said that Joe Plemmons was involved, as were a pair of notorious Chicago mobsters, w. Who disposed of Helen's body in a vat of molten steel. He said that the two mobsters, Michael and Anthony Spilotro, were murdered by the Chicago Outfit because of their role in Helen's murders. The Spilotro brothers were found buried in an Indiana cornfield in 1986, but federal investigators believe it was for their renegade role in running mob operations in Las Vegas. There was nothing that linked them to the Helen Brach disappearance.

Bailey ended his interview with a Chicago television station with the words, "I definitely didn't kill Helen Brach."

Was he telling the truth? Who knows? The authorities have always believed that multiple people were involved in the demise of Helen Brach -- including Bailey.

To this day, the truth behind what happened to Helen Brach remains unknown. Her case will likely forever be tangled in mystery. But if nothing else, keeping Richard Bailey off the streets, and convicting Kenneth Hansen of three murders that had long been cold resulted from the search for the missing woman.

That means that a little good came out of something terrible. Perhaps that's the best that we can hope for.

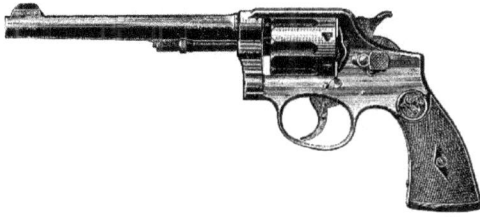

1978: Lost in an Illinois Snowstorm

Dennis Reynolds vanished on February 4, 1978, from a road in rural downstate Illinois. His car was found in a ditch that was filled with snow. It looked as though he had slid off the road in the storm that was blanketing the area with white. The car doors were locked, windows were broken, and Dennis's jacket had been left on the backseat. Everything was there —- except for Dennis.

He disappeared that day, never to be seen again. The police department in nearby Litchfield, Illinois, declared him missing. Days, then weeks, then months passed. His last paychecks were never cashed. He missed family weddings and funerals. But there was simply no sign of him.

His sister, Cynthia Billiter, knew that Dennis was more than just missing. "We all did," she later said. "We knew he was never coming home. He wasn't missing. The police treated this as a joke, like somebody would run away in a blizzard. But we knew better. Dennis was 24 years old, long hair, party boy. A hippie. Maybe the police would have looked harder if it was someone with a better profile. Dennis had his issues, no doubt about that. He drank too much. He did too many drugs. But he would have never just picked up and walked away. Not in the middle of a blizzard."

His sister, Sherry Mueller, added, "He loved his family. That's why this made no sense. He was so close to his mom. And he took care of his little brother Jimmy. When Dennis didn't come home, we knew. We just couldn't prove it."

The frustration of Dennis's sisters has only grown after more than four decades. Litchfield has seen five police chiefs come and go since the young man disappeared. Such turnover doesn't help cold cases —— especially ones that are this cold.

Dennis Reynolds

The winter during which Dennis Reynolds disappeared was one of the worst in Illinois history. The first blast hit downstate Illinois on November 23, 1977, the day before Thanksgiving. That evening, the temperature dropped from 40- to 2-degrees. The wind picked up and the snow began to fall. It seemed as though it never stopped that winter. The temperature remained below freezing for the next 43 days. There were 100 miles per hour wind gusts recorded and wind chills dipped to -60 degrees below zero. More than one inch of snow fell every single day for the next 50 days in a row. Before it was over, more than 82 inches of snow was on the ground. Litchfield, – like so many other Central Illinois towns, – was covered in snow for the next three months.

Central Illinois schools, businesses, and airports were closed indefinitely. The mail stopped being delivered. The National Guard was called in. Fire departments were unable to get to burning homes to put out the fires. Babies were born in homes, cars, and restaurants. At least 24 Illinois residents died while stranded in cars that winter.

The worst snow fell from late January to mid-February. More than 18 inches of snow fell, accompanied by sub-zero temperatures. Like other towns, Litchfield was paralyzed.

And in the middle of this, on February 4, 1978, Dennis Reynolds drove his car to his girlfriend's house. He never made it there.

It was bitterly cold on the day that Dennis vanished. Snow began falling that afternoon around 2:00 p.m. and the temperature dipped to below zero. That evening, Dennis left home, where he lived with his parents, picked up his best friend, and went to a local bar. A few hours later, when he dropped his friend off, he told him that he was going to visit his girlfriend. However, police records show that his girlfriend was not home that night. Of course, in those days before cell phones, there was no way for Dennis to know that.

He drove away from his friend's house with a wave and was only seen one more time -- walking along the road outside of town, probably on his way to seek help for his stranded car. And then he was gone.

Dennis's car was discovered the next day, across the street from his girlfriend's house, stuck in the ditch. There was no sign of Dennis, other than the jacket that had been strangely left behind.

His family, of course, never believed that he simply walked away – or ran off to start a new life, as was suggested by the police. There were no clues —- no body, no crime scene – so it seemed likely, officers in charge of the case believed, he had just abandoned the car and left town. Protocols for missing adult males were different in 1978 than they are today.

Dennis's family, desperate for answers, tried to find him themselves but had no luck. Eventually, they even called in a psychic. According to Sherry Mueller, "They said he was still in his clothes, in water, at the bottom of a well." And then a second psychic came in from California. They gave the same answer – "In his clothes, in water, at the bottom of a well."

But searches turned up nothing. If Dennis was still somewhere nearby, no one could find him. The family hoped that the police were right. They prayed that Dennis had just taken off on his own, even if they never really believed it.

The case became unbelievably cold. As time passed, it should have been realized that Dennis had not left town voluntarily and should have been looked at more seriously —- but it wasn't, until it was probably too late.

Sergeant Jason Black of the Litchfield Police Department began looking into the case when he was still a dispatcher in the late 1990s. "I would read it every chance I had. Boy, was it thick," he said in a 2019 interview. "But then, at some point, we realized the file got lost. It was as if the case never existed."

Time went by. There were new cases and changing priorities, and the cold case was officially on the back burner —– for those who knew it existed. Eventually, though, Black began reworking the case during his spare time. He made contact with Dennis's sisters, Cynthia Billiter and Sherry Mueller in 2007. What had been a missing persons case was clearly something bigger now, and Black began working with the sisters to build a new case file from scratch.

They are aware that, after all these years, it's not realistic to look at the case again with too many hopes or expectations. But the sisters do have their own theory about what happened to Dennis —– a theory based on the rumors that have swirled around Litchfield for decades.

It's been said that Dennis had been abusive to the girl that he was dating. The girl had two brothers, and months before he vanished, Dennis was involved in a fight with the brothers that left him in the hospital, clinging to life after being beaten with a baseball bat. Cynthia and Sherry say that Dennis was warned that he'd be killed if he ever went near the girl again. Scared, he stayed away for almost six months, but then he decided to no longer heed the warning.

It was her house that he was driving toward on the night he disappeared.

Police records show that one of the brothers passed a polygraph test after Dennis vanished. The other brother – and Dennis's girlfriend – refused to take one.

Will Dennis Reynolds – or more likely, his body – ever be found? He will if his sisters and Sergeant Black have their way. At the time of this writing, they are deeply involved in the re-investigation of the case. Only time will tell if answers will be found.

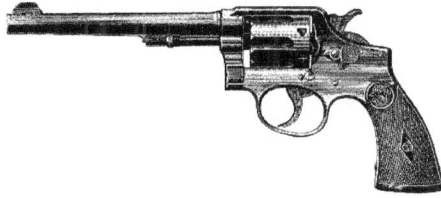

1992: The Vanishing of the "Springfield Three"

On June 6, 1992, two Missouri teenagers and one teen's mother vanished without a trace after a graduation ceremony and have never been seen again. It was a shocking and tragic end to what should have been the event of a lifetime, and it remains a haunting, unsolved mystery to this day.

Best friends Suzanne "Suzie" Streeter, 19, and Stacy McCall, 18, had just graduated from Kickapoo High School and they spent the evening celebrating with friends. They visited several different graduation parties and then decided to go to Suzie's house —– which she shared with her mother, Sherrill Levitt, a 47-year-old cosmetologist —– for the rest of the night. Sherrill was probably happy to see them. Her night had been quiet. She had been on the phone with a friend, talking about painting furniture, until about 11:15 p.m.

What happened after their arrival remains a chilling puzzle.

Since all of Suzie and Stacy's belongings were later found at Sherrill's house - purses, clothes, makeup - it was assumed that they did make it there. Their cars were also in the driveway. But when friends arrived at the Levitt house the next morning, Suzie, Stacy, and Sherrill were missing.

A group of graduating friends all planned to go to the Whitewater water park the next day, so friends Janelle and Kirby came to the Levitt house at 8:00 a.m. on June 7. They knocked, but there was no answer. They went home and then returned at noon, thinking that perhaps the two girls had left for the water park without them. As they approached

The "Springfield Three" — Stacy McCall, Suzanne Streeter, and Sherrill Levitt

the house, they saw that the porch light was broken. They swept up the glass, – trying to be helpful, – but they unknowingly contaminated a crime scene.

Janelle and Kirby checked the door and found it unlocked. That was their first inkling that something might be wrong. When they entered the house, though, everything seemed fine. There were no signs of a struggle. The house was empty, as if they had simply walked away. But to where? Their cars were parked in the driveway, but Suzie, Stacy, and Sherrill were nowhere to be found.

Just before the two teenagers left, the telephone rang. Janelle answered. The caller didn't identify himself but began making lewd comments, so Janelle hung up, assuming it was a prank call. She and Kirby left the house.

A little while later, Stacy's mother, Janis McCall, arrived at the house. She had tried to call, but there was no answer, so she had driven over. She hadn't heard from her daughter since early the previous evening. There was no answer when she knocked, so she went inside. She looked around and found Stacy's belongings. Her daughter's underwear and t-shirt were missing, but the rest of her clothes were neatly folded on a chair. It looked like both girls had removed their makeup in the bathroom the night before. Janis also found all three of the missing women's purses lined up on the floor outside of Suzie's room, which seemed odd. The television was on, and Janis saw there was a message flashing on the answering machine. When she tried to listen to it, she accidentally deleted it.

She was convinced that something was wrong. It had been 16 hours since the three women had been seen. Janis and her husband decided to contact the police. When the authorities arrived, they tried to nail down just how many people had been inside of the house, possibly contaminating the crime scene, and tried to figure out what had happened. It was a baffling situation but suspects soon emerged.

The first suspect was Sherrill's son, Bartt Streeter, who had recently argued with his mother and sister about his drinking problem. But Bartt had a solid alibi and was soon ruled out. Authorities also questioned Suzie's ex-boyfriend, Dustin Recla. He'd been in trouble before. A short time back, he and a friend were arrested for vandalizing cemeteries. Suzie had given a statement to the police that stated that the boys had been digging up graves and stealing gold teeth from the corpses. Threats had been made against Suzie and her mother. When questioned, though, the boys were cooperative and were also ruled out as suspects.

The investigation then focused on Robert Craig Cox, an Army veteran who had been arrested and convicted of a woman's murder in Florida. The case was overturned due to a lack of evidence. In 1985, Cox was convicted of two different abduction attempts and sentenced to nine years in prison. His case was appealed and overturned in 1992 when a judge ruled that the evidence only gave the suspicion of guilt rather than proof of it. He was released in 1992 and sent to live with his parents in Springfield, Missouri —– which put him in the right place at the right time to have been potentially involved in the disappearance of the three women.

Cox worked as an electrician, which the police speculated could have given him an excuse to enter the home. They also found that Cox had previously worked with Stacy's father at his car lot. Cox's girlfriend gave him an alibi at the time but, years later, she admitted that she lied. Cox had convinced her to make up the story if the police asked where he was during that weekend in June. Her story seemed solid at the time, so the police had no choice but to let him go.

But Cox found it impossible to stay out of trouble. A short time later, he was arrested for an unrelated crime. Detectives still believed that he had something to do with the missing women and took the opportunity to question him again. Cox laughed at them. He said that he knew the women were dead and, he claimed, he knew where their bodies were buried. Was he telling the truth? The police didn't know. Cox loved attention, and this was the perfect way to get it. He was their most promising suspect, but he wouldn't talk, and they had no hard evidence against him. Eventually, the case went cold.

The case of the "Springfield Three" officially remains open. Tips and stories have led to nothing but dead ends over the years. Theories abound. Some say they were victims of sex trafficking, while others claim they were carried off by a satanic cult. One tip —— claiming that the women were buried in the foundation of a parking garage at a local hospital —– was so convincing that the authorities tore up the concrete to look for them. And they found nothing.

What happened that night in 1992? There was no sign of a struggle. The three women were simply gone. They were declared legally dead in 1997, but the questions that linger still weigh heavy on surviving family members and on detectives who refuse to close the case.

Where are the "Springfield Three?" After all these years, no one knows.

1995: The Vanished Reporter

In the early morning hours of June 27, 1995, a young woman named Jodi Sue Huisentruit, television news anchor for KIMT-TV in Mason City, Iowa, mysteriously vanished soon after telling a colleague that she was on her way to work. There were signs of a struggle outside of her apartment but aside from that, no trace of her has ever been found.

Jodi grew up in Long Prairie, Minnesota. In school, she was part of an award-winning golf team and later attended St. Cloud University, where she studied television broadcasting and speech communication. She graduated in 1990, and after working for Northwest Airlines for a period, she earned her first broadcasting job at KGAN in Cedar Rapids, Iowa. She later worked in Minnesota and then returned to Iowa for her position at KIMT.

The still missing TV news reporter, Jodi Huisentruit, who vanished in 1995

On the day before she disappeared, Jodi participated in a golf tournament and, according to Mason City resident John Vansice, she went to his apartment to view a video tape of the birthday party that he had arranged for her earlier in the month.

Jodi worked hard at her job and took great pride in her position as the anchor of KIMT's early morning news. She went on each morning at 6:00 a.m. but usually arrived at the studio by 3:30 a.m. Her friend and producer Amy Kuns noticed nothing unusual when she called and woke Jodi up at about 4:10 a.m. This had happened before. As Amy later said, "If she's not there between 3:30 and 4:00, I give her a call and say, "'Hey, are you awake?'"

On that morning, she recalled that when Jodi answered the phone, she was only concerned with being late. She loved the show and wouldn't miss it for anything. She told Amy, "I'll be right there."

But when she didn't show up by 5:30 a.m., Amy called again. She got her answering machine. At 6:00 a.m., Amy had to step in and deliver the news in Jodi's place. An hour later, after repeated calls to Amy's apartment, staff members called the police. When they arrived at the apartment, Jodi wasn't there but they found her shoes, hair dryer, and keys on the ground near her red Mazda Miata.

Jack Schlieper was the chief of police in Mason City at the time. He told reporters that there had been signs of a struggle around the car, including drag marks. The vehicle was processed for fingerprints and an unidentified palm print was lifted from the surface of the car.

During the investigation, special K-9 units quickly began a search of Jodi's apartment complex and the banks of the nearby Winnebago River. At least three neighbors in her apartment complex said they heard screams around the time that Jodi would have been leaving for work. In addition, a neighbor who lived nearby reported seeing a white van with its running lights on parked in Jodi's parking lot at about the same time. This van was never positively identified.

That evening, KIMT's lead story was the devastating news about one of its own.

Detectives searched the newsroom and went through Jodi's desk, hoping to find evidence of an angry or obsessed viewer. Some believed that it might have been Jodi's friendliness and warmth that made her a target.

News Director Doug Merbach said, "You know, she went grocery shopping and it took her two hours because she talked to three people along the way. And she always had time for everybody."

Jodi's sister, JoAnn Nathe, feared Jodi was too trusting of her viewers and that her openness with them led to her disappearance. "I worry that she, you know, was too personable, revealing too much maybe, of what she did day-to-day."

As the investigation progressed, the local police called in the FBI for assistance and soon, Jodi's story was national news. Tips and leads flooded the small-town department, and while many of them led nowhere, investigators did discover that Jodi had reported a possible stalker nine months before she disappeared. In October 1994, she reported an incident of a black truck that followed her while she was out jogging on a nearby trail. The police never got to the bottom of the incident and Jodi didn't report any further harassment.

However, on the day before she disappeared, she did tell some of her friends at the charity golf tournament that she had been receiving prank phone calls. She mentioned that she was going to have to change her phone number or go to the police. Were the calls somehow connected to her disappearance? No one knows.

In September 1995, the Huisentruit family hired private investigators to work the case, which led to appearances on several national television shows, including *America's Most Wanted* and *Unsolved Mysteries*. In November 1997, investigators and members of Jodi's family traveled to Los Angeles to meet with three prominent psychics. This meeting was televised and served as the pilot for the *Psychic Detectives* television show. Although each show generated a large volume of leads, none resulted in concrete evidence or the identification of a suspect.

But some of the investigators in the case had already started to focus on a person of interest – Jodi's friend, John Vansice, whose apartment that she had visited on the evening before she disappeared to watch a videotape from her birthday party.

Vansice, who was 22 years older than Jodi, lived in the same apartment complex and often met Jodi and her friend, Ani Kruse, at a local bar for drinks. He was a recently divorced seeds salesman who struck up a friendship with the young woman, but many of the people in Jodi's life believed that his interest in her went beyond just friendship. Two weeks before Jodi disappeared, Vansice helped Ani throw a surprise birthday party for her. On the weekend before Jodi vanished, she and Ani were out on Vansice's boat – a boat that he named after Jodi.

Robin Wolfram, a reporter who worked with Jodi at KIMT, suspected that Vansice had feelings for Jodi that weren't mutual. And something that he said to her in an interview after Jodi disappeared sent chills down her spine.

During the 1995 interview, Vansice told her, "I have named my boat after her, because just -- just because she's Jodi ... you can't help but love that woman; you can't help but love her."

"When he said I named my boat after her, that's when I said, 'Ugh, that's an obsession,'" Robin later recalled. "I remember holding on to the microphone and just feeling so ill at ease and thinking to myself, I think he might've done it."

Jodi had befriended him during what seems to have been a turbulent time in his life. He was not only recently divorced, but he'd been ordered to install a Breathalyzer device in his van after a series of arrests related to drunken driving.

When friends tried to warn her about Vansice, Jodi brushed off their concern, explaining that he was more like a father to her. Even when they were concerned about what seemed like an obsession, she laughed about it.

Could her lack of concern have led to her death?

Perhaps, although in the fall of 1995 the police confirmed that Vansice had passed a polygraph test, but there was still concern about his obsession with Jodi. That hasn't gone away. As recently as 2017, the Mason City police obtained a search warrant for GPS information on two of Vansice's vehicles. The police have refused to talk about any specifics in the case, and Vansice refused to comment after he was tracked down by reporters.

Vansice remains on investigator's radar – and he's not alone.

In late January 1998, investigative reporter Caroline Lowe at WCCO in Minneapolis, began looking into Jodi's disappearance. She had been covering a terrifying series of rapes in the Minneapolis-St. Paul area. The rapist was Tony Jackson, who was arrested in 1997 after handcuffs, a gun, and duct tape were found in his vehicle during a routine traffic stop by police.

When Detective Jay Alberio began digging into Jackson's past, he found that Jackson had been living in Mason City, Iowa, when Jodi disappeared —– two blocks from the station where she worked.

Caroline Lowe found that Jackson had once been a promising basketball player at Iowa's Waldorf College but that he had been kicked off the team for violent episodes. "He was a star basketball player," she said. "Problem is, he would do well and then he would snap. He would get into violent episodes with people, and he was kicked out of the college."

Then, a year-and-a-half before Jodi disappeared, he enrolled at North Iowa Community College in Mason City, where he showed an interest in broadcasting. He started watching the local broadcasters, hoping to learn from them, including Jodi. Detective Alberio theorized that he might have watched Jodi on television, known her scheduled, and even stalked her.

Caroline Lowe learned something else that troubled her. She spoke with an ex-girlfriend of Jackson's who said they broke up five days before Jodi vanished. As the girlfriend told Lowe, "it was, it was violent, very violent. I mean, it was a totally different person. It was like the devil stepped inside of him and just took over." She also described how he had tried to choke her. Although Jackson was arrested for the attack, the charges were ultimately dropped when the woman moved away and declined to proceed. Four months later, he went on to commit the Minneapolis rapes.

Tony Jackson was sentenced to the equivalent of life in prison for a series of rapes in Minnesota. Still, Caroline Lowe kept digging into any connection to Jodi's case. She learned about a former jail mate of Jackson's. He told Lowe that Jackson had bragged about raping and killing an anchorwoman in a rap song. The jail mate had even written the lyricsm down – "she's a-stiffin' around Tiffin in pileage of silage in a bylow, low below..."

Thinking that might mean Jodi was buried in a farm, near a silo, in the town of Tiffin, a few hours from Mason City, Lowe headed there. She brought law enforcement and cadaver dogs to search for human remains. Two of the three dogs alerted, which was a sign that something had been there. Boards that were found at the scene were sent to the State Crime Lab, but the lead went nowhere. There were no forensics connecting Tony Jackson to Jodi.

On May 5, 1999, the Mason City Police issued the following statement: "After conducting a thorough investigation which included interviews, crime laboratory analysis, records review, and polygraph examination, Tony Jackson is not considered, at this time, a viable suspect in the investigation."

Since Jodi's disappearance, police and private investigators have conducted more than 1,000 interviews relating to her disappearance. None of the leads have ever resulted in any conclusive evidence pointing to a suspect in her disappearance, In May 2001, Jodi was declared legally dead.

Tragically, all these years later, no clue leading to the location of Jodi -- or her body -- has ever been discovered. But the police refuse to give up. The case continues to be investigated, and after the recent search warrants to get access to John Vansice's GPS information, it has stayed in the news.

The Mason City police refuse to comment on any possible suspects, but they have made it clear that they are not going to stop looking for information in the case. Who knows? This might be a story that can finally be removed from the annals of the "unsolved" after all.

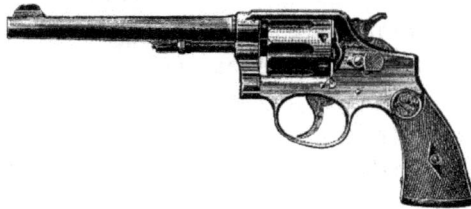

1997: The Run That Never Ended

On July 24, 1997, a young woman named Amy Wroe Bechtel from Lander, Wyoming, went out for a run and never came back.

That morning, she had told her husband, Steve, that she was planning on doing several errands in town after teaching a children's class at the Wind River Fitness Center. She stopped in at the Camera Connection photo store after class and then dropped by Gallery 331, where Amy's conversation with owner Greg Wagner is the last confirmed sighting of her before her disappearance.

After leaving the gallery, she drove to the area near Shoshone National Forest to map out the course of a 10K run that she was helping to organized.

At 4:30 p.m., Steve Bechtel returned home and found that Amy wasn't there. Six hours later, he called the local police with a strange message, "Uh, yeah, hey, I've got a person missing here, I think, and I wondered if you had a spare around anyplace?"

The next day, her unlocked car was found about a half-mile from Frye Lake, which was to be at the end of the 10K run. There was no sign of Amy but her sunglasses, a to-do list, and her car keys had been left on the passenger seat. Her wallet was missing. There was no sign of a struggle either inside or near the vehicle.

Amy Wroe Bechtel —— 24-year-old Olympic marathon hopeful, amateur photographer, friend, employee, daughter, sister, wife ——- was never seen again.

At the time of Amy's disappearance, she and her husband lived on what was known as Lucky Lane in Lander. At the northwestern edge of town, facing the Wind River Range, was a row of 10 identical frame houses filled with people just like Amy and Steve —— young and athletic runners, climbers, and outdoors people. It was sort-of a little bohemia of mountain-town athletes.

Todd Skinner, 39, and his wife, Amy Whisler, lived in no. 10. Todd had led four of the most notable first free ascents in recent years —— at Half Dome, El Capitan, Proboscis in the Yukon, and Nameless Tower in Pakistan. Amy was also a climber. Todd's sister, Holly, lived in no. 8. And, until July 25, Amy had lived in no. 9 with Steve, one of Todd's Half Dome and Nameless Tower partners.

Steve and Amy had met at the University of Wyoming in Laramie in 1991, took exercise classes together the following spring, and were dating by the fall of 1992.

Amy was the youngest of four closely spaced siblings. Their father, Duane Wroe, was a retired city administrator at the time Amy vanished. He was a tough, intelligent man and a former heavy drinker. The family moved to Jackson in 1973, not long after Amy was born, and he served as the city manager there, and later in Douglas and Powell. He kept his hand in politics even after retirement and spent much of his time building furniture. Amy's mother, Jo Anne, was a quiet, insightful woman who spent most of her career teaching handicapped preschoolers. By 1997, she was still substitute teaching in the Powell school system.

Amy started running in the sixth grade. She wasn't, by all accounts, very good, but she kept at it through high school and at the University of Wyoming. By her junior and senior years in college, she was winning every race she entered. She was captain of the cross-country and track teams and, after

Amy Wroe Bechtel, who tragically vanished in Wyoming in the summer of 1997

college, continued to compete in regional and national events. In 1993, she ran the Boston Marathon, and even though she finished about 33 minutes behind the 1996 American Olympic marathon qualifying time, Steve Bechtel proudly told anyone who asked that his wife was hoping to qualify for the 2000 Olympics.

Steve grew up in Casper, Wyoming, the son of Thomas Bechtel, an architect, and his wife, Linda, the director of a school for developmentally disabled children. He had a younger brother, Jeff, and an older sister, Leslie.

When he was a teenager, Steve became obsessed with rock climbing. Even though most believed he didn't have the build or the strength for the sport, Steve —- like Amy with running —- progressed through sheer determination. To the folks on Lucky Lane, Steve was a funny guy, always with jokes and a light-hearted attitude about everything, but he was dead serious when it came to his sport. He was described as unusually intense. When Todd Skinner began putting together a five-man team for Pakistan's Nameless Tower, he picked Steve for his bulldog tenacity and his ability to be positive. Skinner called him "the heart" of the team.

The Lucky Lane folks were all regarded as good people. They wasted little time with bad habits. Most described themselves as middle-roaders of sports —– not the old ones who talked about how it used to be done, or the young ones who were always in search of a thrill. They channeled any energy they'd use for bad habits into sport and what they had left over into small-town camaraderie. They had potlucks and back-yard get-togethers. They kept their doors unlocked and shared equipment, climbing plans, social lives, and workplaces. Todd Skinner was part-owner of the sports store where Amy and Steve worked, and he owned the house that they rented.

At times, the come-in-without-knocking communalism of Lucky Lane wore on Amy's need for privacy. According to Jo Anne Wroe, Amy wanted a home of her own and couldn't wait to move to a new place, closer to downtown. Amy and Steve were planning to move and, in fact, Amy's original plan for July 24 was to drive three hours north to her parent's house in Powell, Wyoming, to pick up furniture that her father had been refinishing for the couple. She changed her mind because she had so much to do that day.

Jo Anne would later call that Amy's "almost moment."

But on the morning of the vanishing, Amy and Steve had a busy schedule. They had the day off from Wild Iris Mountain Sports, the local outdoors sports equipment store where both worked part-time for Todd Skinner. Steve's plan was to drive to Dubois, about 75-miles away, and meet his friend, Sam Lightner, and scout some new climbing routes. Amy drove her white Toyota Tercel station wagon to Wind River Fitness Center, another part-time employer, where she taught an hour-and-a-half kid's class in weight training. She was upbeat, gym owner Dudley Irvine said, though a little high-strung because she had a lot to do that day.

Three days earlier, Amy and Steve had closed on the house she'd wanted near the center of town, away from Lucky Lane. She was also busy organizing a 10K hill climb for September 7. The runners would traverse a series of switchbacks outside of town and then jump into Frye Lake before finishing the event with a picnic.

Amy had made a to-do list for the day:

- run and lift
- recycling
- call phone co.
- electric
- gas
- insurance
- get photo mounted or matted
- flyers for race
- get more boxes
- mow lawn
- call Ed
- close road?
- have Karn do drawing

We know that Amy taught the fitness class and picked up the center's recycling. She contacted the telephone and electric companies. She stopped in at the Camera Connection on Main Street and asked owner John Strom about several photos that she planned to submit in a competition.

Strom remembered that Amy was in running clothes: yellow shirt, black shorts, running shoes. She seemed cheerful and busy. Amy was 11 days short of her twenty-fifth birthday. Friends described her as athletic, small, lithe, determined, thoughtful, even-tempered, and 13 months into a new marriage. John sent her to the framing shop upstairs from him to see about matting. That was in the mid-afternoon.

She talked with Greg Wagner at Gallery 331 about her photos. He later recalled that in the 20 minutes or so that she was in the store, she looked at her watch two or three times. She left the store around 2:30 p.m.

After that, what Amy did and where she went becomes subject to speculation.

Steve Bechtel returned from his meeting with Sam Lightner about 4:30 p.m. and found the house empty. He and Amy were not in the habit of leaving notes about their whereabouts, and Steve was home earlier than he planned, so there was no cause for concern. After a bit, he spoke with Todd and Amy next door, but they hadn't seen Steve's Amy since around noon. He turned down an offer to get pizza with some of the Lucky Lane folks and waited around for Amy. He had no idea where she had gone. He assumed it was for a run. Her climbing gear and camera were still in the house, but her jeans and t-shirt were on the bedroom floor. Her running shoes were gone.

Around 10:00 p.m., Steve called Amy's parents to see if perhaps she had driven there at the last minute. When they asked if anything was wrong, Steve, who later said that he was starting to worry at this point, casually lied to them. "No," he said.

Todd and Amy next door had gone to a movie that evening and arrived home around 11:00 p.m. to find that Amy had still not come home. By this time, Steve had already called the Fremont County sheriff's office, which sent two deputies to the house, alerted the night shift, and began to organize a search team to go out at daybreak. Todd and Amy, meanwhile, went out to look for Amy's car. They drove downtown and then followed what's locally known as the Loop Road, a 30-mile drive through the Shoshone National Forest.

At about 1:00 a.m., Amy Whisler called Steve on her cell phone, and told Steve that they had found his wife's Toyota station wagon at a placed called Burnt Gulch, in the mountains and about 45 minutes outside of town. The car was unlocked. The keys were under Amy's to-do list on the passenger seat, next to an expensive pair of sunglasses. Her wallet was not in the car. Nothing —— except for Amy's absence and the missing wallet (she never carried it when running) —– seemed out of the ordinary. It was as if she had simply parked the car and walked away.

Steve and his friend, Kirk Billings, grabbed lanterns, a sleeping bag, and matches and drove to Burnt Gulch. The little group wandered into the edge of the forest with flashlights, calling for Amy. There was no response.

They called for more volunteers, and long before dawn and before the arrival of the official search team, there were a couple of dozen people looking for Amy. No attempt was made to preserve the integrity of what was later presumed to be a crime scene. No one knew a crime had been committed. They were looking for a missing runner.

"I expected her to come stumbling out of the woods," Kirk Billings said. He had no idea that his friend would never be seen again.

Getting lost or injured in the mountains around Lander was like having your house catch on fire when you live next to the fire station. Scores of rescuers, athletic and mountain-wise, live in and around the city. Amy's disappearance prompted an all-out response from the county's search-and-rescue volunteers. By the weekend, the group of volunteers and county officials had grown to more than 200.

Dave King, the Fremont County sheriff's deputy who became the lead investigator on the case, stated, "We know what we're doing. We have 50 activations a year. We have specialists in steep-angle searches, swift water searches, cave rescues. We have trackers, air spotters, and cadaver dogs, which can supposedly catch scents even underwater. We can bring people out via Life Flight or horseback or on a stretcher. Me? I round up volunteers. I provide the authority and take the blame for bad decisions, but I'm not the expert. I feel foolish sometimes – directing traffic that includes people who have written books about mountain search-and-rescue."

In other words, Amy had the best people possible looking for her.

Investigators had discovered, on the bottom of Amy's to-do list, a milepost description of landmarks that she had apparently jotted down, while looking at the odometer in her car, along the first section of the proposed 10K race route. This was another indication that Amy had driven herself up into the mountains before she disappeared. Because of this, officials focused on the upper sections of the Loop Road for the search.

The route began as a paved road on the outskirts of Lander, running along the Popo Agie River through Sinks Canyon State Park. Beyond Sinks Canyon, the pavement turns to gravel and rises 1,500 feet in six miles to Frye Lake —– the hill climb that Amy was scoping out for the 10K. Still heading up through the Shoshone National Forest, the road passes campgrounds, firewood-gathering areas, Louis Lake, and hiking trailheads. It crests above 9,000 feet and then descends to connect with Wyoming 28 near the tiny mining towns of Atlantic City and South Pass City.

The Loop Road was essentially a horseshoe tipped on its ends. A vehicle has one way in, one way out. During the day, there was a little traffic, but at night, it was nearly abandoned. It felt empty, close to the stars. About halfway along the road, the loop passed through a fire-thinned forest of lodgepole pines. A rutted side road used by firewood cutters led off into the trees toward Freak Mountain. This was Burnt Gulch, the place where Skinner and Whisler found Amy's car.

In the days that followed, searchers painstakingly scoured roughly 20 square miles around Amy's car. They literally combed the five-square area closest to the Toyota. They walked in a line, four men across, the length of the Loop. They covered the distance in a "critical separation" search, in which volunteers, depending on the terrain, maintain only enough distance between themselves so as not to miss anything.

Horses joined the hunt, and then cadaver dogs, and the National Guard. There were ATVs and dirt bikes. A search plane flew overhead. Helicopters, including one with infrared sensors, buzzed the mountains for hours at a time. Radios passed reports back and forth along the Loop, over the mountains, and deep into the woods. Passing motorists were stopped and questioned. The search lasted from dawn to dusk for more than a week.

If Amy was out there, she should have been found.

If she had been attacked by a mountain lion or a bear, searchers would have found broken underbrush, pieces of clothing, bloodstains. If she had become injured or lost, the searchers should have come upon her – probably very quickly. This was a skilled operation carried out by experts in the field, but there was nothing. There was no sign that Amy had been out in the woods at all.

Each day, the volunteers returned to camp exhausted and baffled. There was not, according to Deputy Dave King, not a drop of blood, a scrap of clothing, a single verifiable track, a sign of a scuffle – nothing to indicate that Amy was ever present, alive or dead, on the mountain.

There was only a car, some keys, sunglasses, and a to-do list that would never be completed.

Five days after Amy disappeared, it was realized that volunteers were finding no clues to her vanishing in the forest and things changed from a search-and-rescue operation to a full-blown criminal investigation. Soon after, 25 FBI agents arrived in Lander, set up shop in the sheriff's office, and started questioning anyone who might know where Amy had gone.

Everyone seemed to have an opinion – it was a serial killer, Amy had run away, she'd been kidnapped by "mountain men," like a young woman had been in 1984, her body was at the bottom of the lake, or most commonly, "her husband did it."

Hikers and runners in Lander, especially women, began looking over their shoulders, started running in pairs or with a dog, or with pepper spray. And then the yellow ribbons appeared – on trees, parking meters, and telephone poles. They all begged Amy to come home.

As more time passed, leads – both possible and far-fetched – poured in.

Jim and Wendy Gibson, owners of Lander's Pronghorn Lodge, told investigators they passed a slender blond woman wearing dark shorts running away from town on the Loop Road late on the afternoon of July 24. They were taking some relatives from Nebraska up the mountain for some sightseeing. On the way back to town, at Burnt Gulch, Wendy noticed a "dirty white vehicle" parked there but had no reason to connect it to the runner they'd seen earlier. Wendy remembered seeing "something red" in the car that reminded her of camping. A little closer to town, they noticed a gray truck with a half load of logs on the road. A shirtless man was standing near it, holding a plastic container.

There was also a report of gunfire on the night of July 24 at Louis Lake, eight miles from Burnt Gulch, and a man's voice yelling, "Come on, you sissy, do it, do it!"

A young boy found a bottle in the river near Main Street in Lander. Inside of it was a note: "Help, I'm being held captive in Sinks Canyon. Amy" The handwriting, not surprisingly, was not Amy's.

By the end of August and into early September, the search had moved from the mountains to town. The investigative blitz carried out by the FBI lasted for a week-and-a-half and then they gave up and went home. A room in the sheriff's office became the new command post for law enforcement. On Lucky Lane, Todd Skinner's garage was converted into a headquarters for everyone else. Volunteers manned phones there and printed flyers. They eventually mailed out more than 80,000 flyers, searching for anyone with information about the disappearance and offering a $10,000 reward.

More leads came in but again, they went nowhere.

As the official investigation stalled out, the authorities went looking for a new suspect —— or at least one that they had been considering but had not pursued in the way that they would for many years to come: Steve Bechtel.

The vast majority of violent crimes against women are committed by a friend, acquaintance, or a relative of the victim. The authorities were interested in Steve as well as a small number of men who had exhibited particular interest in Amy or her running career, but no one but Steve had emerged as a clear suspect.

Detectives interrogated Steve on August 1, 1997, falsely claiming to have evidence proving he had murdered his wife. They also claimed that a woman driving through the area from where Amy disappeared claimed to have seen a truck matching Steve's in the area with a blond-haired woman in the passenger seat, but she was unable to positively identify it was him.

Steve maintained that he had nothing to do with Amy's disappearance, even after FBI agent Rick McCullough accused him of murdering her on August 5. Steve had an alibi. He was with Sam Lightner in DuBois, scouting a climbing spot on the day Amy had vanished in the mountains. But, as many have pointed out, there has been no third party found to corroborate the two climbers' story.

After a search of the couple's property, detectives discovered Steve's journals, which contained poetry or song lyrics sometimes with violent overtones, describing violence towards women and, specifically, Amy. The authorities —— FBI agents, lead investigator Dave King, and Sheriff Larry Matthews —— as well as many townspeople and even Amy's parents, wanted Steve to take a polygraph test and clear himself of suspicion in the case.

Steve, who had hired an attorney by now, refused.

They took the position that if Steve was innocent, he had nothing to lose by sitting for a lie-detector test. Steve, his close friends, and his lawyer, Kent Spence, felt differently. They said that Steve had already submitted to four formal interviews with the investigators and pointed to many studies about the unreliability of polygraph tests. Further, Steve and Spence accused the police of following false leads, relying on "profiles" of perpetrators, and wasting their energy badgering Steve when they could be tracking down worthwhile leads and suspects.

But Steve's refusal to take a polygraph test raised suspicions for many Lander residents and, of course, the media.

Amy's brother, Nels, was especially angry at Steve's reluctance to take the polygraph test and cooperate fully with investigators. Nels told the sheriff about one night when Amy and Steve were over for dinner. Nels noticed that Amy was bruised. Amy made a joke, saying that Steve can get a little rough sometimes. Nels found Amy's reaction odd, saying, "Amy just laughed it off, would not look me in the eye, and I said, that is not a normal reaction, particularly for Amy."

Duane Wroe agreed with his son. Jo Anne said little. Amy's sisters, on the other hand, remained publicly loyal to Steve.

More time passed and the reward for information about Amy grew to $100,000. Two months after the disappearance, the Amy Bechtel Hill Climb took place. Steve was there, publicly talking about the search for Amy. Members of her family came, too. Sinks Canyon was searched by divers. Old mine shafts in Atlantic City were searched. At a University of Wyoming football game, the scoreboard lit up with Amy's photo and a photo number to call with information.

But still, there was no sign of Amy.

Steve remained the prime "person of interest" in Amy's disappearance for many years. Authorities visited the Bechtels' house on Lucky Lane with a search warrant to conduct Luminol searches, looking for bloodstains, as well as cadaver dogs. They also followed a tip that Steve had buried Amy beneath the driveway of their new home before the concrete was poured. Neither search turned up anything.

With no other suspect, though, it didn't matter. In July 2007, the 10-year anniversary of Amy's disappearance, Roger Rizor, the detective who succeeded Dave King on the case, commented on the cold case to the *Billings Gazette.* "In my mind there is only one person that I want to talk to, only one person who has refused to talk to law enforcement," he said, "and that's her husband,"

Steve remained the prime suspect —– but it's possible that the police were leaving another suspect off their list.

In the midst of the investigation, a tip came in from a man named Richard Eaton, who told sheriff's detectives that his itinerant brother, Dale Wayne Eaton, may have been involved in Amy's disappearance. But the investigation was focused on Steve Bechtel at the time and the tip was either ignored or slipped through the cracks. No one followed up on it, which may have allowed the man who became known as the "Great Basin Killer" to continue to kill until he was finally arrested in 1998, more than a year after Amy had vanished.

Richard knew that his brother had been in trouble already and knew that Dale had been camping in the Burnt Gulch area at the time Amy was last seen there. This was a favorite hunting and trout fishing spot for the Eaton brothers. The police dismissed Richard's tip as a man looking to collect on the reward. In addition, Dale's niece claimed that he had been visiting her in Greeley, Colorado, on July 24. It later turned out that she lied.

Meanwhile, Dale Eaton was involved in an attempted kidnapping. In an area called Patrick Draw —–– less than a three-hour driver from Lander —– Shannon Breeden, her husband, Scott, and their five-month-old baby, Cody, were traveling when their van broken down at a pullout along Interstate 80. Dale Eaton stopped his off-green Dodge van and offered them assistance. Once he got them into his van, he pulled out a rifle and directed Shannon to drive them south of the highway into the desert. Shannon accelerated and turned in a tight circle instead, which enabled Scott to jump out of the van with the baby and Shannon to get to the other side. Scott grabbed Eaton and hit him over the head with the rifle butt. After a struggle, Eaton was stabbed with his own knife and the family escaped.

Eaton was arrested but his attorney worked out a plea deal that had him spending only 99 days in jail for the attempted kidnapping of the

Breeden family. A sample of his DNA was taken while he was incarcerated, which would come back to haunt him.

His jail time turned out to be easy. Due to prison overcrowding, he was allowed to work on welding and construction jobs while living in a half-way house. Despite strict parole conditions, he failed to show up for work on June 16, 1998, and a warrant was issued for his arrest. The police finally spotted his van more than a month later near Dubois in the Bridger-Teton National Forest. He was arrested and a shotgun was found in his van, leading to his imprisonment on federal weapons charges.

In July 2002, investigators were looking into cold cases, including the March 25, 1988, rape and murder of 18-year-old Lisa Marie Kimmell. She had been driving alone from Denver to Billings, Montana, in her black 1988 Honda CRX, which had Montana plates with LIL MISS on them. She was planning to visit her boyfriend in Cody, but never got there. Eight days later, two fishermen found her body in the North Platte River near Casper. Autopsy results showed that she had been raped, bludgeoned, and stabbed. When investigators studied the DNA taken from semen on Lisa's body, they found a match – Dale Wayne Eaton.

Lisa's case quickly heated up again.

After Lisa had been buried, a strange note signed "Stringfellow Hawke" was found on her grave. An analysis of the handwriting matched that of Eaton. Then, following a tip from neighbors who remembered seeing Eaton digging in his yard, investigators found Lisa's car buried on his property in Moneta, which was less than two hours from Lander. They found an abandoned school bus on the property, where it was believed that Eaton held Lisa captive, repeatedly raping her before killing her.

Had there been other victims? Inside of Eaton's trailer, authorities also found clothing and purses that belonged to at least a dozen women. There were also newspaper clippings about murdered and missing women —- including Amy Bechtel. An FBI profiler who examined the case said that Eaton's behavior pointed to him being a serial killer. He had been possibly operating in the area since at least 1988, long before Amy Bechtel disappeared.

In the subsequent trial, Eaton was found guilty of first-degree murder and sentenced to death by lethal injection. He received a stay of execution in December 20099 after his lawyers argued that he was mentally unfit to be executed. In November 2014, a U.S. District judge overturned his death sentence, but he continues to serve a life sentenced today.

In 2010, investigators in Amy's case traveled with an FBI agent to try and interview Eaton but he refused to speak with them. Whether or not he had anything to do with Amy's disappearance will likely never be known.

After Amy disappeared, life eventually moved on in Lander. Amy remains gone, but not completely forgotten. In time, she was declared legally dead, and in 2004, Steve married Ellen Sissman, with whom he had two children.

But the shadow of Amy will always be there, over his life, and over the mountain town that she called home. Her mystery will likely remain forever unsolved.

2006: The Missing Medical Student

In these modern times, it has become harder and harder to just disappear. With cell phones, computers, online tracking, GPS data, and CCTV cameras, it's difficult to just vanish —- or even to make someone else vanish. We are a much more closely-connected society than we were even a few decades ago, so, theoretically, unsolved disappearances shouldn't happen as often as they once did.

Right? That's the theory anyway, but unfortunately, it's not always that way in the real world.

On the night of March 31, 2006, an Ohio State University medical student named Brian Shaffer went out with some friends to celebrate the start of spring break. When they were separated from him in the crowds, they assumed that Brian had gone home.

However, a security camera near the entrance to a bar recorded him briefly talking to two women, just before 2:00 a.m. on April 1. A moment later, he went back inside of the bar – and apparently, never came out.

Brian Shaffer has not been seen or heard from since.

Brian grew up in Pickerington, Ohio, a suburb of Columbus. He was the oldest of Randy and Renee Shafer's two sons. He graduated from high school in 1997 and went to Ohio State University (OSU) in Columbus for his undergraduate degree. Six years later, he graduated with a degree in microbiology. Following that, he began his studies at the OSU College of Medicine in 2004. He was in his second year of studies when his mother, Renee, died from Myelodysplastic syndrome, a rare type of cancer in which immature blood cells in the bone marrow do not mature and do not become healthy blood cells. His mother's death was hard on him. Although his friends later said that he handled it well, it took him a long time to come to grips with the loss.

He shared his grief with his girlfriend, a fellow second-year medical student named Alexis Waggoner. She – as well as her family and friends – believed that Brian planned to propose marriage to her in April during a trip to Miami that they had booked. He often joked about how much he loved Florida and the Caribbean. He told his friend that even though he was going to become a doctor, his real ambition was to start a band and become the next Jimmy Buffett.

Brian had a good life ahead of him, which makes the idea that he disappeared on his own hard to imagine.

On Friday, March 31, classes at OSU ended for spring break. Brian and his father, Randy, celebrated the occasion by going out for a steak dinner together early in the evening. Randy later recalled that his son seemed exhausted from having pulled several all-night study sessions

Medical student Brian Shaffer and his girlfriend, Alexis Waggoner. Brian remains missing

for important exams earlier in the week. He didn't think that Brian should go out with friends that night as he planned, but he never mentioned that to his son.

At 9:00 p.m., Brian met up with William "Clint" Florence at the Ugly Tuna Saloona, a bar located in the South Campus Gateway complex on High Street. An hour later, Brian called Alexis. She had returned home to Toledo to visit with her family for a few days before she and Brian departed for Miami. After that, Brian and Clint went bar-hopping, visiting several other places as they worked their way down to the Arena District. At each stop, according to Clint, they each had at least one shot of hard liquor.

Just after midnight, they met Meredith Reed, a friend of Clint's, in a bar called the Short North. She gave them a ride back to the Ugly Tuna Saloona, where they had started the night, and joined them for another round. While they were there, Brian got separated from his friends. Both later reported that they tried to find him, but he didn't seem to be in the bar. They left with other patrons when the bar closed at 2:00 a.m. and waited outside for Brian, still believing he was inside somewhere. When he was not among the crowd leaving the pace, they assumed that he had gone back to his apartment without letting them know – the legendary "Irish Goodbye."

Alexis and Randy Shaffer both tried to call Brian later that weekend, but he didn't answer or return their calls. On Monday morning, he didn't show up for the flight to Miami that he and Alexis had scheduled long before.

Things now looked serious. Randy Shaffer called the Columbus police and reported his son missing.

The authorities began their search for Brian at the Ugly Tuna, the last place he had been seen. The area around South Campus Gateway could be a risky area for crime so the bar had installed security cameras. The Ugly Tuna was located on the second floor of a building and had one entrance at the top of an escalator. Anyone entering or leaving could be seen by the surveillance cameras. Detectives reviewed the footage, which showed Brian, Clint, and Meredith going up the escalator to the bar's main entrance at 1:15 a.m. Then, at 1:55 a.m., Brian was seen outside of the bar, talking briefly to two young women and saying goodbye. From there, he moves off camera toward the bar, apparently going back inside. The camera did not record him leaving a short time later when the Ugly Tuna closed.

It was possible, investigators admitted, that he could have changed his clothing in the bar or put on a hat or kept his head down, hiding his face from the camera when he left. Or the cameras might have missed him – one panned the area constantly and the other operated manually. They looked for him but the quality of surveillance cameras in 2006 – especially cheap ones outside campus bars – was not the best.

There was one other way that Brian could have exited the bar that night —– the service door in back. Not only was this door used exclusively by staff, but it also opened onto a construction site that would have posed a dangerous situation for a sober person, let alone someone who had been drinking all evening.

Since Columbus had the most security cameras of any city in Ohio –more than Cleveland, Cincinnati, and Toledo combined – officers checked the footage from nearby bars to see if their cameras could explain how Brian left the Ugly Tuna.

There was no trace of him. Brian had re-entered the bar and, impossibly, he never came out.

The search spread out from the Ugly Tuna, with officers, often accompanied by police dogs, checking the streets, inspecting dumpsters, and asking residents of they had seen him. The police even searched the sewer system but found nothing. At Brian's apartment on King Avenue, – six blocks from the Ugly Tuna, – they found his car still parked outside. Nothing had been touched inside the apartment. Flyers with Brian's picture —— showing a tattoo on his upper right arm of the stick figure logo from Pearl Jam, one of his favorite bands, were posted widely. Pearl Jam's lead singer, Eddie Vedder, even took time out of the band's set in Cincinnati to put out a call for information about Brian.

After searching miles away from the bar in every direction, the police began to consider other possibilities besides an accident or foul play. Since his mother had recently died, it was speculated that he had gone away temporarily to grieve alone. This suggestion was soon dismissed when Brian failed to return. In addition, no money was withdrawn from his bank account and his credit cards went unused. His family and friends insisted that he would not have gone away voluntarily.

Thanks to attention from Pearl Jam, Brian's disappearance sparked an international search effort. Possible sightings came in from Michigan, Texas, and even as far away as Sweden. But none of the tips proved to be useful. Brian was simply gone.

Those who had been with Brian that evening, including his father, were asked to take polygraph tests. Meredith Reed and Randy Shaffer agreed and passed theirs, as did anyone else he spent time with, including the two women that he was talking with outside the bar. The only person who never took an exam was Clint Florence. Reportedly, he refused the test because he felt he had told the police everything he knew about that night.

For months after Brian vanished, Alexis called his phone before going to bed every night. Usually, it went straight to voicemail but one night in September 2006, it rang three times. There was no answer, but the call pinged off a tower in Hilliard, Ohio, about 14 miles from Columbus. Unfortunately, Cingular, Brian's wireless carrier, admitted that the rings were likely a glitch in the system, rather than Brian turning on his phone.

As time went on, Randy Shaffer, like Alexis, refused to give up on the chance that Brian might be found. A psychic that he consulted told him that Brian was dead and that his body was in water near a bridge pier. He and Derek, Brian's brother, along with a group of friends, bought waders and started spending their free time along the shores of the Olentangy River, which flows through Columbus adjacent to the OSU campus.

No trace of Brian was ever found.

Heartache followed Brian to wherever he'd gone. In September 2008, during a heavy windstorm in Central Ohio, Randy Shaffer was out in the yard of his home clearing debris. A branch fell from a nearby tree and fatally struck him. Neighbors discovered his body the next morning.

After his obituary ran online, a condolence page was posted. One of the notes read, "To Dad, Love Brian (U.S. Virgin Islands)". This suggested to some that Brian might have faked his disappearance to start a new life somewhere else. After investigation, though, it was determined that the note was posted from a public computer in Franklin County, Ohio. It was determined to be a cruel hoax.

Shortly after Randy's death, Neil Rosenberg, an attorney for Clint Florence, wrote to Don Corbett, a private investigator who volunteered his time to help the Shaffer family find Brian. He wanted to discuss his client's refusal to take a polygraph exam. Rosenberg suggested that he had learned that the Columbus police who were investigating the case believed that Brian was alive.

He wrote, "If Brian is alive, which is what I'm led to believe after speaking with the detective involved, then it is Brian, and not Clint, who is causing his family pain and hardship. Brian should come forward and end this." Florence, he said, did not have anything to hide; he had merely told everything he knew from the beginning and did not see the value of doing so again.

But many of those involved were angry with Florence for not helping further with the case. "As soon as the detective started getting involved, that's when he pretty much had no contact with anybody," recalled Derek Shaffer, Brian's brother and last surviving immediate family member. "I've always thought he definitely knows something—just won't come forward with it."

Derek still believes it's possible that Brian is alive, and Clint knows where he might have gone. "If Brian did take off somewhere, if that is the case, we just always had a strong feeling that Clint would possibly know that," he said.

Alexis Waggoner also thinks that Clint is withholding information. However, she eventually started to believe that Brian was dead and did not run off. "I can't imagine he would have just done that," she said.

Even today, 13 years later, the Columbus police have said that they are still receiving art least two tips each month about Brian's case via the local Crime Stoppers hotline. None of them have turned out to be useful, though.

The evidence in the case has filled four boxes of files. One of the original investigators has gone on record saying that, after an extensive review of the camera footage from the Ugly Tuna on the night Brian disappeared, they can say with "100-percent certainty" that Brian did not leave the bar through the front door. But he declined to offer any of the theories that investigators have.

What happened to Brian Shaffer that night in 2006 remains a mystery. He has never been seen again. He never used his cell phone, his credit cards, or his bank account again.

How – and why – he vanished that night may always be unknown.

2008: The Last Drive Home

Shortly after midnight on May 14, 2008, a young man named Brandon Swanson drove his car into a ditch on his way home from celebrating the end of the spring semester with fellow students from Minnesota West Community and Technical College. The crash was minor and, unhurt, Brandon got out of the car and called his parents on his cellphone. Unsure of his exact location, he told them he believed he was near Lynd, Minnesota —– he could see the lights, he told them.

Roused from sleep, his parents hurried to the car to go and pick him up. They drove for more than a half-hour but were unable to locate him. Brandon remained on the phone with them the entire time as he walked toward town. Then, suddenly, after 45 minutes on the line with them, he cried out and the call abruptly ended.

Brandon Swanson has not been seen or heard from since.

Brandon Swanson, age 19 at the time of his disappearance, grew up in Marshall, located in the southwestern corner of Minnesota. He was an avid reader and had worked at the local Hy-Vee grocery store for four years. Brandon graduated from Marshall High School in 2007 and decide to study wind turbines for a year at Minnesota West Community and Technical College in Canby.   After that, he intended to enroll in a four-year college and go into a career in the sciences.

He had his whole life ahead of him but it would be tragically cut short.

Classes at Minnesota West ended for the year on May 13, 2008. Brandon stayed in Canby for the evening to celebrate with friends. He attended two different parties and, according to friends, had a few drinks, but not enough alcohol to make him seem visibly intoxicated.

Just before midnight, Brandon left Canby to make the 20-mile drive home to his parent's house. Along the way, though, he ran into trouble. It's unknown how, or why, it happened, but Brandon swerved off the road and ran his Chevrolet Lumina into a ditch. He tried to back out, but it was no use. The car was stuck.

Just before 2:00 a.m., the telephone rang at his parent's house. It was Brandon, calling from his cell

Brandon Swanson

phone. He explained the problem and told them that he was unable to move the car. He wasn't hurt, he assured them, but he needed them to come and pick him up.

Brandon's parents, Brian and Annette, got in their truck and began driving toward where they believed their son had been stranded. He stayed on the phone with them, although the call dropped several times and they had to keep calling back. Brandon had stayed with his car and he tried to signal his parents by flashing his lights on and off, but his parents still couldn't find him.

Finally, he gave up and told them that he was leaving the car to walk toward lights that he could see up ahead. He believed he was looking at the small town of Lynd, which was about seven miles southwest of Marshall, where the family lived. He told his father to drive to the parking lot of a local bar in town and wait for him there. Brian drove in that direction, keeping Brandon on the phone as he did.

Shortly after 2:30 a.m., Brandon suddenly interrupted his father on the line. "Oh, shit!" he called out. A moment later, the connection was lost.

Brandon Swanson has never been seen or heard from again.

Brian and Annette continued to drive for the rest of the night, frantically looking along the roads around Lynd for their son. At 6:30 a.m., they called the police. Officials in Lynd initially told them that it was hardly unusual for a young man of Brandon's age to stay out all night after the last day of college classes. Annette specifically recalled that one of the officers told her that it was her son's "right to be missing."

After Brian and Annette again explained the situation and the abrupt end to Brandon's call, the Lynd police did start a search. A patrol of the area around town found no trace of Brandon or his car, however. They requested help from Lyon County Sheriff Joel Dahl and additional officers began searching the nearby roads. The sheriff's office obtained Brandon's cell phone records, which revealed that Brandon had not been calling from near Lynd at all —- he was near Taunton, northwest of Marshall —- and 25 miles from Lynd.

Brandon's abandoned car was quickly found in a ditch off a gravel road along the Lincoln County line. Lincoln County Sheriff Jack Vizecky added more officers to the search for the missing young man.

Brandon's Lumina had gotten hung up on the top of an incline at the edge of the road. The car wasn't damaged, but it tipped in a way that the wheels couldn't touch the ground on one side. This is why Brandon was unable to move it. There was nothing else wrong with the car. The grass and gravel that surrounded the car made it impossible to find tracks and to determine which direction Brandon might have started walking.

His cellphone had been routed through a tower at the intersection of County Routes 3 and 10 near Minneota, another small town. The authorities were later able to discover that the call had come from within five miles of the tower, which narrowed the search field. Since part of the area within that range included Yellow Medicine County to the north, officers from that jurisdiction also joined the search.

From the area where the call was placed, it was noted that a red light atop a Taunton grain elevator could be seen. It was possible that this was what Brandon saw and led him to believe Lynd was in walking distance from his accident.

The authorities searched the entire area, using small planes to view the prairie from above. Search dogs were also brought in from Minneapolis-St. Paul. A team of bloodhounds from nearby Codington County, South Dakota, picked up a trail that led them three miles northwest to an abandoned farm, then along the Yellow Medicine River to where it appeared to enter the water. Brian recalled that Brandon had mentioned passing fences and hearing nearby water but didn't understand why his son would have left the road.

Fearing that Brandon might have stumbled into the water and drowned, boats from the state's Department of Natural Resources were deployed along the river. Deputies also walked the river's banks, and horses and ATVs covered the surrounding area.

But there was no sign of Brandon.

After a few days, most search efforts were discontinued. Whatever had happened to Brandon had left the police baffled. A few police officers, bothered by the case, walked the banks of the Yellow Medicine River in their free time, and the Swansons left their porch light on all night every night as a symbol of their hope that Brandon would eventually return or be found.

To this day, they still do.

The search for Brandon resumed in the fall, after fields that had been planted around the time of the disappearance had been harvested. Dogs used for these searches followed the scent of human remains into an area northwest of Porter, which had not been searched back in May. No remains were found, though.

Efforts picked up again in the spring, after the winter snows had melted but before the fields had been planted. By this time, 122 square miles had been thoroughly searched.

Two years after Brandon vanished, the Minnesota Bureau of Criminal Apprehension took over as the lead agency on the case. It set up a tip line, which generated more than 90 leads and moved the search area towards Mud Creek, a tributary of the Yellow Medicine River.

Even with renewed interest in the case, Brandon has never been found. Despite the trail that led toward the Yellow Medicine River, Annette Swanson does not believe her son drowned there. After following the scent to the water, the search dog had crossed it and continued on the other side to the Yellow Medicine County line, where it stopped. There was nothing to indicate Brandon had been in the river. Brian Swanson has recalled that, any alcohol his son had consumed earlier in the evening notwithstanding, he did not seem disoriented or confused during their phone conversations.

There seems to be little chance that Brandon is still alive, although he could have intentionally disappeared. If he did, then his ruse was an elaborate one and his parents stated that it was unlikely he would have done that.

If Brandon did not run away or die by accident, then this only leaves foul play. Could someone have followed him home from the last party he left and grabbed him when they saw the chance? It seems unlikely that anyone was lying in wait for him since Brandon got lost on the way home and drove in the wrong direction from home. Could he have gone somewhere else after the party – or met someone – and come to harm? Or was he a victim of pure chance? A killer on the road who saw and opportunity and took it?

We may never know.

As tragic as the case of Brandon's disappearance was, some small amount of good did come out of it. Annette Swanson was struck by the initial response of the police, and she and Brian began lobbying for changes in state law that would require an investigation into the case of missing adults under the age of 21. "Brandon's Law," as it became known, became official in 2008. Annette knew that it wouldn't help in her son's case, but it might save other lives in the future.

Sometimes, that's the best that we can do.

THE END

What do we make of people who simply disappear one day and are never seen again? As noted in the introduction to this book, there are numerous reasons why people vanish – murder, abduction, suicide, and voluntary escapes from reality among them. And then there are the more unnerving cases, where no rational explanation seems to exist. How, or why, do such things happen?

Are they incidents linked to the supernatural, or could there be more mundane explanations for many of them? In the course of this book, I have chosen only those disappearances that seemed the strangest to me -- the most inexplicable and, in many cases, the most disturbing. I certainly do not claim to have collected every unsolved disappearance in history — -- far from it, which is disturbing in itself -- and some readers will notice the glaring lack of inclusion for what some believe is a prominent paranormal disappearance mystery spot – the Bermuda Triangle.

The fact that the Bermuda Triangle is missing from this book was not an accident on my part. While the area of the Triangle is certainly marked by many strange occurrences, I don't believe there is anything paranormal to it at all. In fact, after years of collecting stories of unsolved vanishings, it became readily apparent that Triangle boasts no more disappearances that other parts of the world's oceans.

The Bermuda Triangle, also known as the Devil's Triangle, is a region in the western part of the North Atlantic Ocean in which a number of aircraft and surface vessels are alleged to have disappeared under mysterious circumstances that fall outside the boundaries of human error, piracy, equipment failure, or natural disasters.

Popular culture has attributed some of these disappearances to the paranormal, a suspension of the laws of physics, or activity by extraterrestrial beings, but in many cases, this couldn't be further from the truth. Documentation shows that many of the incidents allegedly connected to the Bermuda Triangle have been inaccurately reported or have been embellished by later authors – much like the story of Oliver Larch, which was first written about by Ambrose Bierce.

Of course, this is not to say that there have not been strange disappearances in the area, or that unsolved disappearances don't exist, it's just that the mythos surrounding the area is much greater than it deserves to be.

The boundaries of the Bermuda Triangle have been designed to be from the Atlantic coast of Florida to San Juan, Puerto Rico, and on to the mid-Atlantic island of Bermuda. Most of the alleged disappearances are concentrated along the southern boundary around the Bahamas and the Florida Straits.

But just how dangerous is this area? Apparently, not very...

The area is one of the most heavily-sailed shipping lanes in the world, with ships crossing through it daily, bound for ports in the Americas, Europe, and the Caribbean Islands. Cruise ships are also plentiful, and pleasure craft regularly go back and forth between Florida and the islands. It is also a heavily flown route for commercial and private aircraft heading towards Florida, the Caribbean, and South America from points north. If this was some sort of paranormal "wormhole," wouldn't disappearances occur much more often?

You'd certainly think so, right? So, how did such stories get started?

The seeds of the Bermuda Triangle legend were first planted by an Associated Press dispatch on September 16, 1950, in which reporter E.V. Jones took note of what he characterized as "mysterious disappearances" of ships and planes between the Florida coast and Bermuda. Two years later, in a *FATE* magazine article by George X. Sand, he recounted "a series of strange marine disappearances, each leaving no trace whatever, that have taken place in the last few years" in a "watery triangle bounded roughly by Florida, Bermuda and Puerto Rico."

M.K. Jessup picked up some of the stories for his 1955 book, *The Case for the UFO*, which suggested that aliens were responsible for the disappearances, an idea that was echoed by other authors. It was Vincent H. Gaddis who actually coined the catchphrase that entered popular culture when he wrote an article for the February 1964 issue of *Argosy* called "The Deadly Bermuda Triangle." Soon, nearly every new book on true mysteries included chapters on the Bermuda Triangle, and claims began to be made that the area was populated by an intelligent, underwater civilization, which was stealing ships, planes, and people from our world.

The first book to be written about the Triangle was a self-published work called *Limbo of the Lost* by John Wallace Spencer. It was re-published as a Bantam paperback in 1973 and attracted a huge audience, as did the 1970 documentary, *The Devil's Triangle*. Bermuda Triangle fever peaked in 1974 with the publication of *The Bermuda Triangle*, a major bestseller by Charles Berlitz and J. Manson Valentine. Two other paperbacks, *The Devil's Triangle*, by Richard Winer, and *No Earthly Explanation*, by John Wallace Spencer, also racked up impressive sales.

The heart of the Bermuda Triangle mystery seems to revolve around the alleged "scores" of vessels that had vanished in the region. Among the most notable were:

Flight 19

United States Navy Flight 19 was a training flight of TBM Avenger bombers that went missing on December 5, 1945, while over the Atlantic. The squadron's flight path was scheduled to take them due east for 120 miles, north for 73 miles, and then back over a final 120-mile leg that would return them to the naval base. The flight, however, never returned.

The impression is given that the planes encountered unusual phenomena and anomalous compass readings, and that the flight took place on a calm day under the supervision of an experienced pilot, Lt. Charles Carroll Taylor. Adding to the intrigue is that the Navy's report of the accident was ascribed to "causes or reasons unknown." Adding to the mystery, a search and rescue Mariner aircraft with a 13-man crew was dispatched to aid the missing squadron, but the Mariner itself was never heard from again. Later, there was a report from a tanker cruising off the coast of Florida of a visible explosion at about the time the Mariner would have been on patrol.

While the basic facts of this version of the story are essentially accurate, some important details are missing. The weather was becoming stormy by the end of the flight, and naval reports and written recordings of the conversations between Taylor and the other pilots of

Flight 19 do not indicate magnetic problems. That part of the story was invented to make things seem more mysterious and likely, to link it to UFOs.

Missing planes? Yes. Something paranormal? Probably not.

Mary Celeste

The mysterious 1872 abandonment of the brigantine *Mary Celeste* is often -- but inaccurately -- connected to the Triangle, even though it was obviously found off the coast of Portugal. I believe the *Mary Celeste* has been thrown into the Bermuda Triangle mess to give it credibility by placing a real-life mystery there. It's also possible that some writers have confused it with the loss of a ship with a similar name, *Mari Celeste*, a paddle steamer that hit a reef and quickly sank off the coast of Bermuda on September 13, 1864. There was, however, nothing mysterious about the accident.

Ellen Austin

A ship called *Ellen Austin* supposedly came across an abandoned vessel and attempted to salvage it in 1881. A crew was placed on board and the derelict was sailed for New York. According to the stories, the derelict disappeared while en route. A check of Lloyd's of London records proved the existence of a ship called *Meta*, built in 1854. In 1880, *Meta* was renamed *Ellen Austin*. There are no casualty listings for this vessel, or any vessel at that time, that would suggest a large number of missing men were placed on board a ship that later disappeared.

U.S.S. Cyclops

The incident resulting in the single largest loss of life in the history of the United States Navy, not related to combat, occurred when the U.S.S. *Cyclops*, under the command of Lt. Commander G. W. Worley, went missing without a trace with a crew of 309 men, sometime after March 4, 1918, after departing the island of Barbados. Although there is no strong evidence for any single theory, many independent theories exist, some blaming storms, some capsizing, and some suggesting that wartime enemy activity was to blame for the loss.

Theodosia Burr Alston

As noted in an earlier chapter, Theodosia Burr Alston was the daughter of former United States Vice President Aaron Burr. Her disappearance has been cited at least once in relation to the Triangle. She was a passenger on board *Patriot*, which sailed from Charleston, South Carolina, to New York City on December 30, 1812, and was never heard from again. Both piracy and the War of 1812 have been offered as explanations, but her ship was well outside the area of the Triangle when it vanished. In this case, a prominent personality was included in the stories of the Triangle in order to give the location more credibility.

Joshua Slocum

The same thing has happened with famed sailor Joshua Slocum and his ship, *Spray*. The once-derelict fishing boat was refitted as an ocean cruiser by Slocum and used to complete the first ever single-handed circumnavigation of the world, between 1895 and 1898. In 1909, Slocum set sail from Vineyard Haven, Massachusetts, bound for Venezuela. Neither he nor the *Spray* were ever seen again. There is no evidence they were in the Bermuda Triangle when they disappeared, nor is there any evidence of paranormal activity.

Carroll A. Deering

A five-masted schooner built in 1919, the *Carroll A. Deering* was found hard aground and abandoned at Diamond Shoals, near Cape Hatteras, North Carolina, on January 31, 1921. An earlier chapter delved into the missing men and the possible mutiny of the crew —- but again, it was nowhere near the Bermuda Triangle when events occurred, despite claims that place the ship there.

Douglas DC-3

On December 28, 1948, a Douglas DC-3 aircraft, number NC16002, disappeared while on a flight from San Juan, Puerto Rico, to Miami. No trace of the aircraft or the 32 people onboard was ever found. From the documentation compiled by the Civil Aeronautics Board investigation, a possible key to the plane's disappearance was found, but barely touched upon by the Triangle writers: the plane's batteries were inspected and found to be low on charge, but ordered back into the plane without a recharge by the pilot while in San Juan. Whether this led to complete electrical failure will never be known, but it certainly offers a very real possibility for the disappearance of the plane that has nothing to do with aliens and mystery spots.

Star Tiger and *Star Ariel*

G-AHNP *Star Tiger* disappeared on January 30, 1948, on a flight from the Azores to Bermuda and G-AGRE *Star Ariel* disappeared on January 17, 1949, on a flight from Bermuda to Kingston, Jamaica. Both were Avro Tudor IV passenger aircraft operated by British South American Airways. Like the U.S.S. *Cyclops*, no explanation exists for where these two aircraft went. Their disappearance remains unsolved.

S.S. Marine Sulphur Queen

Marine Sulphur Queen, a T2 tanker converted from an oil to sulfur carrier, was last heard from on February 4, 1963, with a crew of 39 near the Florida Keys. *Marine Sulphur Queen* was the first vessel mentioned in Vincent Gaddis' 1964 *Argosy* magazine article, but he left it as having "sailed into the unknown," despite the Coast Guard report that not only documented the ship's badly-maintained history, but declared that it was an unseaworthy vessel that should never have left port. Other authors embellished the story even further, making it a part of Triangle lore. It wasn't.

Raifuku Maru

One of the more famous incidents that allegedly occurred in the Triangle took place in 1921, when the Japanese vessel *Raifuku Maru* went down with all hands after sending a distress signal that allegedly said, "Danger like dagger now. Come quick!". This message has led writers to speculate on what the "dagger" might have been, with a waterspout being the likely candidate.

In reality, though, the ship was nowhere near the Bermuda Triangle, nor was the word "dagger" a part of the ship's distress call. It was actually, "Now very danger. Come quick." The Raifuku *Maru* left Boston for Hamburg, Germany, on April 21, 1925, and got caught in a severe storm and sank in the North Atlantic with all hands.

Connemara IV

This vessel was a pleasure yacht that was found adrift in the Atlantic south of Bermuda on September 26, 1955. It is usually stated in the stories that the crew vanished, while the yacht survived being at sea during three hurricanes. However, that's not really accurate. The 1955 Atlantic hurricane season lists only one storm coming near Bermuda towards the end of August – Hurricane Edith. Two other storms around the region include Flora, which was too far to the east, and Katie, which occurred *after* the yacht was recovered.

As it turned out, the *Connemara IV* was in port and empty when Hurricane Edith caused it to slip her moorings and drift out to sea. There was nothing mysterious about its discovery at all.

As the reader can see, the "scores" of mysterious disappearances that have occurred in the Bermuda Triangle have been narrowed down to three. Based on the sheer number of other ships and planes that pass through the area without incident every day, there doesn't seem to be anything "mysterious" about the area.

Sadly, hardly any of the books or articles about the Bermuda Triangle that exist show much evidence of original research. A quick read makes it obvious that each of the chroniclers were just re-writing each other's work.

In 1975, Lawrence David Kusche, a research librarian from Arizona State University, published a devastating debunking of the Triangle with a book called *The Bermuda Triangle Mystery—Solved!* He called it a manufactured mystery and did the archival digging that many other writers had neglected. Weather records, reports of official investigators, newspaper accounts, and other sources showed that Triangle literature had played very loose with the evidence. In the book, he concluded that the number of ships and aircraft reported missing in the area was not significantly greater, proportionally speaking, than in any other part of the ocean. Also, in an area often hit by tropical storms, the number of disappearances that did occur was not disproportionate, unlikely, or mysterious. Oddly, though, most of the Triangle writers failed to mention such storms. He also found that the number of disappearances had been exaggerated by sloppy research. A boat listed as missing would be reported, but its eventual (if belated) return to port may not have been mentioned. Other disappearances that were cited never occurred at all. For example, one plane crash was said to have taken place in 1937 off Daytona Beach, Florida, in front of hundreds of witnesses, but a check of the local papers revealed nothing.

Other, official sources supported Kusche's findings. In April 1975, Lloyd's of London noted that, according to their records, 428 vessels had been reported missing throughout the world since 1955. "Our intelligence service," officials at the legendary insurance company wrote, "can find no evidence to support the claim that the 'Bermuda Triangle' has more losses than elsewhere. This finding is upheld by the United States Coast Guard whose computer-based records of casualties in the Atlantic go back to 1958."

In the wake of these statements, only silence was heard from the proponents of the Bermuda Triangle mystery. They were unable to mount a credible defense, and because of this, the claims that the area was an authentic anomaly began to suffer. Despite occasional reappearances in supermarket tabloids, and the long memories of paranormal buffs who read about the region when they were first getting interested in the unexplained as children, the Bermuda Triangle survives as only a footnote in the history of passing sensations.

Mysteries are not simple. They can drive a would-be problem solver to distraction, confusion, and frustration, and in the case of the unexplained, they often deny us the satisfaction of a resolution. They mock our belief that just because we have accumulated a pile of startling evidence, that answers will surely come to us.

Most of the disappearances chronicled in this book will never be solved and will continue to beckon to us in the years, decades, and perhaps centuries ahead. I hope you have enjoyed the enigmas that filled these pages, and that they have given you something to think about in the dark hours of the night.

If one of these stories, or many of them, give you at least one sleepless night, then my job here is done.

BIBLIOGRAPHY

Aron, Paul - *Unsolved Mysteries of American History*, John Wiley & Sons, New York, NY, 1997

Axelrod, Jim – *Jodi Huisentruit Mystery: The Decades-Long Search for the Missing TV News Anchor*, CBS News, Article, 2019

Balloch, Jim - *Search in Smokies for lost boy, Dennis Martin, produces lessons for future searches*, Knoxville News-Sentinel, 2009

Bellamy, John Stark II – *Death Ride at Euclid Beach*, Gray & Company Publishers, Cleveland, OH, 2004
————————— - *The Killer in the Attic*, Gray & Company Publishers, Cleveland, OH, 2002
————————— - *The Maniac in the Bushes*, Gray & Company Publishers, Cleveland, OH, 1997
————————— - *Vintage Vermont Villainies*, Countryman Press, Woodstock, VT, 2007

Boar, Roger & Nigel Blundell – *Mystery, Intrigue and the Supernatural*, Dorset Press, New York, NY, 1987

Canning, John - *Great Unsolved Mysteries*, Chartwell Books, Secaucus, NJ, 1984

Carlo, Philip - *The Ice Man: Confessions of a Mafia Contract Killer*, New York, St. Martin's Press, 2006

Churchill, Alan – *Pictorial History of American Crime*, Bramhall House, New York, NY, 1964
————————— – *They Never Came Back*, Ace Books, New York, NY, 1960

Citro, Joseph A. – *Passing Strange*, Chapters Publishing, Shelburne, VT, 1996

Clark, Jerome - *Unexplained!*, Visible Ink, Canton, MI, 1999

Colander, Pat – Thin Air, Contemporary Books, Chicago, IL, 1982

Collins, Paul – "Vanishing Act," *Lapham's Quarterly*, New York, NY

Crofton, Ian – *The Disappeared,* Quercus Books, London, 2008

Cyphers, Bob - *Cold Case: Dennis Reynolds vanished during the Blizzard of 1978. He hasn't been seen since*, Article, KMOV, 2019

Davies, Rodney - *Supernatural Vanishings* , Sterling Publications, New York, NY, 1996

Dolnick, Edward – *Down the Great Unknown*, Harper Collins, New York, NY, 2001

Edwards, Frank – *Strangest of All*, Citadel Press, New York, NY, 1956

Eppinga, Jane – *Unsolved Arizona,* History Press, Charleston, SC, 2015

Fanthorpe, Lionel & Patricia – *Unsolved Mysteries of the Sea*, Dundurn, London, 2004

FATE magazine - Various Issues

Fay, Charles Eden – *Mary Celeste: The Odyssey of an Abandoned Ship*, Peabody Museum, Salem, MA, 1942

Ferri, Jessica - *Can't Wait Any Longer: The Chilling Disappearance of Jean Spangler*, Article, 2017
-------------- - *Sharon Kinne: The Housewife Turned Killer Who Vanished Without a Trace*, Article, 2018

Fort, Charles – *The Book of the Damned: The Complete Books of Charles Fort*, Penguin, New York, NY, 2008 edition

Fox, Regina - *Unsolved Ohio: The bizarre disappearance of Brian Shaffer from campus bar*, Article, 2019

Gehr, Danielle - *Jodi Huisentruit went missing 24 years ago. Today, the search for the Iowa TV journalist continues*, De-Moines Register, 2019

Godwin, John - *This Baffling World 2*, Hart Publishing, New York, NY, 1968

Hanks, Micah - *The Disappearance of Dennis Lloyd Martin: 50 Years Later*, Article, 2019

Harrison, Michael – *Vanishings*, Trafalgar Square, London, 1981

Hicks, Brian – *Ghost Ship*, Ballantine Books, New York, NY, 2004

Hoffman, Carl – *Savage Harvest*, William Morrow, New York, NY, 2014

Hunt, Gerry - *Bizarre America,* Berkley Books, New York, NY, 1988

Keel, John A. – *Our Haunted Planet*, Fawcett, New York, NY, 1971

Kolb, Ellsworth - *Through the Grand Canyon from Wyoming to Mexico*, MacMillan, New York, NY, 1914

Landsburg, Alan – *In Search of Missing Persons*, Bantam Books, New York, NY, 1978

Lawler, Andrew – *The Secret Token*, Doubleday, New York, NY, 2018

Levin, Peter – *Album of Famous Mysteries*, Syndicated Newspaper Column

Harry Maihafer - *Oblivion: The Mystery of West Point*, Potomac Books, New York, 1996

Martinez, Lionel - *Great Unsolved Mysteries of North America,* Book Sales, New York, NY, 1988

McThenia, Tal and Margaret Dunbar Cutright – *The Case for Solomon*, Simon and Shuster, New York, NY, 2012

Miller, Lee – *Roanoke*, Arcadia Publishing, South Carolina, 2000

Miller, R. DeWitt - *Impossible, Yet it Happened!*, Ace Publishing, New York, NY, 1947

Monaco, Richard - *Bizarre America 2*, Berkley, New York, NY, 1992

Nash, Jay Robert - *Among the Missing*, Simon & Shuster, New York, NY, 1978
————————— - *Murder, America*, Simon & Shuster, New York, NY, 1980

Outside Magazine (editors) – *The Darkest Places*, Rowan & Littlefield, Lanham, MD, 2019

Platnick, Kenneth - *Great Mysteries of History*, Stackpole, Pennsylvania, 1971

Pruitt, Sarah – *Vanished!*, Lyon Press, Guilford, CT, 2018

Roberts, David - *Finding Everett Ruess*, Broadway Books, New York, NY, 2011

Rusho, W.H. - *A Vagabond for Beauty*, Gibbs and Smith, Layton, UT, 1983

Schneck, Robert Damon – *The President's Vampire*, Anomalist Books, San Antonio, TX, 2005

Schumacher, Emile – *More Strange Unsolved Mysteries*, Paperback Library, New York, NY, 1969

Sloane, Arthur A - *Hoffa*. Cambridge, MA MIT Press, 1991

Steiger, Brad - *Strange Disappearances*, Lancer Books, Canada, 1972

Strange magazine - Various Issues

Swancer, Brent - *Some Very Strange Information on the Bizarre Vanishing of Dennis Martin*, Article, 2017

Sweeney, Gary – *The Babysitter Who Vanished: What Happened to Evelyn Hartley?* Article, 2018

———————— - *The Chilling, Unsolved Disappearance of William and Margaret Patterson*, Article, 2017
———————— - *Vanished: The Unsolved Disappearance of Paula Jean Welden*, Article, 2016

Taylor, Troy – *Into the Shadows*, Whitechapel Press, Alton, IL, 2002
———————— – *Out Past the Campfire Light*, Whitechapel Press, Alton, IL, 2003
———————— - *Suffer the Children*, American Hauntings Ink, Jacksonville, IL, 2018

Taylor, Troy and Lisa Taylor Horton – *Haunted Jacksonville*, American Hauntings Ink, Decatur, IL, 2014

Tilstra, Elizabeth - *Police Gave This Child to the Wrong Family*, Article, 2016
———————— - *The Vanishing Crew of the Carroll A. Deering: A Maritime Mystery*, Article, 2015

Tofel, Richard J. – *Vanishing Point*, Ivan R. Dee, New York, NY, 2004

True Crime Files (Christine) - *The Disappearance of Brandon Swanson*, Article, 2019

Walker, Dale – *The Calamity Papers*, Forge Books, New York, NY, 2004

Weber, Stephanie - *The Chilling, Unsolved Disappearance of Virginia Carpenter*, Article, 2017
———————— - *27 Years Later: The Haunting Disappearance of the Springfield Three Remains a Mystery*, Article, 2017

Wilkins, Harold T. - *Strange Mysteries of Time & Space*, Citadel Press, New York, NY, 1959

Wilson, Colin - *Unsolved Mysteries Past & Present*, Contemporary Books, New York, NY, 1992

Wilson, Colin and Damon Wilson - *Mammoth Encyclopedia of the Unsolved*, Running Press, New York, NY, 2000

Winer, Richard – *Ghost Ships*, Berkley, New York, NY, 2000

Wisner, Bill – *Vanished, Without A Trace*, Berkley, New York, NY, 1977

Yankee Magazine – *Mysterious New England*, St. Martin's Press, New York, NY, 1971

Personal Interviews & Correspondence

Special Thanks to:
April Slaughter: Cover Design and Artwork
Lois Taylor: Editing and Proofreading
Beth Racey: Editing and Proofreading
Lisa Taylor Horton and Lux
Orrin Taylor
Rene Kruse
Rachael Horath
Elyse and Thomas Reihner
Bethany Horath
John Winterbauer
Kaylan Schardan
Maggie Walsh
Cody Beck
Becky Ray
Tom and Michelle Bonadurer
Susan Kelly and Amy Bouyear
And the entire crew of American Hauntings

ABOUT THE AUTHOR

Troy Taylor is the author of nearly 130 books on ghosts, hauntings, true crime, the unexplained, and the supernatural in America. He is also the founder of American Hauntings Ink, which offers books, ghost tours, events, and weekend excursions. He was born and raised in the Midwest and currently divides his time between Illinois and the far-flung reaches of America.